Jew and Philosopher

SUNY Series in Judaica: Hermeneutics, Mysticism, and Religion
Edited by Michael Fishbane, Robert Goldenberg, and Arthur Green

Jew and Philosopher

The Return to Maimonides in the Jewish Thought of Leo Strauss

Kenneth Hart Green

STATE UNIVERSITY OF NEW YORK PRESS

Published by
State University of New York Press, Albany

© 1993 State University of New York

For information, address State University of New York Press,
State University Plaza, Albany, N.Y., 12246

Production by Cathleen Collins
Marketing by Fran Keneston

Library of Congress Cataloging in Publication Data

Green, Kenneth Hart, 1953–
    Jew and philosopher : the return to Maimonides in the Jewish
thought of Leo Strauss / Kenneth Hart Green.
        p.   cm. — (SUNY series in Judaica)
    Includes bibliographical references and index.
    ISBN 0–7914–1565–1 (hardcover) — ISBN 0–7914–1566–X (pbk.)
    1. Strauss, Leo—Contributions in Jewish philosophy.
2. Philosophy, Jewish.   3. Philosophy, Medieval.   4. Maimonides,
Moses, 1135–1204.   I. Title.   II. Series.
BM755.S75G74   1993
181′ .06—dc20   92-31572
                                                          CIP

10 9 8 7 6 5 4 3 2 1

To my sons,
Alexander, Daniel, and Jonathan

"Therefore put these My words
in your heart and in your soul,...
And teach them to your children."
(Deut. 11:18, 19)

RECHA: "Ah, I see, on Sinai! Very good! Now I'll learn at last from one who really knows whether it is true..."

TEMPLAR: "What would you like to know? Whether it's really true that the very spot can still be seen, where Moses stood with God when..."

RECHA: "No, that's not it. Wherever he stood, it was before the Lord. That's all I need to know. But what I'd like to verify is this: Is it really true what people say, that it's much less difficult to go up this mountain than to come down again? For, you see, all the hills I've climbed, I've found the opposite to be true."

—G.E. Lessing, *Nathan the Wise*
Act 3, scene 2.

CONTENTS

ACKNOWLEDGMENTS

THE PRESENT STUDY BEGAN as a doctoral dissertation, supervised by Marvin Fox, at Brandeis University. In the course of preparing this study for publication, which is a thoroughly revised version of that original work, I received generous help from many teachers, friends, and organizations.

I would first like to gratefully acknowledge by name several institutions whose financial aid through fellowships made it possible for me to work on the original dissertation and on the revised version: the Social Sciences and Humanities Research Council of Canada, the Memorial Foundation for Jewish Culture, the Woodrow Wilson National Fellowship Foundation, and Brandeis University. I would also like to thank both the Tauber Institute (and its first director, Bernard Wasserstein), whose Doctoral Research Award allowed me to travel to Chicago in 1984 to do research in the Leo Strauss Archive at the Library of the University of Chicago, and University College at the University of Toronto, whose Harcourt Brown Fellowship allowed me make a subsequent research trip to the Archive in 1991. In this connection, I would like to express my gratitude to Joseph Cropsey, who kindly permitted me to do research in the Archive, and who has been of great assistance to me ever since in relation to my continuing work on the Jewish thought of Leo Strauss.

There are a few individuals to whom I owe a special debt, and without whom I may never have persevered in the face of such a long and arduous task. I must begin by thanking Emil Fackenheim for igniting in me the spark and passion of Jewish philosophy, and for first pointing me toward Leo Strauss as a great modern Jewish thinker. To the late Alexander Altmann I will always be grateful for his showing such gracious kindness to a young graduate student, and for sharing the brilliance of a mind that never seemed to grow old. To him I also owe a sizable debt for this one point which he insisted on: that I not escape into viewing Strauss as just a "pure" philosopher and scholar of Judaism, but rather exert myself to recognize him as a man who never forgot he was a Jew in any aspect of his thinking. I would also very much like to thank Zev Friedman for his friendly prodding, and especially for numerous fruitful discussions on Maimonides and *The Guide of the Perplexed* during the years since my return to Toronto in 1985. I owe the greatest debt to my teacher Marvin Fox, for showing faith in me from the beginning, and for sustaining it to the end. His wise understanding helped me to see light beyond the shadows that seemed at first to surround the Jewish thought of Leo Strauss. To me, he will always exemplify in his person the truth of Maimonides' insight that intellectual knowledge of God, if it be true to its claim, must issue in a higher moral excellence.

Above all, I would like to thank my wife Sharon, whose help is beyond measure, for all the painstaking labor that she put into bringing this work into being. Her constant encouragement, critical acumen, and unflagging sense of humor made what would probably have been an onerous task into a truly joyous undertaking.

PREFACE

THE ORIGINAL AIM of this study was to probe the complex figure of Leo Strauss in order to grasp how his compelling works on Judaism fit in with his philosophic thought as a whole. I was well-acquainted with Strauss as one of the leading contemporary political thinkers, and it intrigued me that this same man had also been responsible for producing a strikingly impressive assembly of works on Judaism. That these works were almost uniformly characterized by their scholarly exactitude and erudition, their intellectual incisiveness, their expansive reach, and their literary felicity, only served to heighten their appeal and interest to me. Moreover, as I was becoming increasingly aware, Strauss's works on Judaism had exercised a deep and pervasive influence on his contemporaries, irrespective of whether they were willing to acknowledge it. What was curious, however, was the fact that Strauss's Jewish writings had scarcely been recognized for their fundamental contribution to contemporary Jewish discourse, nor had his Jewish thought been adequately explored in any truly systematic fashion.

Taking this latter task upon myself, what emerged from this effort was a discovery of the "other" Leo Strauss—not only a distinguished Jewish scholar and commentator, but also one of the most important Jewish thinkers of the present century. But this insight did not occur to me all at once. At first, I began with the idea of making an examination and analysis of the scholarly contribution of Strauss's works on Judaism, culminating in a critical assessment of their uniqueness and degree of originality. I had been prepared by others to look at these works as merely peripheral to, or at most supportive of, his main philosophic concerns, since it had been argued that these works in their peculiarly Jewish form were supposed to have been determined by his purely personal experience.

But following long and careful reflection on the entire corpus of Strauss's writings, I reached this pivotal conclusion: that the Jewish thought of Leo Strauss stands firmly and separately as a central pillar of his entire thought. The present book reflects this belief. It is a full-fledged critical study of Strauss's Jewish thought, which I believe to be the first book of its kind. This study, it is hoped, will help to convince readers that grasping Strauss's Jewish thought is crucial for giving a proper account of his philosophic thought, and that it is certainly of much greater significance on its own than has been hitherto recognized.

My evidence for such a bold claim is grounded in an interpretation of what I perceive to be the core part of his Jewish thought, specifically what I call "the return to Maimonides." From this reading, I believe it is possible to discern that Leo Strauss was not only a powerful, original, and provocative Jewish thinker, but also that his Jewish thought may be essential for grasping the true character of his still controversial political thought. Indeed, I go so far as to suggest that Strauss's "return to Maimonides" may prove to be the key to the proper and deeper understanding of his philosophic thought as a whole.[1]

Tracing the origins of Strauss's thought to his youthful writings on Judaism, I try to show how the overarching figure of Maimonides began to loom ever larger as his thought progressed. However, as I further strive to demonstrate, Strauss's turn to Maimonides was rooted in one prior decisive conviction that Strauss adhered to unchanged in spite of other significant variations in his thought. This was his conviction about the moral and intellectual bankruptcy of contemporary philosophy, a bankruptcy that he regarded as issuing in a grave "theological-political crisis" both for modern Judaism and for modern Western civilization. Strauss suggested that the most serious and deepest reason for this bankruptcy was philosophy's surrender to "radical historicism" (i.e., Heidegger). He believed it led to the self-destruction of reason and the misguiding of religion, and was based finally on the abandonment or "forgetfulness" of truth.

But why, it might be asked, did Strauss choose Maimonides as his model and prototype? Returning to medieval Jewish philosophy, and reaching a fuller and fairer appreciation of it than most of his scholarly contemporaries in Jewish philosophical research, Strauss started to view Maimonides as a type of exemplar. By this I mean to say that Strauss came to see Maimonides as a uniquely wise thinker and teacher who arose in the midst of a similar crisis, and who had been able to resolve the crisis by achieving a "perfect," though unconventional, balance between philosophy, religion, morality, and politics. In this study, I even suggest that Strauss in his final conception presents Maimonides the Jewish thinker as the highest type of philosophic thinker, and as one still eminently worthy of imitation.

This book also attempts to clarify how Strauss's penetrating explorations into Maimonides' thought developed in three distinct stages, culminating in his single-handed rediscovery of Maimonides' "esotericism." The theme of "esotericism" is investigated beyond the hermeneutical issues in order to reconstruct what Strauss claimed to uncover as its fundamental philosophic premises. These are premises, as Strauss would maintain, from which Western philosophic thought itself first became what it is, and in which it remains rooted, insofar as its roots are still healthy. Strauss saw his attempt to reclaim a forgotten wisdom from Maimonides as something done for the sake of modern sensibility; he regarded such wisdom as a corrective to certain inherent tendencies, not to say excesses, of modernity.

Strauss wisely perceived that preserving the virtues of modernity while saving it from its own vices is of special concern to modern Judaism, since modern Jews have been both some of the greatest beneficiaries of modernity's promised blessings as well as some of the greatest sufferers from its unanticipated "deficiencies." This leads me to the further suggestion that Strauss's teaching about Jewish philosophy, religion, and politics, and his wisdom about Jewish history, are deeply relevant to modern Jewish concerns, and that Jewish thinkers can learn a very great deal from him, whether they agree or disagree with his often controversial conclusions.

To what position did Strauss's reservations about modernity lead him in terms of its impact on Judaism? Strauss's solution to modern Jewish spiritual problems begins with the very sources of Judaism. Its texts were formerly often viewed as obsolete relics of ancient or medieval history, but he himself continuously turned to them in his untiring search for wisdom. Among other things, it is hoped that this study shows how one of the many ways in which Strauss expressed himself clearly as a Jew was in his serious resort to the "old" Jewish books, with the hopeful conviction that these could yield crucial new insights for the modern Jew. It seems that, in Strauss's view, the thinking modern Jew is still vitally in need of the wisdom embedded in these premodern Jewish texts, which ironically shed fresh light on modernity. From such studies in the sources, texts, and history of Judaism, he believed that one can learn to see the true promise of modernity in its original dimensions, as well as learn not to be blinded by this very promise as to its inherent and necessary limits.[2]

Whether Strauss is right in his benevolent critique of modernity, and in his relying on Maimonides for the grounding of this critique, cannot be decided by the present study, although I do hope that by its comprehensive view of Strauss it will help to clarify the fundamental issues. By way of a conclusion, I will venture the following prediction: Jewish thinkers will gradually begin to turn to Strauss in ever-greater numbers and with ever-greater frequency. Certainly few other modern Jewish thinkers possess the expansiveness of vision and the profundity of insight into the history of Jewish thought and religion, and into the history of Western philosophy, which Strauss possessed with such abundance and forcefulness. He was one of the first to seek to make Jewish thinkers aware of the dire need to face the contemporary crisis, to provide them with a powerful overview of its unique configuration, and to help guide them toward a possible resolution of the crisis grounded in an adequate understanding of its peculiar character and causes. And if in future years Jewish thinkers do indeed begin to focus their thought on debating the merits of modernity for Judaism in light of the perspective on the issues offered by Strauss, they will undoubtedly find themselves either guided by or opposed to Strauss's claims for his rediscovered "Maimonidean" wisdom. But even were this never to occur, Jewish thought already owes an enormous debt to Leo Strauss, which I believe will one day be gladly and gratefully acknowledged.[3]

INTRODUCTION

LEO STRAUSS is primarily known as a scholar who worked in the field of the history of political philosophy, and who revived almost single-handedly the serious study of ancient and medieval political philosophy.[1] In recent years, it has come to be recognized that he was also a political philosopher in his own right. His thought, often characterized as "conservative," claims to be rooted in what he called "Platonic political philosophy"—a tradition which he traced from Socrates to Lessing.[2] This tradition was subject to a withering critique by Niccolo Machiavelli, who according to Strauss established the true basis for the entire modern tradition through his anti-"idealistic" new thinking about political philosophy. As such, Machiavelli's chief object was to destroy "the great tradition," i.e., the alliance which created the West, the alliance between ancient Greek philosophy derived from Socrates and the revealed or prophetic religions derived from the Hebrew Bible. The last point directs us to the other element in the thought of Leo Strauss—his deep and abiding interest in religion, and especially in the Jewish religious tradition, in which he was raised and to which he continued to swear a devoted loyalty all of his life. Indeed, we may go so far as to assert that this topic was ultimately his main spiritual concern, and that his researches and thought on political philosophy were subordinated to this concern. As he himself unequivocally put it: "I believe I can say without any exaggeration that since a very, very early time the main theme of my reflections has been what is called the 'Jewish Question.'"[3]

Strauss was, of course, predominantly interested in the highest intellectual and moral expressions of the Jewish tradition, but notwithstanding his "noble piety"[4] he claimed to always base his thought on actual experience, and especially on modern, twentieth-century history. He himself was immersed in and affected by it, and he was ever attentive to the implications of Nazi Germany, Soviet Russia, liberal democracy in the English-speaking countries and Western Europe, and Zionism and the state of Israel.[5] Strauss believed that this history manifests a crisis in the modern tradition, a crisis that represents a radical threat to the survival of this tradition, and even to the survival of Western civilization *per se*. Since Strauss believed in the Western tradition, which for him as a Jew and a thinker especially meant Judaism and Western philosophy, he was led to ask whether that tradition could somehow deal adequately with this grave crisis. As a result he was led to

> wonder whether the two ingredients of modern culture, of the modern synthesis, are not more solid than that synthesis. Catastrophes and horrors of a magnitude hitherto unknown, which we have seen and through which we have lived, were better provided for, or made intelligible, by both Plato and the prophets than by the modern belief in progress.[6]

Strauss's Jewish thought, then, like his political philosophy with which it must in some measure be correlated, rests on a fundamental reappraisal and critique of the "modern." But Strauss did not simply reject modern Jewish thought from Spinoza to Buber—first he studied and probed it carefully, next he tried to comprehend both its strengths and its weaknesses, and finally he judged it wanting in several key respects. It is the chief contention of this study that Strauss understood and judged the various modern Jewish thinkers from a standard extraneous to them, and that this standard, which he held up as a truer and better one, was Maimonides. To be sure, the conception of Maimonides' thought which Strauss presents is different from all other modern conceptions of his thought. Strauss presents an original and radical image of Maimonides as philosopher and as Jewish thinker, as esoteric writer, and as a still vital teacher and guide to the enduring perplexities concerning God, man, and the world.

Inasmuch as the critical study and real understanding of the Jewish thought of Leo Strauss is still in its infancy, we do not face numerous opponents whose views we must contest at the very beginning. The commentators on, and critics of, Strauss are recent and still few in number, although this does not make their work unimportant, since even a quick perusal of the literature will show that there have been some very good articles and reviews written. The views of these authors will be encountered chiefly in the notes. In the text itself our aim will be to lay the basis for further discussion by presenting a unified view of

Strauss's Jewish thought as a whole, which we characterize as a "return to Maimonides." In trying to set a new direction for Jewish thought, Strauss needed to tacitly claim that he had been able to rediscover and reconstruct Maimonides' "true thought," a claim which is still highly controversial. It will therefore be our overarching task in this study to grasp what Strauss finally understood by that controversial topic—the "true thought" of Maimonides.

But this leads us to a point that we believe needs to be made with the utmost emphasis. Most discussions of Strauss's work on Maimonides make what we believe is a false step; they assume either that Strauss reached his conception of Maimonides at the very first and by a single stroke, or that what led him to this conception, in terms of its prior stages, is irrelevant for the consideration of what is contained in the final conception. It is our thesis that both of these assumptions are wrong. There are clearly three distinct stages in the development of Strauss's views on Maimonides encompassing his suggestion for a "return," as well as one relevant "pre-Maimonidean" stage. We maintain that passing through these stages was crucially significant for Strauss's development. We further argue that the full comprehension of this development is essential for the adequate appreciation of the lasting achievement of Strauss as a student (and perhaps a disciple) of Maimonides, and for any future critical evaluation of the standing of Strauss's own Jewish thought as a putative guide for the perplexed of our time. These stages reveal Strauss in the process of exhausting the modern alternatives to, and approaches toward, Maimonides.

The present book will consist of the following parts. The first chapter will discuss why the modern alternatives seemed flawed to Strauss; it will consider how he approached and criticized his predecessors. The second chapter will pursue what Strauss regarded as the main modern obstacles to a return to Maimonides, and attempt to reconstruct how he believed they could be surmounted, removed, or dismissed as illusory. The third chapter will examine Strauss's youthful pre-Maimonidean stage as Jewish thinker and scholar, and what happened to arouse his interest in Maimonides. The fourth chapter will uncover Strauss's first Maimonidean stage, in which he used the knowledge of Maimonides the philosophical theologian to criticize Spinoza's critical attack on the Jewish tradition. The fifth chapter explores Strauss's recovery of Maimonides' Islamic predecessors in philosophy and how they led him to the Platonic roots of Maimonides' thought. It probes what Strauss would call Maimonides' "prophetology," a political philosophical approach

to the Bible and Jewish religion which Strauss considered wiser than
that of Spinoza and the moderns. The sixth chapter attempts to uncover
what is philosophically hidden beneath Strauss's rediscovery of
Maimonides as an esoteric writer. It shows how this radically altered
his view of Maimonides as a philosopher, while still leaving Maimonides
in the Jewish fold. The conclusion will briefly summarize the course
of enquiry we have been pursuing in detailing Strauss's developing views
on Maimonides, and recommend some lines for further research and
criticism in approaching the Straussian suggestion for a return to
Maimonides.

CHAPTER 1

"In the Grip of the Theological-Political Predicament"

THE CRISIS OF REASON
AND REVELATION IN
MODERN JEWISH PHILOSOPHY

THE HERO of Leo Strauss's monumental Jewish thought is undoubtedly Moses Maimonides. In fact, it may safely be said that in the entire course of Strauss's Jewish writings—beginning with his first major work, the article "Cohen's Analysis of Spinoza's Bible Science" (1924), and ending with his last major work, the introductory essay in the English translation of Hermann Cohen's *Religion of Reason out of the Sources of Judaism* (1972)—Maimonides is consistently treated with more genuine reverence, and along with this receives less obvious criticism, than any other Jewish philosopher.[1] Indeed, if there is in truth something which may rightly be called "the Jewish thought of Leo Strauss," then it is revealed to the greatest possible degree in Strauss's works dealing with Maimonides.

That this should be so, however, may seem to be a paradoxical assertion for two reasons. First, if we count Leo Strauss among the moderns, as seems fitting, do we not suddenly cut the ground from beneath our feet by taking Maimonides, possibly the greatest Jewish medieval thinker, as the philosophic inspiration for Strauss? How can Strauss be a modern Jewish thinker if his own Jewish thought is nothing but a "return to Maimonides"? Can he possibly mean by this an unmediated or undialectical "return"? Why would a modern Jewish thinker who clearly expresses a passionate interest in the modern theological-political crisis facing the Jews and Judaism[2] and who has diagnosed the complex causes which brought it about, need to preoccupy himself (for nonantiquarian reasons) with a medieval Jewish thinker, however great. Obviously he is not simply an ultramontanist praising the "ancien régime." However conservative Strauss may have considered himself in regard to Jewish religion and politics, he always soberly recognized both the virtues and the limits of the modern situation, and moderately accepted it as an established fact in Jewish life and thought. Hence, his spiritual affinity for Maimonides cannot be confused with any romantic longings for a return to an idealized, noble past. But what then is there in Maimonides for a Jewish thinker of modern sensibility like Strauss?

Second, these Maimonidean studies by Strauss seem, by his own declaration, to be intended solely as efforts of historical scholarship, albeit of a rare profundity and subtlety, rather than as the vehicle for Strauss's own independent thought. But it is my contention that it is not sufficient merely to acknowledge that the unique literary method and the often radical conclusions of Strauss's research in Maimonidean studies revolutionized the field.[3] This undeniable fact may prove him to be a great scholar, but it does not by itself demonstrate how such scholarly research—if it may not be reduced to pure antiquarianism—is necessarily connected with, or even serves, his own Jewish thought. We hope to prove that, for a specific purpose Strauss is merely donning the mantle of an historical scholar. If this is indeed the case, though, why would he not do so candidly, and thus appropriate or employ directly the results of such historical scholarship in his own thought and speculation? In other words, why would a modern Jewish thinker choose to appear in the humble guise of a historical scholar, and to expound his own original thought through interpreting another man's texts?

We cannot attempt to answer these questions[4] until we have probed some of the leading themes and issues which are at the heart of Strauss's interest in Maimonides. These can only emerge from a reflection on what we deem to be the key texts in the exploration of Maimonides by Strauss, who revivified a Jewish thinker previously dismissed as obsolete. It is evident from the paradoxes inherent in Strauss's exposition that this will not be a simple and unequivocal task, and it is further complicated by the existence of significant stages in the development of Strauss's views on Maimonides. Such complexities notwithstanding, it is our argument that Strauss's view of Maimonides, developed over fifty years, manifests nonetheless a substantial unity (this may be equally true of his Jewish thought as a whole). This is not to say that his views on Maimonides did not grow and change, and, as we hope to prove, even may have passed through three distinct stages. Nevertheless, this intellectual development may be more accurately expressed in terms of "a continuous, deepening process"[5] rather than as a radical transformation. Indeed, it is our thesis that once Strauss's view of Maimonides reached its essential form in his very early works dealing with Maimonides, his original insight into Maimonides was never fundamentally contradicted by his later unfolding of its full ramifications.[6]

One other preliminary remark would seem to be in order. In the mid-1930s,[7] Strauss gradually perceived that Maimonides could not be properly and fully understood if one did not take serious account of his literary method. Strauss began to realize that there were reasons why Maimonides wrote in such a deliberately elusive manner. As Strauss saw it, Maimonides' specific instructions for reading the *Guide* and his peculiar manner of expressing himself in it were intended as tools for the select reader to extract hidden or "esoteric" meanings and as obstacles to keep those same meanings safely hidden from the average reader. This discovery, applied to Maimonides' entire text, gave Strauss the key to distinguishing between Maimonides' secret, i.e., true, teaching ("the golden apple"), and his apparent, i.e., diversionary, teaching ("the silver filigree")[8] which deliberately but deceptively overlays it. This distinction clearly shaped everything Strauss later wrote about Maimonides. Indeed, as we hope to elucidate, this literary method and the reasons for using it may have so persuaded Strauss that he employed it himself in some of his subsequent writings. Strauss apparently chose both to conceal his own views from the average reader and to communicate these same views only to the select reader. In regard to his works specifically concerned with Maimonides, Strauss conveyed his own notions "beneath" his discussion of Maimonides' texts (or, as a hostile critic might put it, by subtly reading in his own views as if they were those of the text).[9] In interpreting Strauss it seems we must begin by obeying the rules of his own art of writing (which, as we hope to establish, are ultimately derived from Maimonides, although they must not be simply attributed to him). Strauss's first rule, as we might call it, for reading a serious, esoterically written work, would require that the elaboration of the surface teaching must remain the chief or primary task, and only through paying careful attention to this surface, or exoteric, level and its attendant perplexities, can the deeper, or esoteric, level be reached and be clearly set apart from it.[10]

However, to comprehend in its proper order Strauss's Jewish thought as it developed in his Maimonidean studies, we must begin with the simpler issue which actually preceded the rediscovery of esotericism, for Strauss wrote important works about Maimonides in advance of that rediscovery. This issue may be put in terms of these queries: Why did Strauss originally turn to Maimonides? What "lost wisdom" did he seek to find, especially in *The Guide of the Perplexed?* And what was the fundamental view of Maimonides that accompanied and supported Strauss in this turn? All of these questions may be seen to receive a decisive answer in a statement which appears in the very first line of Strauss's brief yet monumental *Philosophy and Law*: "Maimonides is the 'classic of rationalism' in Judaism."[11] In fact, as we understand him, it does not overstate the case to say that the basic themes and issues that animated Strauss's concern and directed his attention are condensed in this statement as well as in the following twenty pages, which should be looked at as the vindication of it. (Indeed, the constancy of Strauss's Jewish thought is reflected in the striking similarities, even to the repetition of phrases, between his vigorously original Introduction to *Philosophy and Law* and the equally powerful Preface to *Spinoza's Critique of Religion*, despite the thirty years separating them.)[12] For Strauss, Maimonides was the "classic" of not just any "rationalism," but he meant the term in a very specific sense. As he puts it, Maimonides' "rationalism" is "the truly natural model [*Vorbild*], the standard, which is to be carefully guarded from every falsification, which is thereby the stumbling block on which modern rationalism is brought to its ruin." Hence, we already encounter in *Philosophy and Law* a sharp line drawn by Strauss between modern and premodern rationalism, especially of the theological kind. In the division of these two rationalisms, Strauss categorically prefers the premodern, in its Maimonidean phase. It moves in the sphere of the "truly natural" form of reason, which is purer in its conformity with the enduring requirements of man's political nature,[13] yet is also surer and deeper in its treatment of primary theological motives such as creation, miracles and prophecy.[14]

Even so, why should it be necessary for us to turn for guidance in our modern perplexity to Maimonides? Even if he is *the* "classic" representative of medieval rationalism, even of "rationalism in Judaism," still we do not yet know, or we cannot simply assume, as Strauss was well aware, that this is also *the* "true rationalism," let alone *the* true teaching *per se*.[15] In Strauss's justificatory account of this provisional conclusion about what "the truly natural model, the standard" of rationalism in Judaism is, he tells us that his turn to Maimonides resulted from a genuine cognitive encounter which he staged between medieval and modern rationalisms.[16] Here, "clarity about the present" was the sole original interest motivating him, while the medieval was used as a foil, or as "a mere means" to the end of "a sharper cognition of the distinctiveness [*Eigentumlichkeit*] of modern rationalism."[17] Considering "modern rationalism as the source of the present," Strauss wanted especially to know whether it was rationalism *per se* that had caused the present crisis in modern philosophy and society, which were both gradually but discernibly turning against reason itself, or whether it was produced only by the modern species of rationalism. It was for this comparative diagnostic purpose that he first studied medieval Jewish rationalism.[18] In fact, it was in the course of this encounter, or perhaps as its direct consequence, that Strauss began to radically doubt modern rationalism, and overcome his original "prejudice" in favor of its "superiority" as reason and as a moral force.[19] What he now began to radically doubt was its philosophical, theological, and political adequacy to meet the present crisis.

We must equally bear in mind that "clarity about the present" suggests first of all the actual historical situation with which Strauss was faced: the grave difficulties in which the Jews and Judaism were entangled, as reflected by the catastrophic events and revolutionary changes which occurred during his life. As a Jew in the Germany of the 1920s, he was caught "in the grip of the theologico-political predicament," i.e., he experienced in its full intensity the Jewish crisis as well as the crisis of the West in the trial of liberal democracy, both German and otherwise. This predicament affected Jews so deeply because they had tied virtually *all* their hopes to modern liberalism, modern rationalism's moderate expression as interpreted by Spinoza in the light of classical principles.[20] He perceived that since "the present situation of Judaism as such. . .is determined by the Enlightenment,"[21] the crisis in which the Jews and Judaism are immersed and the crisis of modern Western civilization are fundamentally linked. Strauss recognized the need to reconsider modern rationalism in order to comprehend modern Judaism,[22] and as we trace Strauss's "turn" to Maimonides and the medieval rationalist tradition, we must determine what it is about modern rationalism that Strauss rejected.

The concern for "the present situation of Judaism" in Strauss's view does not entail any derogation from "the basic constitution of Judaism," which for him remains "untouched" by the Enlightenment critique of orthodoxy in its Jewish form.[23] Beginning with this phrase, "the [untouched] basic constitution of Judaism," Strauss reiterates in *Philosophy and Law* his careful demonstration in *Spinoza's Critique of Religion* that modern philosophy has never actually "refuted" divine revelation as taught by the Hebrew Bible, despite appearances to the contrary.[24] To Strauss, the present situation not only encompasses those who marginally identify as Jews but also and especially those who are passionately committed Jews of two different types. The first are those committed Jews who have been fundamentally affected by modern rationalism and liberalism; they reject divine revelation as defining Judaism and determine its character in terms of modern political and cultural categories, especially the movement known as secular Zionism. The second are those committed Jews who accept divine revelation but make it theologically conform with modern philosophic or scientific notions and criticisms. This type refers especially to such modern Jewish religious thinkers as the idealist Cohen and the existentialist Rosenzweig; Strauss puts such diverse thinkers under one rubric, by calling their thought "the movement of return."

Strauss fully respects the first type (i.e., adherents of secular political Zionism) as providing an admirable and a "highly honorable" approach but believes it is not a "sufficient" one to meet the full needs of the present.[25] Not only is Zionism "atheistic" in its political basis, but as a purely political movement, Zionism ignores that its "solution" to the "Jewish problem" is inspired by liberalism while simultaneously exposing liberalism's own limitations. Hoping to be efficacious in one sphere of the modern Jewish dilemma alone—in "the restoration of [Jewish] honor through the acquisition of statehood"—political Zionism (with which Strauss originally identified himself completely) "implied a profound modification of traditional Jewish hopes, a modification arrived at through a break with these hopes." In other words, in order to be preoccupied with human honor and put one's faith in the termination of the exile by purely human means, with the end in view of establishing a secular liberal state, it seems one had to have already lost some faith in divine promises, in divine election and special providence, and in the perfection of the divine law. However, precisely for the sake of the very efficacy political Zionism held in view, it had to "make its peace" with Jewish tradition and to recognize the need for a spiritual "return" (*teshuvah*).[26] For no matter how "secularized" one's Zionism was, if one wanted a "Jewish state" and not just a "state of Jews," one needed a Jewish culture—and hence cultural Zionism. With his mature, clear-eyed

"Platonic" vision, Strauss saw that this secular project for creating a Jewish culture as a support and even as a guide for the Zionist political project would never be able to sever itself fully from the traditional Judaism against which it had rebelled, yet to which it could not help but be tied if it was not to forget its roots in the very Jewish history it planned to daringly redirect.

As for the second approach—i.e., contemporary Jewish religious thought, which he termed "the movement of return"—Strauss did regard it as praiseworthy for radically changing in several respects the previous direction of modern Jewish life and thought (which had been formulated in an apologetic vein by post-Mendelssohnian "religious liberalism").[27] However, at the same time Strauss believed that this fledgling movement did not represent a sufficiently fundamental change; he felt it had not yet squarely faced or truly answered the Enlightenment critique of orthodoxy, and so it carried through its "return" with serious reservations about the Jewish tradition. While it readily admitted the source of its reservations as rooted in the Enlightenment (and especially Spinoza), it did not as a "movement" justify them, in any adequately systematic form, but virtually presupposed their necessity.[28] It is no exaggeration to maintain that Strauss's initial point of departure in Jewish theology was to ascertain as precisely as possible what place these reservations about the tradition should occupy in future Jewish thought, and hence also to deal with the question of whether "the movement of return" was warranted by its own premises in considering necessary this limited critique of the orthodox tradition.

The crucial link between modern rationalism and the modern Jewish crisis may be further elucidated if we consider what the primary *cause* of the crisis is, from Strauss's perspective. To Strauss, modern Jews and Judaism, as well as modern Western civilization, are in the midst of a moral, religious, and political crisis engendered by their waning faith in an eternal truth. Since "the authoritative layer of the Jewish heritage presents itself . . . as a divine gift, as divine revelation," the eternal truth which it teaches is rooted in "the irrefutable premise" of belief in the being of "the omnipotent God whose will is unfathomable" and who reveals himself as he wills.[29] While modern rationalism is precisely constituted by the rebellion—whether it be viewed as speculative or scientific—against this "irrefutable" premise, it is a rebellion that Strauss incisively characterizes as nothing but a "moral antagonism." He says it was previously defined by the Jewish tradition as "Epicurean" unbelief.[30] Though not exactly correct in a philosophical sense, this traditional

Jewish attitude certainly captured the *moral* motive in the modern critique of religion. Inasmuch as modern reason or philosophy dogmatically denies the very possibility of divine revelation (though often camouflaging its radicalism for political purposes), it is a denial which it cannot demonstrate, and thus the very basis for modern rationalism is not "evident and necessary knowledge" but rather "an unevident decision." Hence, following Strauss's logic, philosophy paradoxically puts itself in the category of a faith. Yet modern reason, despite its faulty basis, is permitted by ostensibly "enlightened" theology to pass decisive rational judgments about divinely revealed religion; in particular, it is permitted to give criticism of traditional texts and beliefs. Modern reason also asserts an unconditional victory against classical reason; here too it is a matter of assertion, and not demonstration, its persuasiveness deriving perhaps from the successes of modern science in mastering nature.

Yet as Strauss succinctly indicates, in the very "progress" of modern reason and universal homogeneous civilization, its faith in itself as a force of absolute good for man gradually fails and eventually collapses due to both irrationalist philosophical developments and the events of history revealing the dubious benevolence in human self-assertion against nature.[31] (Strauss speaks of "the self-destruction of rational philosophy" in our day.) Modern rationalism, as Jews adapted the Jewish tradition to it, not only leaves Judaism more exposed to attack by its modern critical opponents for its suprarational claims, but also leaves it appearing less inspired than medieval or premodern philosophy ever did in its happy adaptation to such philosophy. However, even in modern rationalism's collapse through "the victory of orthodoxy" or irrationalist philosophy, its virtual antipode,[32] Judaism is not actually helped, as Rosenzweig especially would have us believe. In stark contrast to him, Strauss expounds Judaism undoubtedly in the spirit of both Maimonides and Hermann Cohen, viewing it as a faith which claims only to possess "suprarational," and not "irrational," truths. Hence, the truths which Judaism teaches, according to Strauss's thought, do not contradict reason but only pass beyond what unaided reason can apprehend by its own efforts and abilities alone.[33] He uses as his prooftext a favorite Torah verse (Deut. 4:6), which he often cites in order to emphasize the rational character of the Jewish tradition, saying: "Jewish orthodoxy based its claim to superiority to other religions from the beginning on its superior rationality."[34]

Thus, Strauss began to radically doubt modern rationalism once he started asking whether the modern form of rationalism was "the source of the present" predominantly in a debilitating sense, while simultaneously pondering whether in fact the medievals exemplified in their rationalism a higher and more enduring standard for measuring the present.[35] Strauss regarded himself as faced with a choice, a choice which all modern people face if they reflect upon their spiritual situation and are not fully satisfied by any modern, post-Enlightenment alternative: we may either put our faith in "what cannot be known from the start— that only new, unheard of, ultramodern thoughts can clear away our dilemma"[36] or, if this seems an unreasonable hope, we may with Strauss consider whether "the critique of modern rationalism as the critique of modern sophistry,[37] is the necessary starting point, the constant concomitant, and the unerring hallmark of the search for truth possible in our age."[38] If that is so, we must "approach the medieval enlightenment, the enlightenment of Maimonides, for help."[39] Animated by both theological and political concerns that beset him as a modern Jew philosophically preoccupied with accounting for and justifying his unyielding but problematic commitment to Judaism as a revealed truth, Strauss turned to Maimonides for this help, and never retreated from him, for Strauss's Jewish thought was transformed by the "aid" he received. In fact, we would suggest that the testing of this "tentative" solution[40] emerged as his life's work. In Maimonides, Strauss believed he had genuinely discovered "the truly natural model, the standard" of rationalism in Judaism, and perhaps even in all philosophy, a belief which his subsequent discoveries only confirmed and deepened. Already in *Philosophy and Law* he declares unambiguously against the moderns that "the purpose of the present writing is to awaken a prejudice in favor of this conception of Maimonides, or rather, to arouse a suspicion against the powerful contrary prejudice."[41] The prejudice against Maimonides was first created and enunciated by the supposedly "free" and "unprejudiced" modernist Spinoza, and repeated ever since by his manifold followers.[42]

But what does Strauss ultimately mean to say, in a philosophical sense, by characterizing the premodern as "the truly natural" form of reason, or as we put it, as the purer and deeper form?[43] The fundamental lack of "purity" Strauss attributes to modern rationalism consists in the willfulness of the prior "unevident decision" about the nature of things and in the determination to "construct" the world as it wants the world to be[44] rather than accepting the limiting inferences possible from experience by first grounding itself well in the evident nature of things.[45] To Strauss, if philosophy is the search for truly "evident and necessary knowledge," then the search for knowledge properly commences in the visible world of human experience which is there for us first and plainly evident to be seen with our own eyes. However, the visible world in the beginning can only be intelligibly articulated and authoritatively explained to us through received or authoritative opinion as one's own city and law establish it. Man only moves or rises gradually, through the intellect's probing of opinion in doubting the "necessity" of the city's opinions, perhaps by comparison with other cities' opinions. One is able to dimly divine the truth, which, acting in the capacity of a final cause, draws one from "the given" to an awareness of the whole, especially as it may be reflected in the few generic and permanent features of the one human soul which manifests itself as such across the many opinions.[46] In other words, Strauss discerned that in the opposed starting points of philosophy, classical versus modern, the ultimate conclusions are already contained, if by these conclusions one limits oneself, as he did originally, to characterizing this fundamental difference by the absolute distinction between nature and history. As a result, what is "first for us"[47] is *either* what Plato termed "opinion," which like "the given" or the empirical *per se* helps us to transcend itself by first forming our view of the visible world and only subsequently leading us to ask about "the condition of its possibility"; *or* it is what the Enlightenment termed "prejudice," which is merely received or forced upon us against our true nature, and which as such hinders and deceives us entirely, so that we can only commence true knowing by utterly substituting for this merely given thing some absolute certainty.[48]

And yet "prejudice," as Strauss further discerned, is itself a derivative notion; in fact, as the fundamental polemical notion of the Enlightenment in its fight against orthodox revealed religion, Strauss perceived that "prejudice" is chiefly a "historical category" and not, as it claims, a purely natural one.[49] It is for this reason that Strauss originally wanted both the justification and the dubiousness of " 'prejudice' as a category" to be elucidated in light of the fight with revealed religion[50] rather than devoting himself to its argument with classical philosophy. Indeed, only for the Enlightenment is it "*the* prejudice pure and simple" to maintain that divine revelation is possible or that this possibility has been actualized in the Bible.[51] In fact, the Enlightenment waged its war against "prejudice" primarily and ultimately "with a view to the radical meaning of revealed religion." This "radical meaning" which it dogmatically rejects resides in orthodoxy's maintaining that mankind has a need for divine illumination and hence lacks self-sufficiency in attaining the truth. In Strauss's interpretation, revealed religion fundamentally rejects this world, i.e., the world of ordinary human experience and reasoning, as the final moral standard, or even as a possible source for such a standard, since "how man *is*" is essentially sinful.[52] Instead, it projects that which is known by divine revelation, by a transcendent source beyond man and the world, as the only true basis for a genuine morality, since only "how man *should be*," i.e., in the image of God, is the valid standard.[53] In other words, revealed religion is, like classical philosophy, morally "utopian," although modern philosophy castigates such moral "idealism" as purely imaginative and wishful, and offers its own "realism" as the first truly rational and efficacious teaching. Hence, Strauss's first substantial theological work in 1928 already reached the conclusion that modern philosophy is moved not so much either by scientific discoveries or by "secularization" of religious meanings and values, as it is by a moral passion; this passion is directed against all claims to transcendent sources of truth made accessible in our world through God's action: "The opposition to utopia is thus nothing other than the opposition to religion."[54]

Indeed, modern philosophy, as Strauss consistently maintained, was perhaps directly "caused," and certainly decisively "facilitated," by the passion which he calls "antitheological ire."[55] However, as Strauss subsequently recognized—and this represents a shift in his view—what modern philosophy teaches in opposition to "theology" seemingly applies to the biblical *and* the classical philosophic traditions, both of which are equally "utopian" in the "strict demands" of their moralities and "theological" in the exclusive God (or god) whose truth transcends and fulfills their respective moralities.[56] Classical philosophy shares with the biblical tradition not only a certain common attitude toward morality, but also "the natural world view" which is in a sense presupposed by their common moral attitude.[57] If we put this "natural world view" common to both traditions in the simplest possible language of philosophy, we might articulate Strauss's silent premise by saying that final and formal causes are still valid and are determinative in defining what the nature of a being is, and that, as such, all beings have a natural end or perfection which is peculiar to them. Morally, man is to be viewed in the light of the high or superhuman rather than of the low or subhuman; he is by nature a noble being, and this classical notion is in rough moral equivalence with the biblical teaching that man is "created in the image of God." This "wisdom" about man common to both the Bible and classical philosophy is a necessary element for both in the complete and final perfection of human life. These principles, with their moral and natural ramifications, are repudiated by modern philosophy and science as prejudices which we must escape, and also by modern historicism as positions which we have progressed beyond.

Strauss incisively cuts through these diverse modern positions and exposes their common core in this one presupposition they all share: the belief that we cannot "return" to the "natural world view" because it has been demonstrably refuted. Yet this presupposition may in fact be itself a prejudice that was consciously *created* by modern rationalist philosophy, supposedly on the strength of modern science, in order to further its cause. It was this prejudice, ironically taken for granted by modern historicism, which gave it the ammunition to mount the attack against its own precursor, modern rationalism, as a "refuted" position which can and must be simply gotten beyond, and to which we can never return. As Strauss puts it, "this belief is a dogmatic assumption whose hidden basis is the belief in progress or in the rationality of the historical process."[58] Moreover, this modern "belief in progress," even in its original rationalist form, contains in itself a plain denial of "the theological tradition" rather than merely its "secularization," i.e., the selective translation of the theological whole into parts usable by the secular world. The theological tradition had "recognized the mysterious character of providence," while modern philosophy "culminates in the view that the ways of God are scrutable to sufficiently enlightened men."[59] Accordingly, Strauss reveals the fundamental weakness of the modern rationalist position, and hence of modern philosophy *per se*, by uncovering the irrationalism of its basic premise—namely, that it can penetrate, and move beyond, the realm of God through rationality alone, or as this same dogmatic presupposition might be put purely philosophically, that it can achieve the conquest of chance in mastering nature as this is made possible by modern science.[60]

Although Strauss reached some of these primary conclusions in his first historical and theological studies, he was also previously influenced by the works of the Jewish thinker Franz Rosenzweig, with whom he was acquainted and whom he "greatly admired."[61] The fact that Strauss dedicated *Spinoza's Critique of Religion* to the memory of Franz Rosenzweig expresses the stage of spiritual growth in which Strauss developed the book's main thrust—the move from purely political Zionism to a decidedly theological orientation. The chief thesis of

Strauss in *Spinoza's Critique of Religion* is, like Rosenzweig's thought, rooted in the philosophic vindication of theology or divine revelation, insofar as the exposure of the hollowness of the modern claim to have genuinely refuted this spiritual possibility yields the plausible inference that its truth claim should be reconsidered. Rosenzweig taught him, among other things, that "the natural, original, pristine is *fidelity*"[62]—a notion which, we would suggest, also serves as the human basis for "opinion" rather than "prejudice." Likewise, Rosenzweig represented, by the heroic odyssey of his return to the Jewish tradition and his rediscovery of its deep spiritual sources for sustaining man in life and in death, the genuine possibility of "return" to an ancient truth even in our modern circumstances.

Strauss was familiar with Rosenzweig's "New Thinking," especially in its critique of Hegel, which postulated the victory of orthodox revealed religion against Enlightenment reason as a consequence of the Hegelian system's "final collapse." But taking this Rosenzweigian insight one step further, Strauss discerned that we can no longer assume that this vindication of orthodoxy alone is true. In other words, Strauss recognized that the Hegelian system's "final collapse" *equally* rehabilitates the Enlightenment along with the Bible or genuine divine revelation, since it too was supposed to have been "sublated," or given its best and highest exemplification, in the historical synthesis of Hegelian dialectical reason.[63] In the light of the collapse of the Hegelian synthesis, Strauss next began to wonder whether the Enlightenment, or modern rationalism, could in principle ever achieve its goal, not only of the simply rational society, but of the completed philosophic system[64]—a goal positive science shares but tries to achieve by a different method— since it began its efforts from such a shaky point of departure. It could not refute its chief opponents, biblical orthodoxy and classical philosophy, so it simply set about "constructing" the world and hoped to eclipse them by its successes. This did seemingly work as a strategy for several centuries. (Strauss calls it a "truly Napoleonic strategy.")[65] However, its eventual failure and what Strauss terms our present theological-political crisis should cause us, according to Strauss's logic, to reacquaint ourselves with the Enlightenment's basic premises and arguments and to ask whether they hold as much certainty as was originally claimed for them. In other words, the rationalism of the original Enlightenment returns to life with the collapse of Hegel, although (as one learns in studying the course of modern philosophy) the doubts about it which led it to be subsumed and sublated by Hegel should not and cannot be forgotten.

The Enlightenment, whose assumptions conquered the non-orthodox Jewish world, is the seventeenth and eighteenth century movement inspired by "Descartes' *Meditations* and Hobbes' *Leviathan*"[66]—but which Strauss would subsequently trace to Machiavelli as its "evil" genius[67]—aiming to make man "the master and owner of nature" through science.[68] However, as Strauss discovered, the Enlightenment originated not in a genuine scientific refutation of either biblical orthodoxy or of classical philosophy (i.e., of "the natural world view" shared by both the Bible and by Aristotle),[69] but in an act of will or belief, in a moral choice, even though "the new natural science appears to be the true entitlement (or justification) [*Rechtsgrund*] of the Enlightenment."[70] Only while "the old notion of truth still ruled the minds [*Gemüter*] of men,"[71] i.e., "the idea of an eternal nature [and] an eternal truth," was a continued belief in the promise of modern science made possible.[72] Once the Enlightenment and modern science were "sublated" by modern idealism, which "consummates itself in the discovery of the 'aesthetic' as the truest [*gediegensten*] insight into human creativity" and "in the discovery of the radical 'historicity' of man and his world as the final overcoming of even the idea of an eternal nature, an eternal truth," then modern natural science, which was the glory of the Enlightenment in its fight against orthodoxy, is exposed as merely "one historically conditioned form of 'interpretation of the world' among others."[73] In other words, it "could not long maintain its claim to have brought to light the truth about the world as it is 'in itself.'"[74] As Strauss reads it, "the 'idealistic' construction of itself was already built into [*steckte...in*] its basic approach." This rather cryptic statement can perhaps be better comprehended if we examine a similar statement he made in the Preface to *Spinoza's Critique of Religion* about how Spinoza's philosophic system "prepares German idealism." He says that neither God nor Nature as it is in itself is the most perfect being to Spinoza, but God or Nature as it is in the process of becoming is most perfect: indeed, the movement from the One to the many represents an ascent, not a descent. "Spinoza thus appears to originate the kind of philosophic system which views the fundamental *processus* as a progress: God in himself is not the *ens perfectissimum*. In this most important respect he prepares German idealism."[75]

Furthermore, it was through this idealistic breakthrough that the Enlightenment's "victory" against orthodoxy was actually denied its force and persuasiveness. As Strauss perceived, this leads to a further consequence with respect to the Enlightenment's "original, decisive justification: the demonstration of the unknowability of miracles as such becomes invalid [kraftlos]. For only on the premise of modern natural science is miracle as such unknowable."[76] Hence, idealism explodes the very truth claim of modern natural science, with the sole exception of its own demoralizing comprehension as a substitute—demoralizing because science can no longer aspire to truly know nature, but can only know either its current state as a configuration in our knowledge or the permanent tools by which the human mind constructs how such things may be. Finally, Strauss observes that even a critical view of knowledge which idealism postulates and clings to as the only truth remaining for us about things, is refuted by existentialism, its own "stepchild," as yet another form of "essentialism," i.e., the false belief in "an eternal nature, an eternal truth." Thus, Strauss diagnosed existentialism (in the form of radical historicism) as the very last consistently modern movement, whose pride and supreme claim as a more or less philosophical movement are based on its purer, *self-conscious* willing to construct the world and even man. Simply put, modern reason in the process of freeing itself from theology and the divine will has destroyed itself as reason by eventually reducing itself to human will. It is revealed by Strauss to be motivated not by pure love of wisdom, which would compel it to encounter theology as a serious and worthy opponent (if not as a teacher), but to be motivated by "atheism," or by "antitheological ire," or—with certain modern revisions—by Epicureanism.[77]

It seems plainly evident from Strauss's incisive diagnosis of the crisis in modern rationalism in *Philosophy and Law* (a diagnosis which was never repudiated by him, although it may have been subsequently radicalized) that his original interest in the attempted refutation of orthodoxy by Spinoza and the Enlightenment was by no means determined by a passion for orthodoxy pure and simple, even though he deeply respected it and often appears in the guise of its noble protector. Rather, it is an expression of a decided preference for an eminently reasonable theology, in one for whom "the desideratum of an enlightened Judaism is not to be denied [*unabweislich*]."[78] He "greatly admired" Franz Rosenzweig, but Strauss was not satisfied by his approach, even if he did acknowledge that "Jewish theology was resurrected from a deep slumber" by him.[79] Seeking an "enlightened Judaism," Strauss was "obliged to ascertain whether enlightenment is necessarily modern enlightenment," and hence he pursued a different path in search of this goal. Ultimately he found this goal only attainable by striving to reappropriate a premodern "Platonic" criterion for measuring "enlightenment,"[80] a criterion which points toward and concentrates on the few who can truly achieve it, and disavows what passes for "enlightenment" among the many.[81]

In his search for modern alternatives which might still be embraced, Strauss is sharply critical of what he calls the "moderate Enlightenment," which attempted numerous "harmonizations" [Vereinbarungen] between the "radical Enlightenment" and orthodoxy. He did not believe it signified a cogent third way in preserving and unifying the best of both modern reason and traditional revelation, for he rejects the very notion of mediation contained in its premise. Strauss concurs with the romantics and the idealists, as well as with "the most equitable historical judgment," that this mediating effort amounts to an "untenable . . . compromise."[82] The "moderate Enlightenment" is first represented by Moses Mendelssohn and his followers in the emergence of modern Judaism. But for Strauss, "modern Judaism is a synthesis between rabbinical Judaism and Spinoza," thus a synthesis between two mutually contradictory doctrines. Mendelssohnian "religious liberalism" can only elaborate and maintain its position either by ignoring the contradictions entirely or by smoothing them over in such a way as to inhibit any exact understanding of their pointedness.[83] In Strauss's estimation, all such harmonizing or synthesizing attempts by the moderate Enlightenment are futile, for it sustains no model or standard beyond the modern (i.e., radical) Enlightenment by which it could measure or criticize its own attempts at synthesis, and hence recognize and reconcile its own contradictions.[84] In fact, Strauss discerned that this movement ultimately failed in its own efforts at "mediation," and actually served as the unwitting advance guard in the Enlightenment's attack against orthodoxy: "in the end, these harmonizations always work as vehicles of the Enlightenment, and not as dams against it: for the radical Enlightenment, the moderate Enlightenment is the best first fruit."[85] The moderates create a palatable and even harmless version of the modern Enlightenment which, once the infiltration is complete and resistance is defused, eventually expedites a complete victory by the radicals.

These same strictures which Strauss applies to the pre-idealistic moderate Enlightenment concerning its subservience to the radical Enlightenment, he also applies, with some modifications, to subsequent philosophical and theological developments, i.e., Hegelianism and the anti-Hegelians. In Strauss's view, the " 'higher' plane of the post-Enlightenment synthesis," with its "interiorizations" of the orthodox tradition's primary assertions, "robs these assertions of their entire sense"[86] as claims about the "external" world. Taking the most fundamental case, Strauss maintains that if these "post-Enlightenment synthesizers" believe God did not "actually create" the world, and if they do not accept as a given this scriptural belief in the divine creation of nature as an entirety, i.e., "as simply true, as the fact of creation," then there is in the Hegelian and anti-Hegelian schools a spiritualizing tendency more or less continuous with their moderate Enlightenment predecessors. This spiritualizing tendency, however, has moved even farther away from any genuine scriptural belief, for it claims to have ascended to a higher synthesis which surpasses the claims of both its constituent theses—i.e., their claims to be *the* truth. But to Strauss, the spiritualizing tendency of this synthesis represents an equivocation, even a vacillation, of a still greater radicalness, which undoubtedly expresses the overwhelming fact that for the " 'higher' plane of synthesis" "the relation of God to nature could no longer be understood, and hence is no longer even of interest,"[87] because it has followed modern natural science in wholly surrendering the belief that it is necessary to infer metaphysical principles in order to explain adequately the physical universe.

Not only does the moderate Enlightenment thus transformed by the Hegelian synthesis still serve the radical Enlightenment in general purpose, but also the two procedures by which it validates its specific claims of harmony or synthesis are for Strauss completely "unscrupulous" as well as "erroneous" in principle.[88] First, it designates the "external" or literal sense of Scripture as a mere relic of "an immature level of formulation of the faith,"[89] even in regard to such seemingly crucial doctrines as creation out of nothing, verbal inspiration, and individual immortality.[90] Second, it "invokes against orthodoxy extreme utterances ventured in the Jewish tradition" as if they were normative, and hence turns them upside down as if the base were "the tip of the pyramid."[91] In his judgment the moderate Enlightenment reads the Bible and tradition as a mere search for prooftexts in order to justify its own preconceived opinions. Strauss undoubtedly counts among the figures who employ such a faulty method not only its spiritual patriarch Mendelssohn, but also the two greatest post-Hegelian Jewish thinkers, namely Cohen (with his "idealizing" interpretations) and even Rosenzweig (with his "new thinking"), both of whom readily admit the

Enlightenment origin of their "reservations" [*Vorbehalte*] toward tradition.[92] *All* "interiorizations" or "spiritualizations" [*Verinnerlich-ungen*] of the tradition's basic and primary assertions are to Strauss, in his radical critique, "in truth denials" of the tradition; for him this "is a fact obvious to the unbiased view."[93] That is because in the very act of "internalizing" or "spiritualizing" their meaning, the traditional assertions are stripped of their claims to be truths about the world in its external, factual sense.[94] This is obscured from view only because we, "so long as we do not make a point of fighting against our prejudices through historical recollection [*Besinnung*], are completely under the spell of the mode of thinking produced by the Enlightenment, and consolidated by its proponents and opponents."[95] Thus, in the very act of reconsidering the Enlightenment's encounter with orthodoxy, Strauss seems to have liberated himself from the Enlightenment-created "prejudice" endorsing its own rational necessity. He emerged in favor of premodern reason, achieving this liberation decisively aided by theology.[96] In the course of his embattled and passionate reconsideration, the theology whose cause he embraces was driven back to its premodern, sounder fortifications. Indeed, he discovered that those fortifications had never actually been destroyed by its opponents; its opponents had merely caused them to be abandoned through a clever diversionary tactic. Yet, how was Strauss enabled to see the great divide and to recognize the enduring validity of the premodern theological approach?

It seems that the key to this great step beyond the dualism established by modern philosophy—a dualism which sets the final choice as between Spinoza and the Jewish tradition, Enlightenment and orthodoxy, even philosophy and the Bible—is to be located in Gotthold Ephraim Lessing. Lessing was not bound by the dualism because he had, as Strauss might have put it, recovered *the* "natural horizon of human thought."[97] Lessing was able to think beyond the modern dualism because he looked back to the ancients who, in his own words (quoted by Strauss), saw with "better" and "sharper eyes" than the moderns who can only claim to "see more."[98] To Lessing, the ancients already penetrated as deeply as possible to all the fundamental principles of philosophy, while the moderns only apply the same to a wider field and elaborate them in a higher number of examples.[99] In other words, Lessing was not captivated by history, for "having had the experience of what philosophy is" in its true, i.e., classical, sense,[100] he used history precisely with the proper philosophic intention of recovering "the natural horizon." It would reflect "the eternal truth" beyond either orthodoxy or Enlightenment, whose conflict had been obscured in his day by polemics and apologetics. In his mature historical studies of the Enlightenment and orthodoxy, Lessing partially vindicated and partially criticized them both, which to Strauss indicates the ironic distance at which Lessing held these two rival parties. According to Strauss's conception, it was Lessing's firsthand knowledge of classical philosophy which enabled him to transcend dialectically these false modern alternatives. He rightly recognized these alternatives as determined mainly by a mere historical accident (i.e., the conflict which occurred in the seventeenth and eighteenth centuries, primarily caused by the modern Enlightenment's peculiarly bellicose character), and thus not by the suprahistorical or necessary truth.[101]

Likewise, Strauss justified his own original researches concerning Spinoza, the leading figure in the Enlightenment's critique of religion, by the need to "reenact" or "repeat" [*wiederholen*][102] "the classic quarrel between the Enlightenment and orthodoxy" as a fight for "the one, eternal truth." He says that in the classic quarrel "the natural desire for truth had not yet been deadened by the modern dogma that 'religion' and 'science' each has in view its own 'truth' coordinated to it."[103] This notion of Strauss's that the search for the single truth may reside in reviving and "reenacting" supposedly obsolete quarrels is reminiscent of the remark made by Lessing about his need for retrieving truths which he might have lost in discarding certain prejudices.[104] Indeed, the proof for the basic failure of the Enlightenment, especially in its attempt to refute orthodoxy, was apparently furnished in substance for Strauss by three things which Lessing taught him.

First, the radical Enlightenment's need to resort to laughter and mockery in order " 'to laugh' orthodoxy 'out' of its position from which it could not be dislodged by any proofs supplied by Scripture or by reason"[105] demonstrates like no other historical fact that orthodoxy's "ultimate premise" is "irrefutable," for this resort to base techniques such as mockery must be considered a desperate measure for rational men. As Strauss remarks trenchantly, "mockery does not succeed the refutation of the orthodox tenets but is itself the refutation."[106]

Second, according to "Lessing's Law [*Regel*]," as Strauss calls it,[107] the Enlightenment's worldly successes (e.g., modern science and modern politics), inasmuch as they are victories against orthodoxy, do not by any means prove the truth of its assertions, for "victories are 'very ambiguous demonstrations of the rightness of a cause, or rather. . .none at all' and thus 'he who is held to be right and he who should be held to be right is seldom one and the same person.' " It is for this reason among others that Strauss regarded it as necessary to abandon one's prejudices and to reenact the classic quarrel between orthodoxy and the Enlightenment. He wished to reach an honest judgment about the truth, by considering "uncorrupted by prejudice" each party's "hidden premises": hence "one must pay attention to the arguments of both parties" equally and fairly.[108]

Third, the critique of the "spiritualizations" of traditional orthodox assertions—a critique carried through with full force by nineteenth-century anti-Hegelianism, and as such laying the basis for the twentieth-century "movement of return"— was, as Strauss discovered, decisively begun by Lessing.[109] In fact, Lessing engaged in such theological critiques, so Strauss contends, actually as "a rehabilitation of the [radical] Enlightenment" in order to isolate the real disputants in the conflict.[110] Following Lessing's lead in remaining free of attachment to either one party or the other, even while "rehabilitating" their most radical arguments, Strauss indeed judges both sides justly. Strauss praises orthodoxy for having withstood its attackers' numerous "ruthless"[111] offensives by adhering mightily to "the irrefutable premise" on which it is firmly grounded and also because it defends a noble set of moral ideals.[112] Similarly, in addressing himself unpolemically to the Enlightenment (i.e., not as if it were a spent force, despite what its post-Kantian and romantic critics maintained against its "dogmatic" rationalism), Strauss vigorously praises it for not arguing "the great issues" with "trivial premises." He says it does not deserve to be treated as "a contemptible adversary,"[113] despite what he admits is its "atheistic" modern Epicureanism.

The dialectical approach which Strauss employs for "reenacting" the quarrel may have been borrowed from Lessing as well. Lessing was also able to criticize sharply those parties which he considered either guilty of a faulty compromise (e.g., Mendelssohn) or immersed in a pious self-deception (e.g., Jacobi). Learning from Lessing this agile and independent style of thinking, Strauss was able to reach strikingly judicious and unprejudiced conclusions about the Mendelssohn-Jacobi *Pantheismusstreit*. He also came to understand what Lessing was trying to get at in his use of a dialectical style which seemed to go out of its way to be paradoxical: he was striving to provoke his friends in both camps to a less dogmatic, more probing form of thinking, one which escapes modern prejudices and ripens into a deeper, classical freedom of thought. It is thought which allows itself a full radicalism of theory while moderating itself by prudence in practice.[114]

On the one hand, Lessing may have wanted to shock and perplex his friends in the moderate Enlightenment of Berlin by viewing orthodoxy so appreciatively following the acrimonious controversies that he had just been waging with the orthodox Pastor J. M. Goeze. This Lessing clearly did by "vindicating" Leibniz's strange assertion of pure orthodox beliefs in his fight against a contemporary heterodox theologian. But Strauss helps us to perceive beyond this apparent "vindication" [*Rettung*] that Lessing may have wanted to prove, among other things, that either an honest avowal of faith in the strict orthodox tradition or an unambiguous Spinozistic philosophic "atheism" is preferable to acquiescing in anything like Mendelssohn's pantheistic "purified" Spinozism, which Strauss aptly calls "semi-theism."[115]

On the other hand, Lessing's seemingly simple, though not entirely unironic, identification of philosophy with Spinoza may have aimed to shock men like Jacobi into keeping away from what he discerned in them as budding romanticism, or a nostalgia for "the lost belief." In Lessing's view, Jacobi (and the romantic philosophers who followed him) could no longer believe in the orthodox religion because modern rationalist philosophers (like Spinoza) had convinced him that it could not be true, but he could not bring himself to sever his *inner* attachment to the faith. This resulted in his assuming an attitude of "equivocal reverence" for the orthodox tradition, i.e., of venerating its past greatness while keeping it safely "at arm's length." According to Strauss's reading, Lessing was apparently hinting that they plainly err if they consider this to be either genuine religiosity or genuine speculation, since the belief which they thus try to recover has been infected with atheism through its very exposure to, and immersion in, modern rationalistic philosophy. Like its moderate Enlightenment opponent, this erstwhile romanticism too is a compromise or a synthesis with Spinoza and the radical Enlightenment. As it seemed to Strauss, Lessing intended to express that a pure atheism is preferable in its honesty to a half-hearted faith which consists mainly of nostalgic longing.[116]

However honest or sincere this atheism may seem, "conscientious" atheism is scarcely Strauss's own last word. Indeed, Strauss was induced to wonder about the theological and political adequacy of modern rationalism precisely once its fundamental atheism was exposed.[117] Its atheism seemed to Strauss somehow connected with its issuing in a decided irrationalism.[118] As Strauss declares, atheism is "admittedly undemonstrable"; hence, atheism cannot be "made a positive, dogmatic premise." This logic remained binding only so long as the "old love of truth" ruled philosophy—but it is not necessarily so with the new "intellectual probity," which, godlike, claims that it can search and know its own heart with purity.[119] Strauss contends that such a "terrible thing as atheism"[120] is only a tolerably valid term if it hesitatingly articulates the experience represented by negative, skeptical probing, by free enquiry, and if it is meant primarily as a tentative method of standing in doubt of "authority" ("authority" being the source of every "orthodox" opinion or prejudice).[121] As such, even the Enlightenment, having established itself as an "authority," must be doubted by the authentic "atheist" (which may be done in the manner of Lessing, who recognized that the best way to contend against this new authority was through its old chief adversary, orthodoxy). This doubting, which is not bound by any dogma, even a dogmatic atheism, is distinguished by genuine open-mindedness, or by true "free thinking," because it is free with respect to the opinions commanded by authority. Consequently, it is pursued not in order to attain immediately one absolutely certain thing by doubting everything possible, as with Descartes in his grounding of modern philosophy,[122] but in order to acquire the truly philosophic "attitude,"[123] as Strauss conceived it, which by its nature requires one to "dialectically" transcend false alternatives and their claims to be the complete and final wisdom.

Thus do we arrive at the Socratic "dialectical attitude," which in Strauss's scheme is the peculiar characteristic of the true philosopher. In fact, according to Strauss, it was this "dialectic" that was, in the very beginnings of philosophy, originally applied to the conflict of opinions about the good and about the whole in the diverse divine codes. Philosophy was a search for what is good "by nature" rather than by ancestral tradition, as well as a search for an adequate, evident, and necessary "articulation of the whole" rather than for its mythic presentation.[124] Therefore, Strauss (following Lessing) proceeds differently from the Enlightenment in method, and likewise moves away from it in goal, because he keeps in view the *possibility* of a truth which transcends all "authoritative" opinions or prejudices but which is fleetingly reflected in them and to which only they first point us. Hence we must ascend "dialectically" *through* them, be it only for the sake of their directing us to "a fundamental awareness of the whole," philosophically known as the eternal truth, or nature, or even God. "In other words, the opinions prove to be solicited by the self-subsistent truth, and the ascent to the truth proves to be guided by the self-subsistent truth which all men always divine."[125] In light of these considerations, as well as the further statement which Strauss proffers concerning what, according to him, is the one universal thing which "all understanding presupposes"—"prior to any perception of particular things, the human soul must have had a vision of the ideas, a vision of the articulated whole"[126]—it is, I believe, entirely accurate to designate Strauss as what we might call a "cognitive theist."[127]

CHAPTER 2

Is a "Return" to Maimonides Possible?

THE OBSTACLES AND
THEIR SURMOUNTING

STRAUSS SEEMS TO HAVE ACHIEVED a standpoint from which he could view the antagonists, Enlightenment and orthodoxy, free of partisan passion, and yet could still remain vitally interested in the examination of their "classic quarrel" and its "great issues."[1] Indeed, this is the standpoint that Strauss identified with Maimonides. Strauss attained his first striking comprehension of the Maimonidean standpoint by analyzing, in comparative terms, the philosophic flaws and the natural limits in Spinoza's critique of orthodox revealed religion; Strauss always regarded Spinoza's powerful criticism as a great help in sharply formulating the decisive points of conflict.[2] As I mentioned previously, Strauss's comprehension of the Maimonidean standpoint was certainly deepened but never surpassed in his subsequent development, however one judges its direction.[3] As a *fundamental* standpoint, which somehow harmoniously embraces both natural reason and divine revelation, Strauss clearly recognized and distinctly maintained its basic connection with Plato, but this does not make it purely and simply Platonic. Strauss believed that Maimonides probed the meaning of the Platonic standpoint deeper and carried its ramifications further than anyone else in the struggle between what Strauss viewed as the two ultimate antagonists, the Bible and philosophy.[4] Strauss definitely identified this Platonically dialectical standpoint with Maimonides rather than with Lessing, although Lessing taught him a good deal which helped him penetrate the hidden reaches of Maimonides' thought in both its religious and philosophic aspects. Strauss remained loyal to Lessing even while

diverging from him, just as Lessing had conducted himself with regard
to Spinoza's philosophy; Lessing had carefully studied as well as
transcended Spinoza's specific views, while still retaining his general
approach in its uncompromising search for clarity as well as profundity
of active thinking.[5]

What then is the Maimonidean standpoint which Strauss advocated,
and are there any serious substantial grounds for accepting it as a true
and valid standpoint? As Strauss freely acknowledged, we moderns—
with our rigorously mathematical natural science and its sure empirical
method, with the previously unknown "facts" discovered by modern
natural science, and the modern cosmology constructed through these
"facts"—will certainly wonder whether we can honestly turn to
Maimonides' supposedly "natural world view."[6] Strauss asserts that this
world view was shared by the Bible and by Aristotle, and achieved its
most fully developed and harmonized form in the Aristotelian-Ptolemaic
science and philosophy of the Middle Ages when it was combined with
the highest biblical religious teachings by such religious thinkers as
Maimonides. But is not this "natural world view" nevertheless an
obsolete, or "irretrievable, cosmology"?[7] Moreover, if the Bible and
Aristotle do share "the natural world view," we might say that this shared
world view is an additional argument against the Bible.[8] Certainly sharp
modern critics like Spinoza rejected final causality as being a "prejudice"
about God as well as nature.[9] Let us recall for a moment Strauss's
"reenactment" of the argument between orthodoxy and the
Enlightenment, and restate the results which it produced, in the light
of a possible turn to Maimonides. On the one hand, orthodoxy is proven
to be simply irrefutable, because its fundamental premise, "the
omnipotent God whose will is unfathomable," can only be refuted if we
possess the completed "philosophic system," *the* "clear and distinct
account of everything."[10] On the other hand, miracles, orthodoxy's main
evidential support, are proven to be "unknowable" *as* miracles, even
though their possibility has never been refuted, and thus orthodoxy's
chief factual arguments for its fundamental premise are merely believed
but not known—"they cannot claim to possess the binding power
peculiar to the known."[11] However, this is a conclusion that holds true
and is decisive only so long as modern natural science prevails as *the*
final and necessary account of the world.[12] In Strauss's view, the collapse
of this finality and necessity lies in the discovery that modern natural
science is only "one historically conditioned form of 'interpretation of
the world' among others." This removes a very significant obstacle

preventing modern man from seriously considering a return to Maimonides[13] and the classical natural perspective.[14]

Even if it is true that Maimonides' natural science might yet be proved valid, this is still purely a negative argument for the truth of Maimonides' standpoint, since to maintain that its natural basis is *possibly* true does not in any case move us much further toward proving the actual truth of this standpoint. Yet once the principle is accepted that it could possibly be true, a very great divide has been crossed.

In the potential restoration of the Maimonidean standpoint, Strauss nonetheless considered it safer, i.e., more evidently useful and less seemingly antiquated, to comprehend Maimonides' human science first. For while Maimonides' human science may still presuppose to a certain degree something akin to classical natural science or philosophy, it does not require that this natural science either be approached directly or be appropriated systematically. If we carry this logic one step further as his argument requires, it seems for Strauss that Maimonides, like Socrates, was not ultimately "committed to a specific cosmology."[15] Maimonides' human science has enduring human relevance, and its wisdom or virtue in regard to the actual world makes it of interest to us as Jews and as human beings. Our present-day crisis is mainly experienced by us as a crisis in morality or religion or politics rather than as a crisis of nature.

Two fundamental "natural" principles which support classical science are discernible in Strauss's reading of Maimonides: all things are most accurately comprehended in the light of the high (or superhuman) rather than the low (or subhuman); and all things are most accurately comprehended "in the light of the completed thing or the end of the process" rather than in the roots of the thing or the beginning of the process.[16] Put in terms of traditional notions, we may designate these fundamental principles as "natural hierarchy" and "final causes." Strauss obviously rejects the historicist premise that the essential nature rather than merely the existential situation of man and even of Being has ever changed in any decisive respect. Along with this he rejects the belief in progress; in his view this idea originally "determined" the historicist premise,[17] with its radical belief in the absolute mutability of Being through history, i.e., the belief that "Being [. . .] creates itself in the course of History."[18]

What then is the philosophic or natural basis for Maimonides' human science? And why would Strauss have us consider it prior to considering Maimonides' fully developed natural science? It was, we must remember, essentially through this natural science that

Maimonides was able to demonstrate God's existence—surely a matter of higher concern in Maimonides' cognitive scheme than any human relations. (His numerous statements about the dignity of natural science in the striving for human perfection, and certainly about its being a necessary constituent in man's apprehension of God, would seem to put this matter beyond all doubt.)[19] Nevertheless, Strauss would, I believe, have mustered the following argument in favor of human science as prior to natural science.

First, human science does not have ultimate priority but is prior in the intellectual immediacy of common sense, in its appeal to human excellence, and in its moral usefulness to all men. Besides, human science attempts to determine the conditions of the possibility of philosophy as a whole (of which natural science is only a very crucial part). It considers how and why philosophy arises among human beings and how it may be preserved and helped to flourish—thus claiming a priority in material comprehensiveness to which natural science must acknowledge its subordination. Strauss perceived that this priority is reflected by Maimonides' *Guide* in the logic of its literary structure. In Strauss's reading, there is a deeper reason for Maimonides' having chosen to present the *Guide*'s complete argument in the form of an "ascent" followed by a "descent." The *Guide* begins with man dwelling in the world of opinion: it teaches about the human realm and about how to reorient oneself toward the human realm. Prior to everything else, Maimonides wants his addressees to comprehend what the human realm is, i.e., it is the world created by opinion, and the life led according to its authority. This means that human science teaches man to separate from opinion, and to turn toward the search for knowledge of the truth. The first portion proceeds gradually but deliberately from the human context of the philosophic search (introduction and first part, chapters 1–49) to man and his proper relations with God and nature (first part, chapters 50–76) to God by himself alone and how in his perfection he overflows to man (second part). The second portion returns to treat man again, but with a view of how "the typical and atypical addressees" of the book, transformed by studying the first and second parts, should dwell in the human realm (third part).[20] Once the proper groundwork is laid by human science, the crucial decision is then whether natural science will be pursued thoroughly and autonomously by "the typical addressee," since the kind of transition "the typical addressee" makes especially from the first to the second parts shapes how he will read the book as a whole. More importantly, it is the character of this transition that determines how he will use his mind and lead his life, and decides whether he will emerge as "atypical," and hence desire to be as "critical and competent" as Maimonides himself.[21] Thus, Strauss by no means discounts or ignores natural science, even though in reading the *Guide* he approaches it first by way of human science. Indeed, by doing so, he would seem to be following Maimonides' own directions.

Second, in the spirit of both Socrates and Maimonides, Strauss recognized that beginning with natural science represents a grave danger, for it threatens to destroy entirely traditional beliefs and habits by a false confidence. If one attempts to explain all things directly by natural science alone, this tends to lead one to a materialistic reductionism.[22] Further, in bypassing or utterly dismissing authoritative beliefs and habits, as the one "corrupted" by natural science is wont to do, one is likely to miss the decisive lessons even for the interpretation of nature which beginning with human science facilitates. These lessons for interpreting nature, derived from studying the soul and its causes, can only be glimpsed in flashes through true opinion, and the search for true opinion in the authoritative beliefs is the propaedeutic aim of human science as a guide to the ascent to the truth about the *whole*.[23] Strauss also believes Maimonides has a subtler purpose in warning against the immoderate desire, and premature exploration, of natural science. Maimonides' explanation of the five causes why one should not commence one's instruction with divine science is directed not against those who are properly equipped and are also willing to make the enormous effort to master natural science. Instead, it is aimed against those who deny natural science as the necessary preparation for divine science, because their own laziness or lack of natural ability in science keeps them from applying themselves to its correct appropriation. Rather than renounce their desire, which would be healthier for them, their "abundant longing" drives them "to disapprove of their preliminary studies" and to substitute for true scientific knowledge something wrought in the imagination. Indeed, it is this "disease" that afflicts the greater number of "those generally known as men of knowledge," as Maimonides puts it. Thus, Strauss does not discern in Maimonides any denial of "a natural harmony between the human mind and the whole"[24] which might seem to contradict man's natural desire for the complete scientific truth: Maimonides, in his discussion of man's "natural desire for knowledge, warns not against the desire for comprehensive knowledge, but against seeming knowledge."[25]

Third, there is, it seemed to Strauss, greater evidence for the fundamental principles of Maimonides' political teaching than for those of his theological teaching taken in isolation.[26] These fundamental principles of his political teaching are that man has a final end (or telos) which is natural to him and that this end can only be discovered and properly defined in the light of human perfection or virtue. This greater evidence provides a compelling argument for Maimonides' human science inasmuch as his political teaching contains what is requisite for a true and perennial understanding of man always, and may be applied to any society in any place and time, to all political life, even if one disregards for the moment the truth of the theological beliefs in which this life may be rooted. In fact, even these theological beliefs and indeed the society itself cannot long endure if great political leaders, military heroes, religious saints, or philosophic teachers do not arise who are moved to act nobly, and if necessary, to sacrifice personal happiness in order to preserve the society for the sake of a transcendent vision. These men are, as it were, perfect men, for they embody what all men who are not perverse or corrupt spontaneously admire for its own sake. They are recognized both as humanly paradigmatic in their virtue and as possessing a self-evidently greater perfection than ordinary men.[27] This seems to prove that human excellence does not arise either from chance or from the creative human will alone, but follows in consequence of natural principles which govern human life. This signals an inference of naturalness that, in Strauss's view, is evident to any unprejudiced beholder participating in human life. These same natural principles, fundamental to Maimonides' political teaching,[28] appear in his physics and metaphysics as systematic formal and final causes in the world of nonhuman nature. However, they do not seem as evident and necessary to us as the principles governing human life. According to Strauss, this disparity between the natural and human realms especially holds for us moderns because we are trained by modern science and philosophy to believe that formal and final causes are based on superstition, and that the world can be explained adequately by material and efficient causes. Consequently, we are precluded from utilizing these principles for pointing to nature itself as the exemplification of active intelligence in its order and purpose. Nor can these principles be employed to reveal the general governance through the natural order and the specific providential purposes of the divine. Such traditional philosophic employment of natural teleology in theology constitutes in substance what Strauss calls "the simple teleology" or "the teleotheology."[29]

This discussion of why Strauss considered human science prior to natural science leads us to the problem of Strauss's own "cosmology," because it is only in attaining a comprehensive view of the *whole* that one can order the priority of its parts. According to Strauss, we moderns lack a final and complete scheme of the universe by which we might comprehend man, who needs such a scheme in order to be assigned a dignified though subordinate rank in the natural order. The natural and divine science developed by classical and medieval philosophers constituted such a scheme, though Strauss acknowledges it to be for us "an antiquated cosmology."[30] It viewed man in the light of the naturally high, while modern science cannot help but view him in the light of the naturally low. As moderns, we are trained to comprehend nature as operating by uniform, equal laws, illuminated solely by efficient and material causes. We have moved beyond contemplating the universe as a finite whole whose parts articulate a natural hierarchy in the order of beings. This great chain of being culminated with man in the sublunar or lowest sphere, whose distinctive excellence was intellect; and it "located" God, as it were, in or just beyond the highest or all-encompassing superlunar sphere, demonstrating him to be the highest and the most perfect Being, and as the First Cause of the universe. In such a scheme of the universe, Maimonides was able to harmonize human and natural as well as divine sciences at the highest level: man holds the key to his perfection through his natural form ("in virtue of which a thing is constituted as a substance"), through the exercise of his intellect, and in the act of "cognitive apprehension" man approaches God.[31] Moreover, this natural perfection of man in striving for comprehensive knowledge was then for Maimonides also identical with man's supreme religious duty to God—to imitate and love him—because man's link with God was achieved in that specific manner by which he himself was created (i.e., "in the divine image").

But, in Strauss's assessment, this "moving beyond" the classical or natural view of the universe does not represent a genuine progress in understanding. In order to overcome the philosophic and moral crisis we face as moderns, a new cosmology is needed which will explain the universe in such a way as to transcend the mechanistic-mathematical materialism of our modern cosmology;[32] yet will not completely return to the old medieval and classical form, since that manner of interpreting certain natural facts may well be "antiquated." However, even with the inspiration of Strauss's own vigorous restorative efforts in human science as an example to follow, it is still no simple task to perform. As Strauss himself recognizes, the teleological view of man, to be entirely valid and adequate, can only form a part of the teleological view of nature as a whole, but such a comprehensive teleology "would seem to have been destroyed by modern natural science."[33] He believes there is a necessary connection between human and natural science, and he does not want to commit the error of the modern Thomists, who "break with the comprehensive view of Aristotle" (who regarded man and the world as constituted by one ruling conception of nature). Such Thomists, he says, "are forced to accept a fundamental, typically modern, dualism of a non-teleological natural science and a teleological science of man."[34]

Strauss seems to suggest tacitly that the classical teleological view of nature must be revived—in other words, has not been utterly refuted—modern natural science notwithstanding. Strauss seems to "invite" any courageous and radical natural scientist to explore the classical and medieval sources to try to save modern natural science from the crisis[35] to which it has been led by its own mechanistic and materialistic bases.[36] At the same time, he justifies his own procedure, as likewise Maimonides', by claiming that we do not have to be "committed to a specific cosmology" in order to render an account of man in Socratic terms, or in the light of those terms which established human science as known through the classical tradition. Socrates "viewed man in the light of the mysterious character of the whole" and did not believe that ignorance of "the ultimate causes" of the human situation changes what we may know about man as man, so long as we remain aware of this ignorance while striving to relieve it through pursuing comprehensive knowledge about nature even in human science. As such, Maimonides too would have to be regarded, according to Strauss, as one for whom "the quest for cosmology rather than a solution to the cosmological problem"[37] lays the basis for philosophizing. Strauss quotes Maimonides[38] to the effect that "the conflict between philosophic cosmology and mathematical astronomy. . . [was] 'the true perplexity.'"[39]

And yet, for all of this cosmological uncertainty, Strauss seems to suggest subtly that if the medieval teaching about man, which regards him as possessing a final end natural to him—a culminating perfection or virtue in the light of which all other human things are comprehended—could be "proven" or recognized to be the only truly intelligible account of man, one would be well-equipped to argue for the teleological view of nature. Likewise, if final and formal causes are operative for man and for nature, then it may also be requisite to consider the visible world, as we observe it, to be a completed whole, whose perfection does not reside in any future development; we must acknowledge that what of the completed whole is perfect, it already and always possesses. In other words, if such final and formal causes are evident in man, and if such fundamental principles are even *necessary* for the proper comprehension of human nature, they are likelier to be required in the proper comprehension of nature as a whole (though admittedly merely "likelier").[40]

Indeed, if final and formal causes were necessary for comprehending man, they would be demonstrated to be present in nature, if only in the nature of man. Strauss surprisingly acknowledges radical historicism's exacting insight that we need no longer be bound by the modern separation between man and nature. This has been radical historicism's main and incisive contribution to liberating us from modern prejudices, for it turns against its modern philosophical creator and expels nature entirely in favor of history.[41] Experimentally extending such fundamental principles to nature as a whole would be philosophy's natural inclination, as it were, whatever the result it subsequently produced, for philosophy is to Strauss virtually identifiable with the passionate interest in the cognition of everything which it is possible for man to cognize. Or as Strauss succinctly puts it: "Philosophy strives for knowledge of the whole." The whole may be most illuminatingly approached, even if only dimly perceived, through whatever parts of it we can truly and certainly know, especially as these parts fit into, or add to, or finish the whole as partial wholes themselves. Strauss further elucidates his position thus: "To understand the whole, therefore, means. . . to understand the unity that is revealed in the manifest articulation of the completed whole. . . . This view makes possible, and it favors in particular, the study of the human things as such."

We can discern in Strauss's "Socratic" reading of the Maimonidean standpoint why human science is to be preferred as the natural beginning for true philosophizing. Human science alone best provides us with direct access to a completed whole which may reflect *the* whole, assuming only, as Strauss must, that man himself represents a completed whole, possessing a nature or a soul, and that human excellence or virtue or perfection is the true intention of human life, with all other human things to be viewed in its light. This amounts to nothing other than the knowledge of man, whose life is diverse in intentions but is experienced as a unity, especially by those wise men who seem to know what ends it is best for man to pursue. "As knowledge of the ends of human life, it is knowledge of what makes human life complete or whole; it is therefore knowledge of a whole. Knowledge of the ends of man implies knowledge of the human soul; and the human soul is the only part of the whole which is open to the whole and therefore more akin to the whole than anything else is."[42] Hence, while "this knowledge. . . is not knowledge of the whole," but must be combined with knowledge of nature (especially as perfected in mathematical knowledge) in order to be true wisdom, nature itself seems to sustain our philosophical quest by fostering in us love or desire for that highest wisdom toward which we strive, even though it is seemingly ever unfulfilled.

Strauss thus provides an enduring justification for the classical philosophy which Maimonides embraced and yet also contended with and occasionally even tried to "correct" or "complete." Rather than asserting what man must be by what it supposedly knows about nature, classical Socratic philosophy attempts to account for the whole[43] through first investigating one part which in itself seems to form a completed whole, i.e., the human soul or the human "situation" (insofar as a single essential "situation" characterizes human life). It is this part which we may perhaps know about in some measure with the greatest certainty or with a greater directness of access.[44] Classical philosophy, in the spirit of Socrates, apparently proceeds to nature from the truths which it obtains about man; or, what it teaches about nature is both determined and limited by what it teaches about man. Hence, it must remain free from any commitment to a "specific cosmology," if it professes mere knowledge of its own ignorance. Such "Socratic" philosophizing certainly cannot require or presuppose classical natural science inasmuch as it claims to know the whole: if one being, man, is its beginning and the whole or nature is merely the end, it must recognize how enormously difficult it is even to know ourselves; hence, it must also recognize its accounting for the whole as a mere attempt. The basis for classical philosophy is "the quest for cosmology rather than a solution to the cosmological problem."[45] Any complete solution which it might offer to the cosmological problem must remain tentative and hypothetical.

Nothing in all of this, however, excludes the possibility that Socrates himself held cosmological opinions. Indeed, both from Strauss's own argument and from suggestions which he attributes to Xenophon, it seems we must necessarily infer that "there is a Socratic cosmology," although this may only have been either a partial solution to the cosmological problem or only the fundamental principles which point to a complete one. This also does not require us to conclude that Socrates taught his cosmology directly to anyone, even though his wisest students may have been able to deduce it for themselves. What Socrates actually taught publicly then—his theological-political doctrine proper, which

Strauss calls the "teleotheology"—may be the best clue we possess to his private teaching. In any case, the "teleotheology" which persisted until Maimonides' day and beyond it, perhaps until Spinoza's apparently devastating critique, was the teaching by which, according to Xenophon, Socrates made his companions pious. It reveals man as the being who is divinely ordained to perfect himself in the quest for the whole and in the life of virtue. And for Strauss too, it seems to contain in itself the greatest probability of truth: final and formal causes and natural hierarchy must be maintained as fundamental natural principles if an adequate human science is to be attained. A human science is only considered adequate if the possibility of philosophy and its harmony with the life of man in the city can be enunciated correctly and persuasively.[46] Likewise, in the case of Maimonides, "the classic of rationalism in Judaism," Strauss would concede that although his cosmology and natural science seem to be antiquated or obsolete, this is so only in *some* respects. Strauss then does not allow this concession to determine entirely his thinking about *all* things, for he would argue that there are fundamental principles guiding Maimonides in his approach to nature which may still be true, valid, and unrefuted.

The endeavor to establish the possibility of a "return" to Maimonides, which we have been following with regard to cosmology and natural science, will be helpful, I believe, in recognizing the decisive philosophic significance of Maimonides' human science for Strauss. In Strauss's reading, Maimonides himself penetrated these issues as deeply and as thoroughly as any thinker ever did, and as a result he apprehended the binding power that this "Socratic" conception of the nature of philosophy possesses. That Maimonides embraced this approach, favoring human science first in pursuit of divine science, was evident to Strauss from Maimonides' conclusively admitting the need for a kind of divination—i.e., lawgiving prophecy—in reaching the highest truth. Even in Maimonides' often radically naturalistic scheme, prophecy itself is depicted as a kind of "divine gift," for God may in some sense "prevent" the potential prophet from reaching his full actualization. This then would seem to suggest that there is no system of final rational truth through which all men may necessarily achieve human perfection. Moreover, in Maimonides' scheme, all theological knowledge and all political rule have their inexorable and fateful grounding, we might say, in "lightning flashes" of illumination, or in something which is akin to them. Human perfection, and hence true happiness, would then seem to be reserved for those few who are so graced by divine providence that they receive divine illumination in their active search for the final rational truth. But there is hope for the many in the very being of the true prophet, who brings to the multitude an imaginative version of the truth in the divine law, which at the very least is the best approximation to human perfection, as knowledge of rational truth, available to most men.[47] Hence, the better the society's order and its opinions, the more directly is it correlated with the degree of truth and justice apprehended in illumination by the prophet who gave it its law.

This is the chief sign of divine providence that is present in every society.[48] Its degree is determinable by the evidence of divinely given human speculative intelligence and moral excellence in the law, and especially in its establishing such universal signs of divinity in human matters as the ultimate goals of human striving, particularly for those men who faithfully obey the law and who are in turn shaped by it. Indeed, Maimonides puts the prophet and his divinely given law at the very center of his entire theological teaching (and rightly so, according to Strauss); it is as a result of this that Maimonides' teaching possesses a distinctly political coloration, since it provides the necessary and fundamental basis for any society.[49] Consequently, Maimonides' notion of prophecy does not enmesh him in asserting irrationalities concerning God and nature.[50] In Strauss's reading, those "suprarational" truths taught by the prophet that Maimonides accepts derive only from Maimonides having been compelled by pure reason to acknowledge the unavoidable, and hence natural, human limits in attaining the complete, adequate, and final rational system of truth about the world. If such a system were truly actual, it would necessarily make itself the *unerring* basis and guide for designing any society that wants to be or claims to be rational. In other words, every society would have to conform with this system not just in its general basis or guidelines, but in every specific significant detail—a claim about political truth precisely correlated with speculative (or theological) truth which Maimonides considered beyond the power of man to actualize (and hence a claim which must always descend into dogmatism). Thus, it is the expression of Maimonides' intellectual freedom that, even in his adherence to the basic Platonic-Aristotelian postulates as apparently "systematized" by the lawgiving prophet, he is not tempted to embrace the style of dogmatic rationalism that was to some degree already present in the "systematic" philosophy of Thomas Aquinas.[51]

Following Strauss's lead, we may contrast this Maimonidean scheme with that of Spinoza, who maintains that lawgiving prophecy is just a simple human effort aided by the imagination alone in devising political rules for men. Spinoza says prophecy need not be comprehended in the light of any *transcendent* theological truth or in the light of supreme human virtue. The basic principle guiding this modern approach may be said to be that men of intellect or of virtue are not the natural standard against which all things subordinate in perfection to them are measured; average men are the standard, and the exceptions have to fend for themselves. Once we possess the complete, adequate, and final system, e.g., in the form of Spinoza's *Ethics*—a system which in fact presents man "realistically," or as he is, rather than "idealistically," or as he should be, and hence which dispenses with natural hierarchy and final causality— man can, according to Spinoza, devise through it the principles for a perfect or harmonious society which will potentially resolve all fundamental human contradictions and conflicts. Moreover, man alone makes all civilization, and does not need God's help; even the best society can be constituted by such a simple human effort (once the chief obstacles such as superstition have been removed). The resulting constructed system is the one needful possession for all men to actualize their rationality.[52] The Enlightenment offered itself as such a system, with the help in its construction provided by men like Spinoza; they were constrained to start the modern "historicization" of philosophy in order to achieve their goal, which the classical philosophers would have considered to be ultimately "against nature." Although it required all doubts about its project to perfect man and produce the best society to be rationally dispensed with in the beginning of its efforts, the Enlightenment could only promise the full manifestation or proof of its own truth for man in the *future*. But according to Strauss's unique analysis, this may not be so easy a task to perform now that we have witnessed the limits of the Enlightenment's ability to control or diminish human evil, and now that we are no longer convinced by the decisive claims of modern science to possess the final truth. Its "Napoleonic" strategy worked only so long as we were blinded by its worldly successes.[53] As its failures manifest themselves, religious orthodoxy (especially as rooted in the "enlightened" thought of Maimonides) comes back into sight as a logically possible and morally valid approach.

Strauss discovered that the main reason a return to orthodoxy is not "an impossibility" but is "in fact only a very great difficulty" is that Spinoza may have been "wrong in the decisive respect"—that is, wrong in regard to the possibility of there being a final and complete philosophical refutation of divine revelation as this is made known to man in the Bible by the one omnipotent God.[54] No modern Jewish philosopher had been able to prove this to Strauss, although Hermann Cohen's critique of Spinoza approached such a proof in exposing the nonscientific interest motivating Spinoza's Bible science.[55] Strauss's phrase "wrong in the decisive respect" would seem to be meant in terms of knowing, and not just believing, as Cohen apparently still did, that the Enlightenment system (especially as it was synthesized by Spinoza) is entirely true, or true in its basic premises, which would thus certainly entail the definitive refutation of orthodoxy. As a result, belief in the truth of orthodoxy may nevertheless still be "a very great difficulty," even if it is proved to be a logically possible truth. Hence, Strauss's additional phrase provisionally concedes that "Spinoza has refuted orthodoxy" through his historical and philosophical criticism, insofar as this refutation is not solely dependent upon his system but follows a soundly naturalistic approach. This is meant seriously inasmuch as the religious believer claims to "know" the teachings which biblical orthodoxy propounds as evident and necessary truths; this "knowing" would only be possible if orthodoxy could likewise entirely refute philosophy, which it has never been able to do. Even if orthodoxy's fundamental premise is "irrefutable," that does not render it evident and necessary, and thus in this "irrefutability" there is still not contained a valid demonstration of its truth. In other words, it is much more difficult to prove the truth of orthodoxy than it is to disprove its supposed refutations. Nonetheless, what Strauss calls "the irrefutable premise"[56] of orthodoxy must still be demonstrated to be in conformity with genuine "intellectual probity,"[57] in order for orthodoxy to be believed in; and the *only* rationalist Jewish theologian that Spinoza never defeated in regard to this crucial issue was Maimonides, as Strauss's first researches convincingly prove.[58] But if divine revelation is to inspire true belief in the modern intellect characterized by its probity (i.e., its honesty and sincerity rather than its love of truth alone), then it must be proven to bestow some excellence of soul needed even by the best human minds to exact their sincere acceptance and reverence. Thus, Strauss was provided with another urgent motive for attempting to understand how Maimonides could withstand Spinoza's assault, for it seemed that this same "very great difficulty" also stood in the way of Strauss's own wholehearted return to Jewish orthodoxy.[59] Of course, it is not necessarily the case that the profundity with which Strauss penetrated into the edifice of Maimonides' thought itself resolved or overruled this "very great difficulty," but it went a long way toward persuading him of the great need for divine revelation which Spinoza and his modern followers had so heedlessly discarded.[60]

We now arrive at the problematic task of attending to Maimonides, in the manner of Strauss, for the answer to the question of the relation between philosophy and the Bible (or Enlightenment and orthodoxy) which Maimonides solved through his so-called "allegorical method" of biblical interpretation. This "method" poses an acute difficulty peculiar to us as moderns since, as Strauss shows, we are trained to regard it *a priori* as being radically flawed. However, our doubts about this "method" by which Maimonides' teaching seems to "stand or fall" are, according to Strauss's arguments, doubts that we must recognize as determined by a "prejudice," because they are merely derived from our original or primary loyalty to modern science and philosophy as the binding or final truth. As such, they are not doubts readily given to us by self-evident reasoning or by simple respect for the biblical text. And it is the same ill-famed "allegorical method," irrespective of whether or not such a term adequately characterizes Maimonides' subtle literary method, that we are familiar with as the one which was first vehemently denounced by Spinoza.[61] Spinoza castigated Maimonides, claiming he arbitrarily interpreted and even unscrupulously extorted from the biblical text what he wanted it to teach, i.e., "confirmations of Aristotelian quibbles."[62] To Spinoza, Maimonides failed to respect the biblical text in terms of its literal meaning, which Spinoza himself considered readily comprehensible, although self-contradictory and, except for its moral teaching, entirely unsystematic. Inasmuch as Spinoza's critique of the "allegorical" hermeneutic can be serious and can work, it must move beyond simple opposition to Maimonides. Thus, on the one hand, it must surpass either traditional Jewish "skeptical" theological criticism of Maimonides' presuppositions or traditional biblical commentators' allusions to genuine difficulties in the biblical text (which, however, they still tried to harmonize with the tradition on some literal grounds and hence not in the manner of Maimonides). On the other hand, Spinoza must develop an interested approach to the Bible, which is not sustained by a simple alienation from the tradition, and which pursues an aim not merely of rationalistic execration. Strauss forcefully demonstrates that in developing such a critical approach to "allegory" in favor of literalness Spinoza already "presupposes the constitution" of modern, positivistic, ever-progressing, "ever developing [natural] science,"[63] which by definition knows no limited scientific horizon.

Hence, Spinoza can in fact only succeed against Maimonides by dogmatically denying the right of any exegesis which he would call "allegorical" to interpret the biblical text either in the light of an unchanging truth of natural science (i.e., Aristotelianism)[64] or in the light of the perennial truth of human science that claims to possess sounder fundamental principles than the moderns (i.e., Socrates or Plato). To Spinoza, no man and likewise no book can know what the ever-changing scientific truth, as *specific* laws or conclusions, will be until such laws or conclusions are discovered and subsequently refuted or surpassed in the unending search for scientific or factual truth as postulated by modern positivistic science. Thus, "allegorical interpretation" is subject to exclusion *a priori*, for it presumes to rediscover fixed scientific truths in the Bible; but no such objective truths could have been available to the biblical authors, since positivistic science is always changing and progressing, i.e., it is by definition *unfixed* as content (though not necessarily as "method"). However, according to this argument, one man can surely know, and one book can surely teach, the unchanging philosophic truth as general laws or premises. Spinoza believed his *Ethics* contained in its "clear and distinct" account the only validly enduring first principles of such a science of wisdom.[65]

Yet Strauss perceptively discerns that once Spinoza firmly established that this basic modern notion of positivistic science cannot itself be negated, Spinoza may actually himself have succumbed to using something like this same "allegorical method" so long as its thrust is limited to detecting the Bible's properly moral function. That is to say, if Spinoza claims to know *the* truth about the biblical text's authentic or deeper meaning as simple "natural" morality merely put in the form of imagination (which prophets are limited by), then there must be available to him *the* definitive truth. And it is because he possesses this definitive truth that Spinoza also is able in a sense to interpret the Bible "allegorically." According to Strauss, Spinoza presumed that this truth could not have been fully known until his system arose, and thus he alone was able to use legitimately or correctly this same "method" for biblical exegesis. Spinoza's positivistic conception of the nature of scientific truth as occurring in a gradual ascent beyond man's primitive origin[66] makes the very attempt which Maimonides' method represents (i.e., to recover *the* eternal philosophic truths taught by Moses but concealed by his imaginative presentation for the people's sake) appear *a priori* "useless" and "absurd." Indeed, this mockery will seem valid to the positivist, irrespective of any merit that might reside in Maimonides' arguments about the biblical text's true meaning, and irrespective of whether Spinoza ultimately himself employs the same means but for a different end, simply because he believes positivistic science to be true.

In other words, as Strauss demonstrates, Spinoza's is a purely polemical victory. As such, Strauss is effectively able to banish our doubts about Maimonides' standpoint being somehow illicitly achieved through "allegory": he clears the way for taking Maimonides seriously, pointedly emphasizing that careful attention should be paid to his biblical interpretations, which are actually very subtle in spite of the fact that Spinoza grotesquely caricatured them. Giving heed to these preliminary insights, and having finally been liberated from the strictures of Spinoza, Strauss was enabled to reach the last step by which he completed his "vindication" of Maimonides. Accordingly, he took issue with the form in which the teaching of Maimonides has been cast by contemporary historical scholars, a form unequal to the true greatness which Strauss claimed for it.[67]

Indeed, the two primary modern philosophic doubts about Maimonides' relevance—about his cosmology and about his "allegorical method"—seem to Strauss to lay the basis for the two "historical" prejudices against Maimonides' Jewish thought. Strauss discusses the latter in his critique of Julius Guttmann, who preserves and promotes these two prejudices.[68] To Strauss, these two "historical" prejudices, though opposite to one another, both unjustly blame Maimonides for giving rise to certain wayward trends in subsequent Jewish thought. Either Maimonides is claimed to be the model for the "moderate Enlightenment," which has proven to be deficient by its faultily constructed "mediating" efforts; or he is regarded, perhaps paradoxically, as the model for the "radical Enlightenment," whose fundamental medieval premises in fact represent to Guttmann a greater threat to "the spirit of Judaism" than do those of the modern Enlightenment, moderate or radical.

In response to the first charge preferred by Guttmann, Strauss already in *Philosophy and Law* stresses the "esoteric" character of the medieval "moderate Enlightenment" as contrasted with the "exoteric" character of the modern "moderate Enlightenment." In Strauss's view, Maimonides was not concerned with enlightening the multitude; rather, his primary aim was subtly to educate an elite, all the while striving to keep controversial issues secret from the multitude, who must be satisfied with authoritative (albeit "purified") beliefs. Thus, for Maimonides, genuine "enlightenment" was not meant to be universal—the multitude can never hope to know, and will never want to know, *the* absolute truth. This calls for a decisive differentiation to be made between the premises, the methods, and the aims of "enlightenment" in the two cases, which also entails that "allegorism" certainly is not an adequate term to apply to them both equally. In fact, Maimonides' "allegorical method" is not meant merely to substitute the plainly revealed truths of the intellect for Scripture's metaphorical secrets, as if it were the kernel of truth encased in the imaginative shell. Rather, his "method" advocates the need for communication in imaginative terms for the sake of those who should not be exposed to the truth, and is intended to demonstrate the need for employment of the imaginative mode in the proper education of his select readers. In the process, the select readers will have been taught by Maimonides to appreciate the proper sphere of the imagination and its "truths" in the search for "enlightenment"; and they will have been trained by him, if naturally endowed to do so, to master it themselves in order to make it serve the higher needs and purposes of such "enlightenment."[69]

The second charge revolves around what Guttmann calls "the spirit of Judaism." In the original German version of his *Die Philosophie des Judentums* (1933), Guttmann claims that Maimonides' philosophic "radicalism" (i.e., his elitism, intellectualism, and naturalism) subverts the true basis for authentic Jewish belief just as much as does the "radical" modern Enlightenment.[70] Strauss carefully demonstrates, however, that this argument itself presupposes thoroughly modern notions of what defines "the spirit of Judaism." According to Strauss, he ultimately means to say "biblical personalism" (thus locating Guttmann in the Schleiermacher school).[71] However, these modern notions, especially as Strauss critically presents them, in fact do not treat the fundamental Jewish teachings as deeply as do Maimonides' premodern notions, although in Strauss's reading these very notions are not very successfully comprehended or interpreted in Guttmann's explication of Maimonides' *Guide*. Indeed, Strauss incisively exposes that it is not Maimonides but actually our entire modern Jewish philosophy which fails to preserve adequately this key determining factor defined by Guttmann as "biblical personalism." This is certainly evident through an unprejudiced comparison between Maimonides' enduring strengths and the moderns' glaring weaknesses in regard to crucial theological matters, whether it be idealism's difficulties with "God as reality" or existentialism's difficulties with creation as an actual fact.[72] The supposedly preferable modern notion of "religious consciousness," in which Guttmann stakes his claim to preserve biblical personalism, is according to Strauss's analysis in a state of "critical decomposition" among philosophers themselves. But of even greater significance for

Strauss, "religious consciousness" does not in truth do as complete a justice to "the spirit of Judaism" as does the medieval notion, derived from Plato, of revealed religion as *law*, primarily as divine law, which in Maimonides' scheme preserves both God and creation as genuine actualities for rational belief about the world rather than just as postulated or constructed attitudes in human consciousness necessary as supports for moral sentiment.[73]

Accordingly, not "cosmology" as Aristotelian physics and metaphysics, but political philosophy, indeed *Platonic* political philosophy, is to Strauss the fundamental basis for Maimonides' standpoint.[74] This provides a firm grounding for his views that does as full justice to the truths both of reason and of revelation as may be achieved rationally, inasmuch as in them both, as Maimonides presents them, something is lacking which allows each one to leave room for harmony with the other, to fulfill a need it could not satisfy by itself.[75] Concretely, this would seem to mean that reason cannot produce a compelling religious and moral teaching if it does not adhere to divine revelation; and revelation cannot provide a persuasive account of its theology in such consistent rational terms as would justify its beliefs to *all* men who are bound by its law, if it is not aided by human reason. But this spiritual accord (which was originally a spiritual conflict) issues in an acutely political problem, because it is ultimately concerned not just with the purely abstract theological truth but also with the question of who best rules human society: rationally perfect men or morally perfect men. Likewise, as Strauss views it, Maimonides' solution is political, since he resolves the issue through the need for the prophetic lawgiver who embraces both perfections. In fact, Strauss considered the chief result of his study in prophecy as understood by Maimonides to have been the discovery that this political teaching is crucial for Maimonides' entire theological approach. And in Strauss's overview, this teaching about prophecy can only be properly comprehended if it is recognized that it clarifies with an unparalleled depth of reflection how philosophy and religion can be fruitfully harmonized with one another and can even help one another.

In other words, Maimonides' primary aim is to offer a decisive solution to *the* perennial political and theological problem: which "wisdom" is to rule human life, divine or human?[76] But to Maimonides, as Strauss presents him, this particularly penetrating "harmonization" is viable only if it is carried through in a form that as little as possible compromises the essential as well as existential spirit of each. Such an uncompromising "harmonization" can only occur in the form of a prophet who achieves the final term of human perfection by being both supreme philosopher and lawgiver, and who in being such, establishes through his overflowing perfection the first truly paradigmatic religious community.[77] Both in terms of what Strauss regarded as sound Platonic natural right as well as enduring Platonic natural theology, as they are informed by what is uniquely expressed as divine revelation, it would seem Maimonides especially provided the map by which Strauss discovered in the history of philosophy "a safe middle road between [the two] formidable opponents, Averroes and Thomas." Indeed for Strauss, it was Maimonides beyond all others who struggled nobly and mightily with the great conflict between reason and revelation, and who as such "is probably the greatest analyst" of the "fundamental difference" between the two claims to the comprehensive truth.[78]

CHAPTER 3

The Gradual Awakening

THE "PRE-MAIMONIDEAN" STRAUSS

WE HAVE argued that the preponderance of evidence supports our representing Leo Strauss's Jewish thought as a "return to Maimonides." We have also said that Strauss's original insight into Maimonides was never fundamentally contradicted in his later, more mature thought.[1] But does this contention require us to take the seemingly correlated step, and to claim that this "return" occurred all at once, directly, and completely? Was Strauss's penetration into Maimonides' innermost thought given to his understanding whole and perfected, so as to need no progress from the governing overview to the significant details? We will endeavor to prove that although Strauss's relation to Maimonides reached its decisive form virtually at the beginning of his turn to Maimonides, and remained clear, constant, and unidirectional, there was a remarkable development in Strauss's comprehension of what Maimonides' operative and ruling purpose entailed as to its final consequences. In other words, what may seem to be merely Strauss's subsequent elaborations once he apprehended the essential core of Maimonides' thought, should rather be perceived as a *gradual awakening* to the several layers of meaning contained in the original discovery itself. To be precise, we may isolate three distinct stages[2] that Strauss's Jewish thinking about Maimonides passed through, roughly corresponding to three key works—*Spinoza's Critique of Religion, Philosophy and Law* and *Persecution and the Art of Writing.*[3] Indeed, this pattern of progressive discovery, which testifies to the gradual awakening of Strauss to Maimonides' philosophic wisdom (however "occasional" the original recognitions may have been),[4] can be precisely traced in these three works, and proves not so much to have been constituted by any radical transformations as by "a continuing, deepening process."[5]

However, prior to our examining the three stages, it is instructive to speak in some detail about the "pre-Maimonidean" Strauss, for in this preparatory stage we can discern how he was predisposed, and even grew receptive, to the teachings of Maimonides. In a number of his youthful works, it is possible to observe the direction in which Strauss was already moving from the period of his youth. This direction is perhaps best indicated to us first by his review of Rudolf Otto's *The Idea of the Holy* (*Das Heilige*) in 1923.[6] Strauss commences with a Zionist critique of "the spiritual situation of German Judaism on the whole," a critique which can best be summarized in a phrase he coined some forty years subsequent to this review: "political dependence was also spiritual dependence."[7] Strauss was attracted by Otto's groundbreaking work for two reasons. First, Otto reverses the usual order of spiritual dependency, which was characterized by the constant attempts by Jewish theologians to validate Judaism in terms of German philosophy and culture. Instead, in Otto's work we encounter a German philosophical theologian who is eager to learn from the Jews through the explication of basic Jewish religious texts; indeed, it is precisely in this fashion that Otto elaborates his unique thesis about "the holy." Second, and perhaps most significant for Strauss, was the fact that in formulating this thesis Otto does not simply reduce the "noumenal" to the irrational.[8] To be sure, as Strauss presents it, Otto defines the primary task of modern theology since Schleiermacher to be an orientation to the "irrational" element of God in religion, as a needed corrective to excessive modern rationalization. But as Strauss observes further about Otto's thesis, the rightful concern with the profundity of God's transcendence is aimed at something *substantial* beyond man himself: "the irrationality which religion intends to convey resides not in the depths of the subject, but precisely in the depths of the object. Hence we are not in need of any romantic 'religious philosophy.'"[9] Strauss perceived that we may learn the significant lesson from Otto that the doctrine of divine attributes, "whose most essential form for us is the doctrine of attributes of the Spanish era" (especially as this was fully developed in Maimonides' negative theology), still remains a necessary preface to any adequate Jewish theology.[10]

It was also appealing to Strauss that, in his search to define what is genuinely transcendent, Otto does not need to try to contradict or to subvert the rationalist tradition. This is because he does not root the religiously "noumenal" in the irrational human subject, but assumes it may refer us to something genuinely transcendent: "the irrational in the religious Object is the 'bearer', the substance of the rational predicates, of the 'attributes.'"[11] According to Strauss, Otto argues that the medieval doctrine of divine attributes tacitly presupposes the actuality of the religious experience of divine transcendence, which it tries to formulate intellectually. Likewise, Otto criticizes the modern doctrine of religious experience, which argues for theology's need to root itself in personal revelations. Otto finds fault with this doctrine, in that it tends to a kind of irrationalism, basing itself as it does on subjective encounters with something seemingly "divine," but lacking the means to define it objectively as such. To Otto, if religious experience is possible on a personal level, it must proceed from the intellectual approach to theology. This tradition possesses the rational vocabulary and the historical evidence to describe the "object" which it calls divine, and hence prescribes *objective* limits for those who would seek to reproduce the experience through human intention. Following Otto, Strauss seems to point to just such a rational theological tradition, for as he concludes, "however justified our skepticism toward the doctrine of attributes" of traditional "Spanish" Jewish theology, i.e., Maimonides, it can still fully "obtain our sympathy," though perhaps not our adherence. This theological doctrine can still excite our interest precisely because by "the formulation of its task it already *makes a fundamental subjectivism impossible.*"[12] Here, in one of the earliest writings of his youth, Strauss may already be viewed as searching for a thoroughly rationalist theology, but one which simultaneously does not deny the genuinely transcendent element in religion. It may be said to point to something more or less "Maimonidean," even if he did not yet intend it as such.

Besides wrestling with the question of German Jewry's "political and spiritual dependence" and the question of the philosophical adequacy of the modern theological notion of "religious experience," Strauss struggled in the 1920s with the question of "whether an unqualified return to Jewish orthodoxy was not both possible and necessary."[13] However, this was not susceptible of a simple solution by him because he had already been "converted" to philosophy in great measure by the works of Spinoza. As Strauss poetically put it in his later autobiographical writing: "Vague difficulties remained like small faraway clouds on a beautiful summer sky." These "vague difficulties" eventually appeared to him as formidable storm clouds precisely in "the shape of Spinoza."[14]

Thus, in his two key "pre-Maimonidean" writings, Strauss tries to face squarely the challenge of Spinoza. In the first, "Cohen's Analysis of Spinoza's Bible Science" ("Cohens Analyse der Bibel-Wissenschaft Spinozas," 1924), he unfavorably contrasts Hermann Cohen (who had been previously preferred) with Spinoza in terms of the proper modern approach to the Bible. In the second, "On Spinoza's Bible Science and His Predecessors" ("Zur Bibelwissenschaft Spinozas und seiner Vorläufer," 1926), he strives, among other things, to compare the equally formidable Maimonides with Spinoza with regard to their conflicting approaches to the Bible.

"Cohen's Analysis of Spinoza's Bible Science"[15] is a transitional essay that distinctly reflects this intellectual movement away from Cohen and toward Spinoza, although he never simply exchanged adherence to the one for adherence to the other. Cohen remained for Strauss until the very end the modern image of the proud and self-respecting Jew who engages in philosophic activity; he served as a kind of exemplar, standing for the virtues which he hoped to imitate in the spheres of modern Jewish thought and modern Jewish life.[16] In point of fact, Cohen exercised a formative influence on Strauss's intellectual development: in his youth, Strauss viewed Cohen as one who was able to blend happily a strict devotion to philosophy with a passionate commitment to Judaism.[17] However, Strauss began to drift away from Cohen not only due to gnawing doubts about his neo-Kantian philosophic system, but especially because, unlike Cohen, he had been moved to embrace political Zionism at seventeen and continued to accept it, and also because he grew attracted to Rosenzweig's return to a revised orthodox theology.[18]

Although Strauss was attracted to political Zionism and to Rosenzweig's theology, this ironically led to his interest in Spinoza. Both of these endeavors in "new thinking" tried to claim independence from their origins by issuing strenuous critiques of modern liberalism and the Enlightenment, and by extension, critiques of Spinoza, the Enlightenment "saint." Strauss wanted to examine their critiques for himself in order to decide whether the modern Enlightenment (in its original form) still held water, or whether, as its Jewish critics suggested, it was full of holes. Hence, Strauss was compelled to reconsider Spinoza by those very critics who claimed to surpass him. By way of contrast, Cohen, who seemed to stand in opposition to all that these two critiques represented, might be expected to have defended Spinoza's basic intentions against these critics. After all, Cohen still sincerely cherished the ideals of the Enlightenment, in slightly qualified form, and he even hoped to realize these fully through his own moral, political, and religious philosophy. But strangely enough, as Strauss discovered, Cohen had also been engaged in a vigorous debate with Spinoza both as a vindication of Cohen's own mature turn to Jewish philosophy and in order to prove the superiority of his own liberalism as a progress "beyond" liberalism in its original form (a form best represented by Spinoza). Indeed, the reconsideration of Spinoza, in whom *all* schools of modern Jewish thought are rooted, yet to whom *all* these schools also stand in critical relation, seemed to Strauss to be required. He noted the curious unanimity with which such diverse heirs attacked their common benefactor, while still enjoying his legacy.

"Cohen's Analysis" is a key work in this regard because in it Strauss proceeds to a balanced appreciation of Spinoza by carefully analyzing Cohen's efforts to expose the nefarious intentions concealed in Spinoza's critique of the Hebrew Bible and the Jewish tradition. One could even suggest that it was in writing this essay that Strauss started to achieve a decisive liberation from Cohen's premises, method, and conclusions by contrasting these in a dialectical spirit with those of Spinoza. Indeed, his expanded interest in the crisis of modern liberalism, combined with his growing awareness of Cohen's seriously flawed assault on Spinoza, moved Strauss further away from Cohen and brought him closer to Spinoza. In the course of preparing this essay, Strauss seems to have come to a conclusion opposite to the one reached by Cohen: in almost every sense,[19] Spinoza seems to strike Strauss as superior both to his liberal heirs and to their opponents; he is the deeper thinker about the premises which they all share. Spinoza also attracted him for other reasons: for the vigor, originality, and thoroughness of his attack on his chief opponent, i.e., orthodoxy; for his "prophecy" of Zionism in its consistent derivation from his liberalism; for his greater alertness to "the power of evil in man," which appealed to Strauss since it better helped him interpret what he experienced in the ever present evil of endemic German anti-Semitism; and for the cognitive power and the probing depth of mind as was evident to Strauss especially in Spinoza's boldly original and sharply formulated theological-political work.[20]

Accordingly, in the essay "Cohen's Analysis" Strauss succeeds in clearly penetrating to the crucial point which Cohen failed to recognize about Spinoza: despite Spinoza's protracted argument with the Jewish tradition, he is not as antagonistic to the Jews and Judaism as Cohen supposes. Strauss notes that Cohen's error derives from two sources. First, Cohen virtually identifies the Jewish tradition with Maimonides, an identification which admittedly numerous Jewish thinkers tended toward, but which Spinoza rejected. Second, Cohen does not acknowledge the tremendous debt which he himself owes to Spinoza, since he presupposes both Spinoza's philosophy and even his critique of the Jewish tradition in his own basic philosophic and Jewish standpoints. Strauss illustrates Cohen's misinterpretation of Spinoza by focusing on how Spinoza "used" Maimonides for very specific purposes—purposes which Cohen did not properly apprehend. In this reading of Spinoza, Strauss discerns that Maimonides is presented as *the* "dogmatic" Jew[21] and is employed merely as the antithesis to Spinoza's own position. Maimonides serves either as a foil, as grist for his mill, or as the most articulate representative of the position which Spinoza distinctly rejects,[22] and hence is seen solely in an opponent's light. Since Cohen apparently elevates Maimonides to the highest sphere as *the* most authoritative Jew, Cohen regards Spinoza's attack on Maimonides as an attack on Judaism itself.

But Strauss views the matter differently from Cohen. According to Strauss's suggestion, Spinoza's peculiar purposes are fully comprehensible[23] only if seen in the light of philosophic politics, i.e., the conflict between "ancients" and "moderns" about the proper political relation which should obtain between philosophy and religion. Thus, when Spinoza polemically contrasts the Bible's ostensibly "corporeal" God with what he looked at as Maimonides' imaginatively contrived "incorporeal" God, he does so primarily in order to discredit Maimonides' synthesis of philosophy and the Jewish tradition, rather than to demolish the Jewish tradition purely and simply. Indeed, Spinoza blames Maimonides for cunningly twisting and distorting Scripture's literal meaning; Spinoza perceives this method of "allegorizing" to be an attempt surreptitiously to force Scripture to fit in with Maimonides' own "ancient" philosophic premises and conclusions as if they constituted mere commentary.

Cohen, however, does not acknowledge the primacy of the political motive in its modern form as the ruling notion determining Spinoza's philosophic polemics. In Cohen's philosophy, the theological motive appears to be primary, and it is this which leads Cohen to his judgment that Spinoza's "corporealistic" reading of the biblical God, in connection with his radical critique of Maimonides, not only deliberately falsifies the Jewish tradition, but also is "against the meaning of monotheism" altogether. But Strauss acquits Spinoza of both the charges laid against him by Cohen, i.e., of unmitigated hostility to Jews and Judaism, and of the generally false explication of biblical monotheism. As Strauss recognizes, even in the case just discussed, Spinoza does not necessarily misrepresent the conception of God's nature in Judaism *per se*, but only that in one authoritative view—that of Maimonides.[24]

In other words, it cannot be said that the anti-Maimonidean statements made by Spinoza in the context of his biblical science prove his hostility to Judaism—they only mean, according to Strauss, that he used his Bible science for his political ends which were not simply determined by his origins as a Jew.[25] These political considerations were such that Spinoza called for the separation of church and state, and hence for the liberation of philosophy or science from ecclesiastical supervision so as to guarantee them complete freedom in their own realm. In order to achieve this purpose, Spinoza attempted to deprive Calvinist orthodoxy of its main theological support for its claim to be *the* legitimate spiritual authority in Dutch society, a claim primarily rooted in the Old Testament. Such political purposes would have been fully congenial to Cohen, who was no friend of established religions in the state, as Strauss well knew. Strauss thus vindicates Spinoza against Cohen's critique because he recognizes in Spinoza's treatise a clearer and deeper analysis of the harsh and even radical things which must be done in order to move to a liberal state from a state which is not neutral concerning religion.

Also worthy of serious note are the remarks which Strauss makes in passing about Maimonides in this same essay. Strauss shows that Spinoza attacked Maimonides' "allegorical" method in order to further his assault on the political claims of theological orthodoxy. He did so because he regarded Maimonides' approach as the best available case of a method based on "churchly" or traditional theological grounds. In contrast, Spinoza regarded his own critical and "scientific" historical method of exegesis as not only closer to the literal meaning of the biblical text, but also as politically expedient for the establishment of a secular liberal state not subordinated to either theological beliefs or sectarian religious conflicts about who holds *the* biblical truth. In fact, he viewed his own system as alone providing a soundly calculated rationale for the free and unhampered pursuit of science in such a state.[26]

As Strauss recognized, this philosophical aim of Spinoza (to which theological motives are subordinated) accounts for another feature of his radical divergency from Maimonides, that is, his method of reading the Bible. In Strauss's view, Maimonides is a philosopher who manifests an "attached" attitude to the Bible and tradition, since he viewed them as essentially rationalist in their core. Hence, his method of interpretation aims at demonstrating the fundamental rationality of the tradition by "improving" or "correcting" its faults as mere irrational excrescences; likewise, he strives to prove that the true prophet is the one who exhibits perfect rationality. In contrast, Spinoza is a philosopher with a "detached" attitude toward tradition. He regards the Bible as rooted in the imagination and popular morality which he believes necessarily inhibit man's movement to rationality. Hence, his method of critique, which aims at exposing the rational incongruities in the basic biblical teachings, is chosen because it supports his argument for the simply rational state and free science "no longer standing in the service of religion."[27] In consequence, Spinoza asserted that Maimonides' attempt to reconcile theology and philosophy not only presupposes a "dogmatic prejudice" about the rational usefulness and authority of religion in human life, but also poses the greatest threat to man's reason and to his political life, since both are best pursued in conditions of freedom. These liberal convictions were persuasive to Strauss and at this stage he allowed himself to more or less concur with Spinoza's characterization of Maimonides as an apologist for the orthodox claim to rule,[28] though he certainly was aware of the serious flaws in Spinoza's polemical comments on Maimonides' actual scriptural readings and his method for reaching them.

Thus, Strauss at this stage in his Jewish philosophic development seems to prefer Spinoza as a philosopher because his argument allows one to face honestly the price one must pay for pure liberalism. That is, as a Jewish thinker, it seems one must decide to be either a modern philosopher or a traditional theologian, both of which require crucially different political conditions. However, Strauss was not fully persuaded by Spinoza, partially because he was not satisfied with the actualization of his teaching in the morally lax liberal democracy he knew as a youth. Also, Spinoza seemed to overrule the possibility of an authentic rootedness in the Jewish tradition consonant with reason. Maimonides was only a shadow on the horizon; Strauss still viewed him essentially either in the image of Spinoza's "realistic" Machiavellian polemic or in the image of Cohen's Kantianizing idealization.[29] In fact, Strauss was only just beginning to reach his own understanding of Maimonides in what we may call "Platonic" terms.[30] But Strauss, it would seem, did start to recognize, as an eventual consequence of this study, that neither Spinoza nor Cohen truly comprehended Maimonides, and connected with this, that Maimonides might still hold some serious interest for modern

Judaism. He was *the* authority in Jewish thought, recognized by both Spinoza and Cohen, yet his meaning had not been properly expressed in modern terms by either. If Strauss learned much from Spinoza about both political motives and modern philosophy, and if he defended Spinoza against Cohen's misreading, he also started to discern the limits of Spinoza's teaching precisely in his skewed characterization of Maimonides. And since neither Cohen nor Spinoza correctly understood Maimonides, perhaps what one needs first of all is an accurate elucidation of Maimonides. His Jewish thought, even if not simply applicable to modern Jews, must still be put in proper perspective to judge aright the aims and purposes of Spinoza, the Jewish thinker who claimed to overrule Maimonides once and for all.

The influence of Spinoza's philosophy on Strauss also finds clear expression in the review essay "Biblical History and Science" ("Biblische Geschichte und Wissenschaft," 1925),[31] which appeared one year prior to the powerful essay "On Spinoza's Bible Science and His Predecessors" (1926), the essay in which Strauss was finally to pit Spinoza *directly* against Maimonides. In "Biblical History and Science," a less academic and more personal piece, another hint of a move toward Maimonides may be discerned. Here, Strauss seeks by virtue of a Spinozistic argument to vindicate Simon Dubnow's "scientific" account of Jewish history against Ernst Simon's critique, a critique rooted in traditional orthodox piety. Strauss's vindication of Dubnow's scholarly enterprise proceeds on two grounds. First, Strauss defends Dubnow's employment of Spinozistic biblical science in his presentation of ancient Jewish history. Strauss says Dubnow's reliance on Spinoza's modern critical method is fully warranted by Zionist considerations, since knowledge of ancient Jewish self-rule and its difficulties grounded in purely natural political considerations may be highly useful in the establishment and the maintenance of a future Jewish state. Second, he rejects Simon's call for modern Jewish historical writing to be more pious and less "scientific." Strauss views this type of historical writing, that is "guided by dogmatic and scholastic notions," as something which is finally determined by "theological prejudices," and hence ultimately denies genuine freedom of thought. Now Strauss so argues using the precise Spinozistic terms not because he simply rejects orthodoxy as did Spinoza, but because he, like Lessing, rejects the "trivializing" grounds for accepting it: to Strauss, the primary basis for orthodoxy lies in the Law, and not in the belief in "verbal inspiration and miracles."[32]

But for Strauss, already a "convert" to philosophy, it seemed that orthodoxy does still require rational theological arguments for the Law.

Its central theological presupposition is the belief in God the lawgiver, who created nature and who guides history, a belief which "scientific" history, dogmatically atheistic as it is, can neither refute nor subordinate. *The* fundamental dilemma, as Strauss recognized, is not whether "the Bible, especially the Torah, is the deposit of a centuries-long development—what, indeed, everyone today at bottom assumes—and did not have its singular origin in a dictation at Sinai," but whether "the belief in the power of God over nature," i.e., creation, is an intelligible and even a compelling rational belief which contradicts nothing known by human experience alone.

> Without the power over nature, God is in truth powerless. I am no brute, I demand no miracles—creation would be enough for me. But who today still dares to teach creation....Hermann Cohen...was enough of a Jew to see precisely in the power of God over nature an indispensable moment, not to say the basic meaning, of the idea of God.

By orienting himself with such critical profundity toward the notion of "creation" as the fundamental theological presupposition in which the entire Jewish tradition is rooted, we can observe that Strauss was evidently predisposed, as it were, to a turn to Maimonides.

Thus, in the act of arguing against Simon's theological "dogmatism" and vindicating Dubnow's modern "scientific" history, Strauss makes a seemingly paradoxical shift: he himself ultimately argues for a theological position also, but only one which can be "scientifically" grounded. In fact, among the great Jewish theologians, medieval and modern, it was perhaps Maimonides alone who seemed most able to happily combine theology and science. Maimonides made "the belief in the power of God over nature" the cornerstone of his theological edifice, inasmuch as it is absolutely necessary for the understanding of the Jewish tradition in its deepest opposition to "unbelieving" philosophy.[33] Yet Maimonides also clarified how the Jewish tradition is almost fully consonant with such philosophy once the latter's "unbelief" (as adherence to eternity rather than to creation) is proven never to have been scientifically demonstrated.

At this juncture in the unfolding of Strauss's Jewish thought, we might want to ask whether he reached such conclusions through familiarity with Maimonides, or by thinking through for himself this primary issue of Jewish theology (though undoubtedly with substantial assistance from Spinoza's and Cohen's discussions). It is difficult to give a definitive answer to this historical question with the small amount of evidence at our disposal. All we can say is that a striking affinity with Maimonides is plainly manifested.

The final key pre-Maimonidean writing by Strauss, "On Spinoza's Bible Science und His Predecessors,"[34] constitutes both the first direct encounter which he stages between Maimonides and Spinoza, and a careful but limited preparation for the arguments fully elaborated in *Spinoza's Critique of Religion*. In this work, we can begin to observe a movement away from Spinoza and a definite step toward Maimonides. In Strauss's analysis, the three grounds on which Maimonides and Spinoza can be compared—the theological, the political, and the epistemological—reveal their fundamental philosophical *differences* to be greater than any similarities between them. Strauss makes this assertion in direct contrast to the essential commonality that is often claimed to hold between Spinoza and Maimonides, and which numerous leading modern Jewish scholars (Cohen excepted) have been engaged in trying to establish.[35]

Strauss provisionally assents to Spinoza's theological critique of Maimonides' "dogmatism." Strauss apprehended that for Maimonides, reason is not entirely free in relation to Scripture, although as Spinoza (and Strauss) acknowledge, Maimonides accepts that limitation on reason not because any specific *text* binds him to some irrational teaching.[36] Rather, reasoning about Scripture is theologically controlled by "a definite notion of God," which is still held to stand in conformity with reason, as well as limited by a belief in the actual truth of revelation as a historical fact. At this stage in Strauss's developing views on Maimonides, it is clear that he still "conventionally" accepts Maimonides' doctrine of negative attributes as the key to his highest teaching about God. This negative theology argues that God is with respect to his essence ultimately unknowable. Does Strauss, as a result, believe himself compelled to acknowledge Spinoza's claim to be the deeper, more rational, and less traditional thinker than Maimonides? Strauss was willing to recognize half of Spinoza's claim. On the one hand, Spinoza is correct about his own greater rational freedom with regard to Scripture, inasmuch as he pursues historical-philological criticism; but, on the other hand, Spinoza is not correct in claiming to be the first to follow through Maimonides' theological notions with complete rational consistency. Rather than following through Maimonides' notions consistently, Spinoza tacitly presupposes a radical break between his and Maimonides' views of God. Although the general similarity between the formulation of their basic theological proposition (namely, the identity of intellect and will in God) might seem to belie such a radical break in their notions, it cannot be said that the formula, "the identity of intellect and will in God," ever means the same thing for Spinoza and for Maimonides. For the former, it is the complete immanence of "God" in nature, whose "infinite number of infinite attributes" merely encompasses thought and extension; for the latter, it is God's radical transcendence of nature, so that God is essentially unknowable as he is in himself, and surpasses even any analogical reference to existential or positive attributes.[37]

Keeping in mind this radical difference in their fundamental notions of God, it may now be clarified why Strauss's assent to Spinoza's critique of Maimonides' "dogmatism" had to be called "provisional." Strauss recognized that because Spinoza could not readily "refute" Maimonides' stronger argument for his rationalist theology, Spinoza attacked Maimonides at the point at which his argument seemed weaker: its application to Scripture. Hence, Spinoza characterizes Maimonides' position on Scripture as "dogmatism"; according to Spinoza, Maimonides ostensibly claims the right of rationalist theology, indeed of pure reason itself, to be fully determinative in any proper approach to Scripture. Strauss acknowledges that this is more or less Maimonides' position, and that this position might well be called "dogmatism" by those who reject a rationalist approach to Scripture. But Strauss does not accede to Spinoza's misleading suggestion that Maimonides' "dogmatism" ultimately consists in how he attains or holds his "definite notion of God," and that this in turn theologically controls his further reasoning about Scripture. Strauss rejects this devious Spinozistic suggestion because it does not do full justice to the austere Maimonidean commitment to a genuinely "scientific" approach to Scripture, however much his "science" may seem archaic or obsolete to the modern mind. As Strauss views the matter, Maimonides' "definite notion of God" is based on cogent, purely philosophical arguments, which are themselves not rooted in any "dogmatic" scriptural presuppositions. Besides, Spinoza himself vigorously pursues a rationalistic approach to Scripture, and so he cannot be counted among those who reject the approach of "dogmatism" in principle. This helps to account for Strauss's merely "provisional" assent: it is grounded in the growing awareness that what Spinoza does, in the end, amounts to the same thing as what he accuses Maimonides of. Here it is not approaches to Scripture which are in fundamental conflict, as both are rationalistic, but different notions of reason, God, and nature.

In point of fact, Strauss discerns that Spinoza's historical-philological critique of Maimonides (in regard to his "unfree" approach to Scripture because "prejudiced" in favor of its philosophical reasonableness) is made possible by Spinoza's own prior theological critique of Maimonides for his allowing God any transcendent element. Thus, Spinoza's historical-philological procedure in reading Scripture, which he faults Maimonides for neglecting, derives from his *own* "definite notion of God" and proceeds to entirely "naturalistic" conclusions about Scripture. But since this procedure is fully in conformity with his own rationalistic definition of nature, Spinoza merely substitutes one rationalistic "dogmatism" for another. So Strauss assents to the critique only "provisionally" because he wants to prove methodically that this same critique could be applied to Spinoza's own "critical" Bible science. Here it is possible to observe Strauss developing an exegetical technique which he was subsequently to employ with a characteristic intellectual acuteness. As he incisively shows, the critique, if valid, could readily be turned against itself. As a result, the method of Strauss now brings the analysis to a much deeper level in uncovering the essential argument between Spinoza and Maimonides. The rationalistic approaches to Scripture of both Jewish thinkers are rooted in prior theological assumptions which may or may not be demonstrated, but which can only be judged properly in terms of their purely *philosophic* truth and adequacy.[38]

According to Strauss in "On Spinoza's Bible Science," the fundamental philosophic divergence between Maimonides and Spinoza can be located on purely theological grounds. Moreover, Strauss isolates and reduces the divergence to their supposedly similar theological propositions about the identity of intellect and will in God. Strauss brings to light that what this proposition entails for Spinoza is actually something radically different from the proposition adhered to by Maimonides; and indeed it is this theological proposition in all its ramifications that lays the basis for Spinoza's critique of both prophetically revealed religion and Scripture as well as of its Maimonidean defense.[39] The matter which Strauss is trying to get at in his elaborate discussion can be demonstrated quite simply by quoting declarations from each of the two Jewish thinkers. Spinoza, on the one hand, is able to assert unambiguously: "The human mind has an adequate knowledge of the eternal and infinite essence of God."[40] On the other hand, Maimonides makes such statements as the following:

"His essence cannot be grasped as it really is";[41] and, "there is no device leading to the apprehension of the true reality of His essence. . . ."[42] It is through this crucial, radical difference in regard to the conception of God's nature and the human mind's adequacy to attain such definitive knowledge about God, that Spinoza is able to deny unconditionally divine "creation, lawgiving, and miracles," i.e., the scriptural teachings which guide Maimonides' philosophic reflections. For Spinoza, these are "actions" which are beyond God's power to perform (or perhaps, beneath his "definition"), since his power is defined solely by what is consistent with purely natural, i.e., mechanical, necessity. This is a conclusion which Spinoza can perhaps logically draw with some validity from his basic philosophic premises. But it is *not*, as Strauss recognizes, a necessary philosophical or scriptural conclusion which Maimonides would also be forced to accept if, as Spinoza tacitly suggests, Maimonides like Spinoza had been determined to pursue the key premise (i.e., the identity of will and intellect in God) with the greatest possible consistency to its uttermost limit.

As Strauss discerned, neither philosophic consistency nor loyalty to Scripture is the issue; rather it is fundamental philosophic presuppositions which are in seemingly irreconcilable conflict—presuppositions about what philosophy itself *is*, and about what it can know. The theological proposition possesses only a very limited validity as a common premise for both Maimonides and Spinoza, because they hold to such different notions of what *the* true philosophy consists in: either it is comprehensive cognition of the absolute scientific system which is unequivocally closed to genuine revealed theology (Spinoza), or it is engagement in a thinking activity striving for truth or science yet limited by man's rational powers and hence potentially open to revealed theology (Maimonides).

This primary divergence about philosophy remains true in spite of the fact that Maimonides and Spinoza are united by an apparently common basic attitude to "theory": "theory" or philosophy represents for both the sphere in which the only genuine cognition of God can occur, and for both it is also the highest ground for achieving human happiness or perfection. In this respect, which is not yet for Strauss the decisive respect, they concur on the purely "moral" premise that the theoretical life is the best and the highest way of life for man, even though the natural or cosmological grounds in which they root their common belief are so different. However, Maimonides and Spinoza are in point of fact essentially divided by decisively different conclusions proceeding from their common belief in the supremacy of theory, namely, about the end which it aims for or about the role it can play in reaching the highest truths. In "On Spinoza's Bible Science," Strauss still derives his philosophical approach to the two Jewish thinkers from a more or less conventional modern historical construction. The essential division between Maimonides and Spinoza is seen to revolve around divergent "theological" conclusions, which must be related to their primary divergence on ancient versus modern epistemology, physics, and metaphysics. And it is on this ground that the youthful Strauss, as a modern thinker, must still side with Spinoza, since he doubts whether any natural theology like the one on which Maimonides' entire position rests (as he then believed) can still be valid or true for us with our modern positivistic natural science, which if anything is closer to Spinoza's revised "natural theology."[43]

Furthermore, in Strauss's view the differing attitudes of Maimonides and Spinoza toward philosophy or theory are reflected with greater accuracy by their conflicting political notions about the multitude. In essence, they are divided about how theory should be related to the multitude, and as a result about how the state should be organized. According to Maimonides, "the acknowledgment of a truth is to unite all men, the wise and the unwise," while according to Spinoza the multitude is irremediably "enslaved by its passions" and it cannot be liberated by any "acknowledgment of a truth" in which it cannot truly believe. Certainly Maimonides' case is not especially helped, from Spinoza's standpoint, if *the* truth is identified with revelation.[44] Indeed, Spinoza judges Maimonides guilty of a lack of theoretical objectivity about Scripture; he contends that this lack derives from the fact that Maimonides attributes to revelation a potential rootedness in *the* truth, which is not evident by examining the text honestly, but by unscrupulously "interpreting" it, i.e., by forcing it to conform with his own preformed dogmatic assumptions.[45] According to Spinoza, this scheme ultimately expresses a decidedly political interest, namely, the domineering philosopher's desire to rule through the religious authorities. To Spinoza, this is likelier to result in the rule of ignorant priests rather than enlightened statesmen.

Although it seems as if Strauss, at this stage in his philosophic development, still shared the basic liberal political aims of Spinoza, what began to become evident to him was that Maimonides *also* preferred politics to be rooted in a soundly rational approach, and aimed for it to be guided by enlightened statesmen. This was, of course, directly contrary to Spinoza's insinuation that Maimonides' biblical exegesis was somehow in the service of rule by ignorant or malicious priests. As a result, Strauss started to perceive in this essay that the crucial political difference between Maimonides and Spinoza revolves around what it means to be philosophically "enlightened"—whether philosophy should lead one to a healthy political respect for revealed religion, or whether philosophy teaches one to treat revealed religion as the greatest threat to a healthy political life. It appears Strauss was becoming aware that he was not simply compelled to choose the Spinozistic position in order to defend a "liberal" approach to politics and religion, which rationally delimits to each its proper sphere in the life of man, and which allots to reason a ruling power even while respecting the nonrational multitude and its peculiar needs. Perhaps something like this same "liberal" respect for a rational politics could be maintained through the Maimonidean position while not surrendering the unique truths available through religion. Such a position, even though premodern, also strives to separate politics from religion in such a way as to preserve for the enlightened statesman freedom to act with rational means to achieve rational ends. It is able to do so precisely because it insists on the essentially rational content of scriptural teachings; they express a prophetic perfection which in its determining features is a perfection of reason.

As Strauss views the matter in "On Spinoza's Bible Science and His Predecessors," however, perhaps the most fundamental difference between Maimonides and Spinoza is ultimately neither theological nor political, but epistemological, and revolves precisely around the status of revelation or prophecy in reflecting a necessary human limit.[46] The crucial question is whether unaided human reason can be surpassed by "aided" or "guided" human reason. Though Maimonides and Spinoza seem roughly to agree about the prophet's political function as leader or lawgiver or statesman, they disagree forcefully about what the prophet's theological teachings represent: a cognitive progress in human understanding toward the highest truth (Maimonides) or an overreaching of the imagination beyond its legitimate moral sphere (Spinoza). For Maimonides, the prophet attains a human perfection beyond the philosopher's. This enables him to conceive of a harmonization between Scripture and reason through the prophet, who in following nature surpasses but does not contradict ordinary human comprehension. This is the possibility that is denied by Spinoza, though according to Strauss he does so by staking his critique in "an entirely different conception and valuation of the 'imaginative faculty' " which *a priori* renders his predecessor's endeavor absurd.[47] To be sure, Maimonides' efforts at harmonization seem radically to depend on a "perfect and complete" Aristotelian physics, i.e., on there being two absolute "authorities," divinely revealed Scripture and completed reason as science, which he then tries to reconcile with one another.

At this point, then, there is no doubt for Strauss that with the collapse of Aristotle's physics through the explorations of modern science, Maimonides' method of scriptural interpretation would fall along with it, or would at least be legitimately "discredited" as a conception about Scripture.[48] But over and above Spinoza's critique, Strauss also perceived that Maimonides never reductively identified revelation with reason. For Maimonides, human knowledge can always surpass Aristotle through prophecy, i.e., the prophet always attains to a greater theoretical height than the philosopher, even with regard to superlunar physics and its attendant metaphysics. Thus, as Strauss further discerned, Maimonides' entire approach may not actually have been so finally defeated by the transition from medieval to modern science, since his argument is rooted in a prior epistemological critique of *all* possible philosophy or science: it would seem man was, is, and always will be in need of revelation to know *the* truth about God and the angels, and about creation versus eternity.[49] Maimonides' argument for revelation, deriving from an adherence to theory as man's supreme purpose by nature, must then proceed from one fundamental presupposition: the "insufficiency" of ordinary human reason in apprehending the highest truths.[50] As Strauss puts it in the conclusion to this first analysis of the argument between Maimonides and Spinoza:[51]

> the belief in the dependency of human reason on superhuman guidance with regard to the perfection of theory proves to be the prime condition of the possibility of the agreement of theory and Scripture.

If not for the "insufficiency" of the ordinary human intellect in its ability to attain the definitive and comprehensive truth, philosophers would not have an *interest* in examining the claims of revelation to possess a higher, if not the highest, truth. Thus as Strauss recognized, the philosophical critique of revelation (and indeed its very possibility) in which Spinoza was engaged, requires the opposite belief as its basic premise, namely, the belief in the "sufficiency" of the human intellect for the attainment of the complete and systematic truth.

Hence, we may discern that in surveying this decisive difference between Spinoza and Maimonides, Strauss was in the process of freeing himself from accepting all of Spinoza's presuppositions about the possible supremacy of reason in human life, especially as Spinoza asserted this absolute competence in modern scientific terms. Neither theology nor even politics brought about Strauss's turn toward Maimonides and away from Spinoza, but rather philosophy, or reason, and doubts about the human powers attendant to reason, seemed to move Strauss beyond the modern sphere as best exemplified by Spinoza. These doubts led him to ask about other approaches to reason and to man, ones which may be in greater consonance with the intellectual limits evident in human nature.[52]

Indeed, Strauss was attracted to Maimonides precisely because his "classical" view of philosophy, though uncompromising in its commitment to reason, seems honestly to acknowledge the fundamental problem of proving reason's "sufficiency" in all areas of human life, and ultimately with respect to nature as a whole. As Strauss began to recognize, the modern view held by Spinoza appears in part to be rooted in merely an *assertion* of "sufficiency," whose questionability it tries to evade by presenting itself in systematic or "scientific" form. As a result, Strauss started to wonder whether a thorough reconsideration of Maimonides' philosophy was not necessary in order to test his hypothesis about what he regarded as the fatal flaw in Spinoza's philosophy, i.e., its being grounded not in anything either self-evident or demonstrable, but rather in an *irrational assertion* of reason's "sufficiency." Such irrationality would contradict the very nature of philosophy, which is based solely on what is rational. Having aroused a deep-seated suspicion about the fundamental rational soundness of Spinoza's philosophic position, which to Strauss never seems to have been rectified by his modern Jewish philosophic heirs, Strauss felt the pressing need to think through his doubts about Spinoza with even greater precision. Strauss proceeded to a study of Spinoza's philosophic critique of religion. In the process he hoped to clarify whether Maimonides' philosophic approach was able to escape the fatal conundrum which beset the position of Spinoza and of the modern Jewish thinkers who followed in his wake.

CHAPTER 4

Maimonides as Philosophical Theologian

STRAUSS'S TURN TO MEDIEVAL JEWISH THEOLOGY

THE FIRST STAGE in Strauss's switching of allegiance from Spinoza to Maimonides as the "deeper thinker"[1] emerges with *Spinoza's Critique of Religion*.[2] Though Strauss was not yet deliberately engaged in "a return to premodern philosophy," which he still did not consider possible,[3] it seems that this work represents the first recognition of Maimonides as the superior thinker with respect to the rational soundness of his basic arguments, especially those he employs in defending the Jewish tradition. On similar grounds, this work begins to reveal Spinoza as a seriously flawed thinker. In particular Strauss viewed as merely hypothetical, and hence undemonstrated, Spinoza's claim to have achieved a decisive victory in his fight against Maimonides through supposed rational proofs in favor of his own basic antitheological argument. These "proofs," Strauss began to perceive, were grounded in dubious modern philosophical premises that are by no means universally necessary. Thus, by staging a striking encounter between Spinoza and Maimonides in the contested field of revealed religion, an encounter in which Strauss rigorously tests Spinoza's critique of Maimonides, he reaches a clear awareness of the distinct limits of Spinoza's so-called refutation of Maimonides.[4] In order to comprehend properly this great shift from Spinoza to Maimonides, it is necessary that the primary theological issues directing Strauss's attention be treated so as to discern in what precise sense, according to Strauss, Spinoza's attempted refutation of Maimonides misses the mark (or hits it), and hence whether Spinoza's critique truly leaves Maimonides' position intact.

As Strauss's first major work, *Spinoza's Critique of Religion* is an ambitious scholarly project. It attempts to determine the precise contribution of Spinoza's *Theological-Political Treatise* to the radical critique of revealed religion in the modern (i.e., Enlightenment) philosophical tradition. But it is also a work which possesses a still compelling intellectual and moral vigor, perhaps deriving in some measure from its "existential" qualities, which endow it with a concrete and moving appeal beyond the often arcane scholarly issues it treats. By this, I mean to say that it manifests about its author—a modern Jew fully aware of the challenge to faith evident in biblical criticism—a passionate commitment to Judaism as an ennobling faith, combined with an equally passionate commitment to an uncompromising search for rational truth much in the spirit of Hermann Cohen. At the same time, one receives the impression of a man trying to achieve in an unprecedented fashion an unusual union of what he regarded as the exemplary virtues present in his two "heroes," Spinoza as well as Cohen, yet attempting to move beyond the limits evident in both of them. Thus, with this work, Strauss begins to emerge as a modern Jewish thinker fully in his own right, determined to pursue an independent line of enquiry of his own devising. If the conflict of these two deep commitments contended in his soul, he strove to avoid betraying the one or the other in any essential respect.

It is perhaps best to begin "biographically" in order to comprehend how it was that these two sides to Strauss himself brought him to the first stage in his view of Maimonides. For Strauss, these two fundamental commitments—to Judaism as revealed religion and to rational philosophy—never seem to have been in serious question: they constitute, as it were, his unarguable presuppositions. If for him Jews and Judaism were caught in a grave crisis and if "the self-destruction of rational philosophy" seemed to have been a primary problem for him, he certainly never seems to have considered seriously either leaving Judaism or succumbing to irrationalism. The only acceptable answer to his dilemmas, as both Jew and philosopher, was to somehow encompass both commitments.[5]

As previously mentioned, Strauss's critical yet receptive approach to Spinoza was shaped by the Jewish thought, and by the historical personage, of Hermann Cohen.[6] Strauss first encountered Cohen's system in Marburg. There it had been established as a school by Cohen himself, but when Strauss arrived "the school was in a state of disintegration," since "Cohen belonged definitely to the pre-war world." Although Strauss never seems to have been entirely convinced by Cohen's system of philosophy,[7] he was decisively persuaded by Cohen of the possibility of a modern Jewish philosophy, rooted in the genuine need to wrestle in authentically modern terms with the same fundamental theological issues which occupied its medieval predecessors.[8] Moreover, in this same spirit, Strauss learned from Cohen to respect, and to turn to, the archetypal figure of Maimonides, the Jewish philosophical theologian. Maimonides' critical thinking did not entail an act of disloyalty to Judaism in order to philosophize, as it did for Spinoza, however complex the relations were between philosophy and the classical Jewish sources in Maimonides' Jewish theological reconciliation with philosophy. And while Strauss also regarded Cohen's unhistorical method of interpretation of Maimonides as resulting in philosophically unsatisfactory and even fallacious conclusions, primarily because it left its own thoroughly modern premises entirely unexamined, still Cohen's efforts did provide Strauss with an entry, however dim, into Maimonides' often perplexing and opaque cognitive edifice. As Strauss himself admits, "Maimonides was to begin with, wholly unintelligible" to him until he discovered the Platonic connection through Avicenna. Cohen (as well as Spinoza) taught him to pay careful attention to Maimonides as a serious thinker.

Perhaps directly correlated with his introduction to Maimonides as a still-valid authority and model for modern Jewish thought, Strauss learned from Cohen to treat Spinoza free of the unconditional veneration in which, as a rule, he was held by modern Judaism and indeed by modern philosophy and society as well.[9] First meeting Maimonides favorably in connection with Cohen perhaps allowed Maimonides to serve as a kind of a counterweight to Spinoza's reputation as a modern "saint." To be sure, Strauss was powerfully moved to study Spinoza's *Theological-Political Treatise*, but not originally for any reasons related to Maimonides.[10] Rather, he was attracted to this work for two reasons related to entirely "modern" Jewish historical experiences as well as scholarly interests. First, Strauss was not entirely persuaded by Cohen's "fierce criticism" of Spinoza, since he discerned that Cohen's apologetic motives as an advocate for Jews and Judaism did not allow him to render full justice to the possible truths still contained in Spinoza's arguments. Second, Strauss recognized in this seminal work a key to the essential concern which preoccupied him in his youth, namely, the conflict between the modern Enlightenment (especially its "radical" strain) and Jewish orthodoxy, which the deficiencies of both political Zionism and the Rosenzweigian movement of religious return cast in bold relief for him.[11]

We must also not forget that around this time his friend Jacob Klein was gradually helping to liberate Strauss from the "prejudice" in favor of modern philosophy. Klein himself had been helped to reach this specific insight by his exposure to Heidegger, whose great project it was to "deconstruct" the Western philosophic tradition, to lay bare its deepest roots as prerationalistic and even poetic. But it was also the aim of Heidegger to locate in classical Greek rationalism—i.e., Socrates, Plato, and Aristotle—a superficial turn to things manipulated by the rational human mind. Rationalism was thus seen as a movement away from man's proper concern with pure "Being." Here Klein may be said to have convinced Strauss of something quite in opposition to Heidegger's project: "the one thing needed philosophically is in the first place a return to, a recovery of, classical philosophy."[12] It can be maintained with confidence, I believe, that Strauss was not completely sure about his own response to this challenge until after he wrote *Spinoza's Critique of Religion*; indeed, not until he completed this study was he persuaded that Spinoza was "wrong in the decisive respect," i.e., about reason's ability to refute revelation, and thus about the modern Enlightenment's superior rights vis-à-vis traditional orthodoxy. However, the question of a possible return, raised by Klein, and hence of a better and clearer view of the deepest conflict present in premodern philosophy,[13] was already firmly planted in his mind and began to bear fruit almost immediately.[14]

It was as a result of this gradual awakening to the wisdom and vitality preserved in premodern philosophy that Strauss was led to his keen interest in the premodern enlightenment view of revelation, as exemplified by Maimonides. This may also account for why, in the longest chapter on a single thinker in *Spinoza's Critique of Religion*, Strauss dedicated so much effort to comprehending Maimonides' position vis-à-vis Spinoza's, and Spinoza's critique of that position. Maimonides was just as deeply and uncompromisingly concerned with genuine science and rigorous demonstration as was Spinoza,[15] and was just as devoted to theory and the theoretical life as necessary for human happiness and perfection. But Maimonides viewed revelation with the utmost seriousness, both as a historical given to which he was bound as a *Jewish* thinker, and as a matter of theoretical interest which must be expounded and justified theoretically.

However, before we make any attempt to isolate the precise reasons for Strauss's growing respect for Maimonides at this point in his intellectual development, it is first essential to trace how Strauss's gradual disaffection with Spinoza emerged, as this disaffection is made evident in *Spinoza's Critique of Religion*. Strauss's break with Spinoza seems to parallel his search to define the peculiarly "modern" character of Spinoza's philosophy as it manifests itself polemically in the attack on the Jewish tradition, on the Bible, and on revealed religion. His explorations uncovered the problematic origins of Spinoza's philosophy. He located these origins not primarily in the revolutionary discoveries of modern science or in a speculative response to them, and not primarily in the modern political analysis which bases itself on natural right, but rather in a philosophically and morally questionable rebellion against revealed religion, disguised as "scientific" critique. "The battle [Spinoza] fights against Judaism is a battle against fear of God."[16] Thus, one of the very first things which Strauss does in this work, and which he elaborates on at several points, is to put Spinoza's critique of revealed religion in the context of other prior critiques. It became clear to him in the course of his research that Spinoza's critique represented a peculiar and distinctive blend of the primary "traditions" in which the attack on religion had been developed.

To be sure, in the primary sense "the context to which [Spinoza's biblical] science belongs is the critique of revelation as attempted by the radical Enlightenment." But this is itself only a later form of that earlier "critique of religion which was originated in Greek antiquity," and was merely refurbished for "the age in which belief in revelation predominated,"[17] i.e., the modern era. This peculiarly modern critique of scriptural religion actually preceded Spinoza (although he continued it and carried it to its furthest reaches), and Strauss traces it to such figures as Uriel da Costa, Isaac de la Peyrère, and Thomas Hobbes. But one of the first things which Strauss discerned was that this critique claims to be a "scientific" critique primarily in a positivistic rather than a metaphysical sense. Basing itself ostensibly on recent progress in empirical knowledge, the biblical criticism of this era established its legitimacy by investigating such things as the "doubtful historicity" of miracles, restructuring the Bible's "faulty" historical sequences, and pointing to scribal "errors" in the transmission of the biblical text and in the attribution of its authorship.[18] However, according to Strauss in *Spinoza's Critique of Religion*, it was Spinoza who first recognized that positive science *in itself* possesses no comprehensive account of all being by which it could criticize religion and Scripture as theoretically true or false, and thus holds no necessarily superior ground. It too needs a metaphysical justification, and this is precisely what Spinoza set his mind to provide in his *Ethics*.

What became clear to Strauss, however, is that the metaphysics which Spinoza devised to justify positive science was "more than mere theory" aimed at explaining the universe.[19] His metaphysics is closely tied to a moral interest which it shares with positive science: to free man from the pleasure-destroying fear in which religion mires him. Thus Spinoza's critique of religion and Scripture in both its metaphysical and positive aspects aims not simply to comprehend religion properly or to rationally criticize "false notions of God," but rather to prove through the modern sciences of nature and man that man need not stand "in awe of active and effectual gods." He calls the fear of such gods the "ever-menacing" threat to man's secure happiness and certain pleasure. In other words, modern science and philosophy criticize religion not primarily for theoretical reasons, i.e., disinterestedly, but for moral reasons, i.e., interestedly. They are concerned with the best way of life for man, with what is life-enhancing solely in a "this-worldly" sense, in order to bring man the most secure happiness (*eudaemonia*). Hence, Strauss discerned that the entire modern quarrel between science and religion about true or false theoretical conclusions reached by each side is ultimately not as significant as their quarrel about the practical means necessary to attain the highest ends, and about what the highest ends for man are.[20] By seeing Spinoza in this light, Strauss began to realize that Spinoza's elaborate metaphysics is not in essence any different from the antireligious "science" of his predecessors: dressed in sophisticated metaphysical garb, it is merely a tendentious moral program aimed at the demolition of religion, but still lacking in the rational proofs which would enable it to do so convincingly.[21]

In order to uncover the true motive driving Spinoza's project, Strauss traces his critique of religion (along with his compatriots of the seventeenth-century radical Enlightenment) to the ancient Greek philosophers Democritus and especially Epicurus. By making this connection, Strauss was led to the further "possibility"[22] that positive science is not an enterprise primarily devoted to the pure search for truth irrespective of the results arrived at in the search. He seems to regard this view as a recent idealization which obscures the true origins of modern science; modern science, as Strauss views it, is rooted in Epicureanism, whose guiding light is pleasure, with science as a mere means to its end. To be sure, Spinoza and the radical Enlightenment modified somewhat the fundamental principles of the accumulated Epicurean tradition with due regard for its different aims in the modern era.[23] These modern aims were conditioned by the fight against revealed religion, with its peculiar theological features (i.e., the omnipotent but unfathomable one God)[24] and with its great power to determine political life (i.e., "revelation is necessary for salvation . . . for such conduct of life as leads to beatitude").[25] Strauss was to subsequently dub this attitude "antitheological ire." He further recognized that it was necessary for modern philosophy and science to supplement pure and simple Epicureanism while retaining its original motive. Hence, the radical Enlightenment with Spinoza at the lead actually rooted its critique of religion in three separate traditions—the Epicurean, the Latin Averroist, and the Machiavellian—with their three separate motives for rejecting religion: *ataraxia*, theory, and *virtù*.[26]

The comprehensive modern religious critique associated with Spinoza may be summarized in the following terms. First, religion is rejected not only because it threatens man's peace of mind, but also because it jeopardizes peace in society. Here the updated Epicurean motive of *ataraxia* downplays the purely psychic realm in favor of the social realm, because the latter is regarded as the precondition for achieving the former.[27] Second, religion is rejected not only because it causes distress of mind (with its belief in active and efficacious gods),[28] but also because it awakens hopes and fears which are illusory, and hence distracts men from the true and actual goods that are available to them in this life, whether these be of a material or a spiritual nature. Here Latin Averroism's motive of theory degenerates through popularization, and its "this-worldly" orientation to the theoretical life as the only sure means to knowing truth and escaping illusion emerges as merely a "this-worldly" orientation. Third, religion is rejected because it does not adhere to "the reliance on man's achievement, on labor, on culture and progress," but rather adheres to "the belief in the original perfection of man," which man through his own action fell away from. If man was not originally perfect, he certainly will not desire, nor does he need, suprahuman help to return to what were falsely construed to be the divinely blessed origins.[29] The need for revelation is then dissipated, and the interest in it is exploded, for the past holds no great lost divine wisdom or forgotten moral guidance but only rudeness and ignorance, while the future is the hope for man to build, to reach the as yet undiscovered truth, and to make himself perfect. Hence, there is fostered in Machiavellianism's motive for critique of religion (*virtù*) a peculiarly vehement contempt for revealed religion as debilitating to man's powers, seeing that it respects neither vigorous means nor great ends as appropriate to man's station or as ennobling to man's character in his pursuit of glorious and heroic deeds, especially if they are achieved through deviousness, wits, or might.[30]

From these three separate traditions, with certain modifications to each, Strauss was able to reconstruct Spinoza's definitive modern attack on revealed religion which grounds his Bible science.[31] From Epicureanism, Spinoza learned to treat religion as an illusion natural to the human condition, motivated primarily by fear and by dream. Fear (of the gods and of death) leads man to the religious illusion which provides man with false means to reach his true end, which true end for Spinoza is self-preservation. Dream (in the form of revelation) fosters an illusory religious hope in man (i.e., of salvation by supernatural powers), in that through this man turns to faith and wishing rather than to knowledge and planning; in Spinoza's version of Epicureanism, it is through dream that man doubts reason's adequacy as a guide for conducting human life and for commanding fortune.

From Averroism, Spinoza learned to treat reason as the highest power available to man to assure his self-preservation.[32] However, due to Spinoza's preference for "the Averroist tradition," he emphasizes "the distinction between the wise men and the vulgar" in a greater measure than most of the modern philosophers and carries its logic "to its ultimate conclusion"; that is, despite his hostility to religion, in this political context (expediting the interests of the wise few in conflict with the ignorant many) he is able to "recognize religion as an essential means for the preservation of the state." Due to the "superstitiousness" of most men, i.e., "their hasty resort, moved by fear, to illusionary measures. . . against an illusionary peril," reason is a power used mainly by the strong-minded few, who in pursuing knowledge are always threatened by the weak-minded many.[33] Since the multitude are slaves to their passions and imagination, it is both useful and necessary according to Averroism, for there to arise prophets and like-minded leaders, whose peculiar gift is imagination combined with some moral intelligence, which enables them to rule the people and lead them toward simulated virtue.

> Since *eudaemonia*. . . [through] theory is accessible only to the few who are wise, special precautions are needed for the guidance of the ignorant many, for the sake of social law and order. . . . Religion is a regulator of order in social life.[34]

It is from this doctrine or tradition that Spinoza learned to appreciate the usefulness of Scripture and religion, once it has been defanged by his critique, and made to serve his political project.

From Machiavellianism, Spinoza learned that this holding of the people in thrall through the religious illusion by "kings and priests dominated by their thirst for power and glory" can also pose a threat to free philosophizing as well as to truly great and heroic actions in pursuit of power and glory. It is possible to guarantee the freedom to philosophize in the face of the multitude's hostility by cultivating in politicians another type of canniness mostly unrestrained by religion, and by helping them to perceive the advantages which will accrue to them from an alliance with the modern philosopher-scientist. Such an alliance promises the politicians that they will attain to the rational control of the multitude's passions and imagination, and that they will be enabled to achieve great deeds through such rational control, partly by liberating the multitude from the religious illusion as an "other-worldly" promise, and partly by harnessing them to patriotism through a "this-worldly" love of political freedom. In Spinoza's version of Machiavellianism, he is also able to promise to the multitude—in return for surrender of the religious belief in eternal life that dominates their passions and imagination (i.e., their simulated virtue)—the guaranteed satisfaction of their worldly passions through modern science and technology and through modern liberal democracy.[35]

With this masterful reduction of Spinoza's modern critique of religion to its basic elements and sources, it is simpler to understand how Strauss liberated himself from Spinoza and from the authoritative character of his critique. In essence, Strauss doubted the cogency of his critique of religion because it rests on such a dubious basis: the belief in Spinoza's system as entirely adequate to comprehend all things as "evident and necessary." (In this doubt, a distinctive theme clearly emerges which is reprised at various points in Strauss's work: he was deeply suspicious of philosophic "systems" altogether.) Strauss recognizes that, unlike Maimonides, Spinoza certainly never adequately comprehended revealed religion as it presents itself,[36] as a truly serious challenge to the claim of autonomous philosophy, rooted in its "central assumption," i.e., "God is unfathomable will." In concluding his reflections on Spinoza's metaphysical or systematic (as opposed to positive) critique of religion, Strauss remarks:

> Even if all the reasoning adduced by Spinoza were compelling, nothing would have been proven. Only this much would have been proven: that on the basis of unbelieving science one could not but arrive at Spinoza's results.[37]

Does putting the very basis of Spinoza's philosophical position in doubt consequently imply that Strauss also puts in doubt Spinoza's entire critique of Maimonides? It seems so. Strauss maintains that Maimonides emerges defensively unscathed from Spinoza's attack because Spinoza does not face directly his true philosophic and moral differences from Maimonides—the Epicurean versus the Aristotelian premises with regard to philosophy—which lead them to radically different approaches to religion. Following from this primary analysis, Strauss was able to separate each phase of Spinoza's attack on Maimonides and critically evaluate its cogency. Strauss isolates four main grounds in which Spinoza's critique of Maimonides' position as a Jewish thinker is rooted: Maimonides' attitude to science, and his consequent attempt to reconcile reason and revelation, a claim whose very conception, by its nature, Spinoza tries to prove cannot be sustained; Maimonides' allegorical method of interpretation, which Spinoza views as both an unsound or unscrupulous exegetical principle, and as reflecting his untenable view of prophecy; the use of history in Maimonides' arguments, which is connected with his notion of miracles, but which according to Spinoza is plainly refuted by modern progress in positive science and in the historical-critical method; and the very possibility of revelation, which to Strauss is the matter philosophically most in dispute.[38]

Following his careful discussion and analysis of each of these grounds for Spinoza's critique, Strauss reaches the conclusion that only Spinoza's philosophic critique of the very possibility of revelation possesses any genuine cogency. In point of fact, on the other three issues, Strauss finds Maimonides' position still surprisingly well-fortified against Spinoza's attack. Only the one remaining issue will present any serious challenge to Maimonides' position, but *not* for the reasons which Spinoza adduces. Strauss takes this critique very seriously because the basic premises of Spinoza's entire position are rooted in a denial of the possibility of revelation and because his "system" is staked on such a denial.[39]

With regard to science, Strauss recognizes that Maimonides is just as devoted to its free and honest pursuit as is Spinoza, since it is necessary for both in pursuing and achieving the genuine knowledge of God. Although the former follows Aristotelian science and the latter follows Cartesian science, this difference does not make one more or less "scientific" than the other in terms of basic orientation.[40] It yields a fundamental divergence only in Spinoza's critique of Maimonides' "science of prophecy," his prophetology. Spinoza, as Strauss presents him, seems to treat Maimonides' prophetology as his primary lapse from scientific reasoning into theological dogmatism: as Strauss puts it, Spinoza, who claims to base "his stand on the unambiguous evidence of reason and experience, denies the possibility of such cooperation of intelligence and imagination."[41] But this divergence on prophecy actually depends on a prior divergence about Aristotelian versus Cartesian epistemologies, i.e., on legitimate *scientific* differences.[42]

Moreover, Strauss notes that Maimonides is willing to accept the most radical conclusions reached by science, whatever consequences may seem to follow for religion, provided they are arrived at by genuine and rigorous demonstrations; this is because Maimonides believes science and religion share the same ultimate aim and purpose in both striving for knowledge of God as man's one true end.[43] Indeed, Spinoza seeks to polemically use Maimonides' statement about the world's eternity as reconcilable with the Bible if it had been demonstrated[44] not to prove any lack of devotion to science, but rather (in a devious move to flank his opponent) to expose the flaws in his method of scriptural interpretation, supposedly since it is not rooted in the "literal" meaning.[45]

To be sure, Strauss perceived that this attack on Maimonides' science was necessitated, and even aggravated, by a stinging paradox in the position of Spinoza. This paradox is that Spinoza himself begins with and even actually adopts Maimonides' essential position on "the union of faith and knowledge" in the divine law;[46] Spinoza merely denies that Maimonides carries through this position consistently. According to Maimonides as well as Spinoza, "faith and knowledge" can be discussed and reconciled in identical, almost entirely naturalistic terms, because both share the same view of the aims proper to man in reaching his perfection or happiness, which divine law alone can help him to achieve. Spinoza merely doubts whether this divine law can ever be brought by such human beings as prophets, since their association with the imagination dictates for him that they cannot also be occupied with scientific matters; intellectual excellence and powers of imagination are in diametrical opposition, and are expressed in inverse proportion to one another.[47]

From this vantage point, Strauss astutely observes that it is only Spinoza's further adoption of Cartesian science which leads him in a direct line from his common position with Maimonides to his critique of revealed religion as it is grounded in prophecy by Maimonides.[48] Strauss is aware that Spinoza's adoption of Cartesian science (by which he "constructed his system") necessarily issues in his critique of revealed religion because, in the teaching of Descartes, imagination must be collapsed into sense perception as the sources of deception.[49] Indeed, this fatal flaw of deceptiveness in both sense perception and imagination prevents man from attaining absolutely certain knowledge on which a true science can be built "free. . . from all prejudices."[50] Spinoza merely "draws the conclusion" from Descarters[51] by disallowing the "legitimate cooperation between imagination and intellect"[52] as "a cooperation of both in perfection"[53] in the Maimonidean prophetic act of cognition, so that the prophet for Spinoza does not rise to any more than very ordinary knowledge or cognition.

But to Strauss, Maimonides' position is just as "scientific" as Spinoza's, since Maimonides' prophetology is a true and legitimate product of Aristotelian science. Employing in his prophetology the Aristotelian view of the relations between sensation, imagination, and intellect,[54] Maimonides renders prophecy fully comprehensible as essentially a *natural* rise to the cognitive heights accessible to man as man. Strauss indeed emphasizes that this "prophetology"[55] is grounded in science, since Maimonides and the Islamic philosophers whom he followed based themselves on a dispassionate analysis of the natural faculties of the human soul.[56] Medieval Aristotelian science allows the imagination in certain cases (i.e., once it is freed of the constraints put on it by sense perception during wakefulness) to perform a higher function and to serve as a vehicle or tool of the intellect, especially in dreams during sleep. From this purely psychological analysis, then, there follows "the possibility that the intellect may force imagination into its service for perceiving the supersensory: hence the possibility of prophecy," particularly as it is developed in Maimonides' doctrine. As a consequence of this, Strauss discerns in Maimonides' doctrine that prophecy can be made reconcilable with philosophy on scientific grounds, since prophecy not only requires scientific preparation and talent, but also like the divine law produced through it, prophecy can and must share the same "distinctive aim" with philosophy, i.e., the perfection of man's soul in scientific cognition,[57] culminating in knowledge of God. In other words, Maimonides' position on the reconciliation or union of faith with knowledge does not, as Spinoza's critique tacitly claims, somehow compromise science or forsake it for theological "prejudice." Rather, as Strauss clearly recognized, it builds its reconciliation or union on a different, and not necessarily less rigorous, scientific ground: on "the analysis of the actual order of the world," from which it ascends "to theology and to revelation."[58]

Similarly, Strauss defends Maimonides' hermeneutics, i.e., his "allegorical" method, against Spinoza's scathing critique. Maimonides' approach to Scripture assumes a multilevel biblical text in which beneath the imaginative surface there lies a purely intellectual teaching; and it is on this subterranean level that Maimonides locates the Bible's ultimate teaching and its highest aim. Strauss detects that the most essential element in Spinoza's critique of Maimonides' hermeneutics once again follows directly from their differences about this deepest level of Scripture, or about prophecy. As has just been elucidated, Maimonides attributes to the true prophet the ability to attain philosophical truths and, in some cases, beyond: this is supported by the notion of prophetic cognition as a "cooperation of intelligence and imagination...in perfection."[59] That possibility is denied by Spinoza with his Cartesian epistemology (bolstered by modern science).[60] But for Strauss, Spinoza's attack does not actually touch Maimonides "on his own ground," as it claims to do. In order to do so, Spinoza must first have been able to prove his epistemology (and his attached prophetology) to be truer than Maimonides', and next must have been able to prove it to manifest greater consistency than Maimonides' position. Strauss concludes that Spinoza never actually does this with reference to Maimonides' hermeneutics; instead, Spinoza's entire critique simply assumes his own philosophy as a given. If Spinoza catches Maimonides in any contradiction, it is only on the basis of Spinoza's philosophy, not "on Maimonides' own ground" philosophically.

In Strauss's view, the other two arguments brought by Spinoza against Maimonides' hermeneutics simply "presuppose the alienation from Judaism,"[61] and hence do not meet Maimonides "on his own ground" as a loyal Jew. First, Strauss perceives that Spinoza's reprimand of Maimonides for his unilateral approach to Scripture (i.e., for the "licence with which he adapts Scripture to his preconceived opinions") is merely a borrowing from the revitalized sensitivity to the literal scriptural text promoted "by the Reformation and by humanism." In considering this criticism, Strauss makes a point of stressing that Maimonides' hermeneutics "even in its most venturesome moments. . . [is] guided by concern with Scripture, to which [Spinoza] makes claim, and by virtue of which he has the possibility of rejecting Scripture," while Spinoza's criticism of Maimonides' scriptural hermeneutics "is however in itself not so much a presupposition as a consequence of radical critique of revealed religion." In other words, Spinoza limits Scripture's true meaning to its literal meaning precisely in order to highlight its contradictions and thus to

deny tacitly its "cognitive value,"[62] since he cannot accept the notion
of revelation. Maimonides, because he believed in revelation, "rejected
in principle" the identification of the true with the literal meaning in
Scripture as necessarily leading to conclusions which contradict its
"revealed character."

Second, Strauss discovers a further consequence following from this
debate about Scripture's "revealed character" with direct bearing on the
hermeneutical issue. In a concerted attack on any hermeneutic which
might seem to base Scripture's "revealed character" on a theoretical
grounding, Spinoza criticized Maimonides for maintaining Scripture's
basic harmony with scientific truth. He says Maimonides must assume
"a completion of science" in its essential natural principles and causal
bases, and that Maimonides works with this assumption in interpreting
Scripture and explaining man and the world. To be sure, Maimonides
is undoubtedly "guided by the teaching of Aristotle."[63] But along with
this, Strauss seems to acknowledge critically that even if Aristotle's
science is fallible in several fundamental aspects, and even "in astronomy
and mathematics...has been superseded," Maimonides' classical
Aristotelian *idea of science* remains valid, and has not been actually
refuted by any subsequent developments.[64] Spinoza, however, works with
the modern idea of positive science as eternally progressing and
unfinished, and thus by its very essence never perfect or complete; hence
it cannot be applied to Scripture. Accepting positive science as the guide
to Scripture (which Spinoza tactically requires) would, as Strauss
comprehended, lead to the "absurd consequence" that Scripture's
fundamental "account of creation" would need to be reread and its
meaning redefined with each new scientific discovery. But this modern
positive *idea of science*, as Strauss perceived, would virtually remove
the possibility of identifying Scripture with the eternal truth as revelation, since hermeneutically the discussion of Scripture's true teaching,
especially in regard to its scientific status, would need to be permanently
suspended. Hence Strauss discerned the motive in Spinoza's attack on
Maimonides' science to be once again a concealed attack on revelation.

Strauss also does not side with Spinoza in his argument with
Maimonides about the need for and use of history in analyzing the Jewish
tradition and the divinely revealed texts. Here Spinoza criticizes
Maimonides for accepting the Torah's basic "pregivenness" as divinely
revealed and as established through a "historical proof."[65] Maimonides
is guilty, in Spinoza's view, of not waiting to carefully consider whether
the documentary evidence (i.e., a single book which in teachings alone,

not to mention sources, composition layers, and editorial redactions, is full of unresolved contradictions) can sustain such a "historical proof" *prior to* reaching any conclusions about what specifically, if anything, has been divinely revealed. For Spinoza, then, Maimonides was not a sufficiently *critical* historian with respect to the Jewish tradition. He argued that if the entire traditional and textual edifice is rooted in a supposed fact, the grounds supporting the fact should be tested and authenticated by the most rigorous critical-historical methods to which they are susceptible. And this should be done prior to reaching any conclusions about the miraculous character of "facts," whose historicity should perhaps be cast in doubt.

But Strauss astutely recognized that this critique presupposes two other separate but not unrelated elements in Spinoza's general critique of revealed religion (i.e., the unreliability of tradition and the unknowability of miracles), which are unconnected in substance and motivation with the modern science of historical criticism, however much he tries to use history against Maimonides. Strauss clearly shows that Spinoza's vaunted historical sophistication as a biblical critic may be traced simply to his belief in the essential unreliability of tradition. This accounts for his entire critical approach to Maimonides' attitude to traditional history. But Strauss goes a step further than this and also shows that it is precisely this belief about tradition's unreliability that must be related to, and derived from, Spinoza's "fundamental alienation from Judaism." With an eye to "liberated" modern philosophy and science, Spinoza looked at the Jewish tradition, in its form as a revealed religion, as a rude combination of historically and legally barbaric "superstitions" with philosophically or scientifically primitive "prejudices." He saw these as an imaginative combination originally devised by the wise statesman Moses in order to control an ignorant, passion-enslaved people to make them fit to conquer their enemies and to rule themselves as a free people.[66] Since the Jewish state was destroyed, the Jewish tradition has been a fossilized survival, twisted and distorted for centuries by its ignorant, greedy, and ambitious priestly leaders in order to achieve their own purposes. The Jews are still held in their thrall, which prevents them from decisively moving to any planned, concerted political action for their own worldly benefit. From all this typical "historical" analysis recurring often in Spinoza's work, which simply reduces the religious to the political, Strauss concludes that only radical alienation could justify such a perverse and tendentious approach to the Jewish tradition and meanwhile dare to claim it to be a sounder historical approach than Maimonides'.

Strauss also carefully demonstrates that Spinoza manifests an essential unwillingness to accept any historical fact as providing evidence or proof for a divine revelation, especially if it assumes the form of a miracle. This remains true even when attenuated historical facts are adhered to as proving a miracle, as seems to be the case with Maimonides.[67] In one sense, Spinoza as a modern positive scientist denies the possibility of using history to determine for certain what is a divine revelation, when and where a true miracle occurs, and whether a text or tradition has been divinely revealed, since no single fact adduced, however seemingly decisive, could settle the matter once and for all. On the principles of positive science, there must always be a willingness to consider further fresh historical evidence which could decide the matter one way or the other. Decisions about all such historically based matters would need to be held in permanent suspension. As Strauss puts it: "On the premises acceptable to the positive mind, the factual character of revelation is as little to be established as the factual character of any other miracle as such."[68]

However, Strauss maintains that the essence of Spinoza's critique of Maimonides on history is *not* rooted in his positivist denial of any miracle as historically knowable—namely, that as a reported breach in the fixed order of nature, a supposedly miraculous event cannot be *known* or proven to be supernaturally caused.[69] Rather, as Strauss perceived, Spinoza's critique is rooted in his metaphysical denial of history as divinely created along with nature, and hence also as divinely guided, or as the possible occasion for miracles. That is, he locates its ground in Spinoza's denial of divine providence. Strauss argues in this seemingly "simple traditionalist" way against Spinoza's claim to a superior attitude to history because he perceives that this attitude on its own does not provide any compelling reason to reject either Maimonides' sophisticated defense of revealed religion or even the most simple orthodox belief.[70] Strauss recognized that it is by means of its irrefutable belief in ultimately mysterious divine providence that revealed religion can resolve apparent contradictions or corruptions in the holy texts or apparent discontinuities or unreliabilities of the holy tradition. Moreover, divine providence can be best demonstrated by one of the greatest of historical miracles—that Jews and Judaism have been preserved in history by the action of God—and not by any singular historical fact whose dubious aspects might subvert its utility as a proof for miracles.[71]

Thus, the positive historical critique both of the Bible, and also of Maimonides' method in reading it as a multiplex book can, as Strauss uncovers, only succeed primarily by referring itself to supposed contradictions in the text (and in the tradition) which it can disentangle or elucidate more simply and less artificially through history. But to Strauss, it cannot be a self-sufficient critique, and hence it fails in its own terms, because it is not by itself adequately and comprehensively equipped to deal with the peculiarities of the revealed text, i.e., they may be traceable to some kind of miraculous origin. In other words, Spinoza's entire critical attitude to what is possible in history—whether his critical attitude refers to gaps in the tradition, supposed reports about miracles, or contradictions in the revealed texts—assumes what it is supposed to prove: God does not act in history, and his providential acts cannot be mysterious. As Strauss succinctly puts it in regard to Spinoza's historical critique of Scripture:

> But what is Spinoza actually proving? In fact, nothing more than that it is not *humanly* possible that Moses wrote the Pentateuch. . . .This is not denied by the opponents. . . . [This is because,] on the assumption that Scripture is revealed, it is more apposite to assume an unfathomable mystery, rather than corruption of the text, as the reason for obscurity. . . [72]

Spinoza can only prove this critical historical approach to be the soundest one if he can prove that miracles *per se* are not possible. Hence, the historical critique presupposes the philosophical critique of revelation, i.e., the denial of *the* basic miracle which substantiates the God who can perform miracles.[73] Everything Spinoza brings to light about history is raised in order to make Maimonides' defense of "the pregiven teaching which was originally revealed"[74] in history seem absurd, because it does not conform either with what is empirically probable[75] or with what "can be mathematically proved."[76] But all arguments from history are ultimately beside the point with respect to Maimonides' position. According to Maimonides' most basic view, "starting from revelation is primarily not starting from a fact established by historical proof."[77] History only enters Maimonides' "context of thought" in its third stage. In fact, Strauss considers Maimonides' position in its "context" as that which can be best characterized as "a nexus of scientific reasoning."[78] According to Strauss, Maimonides' fundamental principle is rooted in science, even if he (as it were, anticipating Kant) first proves the limits of such science: "scientific reasoning shows first of all the limits of itself."

Strauss locates this in Maimonides' scientific "critique of the philosophic proofs adduced for the eternity of the world." Only once such limits have been proven does Maimonides argue, by the "same scientific reason," for the possibility of revelation; and only then does he move to defend by historical arguments the Jewish revelation as genuine because grounded in verifiable historical facts and conditions.[79] By this critical unfolding of the latent process in Maimonides' reasoning Strauss proves that not history but science is the *primary* "context of thought" in which the entire Maimonidean position is rooted and on which it depends.

We are thus led inexorably to the fourth ground for Spinoza's critique of Maimonides, the only ground on which, according to Strauss's analysis, the critique is rooted in a genuinely cogent argument. It is an argument which pertains to all revealed religion, and not just to Maimonides' own "belief in revelation" and to his philosophic vindication of man's need for "supernatural guidance."[80] Strauss recognized that in order to dispose both of the Bible as the basis for all revealed religion and especially of its claim to teach the suprarational truth, Spinoza must disprove or refute philosophically the notion of revelation *per se*. But Strauss argues that revelation can only occur in a certain kind of universe: one in which the human mind can achieve perfect knowledge naturally only to a certain degree, and in which God, who is all-powerful and who "acts with unfathomable freedom,"[81] can satisfy man's yearning for such perfect knowledge insofar as he chooses to let man know. The unequalled cogency of Spinoza's critique of the notion of revelation (and especially as this is philosophically defended by Maimonides) lies in his radical awareness that the possibility of such revelation can only be refuted if the universe and the human mind are so constructed as to disallow it unconditionally. Strauss views Spinoza's entire position as an uncompromising attempt to think through as far as possible the consequences of his critique of revelation. This, in turn, lends his critique its power. Whether Spinoza succeeds or fails in this endeavor, it cannot be denied that he so constructs the universe and the human mind as to prevent the possibility of any revelation from occurring in them.

In point of fact, Spinoza never does achieve his goal in the *Theological-Political Treatise*, as Strauss discloses by paying careful and critical attention to Spinoza's actual arguments. Maimonides was perhaps Spinoza's toughest-minded philosophical opponent. Spinoza attacks his hermeneutical method, his Aristotelianism and "scholastic" attitude to science, his view of man and of Jewish society and faith, his prophetology and attitude toward miracles. However, inasmuch as these attacks do not fall into logical fallacies or meet with other rational limitations, they all assume the refutation of revelation as a human or natural possibility. If, as directed by Strauss, we finally turn to the *Ethics* in anticipation of discovering the truly systematic refutation, our hopes will be disappointed: this system, rather than being a refutation of revelation, presupposes its falsity from the very first page of the *Ethics*. Thus Spinoza never refutes it *in* the system since its falsity is presupposed *by* the system. But why is it necessary for Spinoza to simply presuppose its falsity? What premise is so difficult to refute or even to face directly? To Strauss, the difficulty lies in the following concept: God as unfathomable will. If God is unfathomable will who reveals himself as he wills, revelation is possible. It could be refuted only if man could attain the clear and distinct knowledge of the whole, the knowledge which Spinoza strives to contain in the *Ethics*, the knowledge which in principle makes all causes explicable and hence renders all things intelligible. In a completely comprehensible universe, the mysterious God would be a superfluous hypothesis. Since, according to Strauss, Spinoza never adequately demonstrates his view,[82] the system presented in the *Ethics*, "the clear and distinct account of everything. . . remains fundamentally hypothetical. As a consequence, its cognitive status is not different from that of the orthodox account." For this reason, Spinoza cannot refute, or even "legitimately deny" the *possibility* of the theological view presented in the Bible, i.e., there is then no justification whatever for his not considering the revealing God and revelation *per se* as possibly the truth.[83]

From this reconstruction of the most essential arguments occurring in the encounter which Strauss staged between Maimonides and Spinoza, it becomes clear that even if Strauss did not originally set about to argue in defense of Maimonides' position and against Spinoza's critique, he certainly emerges in *Spinoza's Critique of Religion* as just such a defender of Maimonides' reconciliation between faith and philosophy.[84] The Maimonides chapter in *Spinoza's Critique of Religion* contains the momentous result that Maimonides was not refuted by Spinoza.[85] Now, of course, to say this does not mean to suggest that for Strauss Maimonides can withstand any attack; perhaps some subsequent superior critique could demolish the entire basis for his position. But after all is said and done, something about Maimonides undoubtedly must have been attractive to Strauss even before the arguments made by Spinoza against Maimonides no longer daunted him as decisive refutations. Why did he apparently seek to defend Maimonides' position from the first, and why did he find it not only immune to Spinoza's critique but also seemingly superior to Spinoza's position? Was it just the formal and rigorous structure of Maimonides' specific theological arguments, a structure superior to that of Mendelssohn? Or was it merely the general scientific approach in which he engaged in a purely philosophic defense of revelation, an approach superior to that of Rosenzweig? Was it his stance as a loyal Jew devoted both to Judaism and to philosophy, a stance superior to that of Cohen? Was it (by a kind of *reductio ad Spinozam* argument) that since Maimonides preceded and was not beholden to Spinoza and to his flawed modern premises, this automatically makes Maimonides a superior thinker?

Perhaps the most basic reason for this incipient turn to Maimonides was the decisive awareness that in the point of departure for his philosophizing, Maimonides is more philosophical or "natural," and hence less historical, than Spinoza.[86] I allude, of course, to the key passage (already referred to) in which Strauss isolates "prejudice" rather than "opinion" in Spinoza's analysis of revealed religion, as the pivot on which his critique turns.[87] Here Strauss states that for Maimonides and the premodern enlightenment as such, "the natural, original, pristine is *fidelity*," i.e., to the religion or tradition in which one is rooted, and "what has to be accounted for. . . is the falling away." But to Spinoza and the modern Enlightenment with its positivistic science, "fidelity" (or "obedience") to what they must regard as an obsolete and hence dispensable opinion, is perceived as simple stupidity and as slavery to prejudice from which the mind must be liberated:

> For the age of freedom it is essential that it be preceded by the age of prejudice. "Prejudice" is an historical category. This precisely constitutes the difference between the struggle against appearance and opinion with which philosophy began its secular journey.[88]

The modern Enlightenment, in order to fulfill what Strauss calls its expanded "Epicurean" mandate, must combat religion as the greatest evil in human life because it leads to distracting men away from their true happiness and thus also prevents men from attaining to the possibility of philosophy.[89] Hence, to Strauss, the supposedly philosophic fight of Spinoza against revealed religion is more historical and less natural because it is entirely guided, not by the natural conditions of philosophizing in all times and places, but by a specific historical project, i.e., the modern Enlightenment as the promise to achieve true happiness for all mankind in the immediate historical future.

In contrast, in chapter 6 of *Spinoza's Critique of Religion*, Strauss acknowledges that Maimonides, as the more "natural" thinker, does not succumb to this fundamental "error," and that his approach is fully consistent with the dominant premodern Platonic-Aristotelian tradition. This is apparently because Maimonides does not strive in the beginning of philosophizing to achieve something absolutely certain as purely human knowledge in order to construct "the system" free of all doubt. Such was Descartes's radical intention: to "resolve to doubt of everything in order to free himself once and for all from all prejudices," in order to make "once in one's life—the fresh beginning. . . the entirely primary and entirely decisive beginning."[90] The basis of Maimonides' position with respect to science or knowledge is rather laid in "the analysis of the actual order of the world," and ultimately remains with "the traditional ascent from physics to theology."[91] Spinoza, however, "constructs his system" in the diametrically opposite and irreconcilable spirit of Descartes:

> This system does not begin with the analysis of the actual world-order, but with elements that are beyond all doubt, i.e., with "certain very simple concepts" with which what relates to the nature of God is connected.[92]

But Strauss seems already to be fully cognizant of a further distinctive difference in the modern and premodern positions. The Maimonidean philosophic position may be even more natural (i.e., essential) and less historical (i.e., accidental) than the Spinozistic, not only in its beginning but also in its end. Strauss discerns that this "error" in the modern point of departure derives from the modern Enlightenment "never in fact completely freeing itself from the prejudices" it wanted to eliminate.[93] Like revealed religion, and unlike premodern philosophy, it is full of hope for the future; but in this case, positivistic science is seen as the solution to *all* human problems, and it now uses "its own powers to build the future." In spite of the fact that "the system" can only prepare and project such a final solution to all human problems, the hopes which this promise arouses are unprecedented for philosophy, and its expectations can only be called "messianic," although solely in the most fundamentally human sense of the term.[94]

Notwithstanding these reasons for preferring Maimonides' seemingly sounder premodern philosophical basis to Spinoza's modern presuppositions, Strauss was not entirely convinced by Maimonides' arguments as he understood them. It may be that he overlooked the fundamental principles *unique* to Maimonides' position in accepting the conventional view prevailing in the modern scholarly approach to Maimonides. Certainly, Strauss still conceived of the nature of Maimonides' effort in the Christian scholastic mode which forces philosophy to conform to, and subserve, theological need. Maimonides' position "is presented as a *reconciliation* of reason and revelation,"[95] a possibility which Spinoza claims to disprove. But as Strauss demonstrates, Spinoza also arranges "the [two] elements, namely, philosophy and revelation, which Maimonides believes to be compatible," in such a way as to *also* prove their compatibility. So it seems Spinoza too begins with the basic Maimonidean position, albeit a modern revised version of it.[96]

Indeed, it was Strauss's growing dissatisfaction with the conventional Maimonides which gradually brought him to the next stage in his view of Maimonides as a philosopher and as a Jewish thinker. Connected with this was his awareness that Maimonides was a thinker of such daunting profundity that he had been able to anticipate Spinoza's essential attack. Was there then something in Maimonides' position on reconciling reason and revelation which had been previously missed by Strauss? And then again, was there something radical about Maimonides' thought which lent itself to Spinoza's transformative refitting of the same position— perhaps a greater stress laid on reason than had been previously acknowledged? Moreover, as Strauss probably also began to wonder, if for Maimonides "the compatibility of reason and Scripture assumes the inadequacy of human intellect for attaining perfect knowledge of God" (as Strauss maintains is "true for Maimonides [just as it] is true of all believers in revelation"),[97] why should a Jewish thinker accept man's adequacy to attain perfect knowledge of the world, if only admittedly in the sublunar sphere?[98] On the one hand, why should a man who defends "belief in revelation" and even "interest in revelation" as theoretical exigencies, and hence who "fosters, or even merely tolerates, the concern with supernatural guidance of human life," devote himself to striving to attain genuine or "scientific" knowledge of the final truth for himself alone, as if it had not already been sufficiently provided by revelation as containing in itself the eternal truth?[99] On the other hand, if Maimonides' motives are less pietistic and more purely philosophical, why should he defend a position in which "recognition of *one* [revealed] truth is to unite all men, the wise and the foolish. For faith given to untruth is idolatry, *sin*"?[100] And why should he unconditionally defend Moses' "solution" to all the most basic and significant problems (and rest satisfied with it as if were "*the* system"), rather than ground his claim to the need for the theoretical life in the problematic character of every such resolution attained by man, even if divinely aided or revealed to the prophet? Why did he not root his position in the need of man to examine and to investigate all claims to the truth in order to know and not just to believe? I contend that the chief question which drove Strauss to the next stage in his view of Maimonides, and which he tried to answer in *Philosophy and Law*, was this: why does Maimonides adopt a seemingly self-contradictory position, confirming the supreme duty and natural end of man to be the unconditional search for the highest and even the most comprehensive truth, and yet also denying the adequacy of man's intellect to attain the highest truths by his own efforts and abilities? In other words, Strauss was starting to acknowledge that Maimonides' position did not rest on as self-contradictory and even flimsy a ground as his modern defenders wanted to maintain. Instead, his position seemed to presuppose some less confused, "more radical" reasoning which provided the true basis for Maimonides' apparently disparate and even contradictory primary assertions.[101]

At the very end of the chapter on Maimonides and Spinoza, Strauss reveals in the form of a question to himself the dilemma in which his own presentation is caught and to which it can provide no answer. In defending Maimonides against Spinoza's attack, he was armed with the weapons of rational philosophic criticism, modern historical methods and views, and recent neo-orthodox developments in theology, a combination probably learned from Julius Guttmann's approach to medieval Jewish philosophical theology. Consequently, Strauss needed to assume that in the final analysis Maimonides does not build his position "on the basis of science," but merely uses science to defend "his pregiven Jewish position."[102] This "pregiven Jewish position" is grounded in the simple belief in revelation which, in "the context of Jewish life," provides its primary justification and needs to be vindicated rationally for the benefit of those Jews on whom philosophy exercised a detrimental influence.[103] It was this simple adherence to historical revelation, and to the Jewish life it supports, that accounts both for Maimonides' preoccupation with philosophy and for his attentiveness to shedding light on its limits. Strauss argued in this fashion because already he saw with unusual clarity that "it is not possible for any interpretation of the *Guide of the Perplexed* to disregard the fact that this book is not addressed to philosophers of another faith, nor to unbelieving philosophers, but exclusively to believing Jews."[104] Strauss draws the conclusion from this premise that Maimonides is first of all a Jew rooted in Judaism, a believer who resorts to "unbelieving" philosophy only in order to defend "the assumption of the traditional faith." What "necessarily precedes the stage of philosophic knowledge is obedience in act to the Torah." As Strauss elaborates, Maimonides did not establish

> a pedagogic program by virtue of sovereign philosophy.... He defends the context of Jewish life which is threatened by the philosophers in so far as it is threatened by them.... He elevates Judaism by means of philosophy once again to the heights it originally attained...Maimonides' philosophy is based in principle and throughout on Judaism.[105]

Maimonides, according to Strauss in *Spinoza's Critique of Religion*, is a Jewish theologian committed not to "sovereign philosophy" but to "the assumption of traditional faith" in all its original "pregivenness."

However, Strauss also perceived that it is somehow doubtful that a thinker like Maimonides could have been able to accept this "pre-givenness" by an entirely unreflective act. As Strauss well knew, Maimonides could not be classed with the Kalam dialectical theologians, whose dogmatic method he utterly rejected, even if he shared their aim: Maimonides too wanted to prove true "the doctrine of faith," but would do so only "on the basis of science."[106] In other words, Maimonides' acceptance of the "pregiven Jewish position" surely must itself result from, as Strauss puts it, "some reasoning." And might not a position whose "pregivenness" depends on "some reasoning" suggest by this very qualification that a commitment to science in some sense of the term (i.e., as genuine knowledge) is prior to mere adhesion to any traditional theological belief? Maimonides can perhaps truly accept such belief only subsequent to its scientific proof. Certain expressions of Strauss would seem to point in just such a direction, although they are diametrically opposite to the leading ideas in Strauss's presentation of Maimonides hitherto. The following remark occurs in Strauss's discussion of Maimonides' denial of any possible contradiction between "the philosophical reason and the conclusions drawn from the presuppositions of Judaism" in proving creation preferable to eternity: "the inference of basic tenets of Judaism is also scientific in character."[107] Similarly, Strauss also makes the following unambiguous statement: "The basis of [Maimonides'] position is the analysis of the actual order of the world."[108]

Is there "some reasoning" then of a definite and precise "scientific" character which led Maimonides to accept "his pregiven Jewish position"? Or should one attribute it to "a historical proof for the fact of revelation"?[109] Can "some reasoning" which grounds Maimonides' entire position possibly be traced to a mere theological and dogmatic notion whose only proof is "historical"?

Strauss himself was not satisfied with this resolution to his dilemma. As he states:

> It was our belief that we could justifiably assume that the pre-givenness had a more radical significance, but Maimonides himself casts no light on this more radical significance.[110]

That "this more radical significance" of Maimonides' rooting his own position entirely in "the pregiven Jewish position" could not be based solely on "a historical proof for the fact of revelation" was likely demonstrated to Strauss by two points which were well-known to him. First, Maimonides made an uncompromising commitment to genuine science, which does not embrace history. Second, the proof for an actual fact (i.e., historical revelation) is only the third stage in Maimonides' reasoning;[111] and besides, it does not amount to "some reasoning" from necessity, since to Maimonides as to "the philosophers," the mere assertion of a singular fact in itself "proves" nothing beyond itself.[112] The basis of Maimonides' position might have been located by Strauss in "sovereign philosophy" if one argument that Strauss made had been carried to its limits, but it seemed to him at this point that this argument was connected to other prior and overriding theological considerations; hence it did not lead him to the understanding of the "more radical significance" of Maimonides' rooting himself in the "pregiven Jewish position" which he would reach in his next stage. I refer to Maimonides' purely scientific analysis which led him to ask whether unaided human reason is adequate to attain and comprehend absolute and final knowledge, and to doubt whether the human mind can genuinely achieve cognitive conjunction with "God and the angels" through apprehending the essential truth about all things.

Thus, the intellectual crossroads at which Strauss stood in moving toward a sufficient comprehension of Maimonides' position as a Jewish thinker might be expressed by the following disjunction in defining the position of Maimonides vis-à-vis "the philosophers." Either the basis of Maimonides' position is genuinely scientific, in which case Maimonides too is to be counted among "the philosophers"—but then it must be explained how science leads necessarily to genuinely *Jewish* belief. (The defense of Jewish belief as "scientifically" compelling and persuasive is undoubtedly Maimonides' chief intention in the *Guide*.) Or the basis of Maimonides' position is Jewish life pure and simple, whose "pre-givenness" is grounded in revelation, in which case Maimonides is to be counted among "the theologians"—but if so, there needs to be some accounting for Maimonides' differentiating himself unambiguously from the Kalam, because of his claim to root his arguments for "the doctrines of faith" in a purely scientific, "undogmatic" approach to God, man, and the world. The key which would for Strauss unlock this mystery (as he saw it), and enable him to claim that these are false alternatives, was "the political" in the spirit of Plato's philosophy. Through this insight Strauss moved to the next stage in his developing views of Maimonides, and was able to finally explain the "more radical significance" of Maimonides' rooting his thought in "the pregiven Jewish position."

CHAPTER 5

Maimonides as Platonic Philosopher-Statesman

STRAUSS'S ARGUMENT FOR THE NECESSARILY POLITICAL BASIS FOR THE JEWISH PHILOSOPHIC LIFE

THE SECOND STAGE in the development of Strauss's views about Maimonides is represented by *Philosophy and Law* (1935). This work both continues to investigate some of the leading themes first explored in the previous work and simultaneously makes a decisive break with that work. Strauss thus moves to quite a different notion of Maimonides' Jewish thought in his very endeavor to face directly what I regard as the five unresolved questions raised by *Spinoza's Critique of Religion*. Indeed, the answers that he now reaches shift the ground used as the vantage point for viewing Maimonides' basic aim and method. Let us review here those five difficulties, mentioned in passing during our discussion of the first stage, in order to apprehend how and why wrestling with them brought Strauss to radically redefine Maimonides' primary and ultimate purpose. We will not only assess the problems which drove Strauss to "the second stage" in his rediscovering the lost wisdom of Maimonides, but in the course of our reviewing these difficulties we will try to point in the direction of the solutions to which Strauss next moved.

First, if *Spinoza's Critique of Religion* culminates in a vindication of revelation,[1] it still leaves a crucial matter unsettled because it is essentially a "negative" vindication. By this I mean to say, Strauss merely proves (although it is no small thing) that revelation has never actually been refuted by modern philosophy, contrary to its tacit claim. In order to provide a "positive" vindication, he also should have been able to provide rationally compelling grounds for belief in revelation by a man of reason. As has already been discussed, Strauss was not fully persuaded by Rosenzweig's approach to revelation, although he considered it to comprise the best available modern arguments for orthodox theology yet developed. Strauss recognized Rosenzweig's enduring greatness for taking revelation seriously enough to give a rational account of the necessity for belief in revelation, and hence for making it a vital Jewish philosophical issue again. However, Strauss did not regard this account as sufficiently rational. He perceived that in the decisive respect Rosenzweig too was still enmeshed in the crisis of radical historicism, which Strauss diagnosed as modern rational philosophy in a state of decay or senescence. Strauss started to identify radical historicism with nihilism itself, which he recognized by the symptom of its uncompromising attack on both reason and revelation as guides to what is supposed to be visible in and beyond them—the eternal truth. Certainly Rosenzweig tried to escape the crisis by a leap beyond reason to something mystical or experiential, but Strauss discerned that this leap was necessary only if the grounds from which it was made were themselves sound and evident.

Strauss began to apprehend that the putative need to leap beyond reason rests on an analysis of our situation which is only convincing if we must remain rooted in modern premises. He hoped to preserve the philosophical or intellectual approach through a recourse to premodern premises, even if (or perhaps especially because) they also compel us to accept revelation. Such a prospect Strauss did not regard as a threat to his tentative attempt to rehabilitate rational philosophy, because even in compelling acceptance of revelation, these premodern premises might well prove revelation to be something fully, or at least mostly, compatible with reason. Could it be that Maimonides, to whose Jewish thought Strauss was growing attracted, offered such a rational justification for adherence to revelation, which is to be preferred because it can still persuade reason, and through this not compel submission to anything debilitating to reason? Even with his leaning toward Maimonides, as supported by his recognition of the flaws in Spinoza's criticisms, Strauss still did not know whether Maimonides had been able to provide such a rational proof, with any greater stringency or continuing validity in the substance of his arguments. Hence, he turned to Maimonides' prophetology to answer the question about whether revelation follows reason rather than contradicting or surpassing it, as the most reliable guide to the highest Being knowable by man, to "God and the angels."

Second, and connected directly with the preceding, Strauss was moved by the crisis of reason in modern philosophy to analyze and reconsider Spinoza's rationalistic assault on revelation, as has already been discussed.[2] Radical doubts about modern reason pointed to its genuine collapse, and this suggested that a rehabilitation of revelation was also possible, since the tacit refutations contained in previous "rational" critiques could no longer stand. It was this momentous consequence that was brought to full light for Strauss by Heidegger with his protracted "talk about Being" as revealing itself afresh.[3] To be sure, it was also reflected just as accurately in modern Jewish theology in the "philosophical" endeavor of Rosenzweig at transcending reason toward revelation. However, one of the main results of Strauss's study was the far-reaching conclusion that if biblical revelation remains unrefuted by modern reason, then modern philosophy's claim to supremacy in the field of battle for the truth is rendered doubtful. Similarly, this crisis of reason provoked further doubts about modern rational philosophy's greatest claim to supremacy and success in the field of truth—modern science. With this ominous result it seemed to Strauss that the modern crisis might or perhaps must lead either to acquiescing in the flow of "the new thinking" (which Strauss was inclined to reject by observing the consequences in the example of Heidegger's grave moral failure),[4] or to a genuine turning to "old" views which modern philosophy had claimed to defeat and surpass. This very claim was rendered doubtful by the progressive surrender to unreason of those "committed" to reason in the modern era.

But the return path to what Strauss viewed as "the fundamental alternative"—the primary source for the modern tradition itself, namely, the classical view—seemed to be blocked by two overwhelming obstacles: its ostensible scientific obsolescence with respect to nature and its perceived antibiblical spirit. Strauss disputed the latter on the basis of what he had learned from Maimonides: he claimed the Jewish tradition was fully compatible with classical reason (despite several highly significant qualifications)[5] according to its origins and sources in prophecy or revelation, as he defined these by "rediscovering" their true character and purpose. With respect to the former—its seeming scientific obsolescence—one obstacle was removed by the retraction of the claim by modern science to ground itself in, and to attain to, the necessary truth about nature. Another obstacle was removed by recognizing the greater "naturalness" of Maimonides' reason in comparison with Spinoza's. This forced Strauss to ask whether Maimonides' position, with its classical sources, could possibly still be true and valid.

It was this enquiry that bore its first fruit with *Philosophy and Law*. Strauss also wanted to know what such a foreign type of reasoning as Maimonides' signified in its very basis and meaning as philosophy. Certainly it was plainly differentiable from almost all modern varieties of reasoning which treat philosophy and science as the natural enemies of biblical theology and religion rather than as potential allies in the search for truth. (Hegel is perhaps the most interesting exception to that rule.) Subsequently, by isolating Maimonides' prophetology for study as a key to unlock the *Guide*'s mysteries (if only because Spinoza launched such a fierce assault on it), Strauss located *the* root and principle of Maimonides' prophetology in the philosophy of Plato. To be sure, Strauss was also fully aware that this basic philosophic approach had already been translated for the medieval world by the Islamic philosophers Alfarabi and Avicenna, but their groundbreaking work, as Strauss recognized, did not preclude a Maimonidean move through and beyond them. Strauss discerned that this so-called "Platonic" political philosophy provided Maimonides with a unique and penetrating philosophic access to biblical religion, Jewish theology, and divine law, and laid the basis for Maimonides' entire approach to conciliating reason and revelation. Maimonides learned from, transformed, and opposed himself to his Islamic predecessors. This was also a *political* approach to philosophy because it accounted for a human world guided by divine revelation as necessarily based on the primary state of man and his life in society, and because it justified the human need for enlightenment in relation to the needs derived from that primary state of man in society.

Third, Strauss started to pay closer attention to a factor which had been noted in *Spinoza's Critique of Religion*, but the full significance and bearing of which he had not yet been fully apprised.[6] (To be sure, he would not completely apprehend its true meaning and value until he reached the third stage in his developing view of Maimonides.) I refer to Strauss's alertness to the literary form as a clue to other essential matters, and especially to one of the most puzzling mysteries surrounding the *Guide*: why Maimonides, a man obviously schooled in classical philosophy and devoted to its Aristotelian belief in the primacy of scientific knowledge, was determined to philosophize emphatically as a Jew. Strauss was already not able to rest content with the conventional answer to this question, namely, that Maimonides' book was written with a seemingly simple theological purpose—to justify Judaism in the light of reason, and to vindicate reason as compatible with, perhaps even requiring, Jewish or biblical faith. In other words, Strauss was rightly led to ask himself why a man of such probing philosophic depth and enormous critical passion should want to appear in the guise of a "mere" Jewish scholar and theologian, especially as Maimonides himself vigorously criticizes "mere" scholars and theologians. Again, this brought Strauss to Maimonides' view of prophecy, for it is perhaps only the prophet whom, according to Maimonides, the philosopher should acknowledge as a human being who ascends even higher than himself. By glimpsing the furthest possible visible light as well as the unseen light, the prophet sees enough to return with an authoritative divine law, which helps others to reach the same heights. The questions which remain to be answered are as follows. Why should such a man be necessary to human life? If he is necessary, how is he to be produced? And if he is produced, is what he glimpsed awarded by supernatural grace as a religious experience, or is it a natural light attained by the philosophic intellect? The Maimonidean answer to these questions (which could be summarized in the single question "What is the prophet?") in the end resolves the fundamental theological question at issue between Maimonides and Spinoza, namely, the question of the rationality of the belief in "God as a lawgiver,"[7] which Strauss will decide in favor of Maimonides.[8] However, it should be noted that in the present stage, the issue of the perplexing guise in which Maimonides appears (as "simple" Jewish theologian-scholar) and the related hermeneutical perplexity of Maimonides' "contradictions" did not yet excite Strauss's interest and were not deemed of fundamental significance. Instead, these perplexities, noticed only in passing by Strauss, seem to have been viewed as useful and comprehensible devices employed by Maimonides the philosopher in order to resolve the tension between the divine law and philosophy through the paradigmatic perfection of the prophet.[9]

Fourth, Strauss wondered about Maimonides seeming to accept naïvely the Torah's "pregivenness" (i.e., as binding divine revelation) through a historical proof.[10] Knowing Spinoza's historical criticism as well as he did, and also recalling Lessing's powerful meditation on the substantial ambiguity of any historical proof in trying to demonstrate a philosophical truth,[11] Strauss was sure some such reflections must have been seriously considered by Maimonides, and he puzzled about whether Maimonides' assertion might not allude to, or contain, some "more

radical significance."[12] Why would Maimonides accept such an unsophis-
ticated notion so simply? As Strauss gradually perceived, Maimonides'
prophetology does contain the "radical significance" he was looking for:
like all miracles performed by or for the prophet, they are needed to
convince the multitude about the divine authority and sanction of the
Law, which otherwise they would not discern. The "historical proof" for
revelation is what would be called by Maimonides a "necessary belief."
It is necessary to believe it, less because of history *per se*, but rather
because the fact that the basic Jewish constitution is rooted in such a
"historical proof" guarantees its miraculous origin as divinely ordained:
hence it must be accepted for theological-political reasons in order to
preserve the Jews and Judaism.[13] Why such beliefs are necessary, and how
they are to be differentiated from true beliefs or opinions, can only be
comprehended in the context of Maimonides' prophetology as a whole.[14]

Fifth and finally, the centrality of prophetic revelation in
Maimonides' Jewish thought as the way to apprehend the highest
cognitive truth seemed to follow as a key Maimonidean epistemological
principle for Strauss.[15] Yet this perception also led Strauss to an awareness
of a duality in the thought of Maimonides, which he was at first not
sure how to reconcile or to comprehend. Working with a basic notion
of Maimonides as a medieval scholastic theologian, in the Thomistic
mode, Strauss prior to *Philosophy and Law* explicated Maimonides'
Guide influenced by Guttmann's construction. Thus, on the one hand,
he speaks about Maimonides' "belief in revelation," which he construes
as Maimonides' recognizing the need for "supernatural guidance of
human life." Yet along with this "supernatural" leaning, he also discerned
that Maimonides himself strives to attain decisive knowledge of *the* truth
by his own naturally determined efforts and abilities alone, a striving
which he counsels other men also to pursue; and decisive knowledge
does not signify *only* knowing the proper limits set to human striving,
to speak anachronistically in the Kantian style. On the other hand, if
as would seem to follow, Maimonides claims to pursue the theoretical
life precisely because all resolutions to the perennial questions hitherto
offered remain problematic, why does Maimonides believe "the Mosaic
persuasion" is *the* best answer, preferable to all purely philosophic
solutions? These are the kinds of contradictions plainly evident in
Maimonides' teachings which alerted Strauss to the difficulty of
identifying the *Guide* with any "simple" exercise in reconciling or
synthesizing reason and revelation. Freeing himself from the modern
Jewish scholarly consensus, Strauss with *Philosophy and Law* started

to search for a genuinely coherent account of Maimonides' true intention, by considering the possibility that a consistent thought lay concealed beneath the contradictions. As Strauss was led to further suggest, it was this consistent thought that somehow compelled Maimonides to develop teachings which only seemed to be contradictory. Indeed it was by exploring the full implications of *this* possibility that Strauss was eventually brought in the third stage to see the character of Maimonides' thought in a daringly unconventional light.

It began to seem that the modern Jewish theological and political dilemmas preoccupying Strauss were concentrated in the medieval prophetology of Maimonides. It was this theme on which Strauss started to focus his attention, and which can be seen to dominate what we are calling "the second stage" in his developing views of Maimonides. To Strauss, Maimonides' "scientific" approach to prophecy and revelation seemed to promise that this complex of modern problems could perhaps receive a unified and adequate solution if one fundamental principle could be proven to be rational: the rationality of the belief in God as a lawgiver. Maimonides could offer such a belief as rational because he conceived of the prophet through whom God gives the law as the perfect man, whose perfection is delineated in naturally defined terms. Curiously, as Strauss discerned, Maimonides' attempt through pro- phetology to establish the belief in the rationality of God as a lawgiver is aided by the classical philosophers' attempts to determine rationally according to teleological nature in what human perfection resides.[16] As such, the prophet as the perfect man is a helper of the divine perfection: through a divine "overflow"[17] to the true prophet as wise man, lawgiver, and ruler, he helps to guide other human beings to such perfection. In other words, God is a lawgiver only through the true prophets. Although the prophets rationally know God in unequal degrees, they are defined as a unique kind of human being, as a singular and equal class, because as a class they strive with all the powers at their command to know God, and because as a result they are enabled to help other human beings by establishing a divine law. It is in the possibility of such prophets as perfect lawgivers, whose nature and training are conceived so as to conform with all the stringent requirements entailed by this possibility, that the rationality of belief in God as a lawgiver is vindicated. Likewise the Jewish tradition presupposing such a belief is rationally justified.[18]

Certainly Strauss could not hope to reconstitute in any simple way Maimonides' arguments for the rationality of the belief in God as lawgiver through his prophetology, especially in the face of modern natural science and its claim to be grounded in the truth about nature, which undoubtedly precludes any genuine natural theology as a necessary support for such a prophetology.[19] What, then, could Strauss as a modern Jewish thinker have been hoping to do with Maimonides' theology, if there is still such a gap between his natural science and ours? As has already been thoroughly discussed in chapter 2 (with constant and detailed reference to *Philosophy and Law*), Strauss was not convinced that this difference in the two sciences is a decisive obstacle to a return to Maimonides (though he recognized that it was still a significant and binding difference inasmuch as the authority of modern natural science still holds sway). How could Strauss consider Maimonides' prophetology as a possible guide for Jewish thought in the present and the future? And how could the rationality of the belief in God as lawgiver be properly vindicated for *modern* Jewish thought through a *medieval* rational prophetology, if it is not sustained by a nature through which such a possibility can be scientifically validated, and if the cognitive needs of our historical situation are so divergent?

In trying to evaluate whether the essential contents of Maimonides' perplexing prophetology might still be convincing as a rational science of prophecy and revelation in which philosophy is encompassed by, yet subordinated to, a higher human potential, Strauss discerned that this strange path he chose to pursue had not been entirely untraveled prior to his peregrinations. He was able to receive some key pointers from predecessors which helped him to overturn the modern conventions and prejudices about Maimonides' position, and to reach a truer understanding. Most of these helpful predecessors have been mentioned already in our previous discussions. Hermann Cohen rightly pointed to Plato's decisive and formative influence on Maimonides as even greater than Aristotle's, even if he offered a wrong explanation of its precise import in shaping Maimonides' mind.[20] G. E. Lessing pointed away from the modern Enlightenment toward a deeper and surer guide to philosophic enlightenment for man and society by reverting to the ancient and the medieval philosophical traditions.[21] Strauss's friend Jacob Klein induced him to consider a return to Plato and ancient philosophy both as a possible and a necessary antidote to the nihilistic crisis of reason in modern philosophy (i.e., Heidegger). This helped him to seriously explore Maimonides not for antiquarian reasons but as a possible guide to *the* truth, i.e., as a contemporary teacher and source.[22] Finally, Strauss perceived in a remark by Avicenna about the definitive treatment of prophecy and divine law as contained in Plato's *Republic* and *Laws*, that this could provide a pivotal clue to the proper reading of Maimonides, especially the *Guide*.[23] In other words, it became clear to Strauss through this Avicennian remark, through Cohen's essays on Maimonides, and through carefully rereading Maimonides' *Guide* with its medieval commentators, that the decisive influence on Maimonides as a philosopher had been exercised by Plato rather than by Aristotle, contrary to the entire modern scholarly consensus which had been guiding Strauss's research. Accompanying this discovery of Maimonides' ultimate Platonism was a strong recognition that Maimonides' enterprise was rooted in *political* considerations of a primary and specific character, rather than in "merely" general *scientific* questions; the latter remain "Platonically" subordinate to the problem of man as the most encompassing dilemma in philosophy. Connected with this was Strauss's simultaneous awakening to Alfarabi as a key figure in Islamic philosophy. Maimonides himself pointed to him as being of great significance, and he was the one in whom the medieval tradition of Platonic political philosophy may be said to originate. Alfarabi provided the method of reconciling philosophic reason with divine revelation through the prophet as divine lawgiver, whose law he would "Platonically" call divine because it aims to enable man to fulfill his two perfections, of the body and of the soul, or in the moral sphere and in the cognitive sphere.[24]

Thus, what began to emerge in this stage was Strauss's recognition of how crucial it is to view Maimonides' prophetology in the light of his Islamic philosophic predecessors, Alfarabi and Avicenna. He devotes a substantial amount of *Philosophy and Law* to these two figures for their political and psychological sciences respectively. But the rationalistic account of prophecy and revelation (with regard to its psychological operation and political function) is, as he also perceived in *Philosophy and Law*, not peculiar to these medieval philosophers: it falls in with and modifies somewhat a certain tradition which derives from, and adheres to, Plato's notion of the perfect city as ruled by the philosopher-king in the *Republic* and the *Laws*. Maimonides the Jewish philosopher and the two Islamic philosophers were "students of Plato and not students of the Christians"[25] because Plato faced as an intellectual possibility the same dilemma they faced as an experienced actuality: they were philosophers who wanted the freedom to philosophize, but they were ruled by a law, a divine law, which claimed to comprehend and to command all facets of belief and action in human life. Their defense of prophecy or revelation occurs in a "political" context, according to Strauss, because "political" means reconciling philosophy or the philosophic life with the law or the city, even if that should mean the law in its divinely revealed form or as the city of God. Political philosophy precedes theology and all other matters philosophical for them, not because it is philosophy's highest theme or ultimate concern, but rather because it is rooted in issues surrounding the permanent human conditions necessary to actualize the best possible city, i.e., the divine law, and hence can also be a guide to the permanent human conditions of philosophizing.[26]

A shift in Strauss's comprehension of Maimonides' position now occurs. He begins to see that the chief problem of Maimonides, to which his prophetology was the fundamental solution, was not primarily scientific and theological, as modern scholars had been arguing, but ultimately it was *political*, as Spinoza claimed. But the politics in Maimonides' case, as Strauss here started to recognize, was not (as Spinoza had claimed) the politics of domineering philosophers with an unreasonable passion to rule, but the politics of vulnerable philosophers with a desire to defend the life they were leading and the activity in which they were engaged as fully legitimate with respect to the divine law. Now in such a view, philosophy is not always—indeed is almost never—simply or readily compatible with the city or political life: to be sure, there may be a permanent and unresolvable tension between the two. Divine revelation claims to teach *the* truth ready-made, while human reason claims *the* truth must be searched for and known rather than merely believed in. The response of Maimonides and the Muslim philosophers was to claim divine law authorizes and even commands philosophizing through the duty to know God.[27] Here, Plato seemed to them the best guide to the problem, because for him "political philosophy" ultimately means the politics of philosophy, i.e., how to reconcile the city as comprehensive law with philosophy as the free search for knowledge. Plato's solution held great appeal for them: a divine "revelation" may be necessary as the grounding for society, but in the form of divine law and not *primarily* as dogmatic final truth, hence allowing philosophers the right of free exploration in searching for the proper interpretation. If such a resolution were viable, it could settle the fundamental conflict. The medievals would then only differ with Plato about one thing: what he merely promised or prayed for, and perhaps considered unlikely and due to chance, namely, the coincidence of philosophy and kingly rule, they regarded as historically actualized in the great lawgiving prophets, i.e., Moses, Jesus, and Mohammed.[28]

Hence, Strauss discovered in Maimonides' teaching a view of the philosophic life as fully in unison with the divine law, which permits and even commands those men who are qualified by natural ability and training to attempt to penetrate the divine teaching to its innermost core. Maimonides, as a result, can be simultaneously both a Jew and a philosopher. The one "function" need not contradict the other, since philosophy in this scheme is necessary for what Judaism itself aims for in the perfection of the prophet. But the philosophical life is not a teaching necessary for all men: Maimonides does not want to educate all men about the true significance of certain fundamental principles. In point of fact, the main "enlightenment" he and the other medieval philosophers engage in is "esoteric." It is aimed to make the few, rather than the many, truly rational men, or philosophers.[29] (This is, I believe, the first time that Strauss mentions the distinction between "exoteric" and "esoteric," a distinction to which he will give such pride of place in his third stage. At this point, however, it is evident that he does not yet clearly discern its full implications.) In Maimonides' view, unlike the modern version of "Enlightenment," the multitude of men either cannot, or will not, be remade in the philosophic image; indeed, they will remain hostile to philosophy as a superfluous activity, and probably also view it as detrimental to religious and political life. Accordingly, men like Maimonides were forced to conceal by diverse methods the activities of "enlightenment" and rationalization that this teaching convinced them to engage in. In other words, Maimonides, unlike Spinoza, did not believe in the possibility of actualizing "a simply rational society,"[30] primarily because the classical-medieval notion of what the "rational" man is, and what actualizing such "rationality" in man and society requires, diverges so enormously from the modern notion.

None of this, however, means to say that Maimonides ceased to be a Jew, either morally or speculatively. Even if "the purpose of the divine law is identical with the purpose of philosophy," i.e., human perfection resides in cognizing God, and hence freedom of philosophizing is guaranteed in and by the divine law, still a truly divine law is not *only* characterized by such guarantees. Maimonides in a unique fashion stresses that this view of the true lawgiving prophet not only satisfies a high political need (although it is his primary function), but also that it provides the sole human access to the highest theological truths. This applies especially to the burning issue concerning creation versus eternity, which Maimonides regards as *the* fundamental issue separating Judaism and philosophy. The prophet is superior to the philosopher because through him are revealed truths as well as laws unattainable by "mere" or unaided human reason. Prophecy is hence a response to a twofold human deficiency. First, the human intellect is limited to sublunar nature in which it is sufficient, and so men need prophets for the "supernatural truths" they can convey about "God and the angels," or about the superlunar sphere.[31] Second, unaided human reason alone is unable to furnish man with an adequate divine law which is truly binding, complete, and sufficient to the task of establishing the virtuous city. These two grave deficiencies can only be remedied by one thing: mankind requires the true prophets (such as Moses and those who imitate his perfection), who are perfect in all necessary human faculties (i.e., intellect, imagination, morality, courage, divination, leadership), and who can convey a law which is adequate to meet the complexities and anomalies of ordinary human experience, while orienting it to the highest theological truths by which a virtuous political life should be guided.[32] The Platonic basis for Maimonides' position was thus uncovered by Strauss in prophetology: once divine revelation is accepted as binding law, complete freedom is guaranteed for human reason, and the primacy of the theoretical life for man is rooted in the divine law itself, nay, in the prophet himself. It enables the pursuit of the familiar Aristotelianism with which Maimonides is usually and conventionally identified.[33]

At this stage in his developing view of Maimonides, Strauss seems to have been persuaded that Maimonides, like his Islamic predecessors, was genuinely convinced that the prophetically revealed divine religious law fulfills the political conditions of Plato's ideal city in all essential matters. From this conviction Maimonides can proceed to physics and metaphysics in the manner of Aristotle. It is revealing and significant, however, that Strauss still maintains here in *Philosophy and Law* (as he did in *Spinoza's Critique of Religion*) that "Maimonides acknowledges supernatural truths as such," and "Maimonides unequivocally ordains the essential surplus of the truths of revelation over the truths of reason."[34] It is by making this point so sharply that Strauss now claims to defeat what he regarded as Guttmann's artificial construction of a common medieval Jewish "revelation-believing rationalism," in which Strauss detected a fatal flaw. According to Guttmann, all medieval Jewish rationalists believed in a kind of "double truth" thesis, articulated best by Averroes, which maintains the identity between the truths of reason and the truths of revelation, but they needed and retained a seemingly superfluous revelation only for pedagogical purposes, i.e., to bring reason's truths to the multitude.[35] Here, Guttmann is able to mount a tacit critique of the medieval rationalist tradition for the low regard in which it held revelation.

According to Strauss, however, Guttmann's argument only seems to work because he clearly abstracts from the primacy of revelation as law for these philosophers, and also because he does not refer to its unique and suprarational teachings. Actually, rather than adhering to a "double truth" thesis, unaided human reason is, as Strauss discerned, *the* final and single authority for Maimonides, who was a radical rationalist in matters of truth.[36] But notwithstanding such supreme authority lent to reason, reason itself points to its own limits. It expresses its own possible need for, or authorizes its own legitimate interest in, divine revelation through the prophet. Revelation is the highest source of political laws and also of theological truths, which reason must accept even though these are unproven in its own terms.[37] Hence, even if the divine law does concretize philosophic truths in the form of imagination in order to enable the multitude to comprehend them, the philosopher still only accepts truths which have been determined as such by philosophic reason. Those theological teachings which transcend natural reason are only accepted by the philosopher as true, in line with Maimonides' "most realized form of the medieval prophetology,"[38] because they are communicated by the prophet, who is the most perfect man, and because belief in such teachings was considered mandatory by him in order to support the political order he established. However, for Maimonides, as Strauss presently conceives of him, the true divine law is not merely idealized in such terms but actually fulfills all the requirements of the virtuous city as defined by Plato. Even the most radical philosopher, Averroes, who "esoterically"[39] denied that the prophet brought any "supernatural" theological truths unattainable by natural philosophical reason (which was for him, as it was for Spinoza, sufficient and autonomous), followed this same scheme in recognizing the prophet's full political authority; he "exoterically" defended the freedom of philosophy only because it could be discerned to legitimately accord with divine law and revelation in its ultimate aim and actual commandments.[40]

Thus, with *Philosophy and Law* Strauss reaches the middle and, in a certain respect, the crucial stage in the development of his views on Maimonides. With his gradual awakening to the necessity, the possibility, and the desirability of a return to Maimonides, we witness the "Straussian" Strauss emerging, the Strauss familiar to us as the vigorous advocate for ancient and medieval wisdom in "the great tradition" of Plato and the Bible, especially as these two antagonists were harmonized by Maimonides. This is not to suggest that what followed, the third and final stage, the breakthrough to esotericism with all its attendant rediscoveries, is a matter of slight consequence. On the contrary, it completes and perfects the original insight, and penetrates to the core with regard to his Maimonidean exemplar (and beyond). But it is not the turning point or the "lightning flash" which informed him in which direction to move. The subsequent breakthrough in the third stage boldly executes the promise of the second stage, but it does not require any fundamental change in direction or "orientation"[41] with regard to the basic attitude of Strauss toward Maimonides, although it certainly requires a change in the implications of such an attitude. Our first and second chapters dealt with the necessity and the possibility of such a return to Maimonides; our third through fifth chapters have been an endeavor in delineating its desirability, according to Strauss, as he gradually recognized what Maimonides stood for, as both a Jew and a philosopher. In the conclusion of his Introduction to *Philosophy and Law*, he suggests that we are well-advised, with the available alternatives having been both intellectually analyzed and historically experienced, to turn to Maimonides, "the classic of rationalism in Judaism," for help in the midst of our modern Jewish crisis. This medieval Jewish thinker, as Strauss views him, may offer the morally best and yet most rational approach on the one hand to preserving reason, and on the other hand to vindicating revelation, through a Platonic theological-political wisdom. The same Platonic wisdom employed by Maimonides also happened—not accidentally—to be discovered simultaneously as the basis for Strauss's own philosophic solution to the problem of reason's "self-destruction" in modern philosophy. This solution was a premodern wisdom which paradoxically not only corrects but also saves the modern tradition itself rather than simply rejecting or demolishing it.[42] To Strauss, Maimonides guides the rational Jew loyal to Judaism toward the proper conciliation and tempering of two conflicting and exclusive demands in the human soul: the corrosive but free doubts necessary to the philosophical search for genuine knowledge, and the fundamental but limiting beliefs equally necessary for the stable and decent life of man in society.

In other words, the decisive comprehension of the Maimonidean position that Strauss attained at this moment in his voyage of discovery was what he had been seeking but had not been able to find in any modern Jewish thought. It seemed to point to a Jewish as well as philosophic alternative to the dogmatic atheism presupposed by modern rationalist philosophy, with its Jewish variants, which rejected revelation and theology as even possibly containing in themselves any sources of an eternal and transcendent truth. It also seemed to offer an escape from the nihilism of atheistic modern philosophy as it was first manifested by the postromantic "complex-simple"[43] rejection of modern reason, a rejection that makes itself fully evident in the radical historicism of the contemporary era. This result is not ultimately avoidable, according to Strauss's diagnosis, by recourse in the manner of Rosenzweig to a defense of revelation; however admirable and even definitive this may seem to have been in the context of modern philosophy, it is primarily rooted in the same radical historicism which contributed to modern reason's demise. It seemed to Strauss, especially through his careful and probing analysis of this premodern prophetology in its rational defense of revelation, that the return to Maimonides (assuming it to be possible) offered the only genuine alternative to the preceding two flawed choices. It would allow for both "commitments" which Strauss himself was striving to maintain—to philosophic reason and to Jewish revelation— through the person of the prophet who is the most perfect human being and thus encompasses both separate truths. Hence, to Strauss, the chief point to emphasize in Maimonides' scheme is that prophecy is identified with philosophy as far as this is reasonably possible, while not losing sight of the unique religious and political ends which it serves and is formed by. By so proceeding, Maimonides legitimates himself as a philosopher (as well as legitimating the right of reason) from within the tradition itself. He maintains his activity as a philosopher is in harmony with the innermost purpose of prophecy (i.e., the perfection of the rational soul in knowing God, but only for those who are able), while not requiring every human being, and indeed society itself, to lead its life in accord with the life of reason in the true sense, since it is not the aim of his "enlightenment" to make all human beings purely rational. As Maimonides certainly believed, such aims for man and society may reflect unreasonable hopes which, if "actualized," can eventually threaten reason itself. Strauss himself believed this was evident from the historical consequences of modern Enlightenment. These consequences, which premodern philosophers like Maimonides anticipated by thinking through the problem of reason, have only been fully revealed in the present century, and this leads us to raise once again the connected but crucial question for Strauss of whether the modern Enlightenment was right in its claim to surpass the wisdom of thinkers like Maimonides.

Whether or not such a notion of prophecy is *entirely* believable for us in our modern situation with our historical criticism is not at issue, since Strauss does not suggest that we must accept every literal detail of Maimonides' scheme.[44] Rather, we might let his essential approach and assumptions serve to lay the basis for a reconstruction in Jewish thought along "postcritical" lines.[45] This "postcritical" reconstruction would approximately assume the following appearance: while learning from the post-Spinozist modern Jewish thinkers, it would adhere to the still valid and enduring ancient notion of reason and human nature, in which the search for rational truth is primary and ultimate. But since the search for truth is connected with the prophet who is lawgiver and teacher, it is recognized to be compatible with, if not simply rooted in, suprarational theological teachings. These are opined to be among the necessary beliefs for any healthy, religiously grounded political society.[46] Hence, notwithstanding the search for truth, it is necessary that these teachings be conveyed through revelation as a cognition transcending man's natural or normal powers, according to this Maimonidean view as Strauss presently comprehends it. Further, just as the basis for the constitution of such a society in which the Maimonidean prophet would rule must be theological and supernatural in order to be spiritually, i.e., imaginatively, appealing to and morally constraining on most men, so also must the divine law be conceived as rational in the nature of its final ends so as to ensure political moderation. In other words, the Maimonidean perfect law, even though it is the "law of God," prophetically authorized and supernaturally constituted, still mainly aims for human happiness, which consists in knowledge of the truth, moral rectitude, and physical health. Thus, the good society will be held together and formed by a divine law which rationally aims for man's dual perfection, i.e., that of soul and body, through both true (i.e., theological) opinions and necessary (i.e., political) beliefs. Such beliefs animate the laws in order to unite both philosophers and nonphilosophers in one society conducive to the perfection of both human types. In Strauss's view, Maimonides here correctly discerned that this "Platonic" approach is peculiarly applicable to the Jews and Judaism, since they are constituted by a tradition which has from its beginnings been unambiguously defined as a divinely revealed law brought by the prophet Moses. And with the gradual collapse, decay, or disintegration of the modern alternatives in their claims to self-sufficient truth, Strauss also perceived that we are now uniquely positioned to reconsider afresh how vitally appropriate to our Jewish situation, and even to our situation as modern men, is this Maimonidean analysis, as a liberating guide to our Jewish and modern perplexities. It is liberating precisely by vindicating the lawgiving prophet as the key to our entire Western tradition.

CHAPTER 6

Maimonides as Esoteric Writer

STRAUSS'S REDISCOVERY OF
THE PHILOSOPHERS' CATEGORICAL
IMPERATIVE IN MAIMONIDES' *GUIDE*

THE FINAL STAGE in the development of Strauss's views about Maimonides coincides with the radical change in his belief about the possibility of a return to premodern philosophy.[1] As has already been noted, Strauss commenced his labors as a Jewish thinker by surveying the available options in the field of modern Jewish thought and by searching for a truly well-grounded rational philosophic position which a Jew faithful to Judaism could accept. He progressively understood that the entire field, encompassing even Rosenzweig's reawakening to orthodox theology, was enmeshed in the crisis of modernity which he characterized as "the theological-political problem" and which, as he put it, "remained *the* theme of my investigations."[2] This crisis manifested itself to Strauss by "the modern mind" losing "its self-confidence as a "decisive progress beyond premodern thought," and as a direct result, by its "turning into nihilism."[3] Strauss was not persuaded that a resort to "ultramodern thought"[4] is a reasonable hope for an escape from this crisis, since "ultramodern thought" seemed to him to have been best articulated by Heidegger, whose "radical historicism" Strauss judged to offer the most lucid evidence of the modern crisis rather than any genuine antidote to it. But Strauss's exposure to Heidegger's "radical historicism" was also a formative influence on him in one decisive respect: Heidegger's "unhistorical" return to pre-Socratic thinkers in order to recover the "truth of Being" lost or forgotten by the Socratic (i.e., Western) tradition suggested to Strauss a possibility which had not been entertained by him in his own earlier work critical of, yet linked to, modern philosophy, *Spinoza's Critique of Religion*. What if the ancient and medieval thinkers in the tradition of Socrates were not just worthy predecessors, but perhaps possessed something still to teach with regard to rationalism—something which had not been superseded by the moderns' methodical profundity and scientific rigor? What if a genuine return to the entire premodern "Socratic-Platonic" tradition were perhaps equally possible (if only in the realm of theory, though not necessarily in the realm of practice)?[5] Could they have been actually closer to the truth about the nature of man and his philosophic enlightenment, and about the proper relations obtaining between philosophers and nonphilosophers, than are the modern thinkers who are their critical heirs, and whose conceptions originated in the Enlightenment? The first expression of this insightful hypothesis was in *Philosophy and Law*. In fact, it was roughly at the same time as he was writing this book about Maimonides that he was also writing his book about Hobbes, tracing the rise of peculiarly modern (political) philosophy to what he calls "the break with rationalism" by the moderns (i.e., the break with Plato and Aristotle).[6] This unqualified reference to the premodern as simply "rationalism" betrays his switching of allegiance, indeed, his philosophic "conversion," to the premodern tradition. (Later, in his mature works, he would temper his conscious refusal to characterize the modern approach as "rationalism" at all.) It was this heightened alertness to the crucial differences between modern and premodern philosophy that enabled him to place Maimonides in the premodern, especially Platonic, rationalist tradition, and perhaps also to prefer his Jewish thought for that very reason.

Thus, turning away from the careful and critical examination of Spinoza to his two great predecessors, the modern Hobbes and the premodern Maimonides,[7] Strauss wondered whether a solution to the modern theological-political problem—the collapse of faith in modern reason as an unconditional moral force for good in the progress of civilization—might lie in a return to premodern reason, with all that this would entail for both theological and political doctrines. Strauss's endeavor to reconsider seriously the Maimonidean Jewish philosophic standpoint, to view it afresh in light of both the modern Jewish crisis and premodern theological-political reasoning, would seem to have been completed with his recognizing Maimonides' basic teachings as rooted in what he regarded as the potentially still valid "Platonic" philosophic tradition. Strauss's modern voyage in search of a well-grounded Jewish philosophy, able to preserve both reason and revelation as fundamental principles, would seem to have been brought to a fitting conclusion in his rediscovery of the Maimonidean standpoint (as represented by *Philosophy and Law*). Radically breaking with both modern Jewish theology and modern political philosophy inasmuch as they assert a claim to self-sufficiency and separation from ancient and medieval rationalism, Strauss apparently vindicated a tentative return to Maimonides. To adapt a Maimonidean parable in order to convey Strauss's suggestion,[8] perhaps premodern Jewish thought represents the lost king's palace constructed by Maimonides, the lawgiver, in order to accommodate philosophy to a Jewish home. This palace was situated by him on a habitable island city of premodern "Platonic" provenance that now has been long-forgotten or abandoned. Could it be that in this hospitable spiritual home built by Maimonides the Jewish tradition was allowed to dwell and to flourish with greater naturalness, self-knowledge, and rootedness, and greater assurance of the eternal truth it stood for, than it can in the modern home it currently occupies, which may in point of fact rest on a volcano?[9]

Certainly Strauss would have reached his destination with *Philosophy and Law* if his goal had been simply to tentatively vindicate Maimonides' premodern Jewish thought as possibly a still viable guide to the proper relation between Torah and philosophy, if not also as the true teaching about God, man, and the world. But this was only the penultimate step; the decisive moment in the dramatic unfolding of his thought was yet to occur. To adapt further the Maimonidean "king's palace" parable, Strauss gradually awakened to the fact that he still stood, as it were, in the outer chambers and had not yet been able to penetrate at all to the king's inner court. The fundamentally Platonic (rather than Aristotelian) cast of Maimonides' mind—the "theological-political" orientation in his basic teachings as this first appeared to Strauss in his study of Gersonides', and in turn Maimonides', prophetology[10]—constituted only a beginning rather than an end for his grasp of Maimonides' actual thought. Strauss started to perceive that something was missing in his account of Maimonides hitherto, and as a result he began to pay greater attention to "smaller" textual details as key pieces to a larger puzzle. He began to pay heed to seemingly slight variations of meaning in specific key theological terms as these changed with theme and context, to the diverse modes of expression and literary styles employed in conveying these meanings, and to possible deeper intentions with respect to the author's comprehensive purpose subtly communicated in the structure of the *Guide*.

In several probing essays of a transitional nature—"Quelques remarques sur la science politique de Maïmonide et de Fârâbî" (1936), "Der Ort der Vorsehungslehre nach der Ansicht Maimunis" (1937), "On Abravanel's Philosophical Tendency and Political Teaching" (1937), and his review of Moses Hyamson's edition of the *Mishneh Torah*, Book 1 (1939)—Strauss discerned clues to something hidden, but their full meaning was not yet revealed clearly to him. At first, perhaps put on the alert by Lessing to an ancient philosophical art of "writing between the lines,"[11] Strauss acknowledged "flashes" dimly glimpsed. Eventually, he recognized distinctly that both the concealment of Maimonides' true thought and the keys to its uncovering were deliberately planted by this masterful author in his confusing language and even in his very contradictory teachings. In other words, as Strauss was to discover, the contradictions do not necessarily prove the weakness of Maimonides' mind, but may provide evidence of hidden recesses in the Jewish thinker whose strength of mind kept him from pointing to the truth too plainly. Perhaps Maimonides possessed a private thought which was only obliquely articulated in his public teachings, and which could only be reconstructed with the greatest attentiveness, care, and difficulty, as Maimonides himself, it would seem, considered proper.[12]

These sharp-eyed though merely preliminary insights into what may seem like strangely secretive excesses in Maimonides' manner of communicating his Jewish thought helped to move Strauss along a disused path until he attained to the radical conception known as "esotericism."[13] Strauss first treated esotericism separately and fully in his monograph "The Literary Character of the *Guide for the Perplexed*" (1941).[14] There he focused on Maimonides as an exemplification of the esoteric writer who himself announces his intention to conceal his true thoughts and actually provides a key to his curious literary method with its bizarre subterfuges. Strauss discerned that such an instruction manual for the decoding of Maimonides' often confusing and seemingly haphazard literary manner of expression is intended to allow only the select readers (i.e., "the single virtuous ones") to uncover the clear and distinct meanings, as well as the precisely chosen diction and calculated arrangement, hidden beneath the obvious obscurities and the apparent disorder.[15] Ultimately, Maimonides' detailed instructions in the explication of his riddles, not to mention his help in the detection of clues and his pointers in the noticing of hints and allusions, should permit the select readers to unravel the most well-tied knots—i.e., the deliberate contradictions[16]—by which Maimonides, according to Strauss, locked away his deepest secrets. Strauss next started to apply the lesson he learned so well from Maimonides to the entire philosophical tradition—embracing the Greek, Roman, Muslim, Jewish, Christian, and "secular" traditions—in his still controversial and radical book, *Persecution and the Art of Writing* (1952). What is particularly striking, and perhaps most worth emphasizing for Jewish thought, is that in the book Strauss addresses himself to two otherwise diverse and even seemingly opposite Jewish thinkers—the medieval poet Halevi and the modern rationalist Spinoza—and astonishingly treats them as possessing in common a certain unity and universal typology[17] of philosophic purpose. According to Strauss, despite their great differences on matters of theoretical truth, in the practical realm they share the philosophers' common policy for dealing with nonphilosophers: both Halevi and Spinoza employ an esoteric method similar to the one utilized by Maimonides, and it would seem for roughly similar reasons. Strauss's implicit premise in all of this seems to be that Halevi and Maimonides are to be counted among "the philosophers." But if so, why would he subtly but still shockingly contradict what he explicitly maintains about them both—that "Halevi and Maimonides. . .opposed the *falasifa*"?[18] The critical bearing of such a tacit contradiction in Strauss's own argument will need to be considered subsequently with a sharper focus.

It would seem plain that the esotericism which Strauss rediscovered almost single-handedly does not just pertain to a lost literary category, a forgotten hermeneutical canon, in the history of philosophical writings. This notion would also seem to possess for Strauss not only a deeper philosophic significance relating to what philosophy is and what it necessarily teaches, but also the most comprehensive ramifications regarding what might be termed the ambiguous character of philosophy and the philosopher in human society. Likewise, it would seem esotericism cannot be separated from the theme which began to guide and characterize his researches in *Philosophy and Law* (as is most evident in the title of his Guttmann critique), and which predominates and even defines his work in *Persecution and the Art of Writing*: "the conflict between the ancients and the moderns" in the history of philosophy and in the history of Jewish thought. Although on the surface, this conflict is of a merely historical and scholarly interest, Strauss maintains that it is actually rooted in a still vital and genuinely philosophic controversy.

Indeed, meditation on esotericism, on its premises and on its consequences, is needed, according to Strauss, in order to illuminate the primary challenge facing present-day philosophy as well as Jewish thought. This challenge presents itself in the form of "the two fundamental alternatives" represented by the camps of Socrates-Plato and Machiavelli.[19] And, in Strauss's view, the two camps stand in an opposition to one another that cannot be reconciled. While Strauss undoubtedly leaned toward the ancients and the medievals, his formulation also in a sense reflects a high estimate of the moderns' great critical acumen and probing cognitive powers; he respects them as worthy opponents from whom a good deal can be learned with regard to philosophy. However, this respect was qualified for him by the genealogy of their ideas, which he traced in a more or less direct line from Machiavelli to Heidegger, and by his enduring conviction that modern philosophy is not able to extract itself from, or to resolve by itself, the nihilistic crisis it has been led to invoke against itself. Modern philosophy, while originally committed to a rational philosophy, has been led to lose faith in its own peculiar brand of rationalism, and hence it is no longer a sure guide to the simply rational society it promised to help actualize and even claimed to guarantee (in contrast with the "merely" utopian vision of ancient philosophy).

This grand scheme of things must be looked at in some detail in order to comprehend how Strauss arrived at the peculiar attitude to Maimonides which he formed in the third stage of his developing views. It is clear that Maimonides is a pivotal figure in the gigantic battle of ideas which Strauss presents on the stage of philosophic history. Maimonides' distinction lies in the virtually unparalleled self-consciousness of his arguments for the esoteric method. In paying careful attention to Maimonides' "contradictions," Strauss is not merely moved by a passion for historical research and its "basic condition" alone,[20] nor by aesthetic curiosity about unusual literary techniques, nor by a pious respect for the law which determined the *Guide*'s character as "a Jewish book"; rather, Strauss regarded Maimonides' consummate and even definitive treatment of the need for esotericism in philosophic discourse as the great key to the two most decisive problems, practical and theoretical, affecting "the conflict between the ancients and the moderns." For Strauss, the conflict revolves around, first, the leading versus the supporting function of philosophy in human life (i.e., the political dilemma), and second, unaided human reason as able to attain to the truth it strives for merely by following nature teleologically conceived (i.e., the theological dilemma). Decisively different responses to these dilemmas are offered by the ancient-medieval and by the modern philosophic traditions.

Strauss began to view the responses to these two dilemmas according to the following schema. The politics of the Socratic tradition in philosophy issues in the whole classical-medieval political philosophy, which sets its bearings by surpassing human virtue in imitation of the divine. Hence it can be accommodated to, or harmonized with, highminded biblical faith and morality. According to Strauss, this ancient tradition (as presented by its medieval heirs) did express subtle criticisms and reservations regarding the biblical tradition, but these remained concealed in its private "political" thought on the guiding function of philosophy or pure reason in human society. Paradoxically, however, this same rationalist "Great Tradition,"[21] by it fundamental belief in the highly unlikely "coincidence of philosophy and political power" as the only road to man's worldly salvation, laid the basis for the modern (i.e., Machiavellian) revision. That Machiavellian revision rejects and transforms its progenitor's public accommodations or harmonizations, since these seem to act in vindication of traditional "theology," which it opposes entirely, and because it sets its bearings by worldly, rationally calculating human need. In other words, it believes it can actualize the saving coincidence by a "propaganda"[22] which teaches about the judicious engineering of man's most basic needs so as to satisfy them "rationally" in an entirely worldly horizon. Based upon a "decayed Aristotelianism" which simply denies teleology as natural,[23] it stresses and radicalizes (beyond the original emphasis and significance) the criticisms of the biblical tradition raised so discreetly by its predecessor. The Machiavellian view asserts the competence of reason to rule if properly regulated by desire for glory. This assertion of the virtual omnipotence of reason is limited only by "fortune" or chance, which can itself be conquered. That modern claim to the omnipotence of reason manifests a philosophical audacity which the premodern philosophers would recoil at as *hubris*, for they kept in view recalcitrant human nature. As for the promise to conquer chance, the premoderns would protest against the moderns' arousing such exaggerated hopes. The unavoidable disappointment of these hopes, they thought, would cause a massive defection from reason not intended by those who made the original promise.

Not only in the realm of politics but also in the realm of theology does the enormous difference between moderns and premoderns make itself manifest, as Strauss presents the conflict. The dispute between the Platonic-Aristotelian philosophical theology (i.e., classical-medieval physics and metaphysics) and the biblical God (omnipotent creator of the world and omnipresent guide to man in history) issues in perhaps the highest and most enduring conflict between reason and revelation. It culminates in the heroic medieval attempts at a qualified "harmonization" between the great antagonists in which the claims of both theologies receive their greatest due through Maimonides' efforts to produce a unified view on the ground of creation versus eternity. However, in the modern dispensation, according to Strauss, the "theology" of premodern rationalism is diminished or even eliminated. It is reduced to its purely political drive.[24] As a result, peculiarly modern science emerges, which suspends judgment on the highest things, but is allowed to "torture nature" in the cause of helping man to alleviate his estate and to satisfy his needs. This is because modern science (as guided by Machiavellian philosophy) aims to finally harmonize itself with society by rendering itself useful or salutary rather than threatening. Accordingly, the conflict between reason and revelation is resolved by dispensing with, rather than refuting, revelation, which is viewed as harmful to satisfying man's needs (for which purpose reason claims such omnipotent competence). In the modern project enunciated by Machiavelli, "philosophy is to fulfill the function of both philosophy and religion."[25] That is, it promises to satisfy both the theoretical needs of the few and the practical needs of the many in the rational society guided by science and popular enlightenment, with hope in the historical future for its complete actualization. In lieu of the benevolent but ultimately mysterious providence rooted in theology, there is substituted a ruling human reason calculating for worldly good in the march of history. Through the politics of well-planned human action and technological science, then, reason will provide man with all the real worldly goods whose lack is asserted to be the origin of the need for belief in an ideal God. In other words, modern philosophy is animated by "antitheological ire" because it rejects the notion that man's aim is to somehow transcend this world; it regards the aim to transcend (both religious and philosophic) as receiving its best support from the Hebrew biblical God, who is put beyond the world yet who also guides the world and provides for man, and to whom man desires to be assimilated.[26]

Strauss perceived that the modern rationalist resolution to the human contradictions which prevent the actualization of perfect rationality in human society was achieved by not aiming too high. It set its bearings by how men actually act rather than by how they should act,[27] i.e., it put the main emphasis on the low rather than on the high in the life of man. According to Strauss, the fact that Machiavelli does not orient himself by the perfection of human nature in contemplation is a radical change in the orientation of philosophers toward their own value. As Strauss puts it, this "leads to a radical change in the character of wisdom: Machiavellian wisdom has no necessary connection with moderation."[28] Strauss here refers to "moderation" as if it were a virtue peculiar to "classical" philosophers because according to his notion they recognized, against modern claims to the contrary, how little influence reason can hope to exercise on human action if human action (however noble or glorious) is not able to acknowledge its own limits, or if it does not defer to something which transcends it, i.e., intellectual excellence in man or the justice of the divine.[29]

How, according to Strauss, would these two antagonists conceive of the nature and function of the philosopher in society? The "Machiavellian" (or modern) rationalists would claim that the modern philosopher plays an entirely benevolent or benefactory role in society,[30] and this manifests itself best in the form of modern science and technology. But Strauss claimed to discern that this movement to reconcile the philosopher and society collapsed in the "philosophic" nihilism concealed beneath radical historicism. To be sure, such "philosophic" nihilism, and the leading role it played in the rise of the monstrous twentieth-century totalitarian regimes, is the very antithesis of moderate modern rationalism, which is more or less identical with the Enlightenment "initiated" by Machiavelli and executed by "his great successors."[31] Pressed by a practical concern with the threat to reason, Strauss was led by the Enlightenment's apparent collapse to reconsider the fundamental question about the nature of the philosopher and philosophy, which brought him to the perplexing answer offered in what might be called the archetypal premodern philosophic conception. The premoderns revealed a keen theoretical awareness of the threat[32] posed by the philosopher to society, and accordingly they were concerned with establishing a proper, i.e., mutually beneficial, relation between philosophers and nonphilosophers or society. It is at this point that esotericism enters the discussion, for the philosopher may not be able to eliminate *simply* the danger he represents, since he requires unconditional free thought in order to be what he is; and such unconditional free thought unconditionally communicated may well work to destroy everything the nonphilosophers hold sacred. He may not however require unconditional free speech. Strauss says this may in essence be one of the leading "sacrifices which we must make so that our minds may be free."[33] Hence, in covered speech the philosopher may discover the opportunity he needs to actualize his potential, while not hurting either himself as genuine philosopher or the nonphilosophers as his necessary support.

Thus, Strauss in *Persecution and the Art of Writing* and then in subsequent writings proceeded to meditate on the fate of esotericism in ancient, medieval, and modern philosophy, from Plato and Xenophon through Maimonides to Machiavelli and his assorted disciples. Strauss traces the gradual waning and final disappearance of esotericism in modern (i.e., Machiavellian) philosophy to its most essential difference from ancient-medieval (i.e., Platonic) philosophy:[34] their difference on the standing and character of philosophy itself in human life, and especially on whether it constitutes *the* paradigmatic standard. Their difference may be elaborated further in terms of the following typological queries. Can and should the philosopher ever hope to be entirely at home in, or at peace with, the society of nonphilosophers, i.e., with most men? Can and should the philosopher and the nonphilosopher ever worship precisely the same gods? Is the best or the most virtuous city, i.e., the city ruled by philosophers, actualizable by deliberate or planned human effort? According to Strauss, positive answers to these questions as would be proffered by the modern schools since Bacon would necessitate recourse to a subtle "propaganda" in order to effect forcefully the coincidence of philosophy (reformulated as salutary or benevolent science) with political power; such a goal however could only be achieved once the theological teachings were neutralized or removed as the primary obstacle to such a coincidence. Negative answers to these questions, as would be given by the ancient-medieval schools, would in Strauss's view lead to the creation of a certain "noble rhetoric" not only in defense of philosophy but also of all things humanly excellent, things which harmonize naturally because they all more or less "consist in the proper order of the soul." Such a rhetoric is "noble" because it unequivocally points to the virtuous which, though difficult as well as rare, is the highest end naturally tended toward by *all* human action and intention.[35] But it is still a "rhetoric," however noble, because it is needed to serve as a bridge between different types of men in society with their different virtues, i.e., "the philosophers" versus "the *demos*" or the nonphilosophers.

How then does Strauss account for there being two such disparate types of men in society? To Strauss, the entire citizenry, indeed the city as such, inasmuch as it is unable or unwilling to "defer to philosophy," stands in an irreconcilable opposition of soul to philosophy, which "transcends the city." Even if the philosopher's "noble rhetoric" claims that "openness to philosophy" ennobles the city and defines its "worth," this claim is limited by what these same philosophers themselves should know about the city: it is and must be *essentially* a closed entity. Thus, the two most fundamental human types, each with their own peculiar virtue, "are separated by a gulf: their ends differ radically."[36] Strauss conceives of their different natures as men by referring to these contrasting "ends" as follows: their moralities or ways of life, or the appropriate human ends they hold in view (i.e., love of wisdom versus rootedness in justice); the highest theological truth they aim for (i.e., divine mind versus mysterious or unfathomable will); their means for apprehending such truth (i.e., unaided human reason versus divine revelation); their "political" standing as reflecting unchangeable tendencies in the distribution of human natures (i.e., the few who will be satisfied with nothing less than knowing the demonstrated truths versus the many who will require nothing more than believing the received opinions); and the epistemological standpoint (i.e., the divergence between truth *per se* versus opinion *per se*).

Since these "radical differences" unavoidably lead to grave mutual misunderstandings, if not to fatal conflicts, and since it is virtually impossible to truly reconcile or synthesize such polar opposites even though each continues to need the other, only a "noble rhetoric" can offer the harmonizing belief which reconciles the city to philosophy. Strauss began to perceive that Maimonides and his Islamic philosophic predecessors had developed such a "noble rhetoric" through their medieval prophetology as a "science" of divine revelation. In this scheme, the prophet represents an "overflow" from the divine mind to the humanly perfect medium—in other words, the prophetic lawgiver is a statesman, king, or legislator "of the highest type" because he is also a philosopher.[37] For Strauss, this doctrine constitutes a "noble rhetoric" in defense of philosophy, if not also a settled conviction about revealed religion, inasmuch as it maintains that the true prophet must also be a philosopher. But philosophy is compatible with the divine law only if this "divine" aspect is redefined in purely naturalistic terms as the best or noblest of the human, i.e., as a product of the soul occupied in reasoning about the good and the true as well as about "God and the angels."[38] Such a complete shift in ground as must occur with an apparent reduction of the divine to the human, even if to its best or noblest aspect, represents a fundamental and irreconcilable divergence from how Strauss had in previous works been considering the function of the prophet in Maimonides' scheme. Previously, it had been his view that, according to the Platonic position of Maimonides, any and every premodern city's highest truth must claim to be divinely revealed, i.e., it has miraculous, supernatural, and unique access to the divine through something like prophetic revelation. This prophetic revelation, as the city's "divine" lawgiving, brings to light its basic theological and moral teachings in the form of law, which is called "divine" in the true sense of the word because it also perfects the soul and allows it to move from what is naturally possible or knowable to divinely aided "true opinions" about God, man, and the world.

In other words, Strauss began to acknowledge that the resolution to the conflict between reason and revelation, which he maintained Maimonides had been able to achieve through theologically revising and perfecting the medieval philosophic prophetology, was not as pellucid as he had been convinced it was in the second stage. The harmony of the philosopher and the prophet is not so simply accomplished, mainly because the needs, the purposes, and the actions of the two human types are so radically divergent. For this reason, Strauss begins *Persecution and the Art of Writing* with a brief restatement of the medieval philosophic prophetology;[39] highlighting the ambiguities that arise from its primary and ultimate loyalty to *philosophy*. He leaves undecided in which camp Maimonides made his true home. Indeed, Strauss seems to virtually retract the position on Maimonides' resolution which had been propounded by *Philosophy and Law*, because he cannot believe it is the last word in the comprehension of what Maimonides was doing: ". . . it would appear to be rash to identify the teachings of the *falasifa* with what they taught most frequently or most conspicuously."[40] This statement seems to apply to Maimonides the Jewish thinker just as much as to the Muslim *falasifa*. As such, the "noble rhetoric" peculiar to those philosophers who follow in the tradition of Plato (with whom Strauss unequivocally associates Maimonides), aiming to bridge the gulf separating the philosophic few and the nonphilosophic many, necessarily issues in esotericism as the means of vindicating the philosophers as just, loyal, and law-abiding men.[41]

Moreover, according to Strauss, esotericism pertains to the need to conceal the radical difference between "the two ways of life" available to men in human society, as means to their happiness.[42] Esotericism does not arise *directly* from the controversy concerning human happiness, but it does arise *ultimately* because happiness is not itself the highest good for man, but is a by-product of something else in which it is rooted. These issues are subordinate to the concern with *the* truth, and how man may know it, either by unaided human reason or by divine revelation. This is a division that also reflects a mutual antagonism of the most primary notions about what man's natural end consists in, about what constitutes human perfection, and what is most needful for its accomplishment. It emerged as Strauss's abiding opinion that reason and revelation represent two permanently opposed human poles (namely, belief versus unbelief),[43] which are irreconcilable and mutually irrefutable ("...we can hardly avoid the impression that neither of the two antagonists has ever succeeded in really refuting the other").[44] Both "proclaim something as the one thing needful,"[45] but this "something" is the other's complete opposite: "A life of obedient love versus a life of free insight."[46] Thus, Strauss rejects the possibility of ever achieving a deep and fundamental harmony between reason and revelation, because every attempt has not and cannot do justice in truth to both sides equally:

> In every attempt at harmonization, in every synthesis however impressive, one of the two opposed elements is sacrificed, more or less subtly but in any event surely, to the other.[47]

In this scheme, which Strauss allows to be called "Averroistic" although "with pardonable ignorance,"[48] revelation or prophecy in one form or another is the access to the truth peculiar to the city: politics must employ theology because religion, which imaginatively presents God (or the gods) as an active force devoted to justice, functions in support of the moral life. The philosophic life, however, is devoted to wisdom and claims to transcend the imaginative sphere, and hence assigns revelation to opinion rather than to truth.

Esotericism is thus correlated with the one basic condition of human society which stands in opposition to all philosophy, and of which all serious premodern philosophic writers were keenly aware: this is the disparity between truth and opinion, and thus between philosophy and society or the city.[49] The philosophic way is the search for truth which is genuinely known, and it is the preference for hard and often unattainable questions as against easy and questionable answers; it originates in "the doubt of authority."[50] Esotericism is hence designed to defend philosophy in the terms of the nonphilosophers. It appeals to

the supernatural theological beliefs peculiar to the society in which such
a "defense of philosophy" has been made necessary. This defense is
necessary because of the one fundamental and unchangeable political
condition in which philosophy by its nature must always be rooted and
of which it must always remain aware: "opinion is the element of society."
And it is precisely "opinion" that philosophy (which by its nature is the
endeavor to substitute truth for opinion) must necessarily "attempt to
dissolve" in its search for truth.[51] Moreover, the way of the city is the
building of a common and good life for all men, made possible by opinion
which is generally accepted and thus authoritative. It is produced by a
common agreement which need not agree, indeed may radically disagree,
with the truth as defined by philosophy. In doubting authoritative opinion
for the sake of self-evident and demonstrated truth, the philosopher
represents a grave threat to the city.

Hence, a consequence of this one condition of human society is the
peculiar style of writing employed by philosophic writers. Often this
concealed their true meaning from all but the most careful and
perspicacious readers, i.e., for their fellow philosophers, actual or
potential. It is a phenomenon which may be viewed in two ways. In its
negative light, these writers feared persecution lest they should be
detected holding heterodox opinions. In its positive light, they
"considered their social responsibilities"[52] and willingly "lied nobly"
because they never forgot the radical gulf separating philosophic and
nonphilosophic men, and the damage which can be done to society if
nonphilosophic men begin doubting the city's orthodox or fundamental
opinions. In other words, they recognized the necessity for persecution
of some kind in order to maintain and protect even the best city's most
authoritative opinions.

Consequently, the decisive cause of esotericism could have been
put in terms which are rooted in Platonic political philosophy inasmuch
as esotericism obeys Plato's strategy for "the politics of philosophy."[53]
The wisest philosophers all know they must keep silent about their true
opinions concerning morality (and the noble lie, or the myth, or
the sanctified opinion, which sanctions it), especially concerning its
radically noncategorical character.[54] They are preoccupied solely with
intellectual perfection of the soul and deny the possibility of the soul's
moral perfection; they reserve moral perfection for the body, which as
a mere prerequisite for the "true" perfection must be fundamentally
arbitrary and nonbinding. Thus, the philosophers are not in any way
concerned with either society or its morality as an end, but only as a

means—although they still require or presuppose "social life (division of labor)" for the sake of their own freedom to pursue philosophic perfection.[55] As a result, a central moral determinant of the philosophers' esoteric method as well as their "noble rhetoric" is, as Strauss recognized, to avoid corrupting the masses morally, for the elite need a properly disciplined society which tolerates philosophy in order to achieve the "true" perfection. In point of fact, their "noble rhetoric" rests precisely on the recognition of the need not to subvert, indeed the need to defend, the decent morality and its supporting religion in which most men believe. In other words, the "Platonic" argument in favor of the greatest possible concealment by philosophers in their search for knowing the truth is so crucial because of the deep awareness of the virtually irreconcilable antagonism between ordinary men (or the city) and philosophers. Indeed, such an animus against philosophers is not entirely unjustified, since philosophers in their search for knowing the truth attempt to "dissolve the element in which society breathes,"[56] i.e., opinion. Hence, the philosophers may threaten society directly by subverting the basis for its morality, and they would be responsible for the anarchy or the tyranny which might follow such subversion.[57]

Thus do we arrive at what is for Strauss the fundamental human problem from which the need for esotericism arises among the philosophers and to which they must pay careful heed if they would know themselves and the threat they pose—I refer to their ambiguous relation with morality. Philosophy needs and even presupposes morality, but it also tends to destroy the basis for morality as well as to deny the sufficiency of morality for achieving the final term in human perfection. The doubting of authoritative theological opinion or religious belief, on which all political order rests and in which all morality is rooted, according to premodern philosophy, issues in a perhaps subtle but still corrosive attack on the categorically imperative character of the moral commands. Hence, Strauss's own primary concern with "what philosophy is or what a philosopher is"[58] ultimately reveals his orientation toward determining what the philosopher's proper or "politic" relation with authoritative opinion, society, morality, or nonphilosophers should be, and why the philosopher may need to sacrifice complete freedom of speech for complete freedom of thought. It reflects a deep perplexity in the mind and heart of Leo Strauss himself with respect to his own dual loyalties to philosophy and to the Jewish tradition.[59] His youthful study of Spinoza already made him acutely aware of the fundamental conflict between reason and revelation as something plainly unavoidable due to the necessarily exclusive yet contrary demand which each makes for a perfect human life. Strauss's mature Jewish thought tends unequivocally to emphasize this same fundamental conflict. This might seem to put him in the camp of Spinoza, since Spinoza makes a cardinal point of the disharmony between reason and revelation and the need to separate between them, while Maimonides seems to ground his position in their possible harmony. But Strauss did not regard the insight into the radicalism of that conflict as peculiarly Spinozistic; as in other matters, Spinoza's mode of expression is merely bolder or sharper. To be sure, such greater boldness or sharpness may reflect a characteristic modern attitude,[60] and may have been helpful to Strauss in learning about the basic problem and its character. But this does not mean, and Strauss does not say, that Spinoza's solution to it was superior to anyone else's.

Having reached this point in tracing Strauss's development, it is obvious that he came to view his rediscovery of esotericism as a key to comprehending the history and nature of philosophy, how it has gone wrong among the moderns, and how it might be "restored"[61] to rational health by a return to its ancient and medieval roots. It may well be true that Strauss's concentration on Maimonides' *Guide* was peculiarly helpful for bringing him to this conclusion and for clarifying its implications, but it is not a conclusion which attributes anything essentially unique to Maimonides' philosophic position or which ascribes anything but a distinctly subordinate rank to Maimonides' Jewish thought. It may also be true that Strauss owed a special debt to Maimonides for what he learned from the particularly explicit treatment of these themes and ideas in the *Guide* about what Strauss claimed was universally implicit in all other premodern philosophers: that "all the ancient philosophers made use of two manners of teaching, of an exoteric and an esoteric manner."[62] In this light, one might be right to speak in a purely literary sense about a Straussian "Maimonideanization" of the history of philosophy. It would be most interesting to critically explicate the elaborate literary techniques which Strauss discovered Maimonides to have employed, and to explore how he applied these insights into Maimonides' method of textual reading to the entire Platonic school in philosophy, which he maintained was engaged in an identical activity with Maimonides.[63] Rather than this, however, let us consider whether Strauss manifests just an accidental relation to Maimonides as the occasion for his philosophic discoveries, or whether his relation to Maimonides remains something essential. In other words, is there something about Maimonides' "version" of esotericism with which Strauss identifies himself, and to which he attaches paramount and permanent significance? Does Maimonides' position as philosopher and as Jewish thinker represent something unique in itself, which does not merely reproduce the Platonic idea of esotericism in a Jewish format? To paraphrase Strauss's introductory remark in his critique of Guttmann, if every enquiry into the history of philosophy is also a *philosophic* enquiry, what Jewish philosophic conclusion, if any, may be drawn from Strauss's peculiar affinity for historical enquiry into Maimonides' Jewish philosophy?[64]

Everything which has been elaborated hitherto on the third stage in Strauss's developing views of Maimonides suggests a radicalization both in Strauss's attitude toward the basic dilemma with which Maimonides was faced, and in his conception of the nature of the resolution which Maimonides offered. The basic dilemma referred to is how to reconcile reason with revelation, philosophy and Judaism. As Strauss now formulates this dilemma, Maimonides unequivocally recognizes that "being a Jew and being a philosopher are mutually exclusive,"[65] because the one makes the most fundamental demand of human life something which stands in utter contradiction to what is crucial in the other.[66] The resolution previously referred to is the resort by Maimonides to an elaborate concealment of his own true opinions, his "writing between the lines" so as to hide the truth in a deliberate but decipherable network of contradictions ("a bodyguard of lies") as a necessary subterfuge and precaution for men like himself.[67] This leads to the conclusion that Maimonides' consummate medieval Platonic prophetology, while a useful and even necessary support for his position, is not an adequate resolution in itself to the dilemma of having two mutually contradictory commitments.[68]

If Strauss's approach to Maimonides here treats him essentially as an esoteric writer, even as perhaps the greatest esoteric writer ever, then he seems to presuppose in this final stage that Maimonides is ultimately and primarily a philosopher rather than a theologian. In Strauss's final estimation of Maimonides, Maimonides appears in the guise of a Jewish theologian because, beside his genuine love for things Jewish which he loves because they are his own things, he is also fully alert to what Strauss represents as "the precarious status of philosophy in Judaism,"[69] and hence he needs to vindicate his life as a philosopher who is also a Jew. What "was done. . . in and for Judaism by Maimonides"[70] had already been done in and for their respective cities and communities by the likes of Plato, Cicero, and Alfarabi. The question which naturally arises is whether there remains any unique teaching or position which Strauss discovers in Maimonides. Or, is it a necessary concomitant of this view that whatever is peculiar to Maimonides is attributable to a very simple, but entirely accidental circumstance: that Maimonides happened to be a Jew. If this is all there is to Maimonides' position, then it simplifies matters considerably. It would necessarily follow that he merely adapted the Platonic philosophic teaching (which represents "enlightenment," or true "wisdom" pure and simple) to a Jewish theological and political context which required certain ostentatious flourishes or apparent reservations in matters of religious belief. He would have needed to make these "politic" concessions in order to convincingly appear in the guise of a Jewish theologian.[71] And if, anticipating matters somewhat, Strauss himself also simply adheres "esoterically" to this entire Platonic position, it can also be safely assumed that all statements he makes in the third stage about a unique profundity in Maimonides' Jewish thought are on the same level of seriousness as Maimonides' own "exoteric" teachings: they are useful and necessary teachings rather than true teachings, *pia dogmata* rather than *vera dogmata*.[72] If this were the case, the study of Maimonides undoubtedly facilitated Strauss's own discoveries, perhaps even decisively, but Strauss would still not in any proper sense of the term be a "Maimonidean." Such a term is itself perhaps useful in a Jewish theological context but is still a fictitious term to the mind of a critical philosopher, i.e., it does not refer to anything substantial of a truly philosophic character. The task remaining would be merely to illustrate how Strauss, in imitation of Maimonides, concealed his own true opinions artfully, appearing in the guise of a modern historical scholar. Such a task would call for an "archaeological" literary excavation rather than a "reconstructive" philosophical interpretation.

The final difficulty surrounding Strauss's view of Maimonides in the third stage, then, directs us to touch on the greater difficulty of what Strauss in his own modern Jewish thought is doing. Is there a Maimonidean (and hence, we might add, a Straussian) Jewish thought, which is not merely an exoteric cover for an esoteric adherence to pure philosophy, especially in the sphere of truth? Does Strauss continue to focus on Maimonides for purely philosophic reasons, or is there something in Maimonides' "version" of esotericism which helped Strauss both as a Jew and as a philosopher, which might then suggest a special relation for Strauss between Maimonides' Judaism and his approach to philosophy? In this connection, it must be added: even if the worst case should prove true, i.e., Strauss (as well as Maimonides) is a "pure philosopher," it needs to be acknowledged that in the case of Strauss (as well as Maimonides) it would be the adherence to "pure philosophy" of a loyal and high-minded Jewish citizen who sees no truer or nobler light evident in any other religious or political tradition.[73]

It is my considered judgment, however, that this is not enough. Undoubtedly, Strauss owes an enormous debt to Maimonides as perhaps the key occasion and source for his numerous great discoveries in the historical and philosophic spheres, especially with regard to esotericism and everything encompassed or presupposed by it. But I believe it can be argued persuasively that Strauss's final views of Maimonides are not completely exhausted by the supposition that his interest in *The Guide of the Perplexed* was merely the accidental cause of his discoveries made about philosophy, history, religion, and politics. I believe that there are two inextricably connected grounds on which Strauss bases his final view of Maimonides as a uniquely wise teacher. These two grounds derive in essence from Maimonides' primary position as a Jewish thinker. (To be sure, if Strauss himself ultimately holds to a position which closely resembles the one which he represents as Maimonides' position, as might seem to be the case, then this would also appear to make Strauss a modern Jewish thinker in the manner of Maimonides.) The two inextricably connected grounds to which I refer may be briefly summarized as follows: reason versus revelation; morality versus knowledge.

First, Maimonides' uniquely wise teaching is rooted in what Strauss calls the "ancient conflict" between reason and revelation. By emphaszing "ancient," Strauss seems to suggest that this conflict did not begin with the medieval opposition between "Athens and Jerusalem"—it was already known and dealt with by Plato, for one, in his discussion of the quarrel between philosophy and poetry. Is there, then, anything which Maimonides could add which could be an original or a signal contribution to the discussion? Is he just "putting a Jewish coloration on" a philosophic discussion which in its true character is of no peculiarly Jewish significance?[74] As Strauss well knew, Maimonides was scarcely the only medieval to probe deeply the conflict between reason and revelation. Certainly the monotheistic revealed religions add a new twist to an old dilemma, but were not the most essential elements of the conflict already laid bare in ancient philosophic texts? And did not other medievals, such as Averroes and Thomas,[75] use the same basic approach and deal with just as much profundity with the same basic dilemmas? Does he pick "Maimonides as the representative of all [philosophical] theologians...for the irrelevant reason that he happened to study [him] closely during his youth"?[76]

For several reasons, I believe that this reduction of Strauss's interest in Maimonides from a Jewish and philosophic preference to a mere accident does not do justice to Strauss's ever-deepening "Maimonideanism." First of all, the problem of "Jew versus philosopher," from which vantage point Strauss made his final approach to Maimonides, is for Strauss the key to Maimonides' entire effort at writing his *Guide*, to penetrating its enigmas and contradictions. But it also best reflects the human (and not merely a historical) situation, because it is rooted in the basic conflict between reason and revelation which at its highest is represented by the conflict between ancient Greek philosophic wisdom and ancient Jewish biblical wisdom. In other words, according to Strauss, Maimonides rightly took with the utmost seriousness the two best articulated positions: the Hebrew Bible on the one hand, Plato and Aristotle on the other hand. These are also the most primary sources, and ultimately also the deepest versions, of the teachings in which "the two fundamental alternatives" must issue.[77] Strauss's views about the priority to be accorded to Plato and Aristotle in the realm of reason have already been made sufficiently known. His views about the priority necessarily to be given to the Jewish position on divine revelation are not adequately comprehended if they are merely associated with the Cohenian notion of its greater "originalness" as cultural or historical source. For as Strauss says in his own name, "Jewish orthodoxy based its claim to superiority to other religions from the beginning on its superior rationality."[78] What Strauss seems to mean by this on a deeper level is that the Jewish position is the best conceptualized and articulated "argument" for divine revelation in terms of both its premises and its conclusions;[79] and based on this "superior rationality" its argument was thought through "from the beginning" in explicit and implicit opposition to the essential claims of philosophy.[80] Consequently, what Maimonides most significantly adds to the quarrel between reason and revelation that the ancients did not grasp is the full awareness of how powerful an argument can be made against philosophy. In the Hebrew Bible one thing new has been presented about the nature of God which is not present in any other religious conception—God's absolute moral character.

Strauss was also impressed by what he regarded as Maimonides' depth of comprehension of the problematic character of any supposed resolution to the conflict between reason and revelation. This is reflected for Strauss by the very extent of Maimonides' resort to esotericism in the *Guide* as well as by the double intention which Strauss discovers and which he propounds as still worth imitating.[81] Maimonides seems on the surface to offer decisive solutions based on his great authority to all perplexing problems, thus appearing to close all discussion on certain matters (e.g., the Torah's rootedness in creation out of nothing); this is aimed at those cognitively and morally unfit to pursue further consideration of such matters, in which grave threats to religion and morality may reside. Simultaneously, and on a deeper level, he leaves these same matters open to further consideration and even points in the direction in which they might be fruitfully pursued. He permits and even fosters such investigations and explorations for those fitted to pursue them just so long as their discussion is conducted in the correct manner, i.e., with respect for the very divinely revealed law which makes the best society possible, the society which allows for both types of men to flourish in their separate realms.

The first ground on which Strauss prefers Maimonides' "version" of the philosophic teachings which have been elaborated in the present chapter leads to the threshold of the second ground, with which it is inextricably connected. The second ground—the conflict between morality and knowledge—also rests on an "ancient" awareness, that the most basic difference between men is the difference between the two types of souls, rooted in their different ends: those who strive for moral perfection versus those who strive for intellectual excellence over and above all other things.[82] It is a difference which cannot be "synthesized," according to Strauss, but only roughly or approximately harmonized— one or the other is chosen as the ultimate, and the other must be subordinated to it. What Strauss calls "the natural tension between the city and the philosophers" cannot be nullified, evaded, or eviscerated.[83] It was obscured by the moderns, but it was treated with the greatest possible emphasis by Maimonides (which is perhaps *the* reason for his radical esotericism) as the most crucial actuality which determines human life and how the best life is to be led. It is this emphasis that is a key aspect of Maimonides' greatness in Strauss's view: it also guides his resolution to the conflict between reason and revelation, between "Jew and philosopher."

The reconciliation between "the two wisdoms," Greek reason and Hebrew revelation, is attempted by Maimonides on the ground of wisdom in applied morality versus wisdom in pure speculation, practice versus theory. This attempt might not seem to be that different from the philosophic tradition beginning with Plato and Aristotle, and continued by the Islamic philosophers. But Maimonides, according to Strauss's subtle analysis, overruled his Islamic predecessors because he best understood what was at stake: a sharpened alertness which has been formed by the biblical world view to the cognitive conditions necessary for the survival in any society of the absolute morality made possible by the Bible, together with an awareness of the vital centrality of morality in human life, and an attentiveness to philosophy's frailty in the face of the biblical God. The conflict between morality and knowledge could not be relegated to the mediation by the exoteric-esoteric distinction, because Maimonides clearly recognized that the claim of Moses and the Hebrew prophets (and their Christian and Muslim followers) to knowledge of the truth was greater in the decisive respect than any previous moral and religious claim made against philosophy. Indeed, Maimonides' writings reflect a deeper comprehension of a new and unprecedented dilemma faced by philosophy: namely, can philosophy content itself with treating revealed religion as merely the most recent version of what religion always represented to philosophy? Strauss draws from Maimonides the following more radical and less readily containable alternative, which philosophy cannot so quickly dismiss by its old and familiar arguments in response to religion: absolute divine omnipotence versus "nature."[84] Perhaps neither the Hebrew Bible nor philosophy can refute the other's most fundamental premise if the basic alternative is so defined. But to acknowledge this is already a very serious difficulty for philosophy, one that it cannot evade if it claims to aspire to know the highest truth by human effort alone.

There is another related lesson which Strauss claims to learn from Maimonides. Maimonides did not acknowledge the philosophers' claim to possess a moral teaching, because he did not accept the "natural law" as a genuine morality. It is neither truly natural, nor is it truly rational; moreover, what it does seem to offer as a supposed law, i.e., as a moral teaching which is somewhat like biblical morality, does not unconditionally command or bind. Indeed, not even the philosophers known by Maimonides recognized the natural law as "unconditional," which is what a "genuine morality" would require in the view of Strauss. Morality is, according to Maimonides, entirely conventional until it is grounded by a lawgiver who issues the basic "natural laws" (and essential laws beyond these) as unconditional commandments, and who attaches to them appropriate sanctions.[85] Consequently, the one and only true matter affecting whether something is a "genuine morality" is how good, wise, and reliable the lawgiver is who grounds morality and who makes what are otherwise unbinding conventions into genuine commands with forceful sanctions. But this is a claim that is devastating to all human societies not based solely on revealed morality and religion if it is acknowledged as true by them. It is my contention that Strauss privately accepted this basic analysis, even though he wrote a book in public defense of "natural right." It accords with what Strauss maintains about the deficiencies in the moral teachings of "the philosophers" in his monograph on Halevi.[86] This leads Strauss to the crucial matter of how morality can be made well-grounded, if indeed such a thing is truly possible in human affairs. I believe that he learned from Maimonides to take the Bible most seriously on this issue: Maimonides awakened Strauss to the biblical approach as the most powerful and best formulated articulation ever given to the claims of the moral life and the devotion to justice as the highest truth for man.

In a rare case of speaking in his own name in the midst of a discussion of Machiavelli's antibiblical efforts, Strauss maintains "the Bible sets forth the demands of morality and religion in their purest and most intransigent form."[87] Obviously, as Strauss recognized, the claim that the true aim of human life is moral perfection cannot stand alone. Either it needs to be supported by a true rational account (as Kant most heroically attempted to provide, but Strauss does not seem to have been persuaded by this rational account); or it needs to be established by a true religious belief which proves that this is the final truth about the world, man, and God. As Strauss seems to maintain, it is the religious belief which best supports the search for moral perfection, and it is especially well-established by the monotheism originally presented by the Hebrew Bible, in a form which is beyond the "refutation" of any rational philosophy.[88] If this reading of how Strauss comprehended the conflict between morality and knowledge, and the meaning of morality, is true and accurate, we may conclude that he learned two things from Maimonides, which provided a ground for preferring him as a uniquely wise teacher. First, the Hebrew biblical tradition is the best articulation of the claim for the moral life as leading to human perfection and happiness, especially as directed against philosophy's claim about man's need to search for knowledge. Second, the Hebrew biblical tradition may also contain, in its basing itself on divine revelation by the one God who is all-powerful, the *only* truly sound basis for a "genuine" morality. This alone is a morality that issues in truly unconditional commands, or "categorical imperatives." Assuming only the biblical faith,[89] it cannot be "refuted" by philosophy, and as such philosophers must consider it in the most careful terms and take with the utmost seriousness its claim to the truth.

CHAPTER 7

Conclusion

MAIMONIDES AND STRAUSS

THE TWO GROUNDS for Strauss's special preference for Maimonides' version of esotericism have now been brought to light. In doing so, we reach the end of our consideration of the fully developed views of Strauss on Maimonides. With the entire course of Strauss's "return to Maimonides" having been traversed, we would like to make the following brief concluding remarks.

Strauss himself seems to prefer, and he seems tacitly to counsel others as well, to follow the lead of Maimonides in his version of esotericism. Strauss would seem to prefer Maimonides' version because in it, as a Jew loyal to Judaism and as a philosopher, he devised the most justly balanced and thoroughly sustainable strategy for making the conflicts between reason and revelation, and between morality and knowledge, somehow harmonious and manageable.

In Strauss's final view of Maimonides, these two approaches to truth and to human life, which seem to be irreconcilable, actually are proven to be irreconcilable, but nevertheless in Maimonidean esotericism they are taught how to respect and to learn from one another. Moreover, Maimonides' life and his writings best demonstrate to Strauss how it is possible to be both a philosopher and a Jew, preserving commitments to divine revelation and to Jewish morality as well as to unhampered philosophic thought in their primary integrity. Of course, this is not the same thing as Strauss claiming that Maimonidean esotericism can do full justice in truth to both commitments. There is then for Strauss no genuine "third" approach which is superior to the two fundamental approaches to the truth. To claim to be able to preserve both commitments in their primary integrity is only to claim not to lose anything essential to the true vitality of both. Strauss himself insists we must never forget the question of truth, and the need to choose between these two approaches—but he also never expresses very plainly either his own true answer to it, or his own view concerning Maimonides' ultimate choice.[1]

In the approach of Maimonides as Strauss presents it, these two commitments are not artificially and falsely synthesized with one another. By holding these two commitments and preserving their separateness in full consciousness of the contradictions between them, Maimonides' approach also prevents the thinker (whether philosophical or theological) from readily trying to subordinate one to the other.[2] Rather, each one learns to appreciate the other in the very midst of their continuing encounter and even in their conflicts with one another. Similar to the true meeting between Judaism and Christianity, so also Judaism and philosophy can articulate, and subsequently meet on, a common ground, but only once they recognize "each the noble features of its antagonist." In the best case, each one credits the other for acting from high motives in honestly searching for the truth. Similarly, each one learns to appreciate the other for benefiting it, with both sides acknowledging its opposite for providing it access to higher perspectives than those which it could reach on its own. These higher perspectives would appear in all of the spheres which Strauss explored, and which we have been investigating in his philosophic and scholarly works from his youth to the full maturity of his thought.[3] However, they can only truly meet on a common ground if both sides do not at any point surrender their own approaches to truth. They can only truly learn from one another if they both meet on a common ground of their agreements, and stand on the separate ground of their disagreements. In other words, they should meet in a colloquium of friendly antagonists: noble of soul and purpose, confident in their own claim to truth, and mutually respectful toward one another's claim.[4]

In the Preface, I hope my high regard for the arguments, genius, and achievement of Leo Strauss was made sufficiently evident. At this point in our concluding discussion of Strauss's developing views on Maimonides, it would seem appropriate to focus on some critical difficulties with Strauss's position as a Jewish thinker which remain unsettled, and which will undoubtedly need to be addressed and wrestled with in future Jewish thought.

With regard to Maimonidean esotericism and all that it entails, here we must state unequivocally that in our judgment Strauss cannot be simply criticized or proved misguided on the details alone. Although numerous textual frailties, faulty philosophic points, and dubious logical connections could no doubt be isolated on hermeneutical grounds in Strauss's readings as compared with the texts of Maimonides, these would not touch the most serious issue. That basic issue is Strauss's final thesis about Maimonides as we have been elaborating it in the first, second, and especially the sixth chapters—Maimonides as radical philosopher and esoteric writer. A troubling issue such as this cannot be readily disposed of by emphatically stressing the grave problems that must necessarily arise from Strauss's thesis about Maimonides, inasmuch as this thesis seems to ignore, or to settle in too facile terms, certain obvious and even looming facts. It has been often argued that this thesis is patently false because of the facts of Maimonides' life: since he was a great Jewish scholar, leader, and authority, who immersed himself completely in the tradition's legal minutiae, this obviously proves he was primarily devoted to his faith and his people; in turn, that would be reflected in his approach to the truth. As such, he could not resolve the conflict between reason and revelation by deciding ultimately in favor of philosophy pure and simple, since the facts supposedly speak for themselves, and point to Maimonides chiefly as a Jewish theologian and religious thinker.

It seems however that despite this "argument from the facts," Strauss is able to account for these same facts, and to justify the writings, beliefs, and actions of Maimonides, at least as adequately on his own terms as his critics can do on theirs. In this light, it must be admitted that one cannot so readily dismiss Strauss's thesis. For Strauss, Maimonides was able to resolve the contradictions not by doing away with them, or by necessarily subordinating one antagonist to the other, but by devising a strategy for a *modus vivendi*, i.e., through esotericism, a basic notion which, it would seem, is blatantly contrary to nothing in the life or words of Maimonides. The bigger question is whether or not this is finally an intellectually, morally, or religiously satisfying version of Maimonides. Perhaps this cannot be answered on purely textual or biographical grounds. Those who are not satisfied must root their alternative view in a comprehensive reflection on philosophy, religion, politics, and morality. The alternative conception of these four things, rooted in a different approach toward their natures, must stand on a ground that is as well thought out and solid as the view of Strauss, yet diverges from it in its fundamental principles, and perhaps also in its literary approach, i.e., in how it makes sense of esotericism.

Along with this, however, it must be admitted that the conditional truce and mutual accord—which in Strauss's construction is presented as perhaps the most distinguished substantive achievement of Maimonides—is attained by Strauss partly by proving a genuine stalemate which prevents both sides from assuming a superior position vis-à-vis one another, and partly by a retreat pure and simple to the same esotericism which Maimonides among others supposedly espoused. This is to suggest that Strauss too establishes his own characteristic position on the mutual influence which theology and philosophy necessarily exercise on one another by recourse to plainly concealing his own opinions on the most controversial points of this heated conflict. Strauss apparently leaves matters as he claims Maimonides did, sealing the dispute (for philosophically prudential reasons?) in a conventional accord that actually does not in any true way resolve or tackle directly the fundamental points of contention. What remains for us to decide, if we are persuaded by all or some of Strauss's claims about Maimonides, and through them have been taught not a little about how to probe Maimonides' depths, are two points—one philosophical, the other Jewish.

On the first point, we must ask whether we should remain persuaded in great measure by our modern notions to doubt the possibility, the desirability, or the necessity of a genuine "return" to Maimonides, especially as Strauss construes such a "return," and as he comprehends the Maimonides to whom we are supposed to "return." If we accept Strauss's diagnosis of the modern philosophic and moral crisis as convincing, we cannot but regard this as one of the great challenges that faces present-day philosophy. On the second point, from the Jewish perspective, we must surely ask whether both Maimonides and Strauss do not attain their victories and their reconciliations ultimately from the side of philosophy, and if so, whether they have not been achieved at too dear a cost to the spirit and the substance of Judaism. Around both points the future discussions and criticisms of the formidable achievement of Leo Strauss will probably need to revolve. But in whatever results they may issue, we cannot help but learn from Strauss, for his treatment of Maimonides has been decisive, if for nothing else, in rediscovering him as a still great Jewish thinker and as a perennially wise philosophic teacher.

NOTES

"HBSMP" (*RCPR*)	"How to Begin to Study Medieval Philosophy," as reprinted in *RCPR*
"HFRP*L*" (*WIPP?*)	"How Farabi Read Plato's *Laws*," as reprinted in *WIPP?*
HPP	*History of Political Philosophy*
"HSS" (*PAW*)	"How to Study Spinoza's *Theologico-Political Treatise*," as reprinted in *PAW*
IE*RR*	Introductory Essay to Hermann Cohen's *Religion of Reason out of the Sources of Judaism*
"IE*RR*" (*SPPP*)	"Introductory Essay to Hermann Cohen's *Religion of Reason out of the Sources of Judaism*," as reprinted in *SPPP*
"IHE" (*RCPR*)	"An Introduction to Heideggerian Existentialism," as reprinted in *RCPR*
IPP	*An Introduction to Political Philosophy*
JA	*Jerusalem and Athens*
"JA" (*SPPP*)	"Jerusalem and Athens," as reprinted in *SPPP*
LAM	*Liberalism Ancient and Modern*
"LC*GP*" (*PAW*)	"The Literary Character of the *Guide for the Perplexed*," as reprinted in *PAW*
"LR*K*" (*PAW*)	"The Law of Reason in the *Kuzari*," as reprinted in *PAW*
"MC*L*"	"Machiavelli and Classical Literature"
"MITP"	"The Mutual Influence of Theology and Philosophy"
MMJA, vol. 3, pt. 2	*Moses Mendelssohn Gesammelte Schriften, Jubiläumsausgabe*, volume 3, part 2. Introductions to: "Morgenstunden," "An die Freunde Lessings" and "Sache Gottes oder die gerettete Vorsehung"
"MSPS" (*WIPP?*)	"Maimonides' Statement on Political Science," as reprinted in *WIPP?*

"NM*BK*" (*SPPP*)	"Notes on Maimonides' *Book of Knowledge*," as reprinted in *SPPP*
"NM*LA*" (*SPPP*)	"Note on Maimonides' *Letter on Astrology*," as reprinted in *SPPP*
NRH	*Natural Right and History*
"OA"	"On Abravanel's Philosophical Tendency and Political Teaching"
"OCPH"	"On Collingwood's Philosophy of History"
"OF" (*WIPP?*)	"On a Forgotten Kind of Writing," as reprinted in *WIPP?*
"OIG"	"On the Interpretation of Genesis"
"ONI"	"On a New Interpretation of Plato's Political Philosophy"
"OP*AS*" (*SPPP*)	"On Plato's *Apology of Socrates*," as reprinted in *SPPP*
OT	*On Tyranny*
OT (rev.)	*On Tyranny* (revised edition)
"OVL"	"Der Ort der Vorsehungslehre nach der Ansicht Maimunis"
"PARSPP" (*SPPP*)	"Philosophy as Rigorous Science and Political Philosophy," as reprinted in *SPPP*
PAW	*Persecution and the Art of Writing*
PG	*Philosophie und Gesetz*
"PGS" (*LAM*)	"Perspectives on the Good Society," as reprinted in *LAM*
"PHPW"	"Preface to *Hobbes Politische Wissenschaft*"
P*IHPE*	Preface to *Isaac Husik's Philosophical Essays: Ancient, Medieval, and Modern*
PL	*Philosophy and Law*
"POR?"	"Progress or Return?"
"POR?" (*IPP*)	"Progress or Return?," as reprinted in *IPP*

"PPH" (*WIPP?*)	"Political Philosophy and History," as reprinted in *WIPP?*
PPH	*The Political Philosophy of Hobbes*
PSCR	Preface to *Spinoza's Critique of Religion*
"QR"	"Quelques remarques sur la science politique de Maïmonide et de Fârâbî"
RCPR	*The Rebirth of Classical Political Rationalism*
"Rel"	"Relativism"
RKS	*Die Religionskritik Spinozas*
RMH	Review of Moses Hyamson's edition of Maimonides' *The Mishneh Torah, Book 1.*
SA	*Socrates and Aristophanes*
SCR	*Spinoza's Critique of Religion*
SPPP	*Studies in Platonic Political Philosophy*
"SR"	"Some Remarks on the Political Science of Maimonides and Farabi"
"SSH" (*RCPR*)	"Social Science and Humanism," as reprinted in *RCPR*
TOM	*Thoughts on Machiavelli*
"TS"	"Das Testament Spinozas"
"TWM" (*IPP*)	"The Three Waves of Modernity," as reprinted in *IPP*
"UP"	"An Unspoken Prologue to a Public Lecture at St. John's College (in Honor of Jacob Klein, 1899–1978)"
"WILE?" (*LAM*)	"What Is Liberal Education?," as reprinted in *LAM*
WIPP?	*What Is Political Philosophy?*
"WWRJ"	"Why We Remain Jews (Can Jewish Faith and History Still Speak to Us?)" Hillel House lecture, 4 February 1962

XS	Xenophon's Socrates
XSD	Xenophon's Socratic Discourse
"ZBWS"	"Zur Bibelwissenschaft Spinozas und seiner Vorläufer"

Note: The complete letters of Leo Strauss are as yet unpublished in a critical edition. The unpublished letters quoted or cited in the notes are accessible in the Leo Strauss Archive in the University of Chicago Library.

PREFACE

1. As should be made evident by this work as it unfolds, the view of the present writer is that Strauss was over and above everything else both a philosopher and a Jew. A Jew, as Strauss would have been the first to emphasize, is not just an ethnic designation. This manner of approach to Strauss, however, is not in any way intended to obscure from the fact that Strauss himself often wanted to stress the problematic character of being *both* a Jew *and* a philosopher. In other words, I take it as a given that this was a first formulation by Strauss of a fundamental question—but it is also not Strauss's last word on it. Thus, I believe the following oral remark attributed to Strauss should also be considered very seriously together with his famous statement that "being a Jew and being a philosopher are mutually exclusive." Strauss is said to have remarked "that the Greeks taught the philosophic truth, but that the Jews are still the chosen people." Whether or not this conveys a true *obiter dictum* of Strauss, I believe it accurately and concisely represents a fundamental tendency of his thought evident in his writings. If this is so, then there must have been something in Strauss's deeper views as a thinker which overrode the previously mentioned dichotomy, and which allowed him to pursue his concern to understand *both* what it means to be a Jew *and* what it means to be a philosopher, and yet not be guilty of the muddleheadedness which he attributed to Moses Mendelssohn.

2. The first sentence of Strauss's lecture "An Introduction to Existentialism" for some reason has been silently removed from the published version in *RCPR*, p. 27. This sentence points both to Strauss's abiding Jewish concern and to his belief that this concern extends to, and is involved in, his study of all philosophy, not only of the classical "old books," but also of the dominant new trends: "This series of lectures—a reminder of the perplexities of modern man—should help the Jewish students in particular towards facing the perplexities of the modern Jew with somewhat greater clarity." By such "emendation" of the original text, the editor is responsible, as Alan Udoff put it, for "deleting the deeply suggestive Maimonidean resonances with which the

essay began." Cf. "On Leo Strauss: An Introductory Account," in *Leo Strauss's Thought: Toward a Critical Engagement,* edited by Alan Udoff (Boulder, Colo.: Lynne Rienner, 1991), p. 25, note 39. Cf. also Udoff's review of *RCPR* in the *Review of Metaphysics* 63, no. 3 (March 1990): 648–50, and especially p. 649.

3. The recognition of Leo Strauss has thus far been mainly by his friends (e.g., Gershom Scholem, Alexandre Kojève, Hans-Georg Gadamer) and by his students. The first generation of his students have not been stinting in praise of their teacher. Thus the Jewish philosopher Emil Fackenheim wrote this about what he believes is the true philosophic stature of Strauss: "Perhaps a time will come when Heidegger will be remembered mainly because, without him, Leo Strauss would not have been who he was and became." ("Reply to My Critics: A Testament of Thought," in *Fackenheim: German Philosophy and Jewish Thought,* edited by Louis I. Greenspan and Graeme Nicholson [Toronto: University of Toronto Press, 1992], p. 298; and "Leo Strauss and Modern Judaism," in *Claremont Review of Books* 4, no. 4 [Winter 1985]: 21–23) And the late Allan Bloom boldly suggested that Strauss will be the philosophic standard against which our era will be measured: ". . . I believe our generation may well be judged by the next generation according to how we judged Leo Strauss." ("Leo Strauss," in *Political Theory* 2, no. 4 [November 1974]: 372–92, especially p. 392; idem, in *Giants and Dwarfs* [New York: Simon and Schuster, 1990], pp. 235–55, especially p. 255)

INTRODUCTION

1. For a "Straussian" attempt to summarize Strauss's contribution to the history of political philosophy, see, e.g., "Epilogue—Leo Strauss and the History of Political Philosophy," by Thomas L. Pangle and Nathan Tarcov, in the third edition of *HPP* (1989), pp. 907–38. For his significance in recovering the premodern tradition, see, e.g., Eugene F. Miller, "Leo Strauss: The Recovery of Political Philosophy," in *Contemporary Political Philosophers,* edited by Anthony de Crespigny and Kenneth Minogue (London: Methuen and Co., 1976), pp. 67–99. See also the learned and highly critical study which, however, is built on a false premise, i.e., Strauss's secret Nietzscheanism, by Shadia Drury, *The Political Ideas of Leo Strauss* (New York: St. Martin's, 1988); and T. L. Pangle's brilliant but essentially flawed treatment of Strauss's thought in his Introduction to *SPPP.*

2. Perhaps still the best, most succinct statement on Strauss as a philosopher in his own right is the work of a leading disciple: Allan Bloom, "Leo Strauss," in *Political Theory* 2, no. 4 (November 1974): 372–92; idem, in *Giants and Dwarfs* (New York: Simon and Schuster, 1990), pp. 235–55. With regard to Strauss as a Jewish thinker, Bloom is prepared to discuss Strauss's Jewish thought as an expression of very serious personal concerns, but only insofar as they reflect Strauss's own unique and idiosyncratic experience, and hence Strauss's Jewish thought is only of biographical rather than of genuinely philosophical interest.

By way of contrast, and eminently worthy of careful consideration, is an essay on Strauss and Alexandre Kojève by Stanley Rosen. Though a very different sort of student of Strauss from Bloom, Rosen also regards Strauss as essentially an "Athenian," i.e., as a "pure" philosopher, and hence he expresses no interest in Strauss as a Jewish thinker. See his "Hermeneutics as Politics," in *Hermeneutics as Politics* (New York: Oxford University Press, 1987), pp. 15–17, 87–140. Thus, Rosen lightly dismisses "Strauss's exoteric flirtation with Hebraic tradition" (p. 17). But he also pays a certain heed to the centrality of idealized Jewish concerns in Strauss by introducing "the quarrel between the ancients and the moderns" as turning on "a fundamental difference of theology" (p. 16). He also maintains "Strauss identifies as coeval with philosophy the question *quid sit deus?*" and does not deny it was "for Strauss a real problem in choosing between Athens and Jerusalem." Nevertheless, I believe Rosen and Bloom stand together on the following point articulated by Rosen: "No competent student of Leo Strauss was ever in doubt as to his teacher's choice", i.e., between the Hebrew Bible and Greek philosophy (pp. 112–13). What may lead, in my view, to Rosen's faulty emphasis is his too quickly assimilating Strauss to Kojève: he asserts that in the end they share a fully common notion of themselves as philosophers. This approach, while by no means entirely wrong, blurs the "fundamental difference of theology" which equally divides them. Thus, by relegating the quarrel between Strauss and Kojève to "merely" exoteric teachings which do not express an ancient versus modern quarrel about philosophy itself, Rosen misleadingly defines their supposedly common notion of themselves as philosophers too much in the jocular spirit of Kojève, as "atheists who wish to be gods." With no desire to deny the important differences between Rosen and Bloom, permit me to suggest this about some students of Strauss: could it be that in their approach to their own teacher, they pay insufficient attention to exoteric teaching? How did Leo Strauss present himself? And did Strauss not teach, as they both are wont to quote, that "the problem inherent in the surface of things, and only in the surface of things, is the heart of things"? (*TOM*, p. 13) Was this view not connected with Strauss's effort to restore luster to the reputation of philosophy, which had been tarnished by the modern project of subjecting divine power to natural necessity? And did not Strauss himself, like his teacher Plato, try to restore the honor of philosophy precisely by "subjecting natural necessity to Divine and other more excellent principles"? (Cf. Plutarch, "The Life of Nicias," in *The Lives of the Noble Greeks and Romans*, translated by John Dryden and revised by A. H. Clough [New York: Modern Library, 1932], p. 645; with *PAW*, pp. 12–13.) And should not these philosophical efforts be connected with the moral influence on his students of Strauss's character and integrity, which perhaps cannot be separated from his continuing Jewish commitments? For the impression which Strauss made on Kojève through his students: "I have *talked* philosophy only with your two American(?) students. I must say that as regards philosophical 'eros' and human 'decency,' the young people are OK. They must owe that to you." (*OT* [rev.], p. 265)

3. "WWRJ," typescript, p. 3. This lecture is to be first published shortly
in a volume to be entitled *Jewish Philosophy and the Crisis of Modernity: Essays
and Lectures in Modern Jewish Thought* by Leo Strauss, which will be published
by SUNY Press, and which is planned for 1993–94. That volume will appear
as part of a new five-volume SUNY Series, *The Jewish Writings of Leo Strauss*,
with the present writer as series editor. These volumes will be forthcoming in
the next several years, and will be edited by leading scholars in the field of Strauss's
Jewish thought.

4. The phrase ("edler Pietät") is used by Alexander Altmann in his brief
but deeply respectful German remarks on Leo Strauss. See *MMJA*, vol. 3, pt. 2,
p. VII. With words of sincere veneration, Altmann also paid tribute in English
to the achievement of Strauss as follows:

> The death of Leo Strauss...has removed from the world of Jewish
> scholarship one of its noblest and most cultivated minds, a rare spirit
> of truly philosophical ethos and profound reverence for the Jewish
> tradition.

See "Leo Strauss: 1899–1973," p. xxxvi in *Proceedings of the American Academy
for Jewish Research* 41–42 (1975): xxxiii–xxxvi. Consider also the recent
statement of Emil L. Fackenheim, which pays the highest tribute to Leo Strauss:

> [Strauss's] example has convinced me, more than that of any other
> Jewish thinker alive in my own lifetime, of the possibility, and therefore
> of the necessity, of a Jewish philosophy for our age.

See *To Mend the World* (New York: Schocken, 1982), p. x.

5. Strauss rests his case against the adequacy of Hermann Cohen's thought
on its pre-World War I character:

> The worst things that he experienced were the Dreyfus scandal and
> the pogroms instigated by Czarist Russia: he did not experience
> Communist Russia and Hitler Germany.

See "JA" (*SPPP*), p. 168.

6. Ibid.

CHAPTER ONE

1. Alexander Altmann noted a significantly different pattern in the course
of Strauss's Jewish writings—the unbroken connection with Hermann Cohen:

> Cohen's critique of Spinoza had challenged him at the beginning of
> his career to re-examine the latter's attack on orthodox religion, and
> in *Philosophie und Gesetz* he had quoted Cohen's utterance about
> Maimonides being more of a Platonist than an Aristotelian, thereby

claiming Cohen's support for his political interpretation of Maimonides' *Guide*. Introducing the *Religion of Reason* and, more so, its author to English readers was more than an act of piety. It meant that the circle of his life's course was complete. ("Leo Strauss: 1899–1973," p. xxxvi)

Perhaps we should also observe the curious fact that Strauss only consented to write introductory essays to two English translations, in spite of the number of great works which he commented on and which his students translated. The two books are both great works of Jewish philosophy: Maimonides' *Guide* and Hermann Cohen's *Religion of Reason*. Through this fact does Strauss mean to say something to us about the type of works with which he wanted his name to be permanently associated?

2.   For Strauss and what he calls the theological-political crisis as it affects Jews and Judaism, see "CA," especially pp. 312–14; "BGW"; "TS"; Introduction to *PG*; Introduction to *PL*; "POR?," pp. 17–33, 44–45; "MITP," pp. 111, 117–18; "POR?" (*IPP*), pp. 249–72, 289–90, 308–10; *PSCR*; "WWRJ"; *JA*, pp. 3–7, 22–23; "JA" (*SPPP*), pp. 147–52, 167–68.

3.   The revolutionary change in the study of Maimonides brought about by Leo Strauss's works is discussed by: Marvin Fox, "Prolegomenon," in *The Teachings of Maimonides*, by Abraham Cohen (New York: KTAV, 1968), pp. xvi–xviii, xxiii, xxvi–xxviii; Arthur Hyman, "Interpreting Maimonides," *Gesher* 5 (1976): 46–59, especially pp. 53–56; Warren Zev Harvey, "The Return of Maimonideanism," *Jewish Social Studies* 4 (1980): 249–68, especially pp. 253–55, 265. See also Marvin Fox, *Interpreting Maimonides* (Chicago: University of Chicago Press, 1990), especially pp. 4–5, 15–16, 35, 54–62, 76–78, 85, 335. See also A. L. Ivry, "Leo Strauss on Maimonides," pp. 75–91, and R. Brague, "Leo Strauss and Maimonides," pp. 93–114, in *Leo Strauss's Thought*, edited by Alan Udoff (Boulder, Colo.: Lynne Rienner, 1991). Cf. also H. Fradkin, "Philosophy and Law: Leo Strauss as a Student of Medieval Jewish Thought," *Review of Politics* 53, no. 1 (Winter 1991): 40–52.

4.   In unraveling the mysteries of Leo Strauss, we may perhaps be quite well-advised to proceed first through the obvious perplexities, especially since we may detect a clue to his employing such a method himself in the Greek epigraph to "LCGP" (whose author only—Aristotle—and not the source—*Metaphysics* B1. 995a27–30—is mentioned in the text): "Now those who wish to succeed in arriving at answers will find it profitable to go over the difficulties well; for answers successfully arrived at are solutions to difficulties previously discussed, and one cannot untie a knot if he is ignorant of it." (I quote the translation by Hippocrates G. Apostle, Aristotle's *Metaphysics* [Bloomington: Indiana University Press, 1966].) As Strauss teaches us in his catalogue of what he calls the "additional devices" employed by Maimonides, he mentions "mottoes prefixed to the whole work or to individual parts" as a significant clue extended by the author. (See *PAW*, p. 75; cf. also p. 66: ". . . indeed all quotations in the

Guide, belong to the same class of hints.") Thus, we may suggest that the significance of this Aristotelian epigraph, with which Strauss chose to head this essay, is that it points toward the *contradictions* as the "knot," or as the true "difficulties," in the *Guide*, which we must be made aware of if we are even to begin to comprehend Maimonides' true meaning—and perhaps also Strauss's.

   5.   See Allan Bloom, "Leo Strauss," *Political Theory* 2 (1974): 373–92, and specifically p. 383; idem, *Giants and Dwarfs* (New York: Simon and Schuster, 1990), p. 246.

   6.   Our explication, which locates the decisive move in Strauss's turn to Maimonides, is confirmed by the main text of his own "self-interpretation." Writing in 1962 his spiritual autobiography until 1928 (the research for the original German edition of *RKS* was completed in 1928, but it only appeared in print in 1930: see *PSCR*, see p. 1), Strauss designates as the culminating result of his research in *RKS* the fact that he recognized the need to recover the lost or forgotten wisdom of "especially Jewish-medieval rationalism," i.e., especially Maimonides (as well as its classical basis, Plato and Aristotle). Through this "change of orientation," in which he had first to overcome a "powerful prejudice" (cf. also his Review of Julius Ebbinghaus, *Über die Fortschritte der Metaphysik*, *Deutsche Literaturzeitung* no. 52 [27 Dec. 1931]: 2451–53, as well as *PG*, p. 9, and *PL*, p. 3), he "became ever more attentive to the manner in which heterodox thinkers of earlier ages wrote their books." (*PSCR*, p. 31) One may justifiably doubt whether the Preface is a complete and adequate account of Strauss's spiritual life, as did Gershom Scholem (in his letter of 28 Nov. 1962 to Strauss): "Das einzige, was ich daran auszusetzen habe, ist, dass Sie einige Stadien Ihrer Autobiographie darin zu überspringen." ("The only thing which I would criticize in it is that you seem to leap over several stages in your autobiography.") Responding to Scholem (in his letter of 6 Dec. 1962), Strauss admitted that in the Preface he had "omitted in a way everything which comes after 1928." However, in my judgment, the "in a way" may reflect a substantial reservation about his admission, namely that the Preface does contain everything which followed, if this only be limited to the most essential elements. If one does not want to accept this as the final word, one may turn for a further confirmatory statement to "GA" (pp. 3–4), in which he makes it considerably clearer: it was through his formative preoccupation with Maimonides, and especially his prophetology, that he laid the basis for the crucial conclusions which he ultimately reached about esotericism, philosophy, morality, politics, and religion.

> Maimonides was, to begin with, wholly unintelligible to me. I got the
> first glimmer of light when I concentrated on his prophetology and,
> therefore, the prophetology of the Islamic philosophers who preceded
> him. One day when reading in a Latin translation Avicenna's treatise,
> *On the Division of the Sciences*, I came across this sentence (I quote
> from memory): the standard work on prophecy and revelation is Plato's

> *Laws.* Then I began to begin to understand Maimonides' prophetology and eventually, as I believe, the whole *Guide of the Perplexed.*

It is made quite transparent in what follows in this "account" rendered in 1970 that he was led by Maimonides directly to the fundamental notions which characterize his subsequent work. He also, in some measure yet to be determined, may be said to have derived these fundamental notions from Maimonides. In this light, one must be prepared to consider the possibility that Strauss's life's work may represent a "Maimonideanization" of the history of philosophy. See also his letter of 30 Nov. 1933 to Cyrus Adler; *PG,* pp. 9, 28–29, 118–22; *PL,* pp. 3–4, 19–20, 107–10; *PAW,* pp. 8–11, 19–94, 124–26, 132–33, 181–201; "OF" (*WIPP?*), p. 230. But consider also Rémi Brague, who moderately and sympathetically articulates the view that this whole effort of so-called scholarly research and discovery on Strauss's part was just so much projection of Strauss's own (usually Nietzschean) views onto Maimonides. See his "Leo Strauss and Maimonides," pp. 103–6. In my opinion, this approach taken by both friends and enemies of Strauss, though not entirely in error, gives a wrong impression of Strauss's philosophic enterprise and of his originality. This is because, first, it underemphasizes the seriousness of Strauss's critique of Nietzsche, a critique that issued in Strauss's desire to appear in the guise of a modern historical scholar; and second, because it overemphasizes Strauss's remarks about the present as representing "the third wave of modernity," i.e., as necessarily created in Nietzsche's image. In the view of the present writer, Strauss regarded his own tentative return to Maimonides and to ancient wisdom as an option not fully anticipated by Nietzsche, and hence as something which, if nothing else, would seem to represent either the beginning of "the fourth wave" of modernity, or the only fundamental alternative to the modern altogether. It would mean philosophy as pursued by thinkers like Plato, Maimonides, and Lessing rather than thinkers like Machiavelli, Rousseau, and Nietzsche. See also supra, Introduction, note 1; infra, chapter 3, note 14; chapter 4, note 13.

    7. We must add that Strauss was, by his own admission, "greatly assisted" in these matters by his reading of Gotthold Ephraim Lessing. The issue of the debt which Strauss owed to Lessing is a complex one and deserves a full separate treatment. In "GA" (p. 3), he mentions Lessing already in connection with *RKS:*

> Lessing was always at my elbow. This meant that I learned more from him than I knew at that time. As I came to see later Lessing had said everything I had found out about the distinction between exoteric and esoteric speech and its grounds.

Strauss's probing examination of Lessing was decisively aided by his researches from 1932 to 1937 for the three *Moses Mendelssohns Gesammelte Schriften, Jubiläumsausgabe* volumes which he edited during this period (volumes 2, 3 part 1, and 3 part 2). See Strauss's letter of 28 May 1971 to Alexander Altmann (published by Altmann in his "Vorbemerkung" to *MMJA,* vol. 3, pt. 2; Strauss had completed his work for this volume in 1937, but it only appeared in print in 1974, following his death). In the letter to Altmann, Strauss said that since 1937 he had wanted to write an essay about Lessing in order to present the *Zentrum* of Lessing's teaching "*de Deo et mundo.*" Something like this planned essay, written in 1939, has recently been discovered by the present writer in the Leo Strauss Archive of the University of Chicago Library, and has been published in *Interpretation* 14, no. 1 (1986): 51–59 as Leo Strauss, "Exoteric Teaching." It may in fact be that this specific essay represents the first fruit, in literary terms, of Strauss's great rediscovery of esotericism. (Cf. also *RCPR*, pp. 63–71, for a different edition of the same essay.) Scattered through Strauss's works one notices occasional references to Lessing, often of crucial significance for the argument: see, e.g., *PG*, pp. 17–19, 51–52 and *PL*, pp. 9–11, 43–44 with echoes of the same points in *PSCR*, pp. 28–29, and in the *SCR* text itself, pp. 143–46, and in *WIPP?*, p. 61; *PAW*, pp. 28 note 7, 33 note 13, 182; "*FP*," p. 357 (epigraph), 391 note 97; *NRH*, p. 22; *OT*, p. 112 note 17; "CCM," pp. 106, 107, 114–15; "CLS," p. 190 ("Read Swift—who next to Lessing was the freest spirit of modernity."); and of course the introductions to "Morgenstunden" and "An die Freunde Lessings" in *MMJA*, vol. 3, pt. 2, which deal more or less directly with Lessing through the Mendelssohn-Jacobi dispute about his "legacy." See also infra, notes 98 and 99, and chapter 6, note 14. As for whether Lessing's own esotericism is controversial, one does well to recall Søren Kierkegaard's remark: ". . . no one, no one could carry himself more circumspectly than Lessing, while achieving the still more difficult task of keeping silent though speaking." (*Concluding Unscientific Postscript*, translated by David F. Swenson and Walter Lowrie [Princeton: Princeton University Press, 1968], p. 61)

    8.   See Maimonides' Introduction to part I of *The Guide of the Perplexed*, translated by Shlomo Pines (Chicago: University of Chicago Press, 1963), especially pp. 11–12 (6b-7a) for the "golden apple" parable. In regard to the "golden apple" as a model parable for "a saying uttered with a view to two meanings" (p. 12), we will have to also consider carefully whether the "silver filigree" in Maimonides' *Guide* is achieved by the method of contradictions, especially if, as Strauss categorically puts it: "Contradictions are the axis of the *Guide.*" (*PAW*, p. 74) If so, Maimonides' enumeration of the seven causes of "contradictory or contrary statements" in any book (pp. 17–20) would seem to mean to say ultimately that "in this Treatise" only the fifth and the seventh causes contain the secret to decoding all or most "divergences" in its speech, i.e., just as Strauss would have it, Maimonides claims all contradictions are deliberate. Such a contention undoubtedly receives substantial additional support, as Strauss recognized, from Maimonides' assertion that he chose every word in the book with conscious intention and hence also, as Strauss would have it, every "hidden word," i.e., every silence, either to indicate a true conclusion which is clearly propounded though not necessarily in a single chapter, or to suggest a hidden inference logically inhering in an apparent conclusion.

> If you wish to grasp the totality of what this Treatise contains, so that nothing of it will escape you, then you must connect its chapters one with another; and when reading a given chapter, your intention must be not only to understand the totality of the subject of that chapter, but also to grasp each word that occurs in it in the course of the speech, even if that word does not belong to the intention of the chapter. For the diction of this Treatise has not been chosen at haphazard, but with great exactness and exceeding precision, and with care to avoid failing to explain any obscure point. And nothing has been mentioned out of its place, save with a view to explaining some matter in its proper place. (P. 15)

Cf. also *PAW*, pp. 64–65, 70–74.

9. This notion—that a great thinker may choose to seem to be merely presenting another man's views while not renouncing his own separate voice—has not been regarded as entirely absurd at least since Plato's "Socratic" dialogues. Among the "ancient writers who had not a little to say" (see "ET," p. 51) about the art of "writing between the lines" and the techniques of esotericism (see *PAW*, p. 24), and who were simultaneously even willing to appear in the guise of being mere scholarly transcribers, Strauss would surely have named Cicero, who was one of his favorite "ancients" in several respects (cf. *NRH*, pp. 81–164; *TOM*, pp. 290–91). Indeed, in his works Cicero often seemingly presents the opinions of other men only, but he did not allow this form and manner of expression to inhibit in any way his intellectual freedom, nor even to hamper the exercise of his critical faculty toward these opinions. Cicero articulates his *modus operandi* thus: "And supposing that for our part we do not fill the office of a mere translator, but, while preserving the doctrines of our chosen authorities, add thereto our own criticism and our own arrangement. . ." (*De finibus bonorum et malorum*, translated by H. Rackham [Cambridge: Harvard University Press, 1971], p. 7) Cf. also "OP" (*WIPP?*), p. 230.

10. Strauss's "first rule" is connected with his desire to recover what may be called the "naïve" way of looking at things in general, and not only at how great philosophic books were written. See *NRH*, pp. 76–80, 123–24; *CM*, pp. 10–12, 52–55; *TOM*, p. 13; and Werner J. Dannhauser, "Leo Strauss: Becoming Naïve Again," in *Masters: Portraits of Great Teachers*, edited by J. Epstein (New York: Basic Books, 1981), pp. 253–65, and especially pp. 261–62.

11. *PG*, pp. 9, 119–22; *PL*, pp. 3, 107–10. To be precise, Strauss is citing the judgment of Hermann Cohen on Maimonides, which he is, of course, both in rough accord with and in sharp divergence from. Strauss refers to the monograph "Characteristik der Ethik Maimunis," in which Cohen makes his argument for Maimonides as *essentially* a student of Plato rather than of Aristotle. (See *Jüdische Schriften*, vol. 3, edited by Bruno Strauss [Berlin: C. A. Schwetschke und Sohn Verlag, 1924], pp. 221–89.)

12.   This is not to suggest that *no* significant changes occurred in the views of Strauss from *PL* to *PSCR*—but the fundamental "orientation" remained constant.

13.   *PG*, p. 23; *PL*, p. 15.

14.   *PG*, pp. 18, 21, 87–122; *PL*, pp. 10–11, 13–14, 79–110; *PSCR*, pp. 28–31.

15.   *PG*, pp. 6–10; *PL*, pp. 3–4.

16.   *RKS*, pp. 129–81; *SCR*, pp. 145–92.

17.   It should however be noted that the section and subsection (or chapter) numbers have been restructured for the English translation by Strauss, perhaps in order to make plainer in this version what he considers the central section to be, in accordance with the statement in *PSCR*, pp. 28–31. Thus, if we count the Preface as the first section, then there are eleven sections, the central one of which is the sixth, section 5, i.e., "The Critique of Orthodoxy." Accordingly, the vindication of (especially) Jewish orthodoxy was his main conclusion in the original work. (See *SCR*, pp. 207–9; although cf. also *SCR*, p. 192, and *PSCR*, p. 30.) In this section, Strauss carefully demonstrates that divine revelation, biblical orthodoxy's fundamental principle, was never actually "refuted" by Spinoza's philosophy; and inasmuch as Spinoza's "system," however flawed it may be, represents the true ambition of philosophy in its purest and simplest form, philosophy *cannot* ever "refute" divine revelation. See also *PG*, pp. 18–24; *PL*, pp. 10–16; *PAW*, p. 182; "MITP," p. 117; and *PSCR*, pp. 28–29. However, by renumbering the sections and adding the unnumbered Preface to the English-language edition of 1965, Strauss may have been trying to emphasize in the ambiguity about the central of only ten *numbered* sections that he did not judge this primary demonstration to be the ultimate consequence of the work. Beyond what Strauss wrote about the importance of Maimonides for his future thought in the Preface itself, he pointed here to the possibly but ambiguously central section on Maimonides as yielding (retrospectively) the true first fruit of his labors in this book.

18.   The notion that a critique of modern philosophy can only be carried through in comparison with medieval philosophy, and especially with Maimonides, might seem to be contradicted by statements which Strauss made subsequently about the need for a comparison between modern and classical principles as the only adequate method for escaping modern "prejudices." (Cf., e.g., "ONI," pp. 327–28, with "CCM," pp. 107–8, and *PG*, pp. 9–10; *PL*, pp. 3–4.) However, not only does this essay, and others like it, have to be considered in the context of the man against whom it is directed—John Wild—and the audience for which it is destined—"for students" and for the general American philosophical reader—but one must also connect this statement with the relevant connecting allusions, i.e., the medieval philosophy which "would not suffice" for Strauss here means *Christian* medieval philosophy. (See "ONI," pp. 338, 344–45, 362–64.) Indeed, we now possess Strauss's own evaluation of this essay, and it is definitely clear that he does mean Christian medieval philosophy.

(Cf. "CCM," pp. 106, 108.) In general, Strauss's firmest statements voicing a preference for comparing modern philosophy with classical philosophy alone appear in works whose audience is primarily a Western, i.e., "Christian," one. As shall be brought to light, he considered the link between Jewish and Islamic medieval philosophy and classical political philosophy to be of greater directness and profundity. Cf. the introductions to *NRH* and *CM*. For Strauss's prefaces and introductions as the best key to his own "exoteric teaching," see Victor Gourevitch, "Philosophy and Politics," *Review of Metaphysics* 22 (1968): 58–84, 281–328, and especially p. 61. See also *PAW*, p. 21. For Jewish (and Islamic) medieval philosophy as superior to its modern Jewish (and Christian) counterpart, see *PG*, pp. 33–35, 40–44, 60–62; *PL*, pp. 26–28, 32–36, 51–54. We may now add, to corroborate our thesis here, Strauss's own words directing us along these lines: see "HBSMP" (*RCPR*), pp. 207–26.

19. *SCR*, pp. 178–82; *PSCR*, p. 31.

20. *PSCR*, pp. 1–7, 15–17.

21. *PG*, p. 10; *PL*, p. 4.

22. Perhaps the first thing we should notice about Strauss's approach is the way in which he links the crisis of modern Western civilization with the crisis in which the Jews and Judaism are immersed, and how he uses the difficulties of the one as a dialectical means for revealing the difficulties in the other's situation. On the one hand, the crisis of liberalism, and of the democratic regimes which operate in its spirit, is reflected by its limited ability to facilitate complete Jewish "assimilation":

> the liberal state cannot provide a solution to the Jewish problem, for such a solution would require a legal prohibition against every kind of "discrimination," i.e., the abolition of the private sphere, the denial of the difference between state and society, the destruction of the liberal state. (*PSCR*, pp. 6–7, 20–21)

On the other hand, the Jewish crisis has a great deal to do with the liberal promise, articulated by Spinoza, that it had the solution to Jewish suffering, if this be considered "as a merely human problem." But the Jews have put their hope in a promise, however "sympathetic," which liberalism has never been able to fulfill:

> Finite, relative problems can be solved; infinite, absolute problems cannot be solved. In other words human beings will never create a society which is free of contradictions. From every point of view it looks as if the Jewish people were the chosen people in the sense, at least, that the Jewish problem is the most manifest symbol of the human problem as a social or political problem. (*PSCR*, p. 6)

See *PG*, pp. 9–10, 27–28; *PL*, pp. 3–4, 18–19; *PSCR*, pp. 4, 6–7, 20–21.

23. *PG*, p. 10; *PL*, p. 4. For some remarks concerning belief versus knowledge, or true belief versus spurious belief, cf. *PAW*, pp. 120–21 with

note 175, and p. 104 note 25; "*ET*," pp. 53–54 with note 15. He also refers us to Maimonides' *Guide* I, 50.

24.   According to Strauss, the Enlightenment's leading original advocates were: Machiavelli, Bodin, Bacon, Hobbes, Descartes, and Spinoza. Compare an earlier treatment from the 1920s, e.g., *SCR*, pp. 86–104, 181–86, 215–50, 321–23, 326, with a later treatment from the 1950s, e.g., *WIPP?*, pp. 40–55, 182–91, 200–21. On this point, it must be said that Strauss's view did not change in any substantial respect between the two works. See, e.g., *PPH*, p. 88 note 5, for a recognition already of the decisive influence which Machiavelli exercised on Hobbes. If nothing else, Machiavelli excited Hobbes' (modern) interest in history as a powerful method of liberating philosophy from revealed religion: the "laws" of history suggest a secular power to which even religion must conform, and which can be used to advantage by philosophy.

25.   *PG*, p. 28; *PL*, p. 19.

26.   *PSCR*, pp. 4–7.

27.   The most significant respect in which "the movement of return" (by which Strauss primarily means to say Franz Rosenzweig, "who is thought to be the greatest Jewish thinker" produced by German Jewry) changed the previous direction of modern Jewish theology is in its powerful argument for divine revelation, as not just a received opinion and hence as something which must be "merely believed," but precisely as a present possibility and thus as something which can be "genuinely known." (*PSCR*, pp. 8–9) The other significant respects in which the "new thinking" of Rosenzweig transformed modern Jewish theology Strauss seems to treat more or less critically, especially as compared with Maimonides. His critical treatment embraces: its supposedly "empirical," but actually dogmatic, point of departure in "Israel" rather than in "Torah" (yet for Strauss and the "old thinking" what is actually "primary or authoritative" for Jewish *experience* is "Torah," while "Israel" is merely "the primary condition of [its] possibility"); its revitalized method of biblical interpretation (which however he regards as enmeshed in historicism); its accepting the need for a "principle of selection" in regard to the "traditional beliefs and rules," which refers itself to "a force" possessed by each Jewish person (which he observes is only possible in "the conditions of modern 'individualism' "); its determined stance against "orthodox austerity or sternness" concerning the Law (which in Strauss's view may however be shallower than the orthodox view as regards "the power of evil in man"); and its often doubting attitude toward miracles (which he believes does not sufficiently reckon with God's omnipotence). (*PSCR*, pp. 13–15) See also Michael L. Morgan, "The Curse of Historicity: The Role of History in Leo Strauss's Jewish Thought," *Journal of Religion* 61 (1981): 345–63.

28.   See *PG*, pp. 10–12, 15–17, 26–28; *PL*, pp. 4–7, 8–10, 17–19; *PSCR*, pp. 7–15, 18–28; IERR, pp. xxxiii-xxxv; "IERR" (*SPPP*), pp. 242–44. Strauss's first statement along these lines is also still worth considering, although written in the cause of a romantic Jewish "folk-spirit": "CA," especially pp. 312–14.

29. *PSCR*, pp. 6, 28.

30. Ibid., pp. 28–30.

31. *PG*, pp. 21–22; *PL*, pp. 13–15; *PSCR*, pp. 30–31.

32. *PG*, p. 9 note 1, and *PL*, p. 111 note 1: " 'Irrationalism' is but a variety [*Spielart*] of modern rationalism, which is itself already 'irrational' enough." For Strauss's comments about Mendelssohn's modern Jewish "rationalist" theology in relation to the history of modern philosophy, see *MMJA*, vol. 3, pt. 2, pp. lx–lxx, cxvi–cxx. All translations from the German, following *PG*, will be my own unless otherwise designated. For a critical review of the recent English translation, see Eve Adler, "Leo Strauss's *Philosophie und Gesetz*," in *Leo Strauss's Thought*, edited by Alan Udoff (Boulder, Colo.: Lynne Rienner, 1991), pp. 183–226.

33. It might be asked, is not to "pass beyond" reason also to contradict it? Does reason itself ever distinguish between "suprarational" and "irrational" truths? As it might seem, either a proposition is defensible in terms of reason or it is not, in which case it is not "suprarational" but "irrational." Such might seem to be the Platonic or classical rationalist critique of the possible truth contained in religious propositions as derived from the *Euthryphro*. In response to this, I would argue that Strauss was deeply impressed by Maimonides' pivotal discussion in the *Guide* of the creation versus the eternity of the universe. First, the Hebrew biblical (or monotheistic) challenge to philosophy is fundamentally and radically different from the challenge of Greek (or any pagan) piety—if only because in its articulate and defensible metaphysical claims, philosophy meets a true rival. Second, in matters of physics and metaphysics, rather than morals (which the *Euthyphro* focuses its attention on), the philosophers cannot demonstrate which is *the* true rational and which is *the* irrational position. This lends greater "rational" credence and plausibility to the religious (or so-called "irrational") position. Cf., e.g., infra, chapter 1, note 121, and chapter 6, toward the end. For some passing remarks by Strauss on the *Euthyphro* and monotheism, see *RCPR*, pp. 202, 206.

34. See *PSCR*, p. 30, along with *SCR*, pp. 170–71, 169; *PG*, pp. 54–55; *PL*, pp. 45–47; "HBSGP," p. xxii; *JA*, p. 5; "JA" (*SPPP*), p. 149; cf. also *Guide* II, 11 and III, 31. Maimonides also favored this verse, and his two uses of it in the *Guide* (just cited) suggest that it resonates the same as it did for Strauss: once to defend the compatibility of the Torah with the pure sciences, physics and astronomy, and once to defend the rationality and usefulness of the laws in the Torah.

35. *PG*, pp. 9–10, 28–29; *PL*, pp. 3–4, 19–20; *PSCR*, pp. 13, 31.

36. *PG*, p. 28; *PL*, p. 19.

37. As for Strauss equating "modern rationalism" *per se* with "modern sophistry" (*PG*, pp. 9–10; *PL*, pp. 3–4), here he seems to make an error of simplification in unconditionally identifying the two. He "corrects" this, as it were, in his critique of John Wild. See "ONI," pp. 335–45: "The temptation to identify modern philosophy with sophistry is considerable, and Wild is not the first to succumb to it." (But see also Nathan Tarcov's curious treatment of "ONI"

in "On a Certain Critique of 'Straussianism'," *Review of Politics* 53, no. 1 [Winter 1991]: 3–18.) He subsequently identifies "modern sophistry" with, if anything, "historicism" and relativistic social science. (See *NRH*, pp. 9–13, with 115–19.) Even in Strauss's mature and comprehensive view of the history of modern philosophy, however, it seems that also this peculiarly modern guise in which the natural possibility of sophistry appears has its deeper roots in, and was decisively prepared by, modern rationalism—in which case this small error Strauss made in his youth would not be as significant as the larger truth it possessed in substance. Cf., e.g., "ET," pp. 15–17. But see also *SPPP*, p. 228: ". . .Machiavelli and Socrates make a common front against the Sophists" regarding "the ingredient of politics which transcends speech." For a clear rejection of the characterization of Machiavelli's thought as supposedly originating in "sophism," see "MCL," p. 13. As for "the ingredient of politics which transcends speech," Strauss seems to refer to the body: "the soul can rule the body only despotically, not by persuasion. . ." Still, if Machiavelli does not consider pure thought politically relevant, certainly speech (and action) receive a higher estimation in Machiavelli than they do in the Socratic tradition of philosophy, which regards the naturalness of thought in man as the basis for all natural right. Human nature is not *in general* determined by beautiful speech or by persuasion: only some men can be persuaded in determining their actions by considerations of honor, and only a very rare and specific kind of man is solely determined in his actions by reason. Hence, philosophers must adjust their speech to this reality about human nature. But that very rare and specific man, the Socratic ideal, is of no concern to Machiavelli in determining how political life, and hence political speech, is to be guided. Thus, compare *SCR*, pp. 226–29, and *PAW*, pp. 154–58, 181–84, 191–93, 198, 201, for Spinoza's tactical silences combined with bold assertions, with *TOM*, pp. 232, 294–99, concerning modern philosophy's "considered boldness" as reflecting "a wholly new estimate of man," with its basis in a new view of nature and philosophy. In the new view of nature, man (forgetting his higher self) recognizes himself as "threatened by a stingy, hostile nature" from which he can only save himself by mastering and owning it, and which is only beneficent through free human constructive action. (Cf. *PG*, pp. 20–22, 25–26; *PL*, pp. 12–14, 17–18; *PSCR*, pp. 29–30.) This changes even nature as the standard reflecting "the good" or "being"; as historically comprehended by modern man, now even nature does not mean "to be always" or that this eternal being is good (*NRH*, pp. 30–31). Philosophy itself eventually leaves nature for history: man must retrace his own path "ontogenetically" as his main "philosophic" task in order to know how being has been constructed by man in the form of human civilizations and their supporting "philosophies," and not concern himself with what is by nature. It is, then, denied that true natural knowledge is possible, and man is left only to write the history of opinions as poetic horizons in which he has created his worlds. In *SCR*, Strauss already discerned the root of modern rationalism's primary error in the basic Enlightenment notion of "prejudice," which "is an historical category" rather than a purely natural one, or if it reflects something natural, it is secondary rather than primary. Indeed, its historically derivative character "precisely constitutes the difference between the struggle of the Enlightenment against prejudices and the struggle against appearance and opinion with which philosophy began its secular journey." (*SCR*, p. 181 and generally pp. 178–82, 134–35, 252–54, and *PG*, pp. 45–46, with *PL*, pp. 37–39. Cf. also *PPH*, pp. 152–54, 158–65, for opinion and "dialectic.")

38. *PG*, pp. 9–10; *PL*, pp. 3–4.

39. *PG*, p. 28; *PL*, p. 19.

40. Cf., e.g., *CM*, p. 11.

41. *PG*, p. 9; *PL*, p. 3.

42. *SCR*, pp. 178–82, 191–92.

43. See chapter 1 text supra, near endnote marker 9.

44. Thus, consider these statements about modern natural science: "the new science. . . proved itself in the struggle against orthodoxy, if indeed it did not have its very raison d'être in [such a struggle]" (*PG*, p. 20; *PL*, p. 12); "only on the premises of modern natural science are miracles as such unknowable" (*PG*, p. 23; *PL*, pp. 14–15). Cf. also *SCR*, pp. 60, 212–14; *PG*, pp. 21–24; *PL*, 13–16; *PPH*, pp. 166–70; *NRH*, pp. 169–77; *WIPP?*, p. 47; *PSCR*, pp. 28–29. For "essential differences," or formal and final causes, as still valid or as scientifically unrefuted, see "CPP," pp. 92–93. Consider also: "The rejection of final causes (and therewith also of the concept of chance) destroyed the theoretical basis of classical political philosophy." See "TWM" (*IPP*), p. 87, and also pp. 82–89 generally.

45. *SCR*, pp. 150–51, 158, 160–61, 164, 174–75, 182.

46. *OT*, pp. 213–17; *OT* (rev.), pp. 199–202.

47. *TOM*, p. 134; *CM*, pp. 239–41.

48. *SCR*, pp. 130–31, 178–82, 215, 226, 245–47, 262; *TOM*, pp. 11–12, 51, 175–208, 294–98; *PSCR*, p. 13. See also *DLT*, p. 343, for the necessarily "radical distinction" between "conditions" and "sources" of knowledge in classical philosophy. (This is the famous last paragraph that originally appeared only in the French edition. Unlike the last paragraph, one other paragraph of the original French edition has not been restored even in the revised edition of *On Tyranny* (1991), edited by Victor Gourevitch and Michael S. Roth. See *DLT*, pp. 309–11. The missing paragraph, were it to be added, would appear between the paragraph ending on the bottom of p. 192 and the paragraph beginning on the top of p. 193, in the pagination of the revised edition.)

49. See Gerhard Krüger's review of *RKS* in *Deutsche Literaturzeitung* 51(1931): 2407–12, and especially p. 2410; for an English translation, see *Independent Journal of Philosophy* 5/6(1988): 173-75. Strauss thus seems to have been attempting to "recover" classical "nature" as the true standard for reason through "historical studies," a possibility first exemplified for him by "Lessing's 'dialectic' " ("CCM," p. 107). But modern historical studies, a post-Enlightenment creation, seemingly repeat or presuppose the Enlightenment's belief in a decisive

progress of man beyond both classical philosophy and biblical orthodoxy. (Cf. *WIPP?*, pp. 66–68, 71, 76–77.) He was, as a result, constrained to speak, in an inspired image, of "ascending" from "the second 'unnatural' cave," created by modern rationalism, to the "first 'natural' cave, depicted by Plato's parable." Thus, the return to classical philosophy, to Plato and Aristotle, mediated by Lessing and Maimonides, meant as much as anything for Strauss primarily to learn from the ancients what their obscured or forgotten idea of "nature" signifies in and for our world. (The paradoxical need for history in order to recover nature, and hence for the man who would be a philosopher to appear in the guise of a historian, is one of the first and most enduring principles reached by Strauss in his search for truth beyond modern categories. The difficulty in our comprehending what is conveyed, and what is presupposed, by this notion is not diminished by a recognition of the fact that he seems to attribute his discovering the necessity for such a "recovery" to the crucial awareness of philosophy's radical roots which he discerned in Heidegger's antiphilosophical speculation. For a fuller discussion of the debt Strauss owed to Heidegger, even in their fundamental opposition to one another, see infra, chapter 2, note 13.) It was in this "archaeological" act of recovering the "first 'natural' cave" that Strauss was also fundamentally aided by the reenactment or the remembering of "the polemic against the tradition" (i.e., the modern tradition which created the "second 'unnatural' cave"), which Strauss considered a prerequisite for the philosophic ascent. This was "the polemic against the tradition" that was started by Lessing in his turning the Enlightenment critique of orthodoxy against itself, a polemic later "radicalized" by Nietzsche in his critique of tradition *per se*, as to its very idea or possibility, once modern philosophy's full ramifications were comprehended by him. (For Nietzsche, see e.g. *PG*, pp. 13 note 1, 23–24 with p. 24 note 1; *PL*, pp. 111–12 note 2, 15–16, 113 note 11. It is worth noting further that in Nietzsche's *Ecce Homo* account of *Beyond Good and Evil*, he calls it primarily "a *critique of modernity*." Strauss considered this same book Nietzsche's "most beautiful" book, the one in which he especially " 'platonizes' as regards the 'form' " [*SPPP*, pp. 174–75]. Indeed, he quotes from this account in *Ecce Homo* to support his argument for *Beyond Good and Evil*'s "beauty," but he curiously does not refer to that key sentence, which might seem to have enhanced his preference.) Lessing, directing himself against the moderate Enlightenment in both of its guises, i.e., rationalistic and romantic, disclosed it as a substitute but mediocre tradition which adapted the radical Enlightenment to society by a frail but unsuitable "synthesis." He even exposed it as such a compromise in his rehabilitating the deeper philosophic and political purposes of men like Spinoza, who in their radically antitraditional and antitheological polemic aimed to eradicate all earlier Western philosophy and religion as misguided. It is also noteworthy that in Strauss's consideration of Lessing's "polemic against the tradition," Strauss only seems to be concerned with Lessing's critique of the moderate Enlightenment, and does not even mention Lessing's equally sharp, if not sharper, attacks against strict orthodoxy, i.e., in his eleven *Anti-Goeze* pieces and in the related writings of his dispute with Goeze. In Strauss's own reflections, perhaps the latter did not help him quite as much as did the former, because in his study of Spinoza he had already discerned the natural limits set for any critique of orthodoxy in its being necessarily unphilosophic as polemic. (However, to be sure, Lessing himself had probably recognized the same thing: see the famous letter to his brother Karl, quoted in note 78 infra.) But Strauss also accepted the main substantive thrust in Lessing's critique of orthodoxy, i.e., the right to, and need for, "biblical criticism" as a modern historical and theological discipline, once it has been established. (Thus, see "BGW" as a whole.) However, undoubtedly aided by Rosenzweig, Strauss passed beyond even Lessing in his transcendence of "biblical criticism"'s anti-orthodoxy. (See e.g. *JA*, pp. 6–7; "OIG," pp. 6–9, 14–15, 18–20.) It was probably in this spirit that Strauss entitled the Judaism which he envisioned for the future as "postcritical" Judaism. (See "WWRJ," typescript, Question and Answer section, p. 11; "POR?," pp. 23–24, 27–29, 33, 44–45; "POR?" [*IPP*], pp. 257–59, 263–67, 272–73, 288–89.) It is this very substitute tradition (i.e., in its critique of *the* true Western tradition, which for Strauss means classical philosophy and biblical religion), that has obscured and even managed to "bury" what we might call "the natural perspective" pure and simple, whose true basis the radical Enlightenment originally intended to restore (at least, such was its claim). "The intention of the Enlightenment was the rehabilitation of the natural through the denial (or restriction) of the supernatural; however, its achievement was the discovery of a new 'natural' foundation that, far from being natural, is rather as it were the residuum of the 'supernatural.'" (*PG*, p. 13 note 1; *PL*, pp. 111–12 note 2) The problem seems to arise from the question about whether the "typical" or the "extreme" is the best key to the natural. (See *PG*, pp. 13 note 1, 21–22, 26–27, 36–43, 61–62; *PL*, pp. 111–12 note 2, 13–14, 17–19, 28–36, 52–54; *SCR*, pp. 335–39; "ET," pp. 57–59; "CCM," pp. 111–14; *NRH*, pp. 161–63, 171–77, 202; *TOM*, pp. 221–23, 246–55, 279–80, 297, 299; *WIPP?*, p. 47; *PSCR*, pp. 13, 15–16.) This notion does not change fundamentally for Strauss even with his discovery that Machiavelli, and not Hobbes, laid the basis for modern philosophy, since with all his radicalism Machiavelli still wanted to actualize what the classics merely envisaged. He still moved in the sphere of human nature as delineated by the classics, even if he reached different conclusions about what to do with it. See e.g. *SPPP*, p. 228.

    50. *SCR*, p. 179

    51. Ibid., p. 181. Cf. also *NRH*, pp. 173–76.

    52. In addressing the relations between reason and revelation, it should now be asked whether this goes to the heart of what may be the unbridgeable gap between them, as Strauss subsequently viewed these matters: that man is naturally questionable to reason, but not sinful. Granted, questionableness and sinfulness may come very close to one another at several points, but do they ever meet and join in an essential and necessary way? Similarly, are they morally

"utopian" in the same sense? Does philosophy actually hope to realize its moral ideals for a perfect society? Or does it use them as "heuristic devices," to illuminate the limits of hope for human action on the basis of disclosing what is contained in the human soul, what its natural limits are, and why it resists the form of perfection? And does religious "utopianism" make any sense whatsoever if it does not hope some day to actualize its dream, and to use it as a guide to action, e.g., as messianism might be said to do for Judaism? Here I must acknowledge a debt I owe to Clifford Orwin for raising these questions to me, and in general for his careful reading of the present work in manuscript form. His keen critical sense focused on the problem of reason and revelation in my work, and aided me considerably by forcing me to sharpen my formulations and to clarify my meaning on several specific points.

53. See *PG*, pp. 23–24 and *PL*, pp. 14–15 for the significance of modern science's "Is" and "Ought" (or "fact" and "value") distinction in subverting nature as a standard.

54. *SCR*, p. 226.

55. For modern philosophy's "anti-utopianism," see e.g. *NRH*, pp. 178–79, 200–201. For "antitheological ire," see *SCR*, pp. 178–82, 226–29; *PG*, pp. 31, 25–27 with p. 26 note 1; *PL*, pp. 24, 16–18, 113–14 note 12; *NRH*, pp. 184, 198; *TOM*, pp. 11–13, 198–99; *WIPP?*, p. 44; *HPP*, p. 269. See also the text of chapter 1 supra, near endnote markers 55 and 77.

56. *OT*, p. 205; *OT* (rev.), pp. 191–92.

57. *PG*, pp. 20, 22, 23, 33–45; *PL*, pp. 12, 14, 15, 25–37; *NRH*, pp. 81–95. Cf. also "TWM" (*IPP*), pp. 82–83, for why modernity does not represent a "secularization" process; and pp. 84–89 for the basic accord between the Bible and classical philosophy, and why "Machiavelli rejects the whole philosophic and theological tradition."

58. *CM*, pp. 10–11.

59. *NRH*, pp. 316–17.

60. Ibid., pp. 174–76, 199–202; *WIPP?*, p. 55.

61. "GA," p. 2; "PHPW," p. 1.

62. *SCR*, p. 180; *PSCR*, p. 24.

63. *PG*, pp. 16–17; *PL*, pp. 10–11; *PSCR*, p. 9.

64. *PG*, p. 21; *PL*, p. 13; *PSCR*, p. 29; "TWM" (*IPP*), p. 98.

65. *PG*, p. 21; *PL*, p. 13.

66. *PG*, p. 10; *PL*, p. 4.

67. However, see already *SCR*, pp. 226–29 and *PPH*, p. 88 note 5.

68. *PG*, pp. 20–22, 25–26; *PL*, pp. 12–13, 16–18; *PSCR*, pp. 15, 29–30.

69. *PG*, pp. 22–23; *PL*, pp. 14–15.

70. *PG*, p. 22; *PL*, p. 14. Fred Baumann translates: "The actual grounds for the Enlightenment's right thus seems to be the new natural science." In the unfinished manuscript version of Eve Adler's translation of *Philosophy and Law* (the publication of which is forthcoming), it reads: "Thus the new natural science

appears to be the proper defense of the Enlightenment." (Typescript, p. 18) The original reads: "Die neue Naturwissenschaft also scheint der eigentliche Rechtsgrund der Aufklärung zu sein."

71. *PG*, p. 23; *PL*, p. 15.

72. *PG*, p. 23 and also pp. 13–14 note 1; *PL*, pp. 15 and 111–12 note 2.

73. *PG*, pp. 22–23; *PL*, pp. 14–15.

74. *PG*, p. 22; *PL*, p. 14.

75. *PSCR*, pp. 15–16.

76. *PG*, p. 23; *PL*, p. 15.

77. *PG*, pp. 20, 23–28; *PL*, pp. 12, 15–19; *NRH*, pp. 167–70, 178 note 11, 188–89; *PSCR*, pp. 29–31.

78. *PG*, p. 28; *PL*, p. 19. See also Lessing's famous letter to his brother Karl of 2 Feb. 1774. Lessing defends orthodoxy against the "new theologians" for the sake of philosophy, because in the old arrangement with orthodoxy, "things were fairly well settled. A curtain had been drawn between it and philosophy." Each one allowed the other freedom of action in its own domain. The "new theologians" wanted to remove the curtain and make believers rational; however, in the process of their reforms, says Lessing, "they are making us very irrational philosophers." Likewise, he defends orthodoxy against their Enlightenment-prompted attacks:

> We are agreed that the old religious system is false, but I cannot share your conviction that it is a patchwork of bunglers and half-philosophers. I know of nothing in the world in which human sagacity has been better displayed and cultivated. The real patchwork of bunglers and half-philosophers is the religious system which they now want to set in place of the old, and with far more influence on reason and philosophy than the old ever presumed.

The translation follows Henry E. Allison, *Lessing and the Enlightenment* (Ann Arbor: University of Michigan Press, 1966), p. 84. See also the similar statement of Lessing's in "Die Erziehung des Menschengeschlechts" (1780), paragraph 65. Cf. also Ernest L. Fortin, "Rational Theologians and Irrational Philosophers: A Straussian Perspective," *Interpretation* 12 (1984): 349–56. On what "half-philosophers" are, see "ONI," p. 342, note 15.

79. "GA," p. 2.

80. Cf. *PG*, pp. 28, 46, 53 note 3, 62–67, 113–22 and *PL*, pp. 19, 38, 119 note 71, 53–58, 103–10, for Strauss's first definite statements about how he discovered that "Platonic political philosophy" is the key to this premodern criterion in Maimonides and his Islamic predecessors Alfarabi and Avicenna. Their prophetology was especially pertinent, inasmuch as through it they did not separate the search for "enlightenment" from "philosophic politics," but subordinated its requirements to the unavoidable human difference between the philosophic few and the nonphilosophic many: never will all men be prophets, for they will not want, or be able, to endure the arduous training and way of life it requires.

81. Maimonides' *Guide* was, I believe, enormously helpful to Strauss in wrestling with these "dialectics of enlightenment," since Maimonides deals with these matters with about as much directness as any philosophical writer. To begin with the Introduction to the *Guide* alone, Maimonides puts things most bluntly:

> I am the man who when the concern pressed him and his way was straitened and he could find no other device by which to teach a demonstrated truth other than by giving satisfaction to a single virtuous man while displeasing ten thousand ignoramuses—I am he who prefers to address that single man by himself, and I do not heed the blame of those many creatures. For I claim to liberate that virtuous one from that into which he has sunk, and I shall guide him in his perplexity until he becomes perfect and he finds rest. (Pp. 16–17)

Further, consider *Guide* I, 17, 27, 33, 35. Especially pertinent is a most important chapter—I, 34—in which Maimonides carefully analyses why the search for rational enlightenment and for the attainment of the highest truth ("divine science") is only evident in a very select and rare company of individuals ("these matters are only for a few solitary individuals of a very special sort"). He suggests five causes: the "difficulty, subtlety, and obscurity" of these matters (only a rare few are so naturally endowed and talented as to want, and be able, to wrestle with difficult matters of the mind); "the insufficiency of the minds of all men at their beginnings" (only a rare few are fortunate enough to be provided with *all* of the suitable but necessary conditions in life which enable them to actualize their potential); "the length of the preliminaries" (only a rare few are fortunate enough to receive the proper and essential education, which because it is such a long and arduous process also requires great powers of intellectual discipline and concentration); "the natural aptitudes" (only a rare few are by natural temperament as well as by moral training permitted to start, to continue, and to progress in the study of such matters, which desires in the constitution of man resist for numerous reasons); "men are occupied with the necessities of the bodies" (only a rare few will persevere, because of ardent desire, to devote themselves heart and soul to the search for true knowledge, in spite of the numerous duties which life imposes and the distractions which it abundantly offers).

82. *PG*, pp. 11–12; *PL*, pp. 5–6.

83. *PSCR*, pp. 27, 13, 4–8. See also especially *MMJA*, vol. 3, pt. 2, pp. lxxviii, lxii for Mendelssohn's apparent obliviousness to the irreconcilable contradiction between Epicurean and Jewish moralities.

84. *PG*, pp. 12–15; *PL*, pp. 6–8.

85. *PG*, p. 22; *PL*, p. 14; *PSCR*, pp. 7–8.

86. *PG*, p. 11; *PL*, pp. 5–6.

87. *PG*, p. 22; *PL*, p. 14; *PSCR*, pp. 7–8.

88. *PG*, pp. 12–13; *PL*, pp. 6–7. See also *PSCR*, pp. 16, 18–21: Spinoza, who might be said to have originated the liberal tradition, both political and religious, already "plays a most dangerous game; his procedure is as much beyond good and evil as his God."

89. *PG*, p. 12; *PL*, p. 6.

90. Cf. also "BGW"; "CA," pp. 312–13; *SCR*, pp. 252–56; *PSCR*, p. 27.

91. *SCR*, pp. 200–204; *PSCR*, pp. 23–24; "IERR" (*SPPP*), pp. 244–47; IERR, pp. xxvi–xxviii.

92. *PG*, pp. 11, 16; *PL*, pp. 5, 9; *PSCR*, pp. 14–15, 25, 27.

93. *PG*, p. 12; *PL*, p. 6.

94. *PG*, pp. 11, 14, 22; *PL*, pp. 5–6, 7, 14.

95. *PG*, p. 12; *PL*, p. 6.

96. Strauss acknowledged in both "PHPW," p. 1, and in "GA," p. 2 the debt he owed to the "resurrection" of theology in the 1920s by Barth and Rosenzweig. He does not, however, detail the *contents* of what they taught him, other than mentioning Barth's liberating biblical hermeneutic as he enunciated it in the preface of his commentary to Paul's *Letter to the Romans*. There Barth emphasizes that the truth expounded by Scripture can only be of interest to us if it is just as vital and relevant for us here and now as it was then and there. This amounts to a declaration of independence from the historical approach to Scripture, which can only be exculpated from the charge of participating in historicist triumphalism and reductionism by duly subordinating itself to the eternal truth taught by Scripture.

97. "OCPH," p. 586.

98. Strauss also quotes Lessing's conclusion with seeming approval: "I fear that the entire comparison of the ancients and moderns may boil down to this," i.e., the difference between "better" and "sharper eyes" versus "seeing more." This suggests the contrast between Maimonides' "depth" and Spinoza's "originality" which he speaks of in a subsequent work. Cf. "OF" (*WIPP?*), p. 230, with "ET," p. 59 note 37.

99. As Strauss seems to suggest, Lessing is further intimating by this and by other similar remarks against the moderns that he did not share the belief in there being a greater ultimate or suprarational truth of divine revelation than can be known through natural reason. This is because "unaided" reason cannot pronounce true in terms of itself that which transcends it, although it can recognize such "aided" truths as necessary or wise or blessed inasmuch as they apply to other realms, e.g., morality, religion, or politics. It may have been this belief in a suprarational truth of Scripture that also, *as a philosophic possibility*, laid the basis for the modern, post-Enlightenment belief in "history" as manifesting a decisive "progress" of truth and even of Being. In Strauss's view Lessing would seem to tacitly reject this "progress" in advance by attempting to recover the lost, or obscured, "natural horizon," known best through the ancients. According to Strauss, "the greatest exponents of the ancients' side in the 'querelle [des anciens et des modernes'], that is, Swift and Lessing, knew that

the real theme of the quarrel is antiquity and Christianity." In other words, the conflict between ancient and modern ideals conceals this crucial fact: "the moderns" are powerfully influenced by the Bible and by the Christian theological tradition, and do indeed believe that they vindicate its cause, even if Strauss denies that they do vindicate it by their methods. Strauss carries this interpretation through with an exacting consistency, in that he relegates Lessing's "Die Erziehung des Menschengeschlechts" to "the *completely* exoteric," even though it has often been considered a prophetic anticipation of romantic historicism in its several guises. See Lessing's "Die Erziehung," paragraphs 4, 65, 77; "CCM," p. 106; "ET," pp. 57–59; *PAW*, pp. 12–13, 18; Karl Löwith, *Meaning in History* (Chicago: University of Chicago Press, 1949), pp. 1–6, 17–19, 182–207; Henry E. Allison, *Lessing and the Enlightenment*, pp. 147–61, and especially p. 147 for the "Erziehung" as "an 'esoteric' speculative treatment of the history of religion." See also Henry Chadwick's comments on the esotericism of Lessing in his introduction to *Lessing's Theological Writings* (Stanford, Calif.: Stanford University Press, 1957), pp. 43–44.

100.   Strauss often seems to draw a sharp line in dividing the realms of human knowledge between those things or beings which dwell solely in the sphere of the accidental, i.e., history, and those things or beings which can attain, or are identified with, what is essential, as "the truth about the highest things," i.e., philosophy. Cf. "OCPH," pp. 584–85; "FP," pp. 389–93, 374–77; "ET," pp. 58–59. It is perhaps this radical division between the two realms that causes Strauss to speak Platonically in terms of the need for a "conversion" to philosophy—a complete transformation in the soul of the man who genuinely philosophizes, by turning himself entirely, in soul *and* body, to the love of wisdom. See "ET," pp. 56–57; *PAW*, pp. 108–10; *NRH*, pp. 11–12; *CM*, pp. 112–18, 124–28; *OT*, pp. 211–16; *OT* (rev.), pp. 197–202. By way of contrast, consider "OCPH," pp. 582–86, and "ONI," pp. 326–32 and 333–34, for a defense of history and historical research, i.e., philosophic preoccupation with what is seemingly rooted in the accidental realm: ". . . insistence on the fundamental difference between philosophy and history—a difference by which philosophy stands or falls—may very well, in the present situation, be misleading, not to say dangerous, to philosophy itself." ("ONI," p. 332) Cf. also *PAW*, pp. 12–14. For a discussion of matters related to the role which history *must* play in contemporary philosophy in Strauss's view, see the two essays of Nathan Tarcov, "Philosophy and History: Tradition and Interpretation in the Work of Leo Strauss," *Polity* 16, no. 1 (Fall 1983): 5–29, and his "On a Certain Critique of 'Straussianism'," *Review of Politics* 53, no. 1 (Winter 1991): 3–18.

101.   "ET," pp. 52–54, 57–59, notes 33 and 35; *DLT*, pp. 342–44; *OT* (rev.), p. 212.

102.   For Strauss's fullest elaboration of his notion of "reenactment," see "OCPH," pp. 575, 582.

103.   *PG*, p. 15; *PL*, pp. 8–9.

104.   "ET," p. 54 and p. 57 note 28.

105. *PG*, pp. 18–19, and *PL*, pp. 10–12, with the identical words in *PSCR*, pp. 28–29. Cf. also *SCR*, pp. 145–46, and "BGW" (1925) for the first mention of this principle which he learned from Lessing: "We suppose that the Enlightenment has laughed this orthodoxy to death, and if we today good-naturedly laugh at these Enlighteners, then we forget that there is also still today an orthodoxy." He quotes Lessing by name to prove a similar point: "Not therefore orthodoxy but a certain squinting, limping orthodoxy which is unequal to itself is so loathsome." The quotation is from Lessing's "Counter-Propositions" to Reimarus. See *Gotthold Ephraim Lessings Werke*, vol. 7, edited by Herbert G. Göpfert, et al (München: Carl Hanser Verlag, 1971), pp. 457–91, and especially p. 472.

106. *PSCR*, p. 29; *PG*, p. 19; *PL*, p. 11.

107. *PG*, p. 18; *PL*, pp. 10–11.

108. *PG*, pp. 17–18; *PL*, pp. 9–11.

109. *PG*, pp. 17, 51; *PL*, pp. 9, 53–54.

110. *PG*, pp. 16–17; *PL*, pp. 8–9.

111. See, e.g., *PAW*, p. 109 for a medieval parallel to the philosophers' "ruthless attack" and its potentially disastrous consequences, as reflected in the complete absence of a direct encounter between the philosopher and the Jewish scholar from Halevi's *Kuzari*. Indeed, it is this literary theme and what it represents philosophically that, I believe, animates Strauss's entire monograph "The Law of Reason in the *Kuzari*." I pursue this argument in greater detail in "Religion, Philosophy, and Morality: How Leo Strauss Read Judah Halevi's *Kuzari*," *Journal of the American Academy of Religion* 61, no. 2 (Summer 1993): 225–73.

112. *PG*, p. 18; *PL*, pp. 10–11; *PSCR*, p. 28. See also the text of chapter 1 supra, near endnote marker 25, and between endnote markers 30 and 37.

113. *PG*, p. 10; *PL*, p. 4.

114. See now the recently discovered and published "ET" as a whole. One might be partly justified here in applying to Strauss his own criticism of Nietzsche for having "understood Spinoza in his own image": perhaps Strauss likewise "understood" Lessing "in his own image." (*PSCR*, pp. 25–26) As one critic might plausibly put it, Lessing may not have been so entirely swayed by Platonic dialectics as he was by Spinozistic metaphysics presented with Leibnizian philosophic diplomacy and his own native literary genius. See, e.g., Henry E. Allison, *Lessing and the Enlightenment*, pp. 124–35.

115. *PG*, p. 26 note 1; *PL*, pp. 113–14 note 12; *MMJA*, vol. 3, pt. 2, pp. xxxiv, lxx.

116. *PG*, pp. 26 note 1, 28; *PL*, pp. 113–14 note 12, 19; *PSCR*, p. 30; *TOM*, p. 51. For both Mendelssohn's and Jacobi's "theistic" misreading of atheism as necessarily "antitheism" in Lessing's "Spinozism is philosophy" remark, see *MMJA*, vol. 3, pt. 2, pp. xxxiv, lxx, as well as xxxi, lxxv-lxxvii, lxxx-lxxxii, xc-xci, and *PSCR*, pp. 16–17. In his critique of Collingwood, Strauss isolates the element of modernity in romanticism:

The romantic soul, we prefer to say, is characterized by longing, by futile
longing, by a longing which is felt to be superior to any fulfillment
that is possible now, i.e., in post-revolutionary Europe....True
Romanticism regards the highest possibility of the nineteenth or
twentieth century, "futile" longing, as the highest possibility of man,
in so far as it assumes that the noble fulfillments of the past were based
on delusions which are now irrevocably dispelled....It believes
therefore that the present is superior to the past in regard to knowledge
of the decisive truth, i.e., in the decisive respect....Hence
Romanticism perpetuates the belief in the superiority of modern
thought to earlier thought... ("OCPH," pp. 576–77)

Cf. also *TOM*, pp. 198, 219–21; *PAW*, pp. 157–58.

117. *PG*, p. 28; *PL*, p. 19.

118. *PG*, p. 9 note 1; *PL*, p. 111 note 1; cf. also *OT*, pp. 198, 219–21; *OT* (rev.),
pp. 185, 205–06.

119. *PG*, pp. 22–23, 26 note 1; *PL*, pp. 14–15, 113–14 note 12; "POR?," p.
37; "POR?" (*IPP*), p. 279; *NRH*, p. 169; *TOM*, pp. 11–13, 208–23; *PSCR*, pp. 12–13;
"CCM," p. 112; *SPPP*, pp. 179–81. In "AE" (*IPP*), pp. 148–49, Strauss directs
criticism against the "dogmatic atheism" of modern relativistic social science,
which avows its own unbelief as "intellectual honesty"; as he rejoins, this
"intellectual honesty is not enough. Intellectual honesty is not love of truth."
In other words, it is not compelled by any rational demonstration of the necessary
falseness of every possible divine revelation, but simply proceeds in atheistic
faith as if there were such a refutation. If "a frank atheist is a better man than
an alleged theist who conceives of God as a symbol," then "unreasoned unbelief,
probably accompanied by a vague confidence that the issue of unbelief versus
belief has long since been settled once and for all" is the worst sort of dogmatism,
for this "unreasoned unbelief" is grounded in the deaf and blind refusal even
to consider "the possibility that religion rests ultimately on God's revealing
himself to man." Similarly, in his dispute with Kojève, Strauss suggests that this
concern with "probity," which criticizes philosophers for their motives in desiring
to attain certain cognitive pleasures, rather should recognize that this whole
matter of pleasures is subordinate to the activities philosophers desire to engage
in: "the rank of the various kinds of pleasure ultimately depends upon the rank
of the activities to which the pleasures are related. Neither the quantity nor
the purity of the pleasures determines in the last resort the rank of human
activities." Strauss suggests that this exclusive concern with "intellectual probity"
seems to "gratuitously assume...an omniscient God who demands from men
a pure heart," while what for the Socratic philosopher is "akin to 'the good
conscience'" is something quite different. See *OT*, pp. 211, 218–19; *OT* (rev.), pp.
197, 203–05.

120. *OT*, p. 198; *OT* (rev.), pp. 185–86.

121. *NRH*, pp. 82–90, 123–24; "POR?," pp. 41–43; "MITP," pp. 111–12; "POR?" (*IPP*), pp. 284–88, 290–94. But cf. Victor Gourevitch, "Philosophy and Politics," pp. 294–99.

122. *SCR*, pp. 181–82, 183–86.

123. *PAW*, p. 105 note 29.

124. *NRH*, pp. 90–93, 124; "MITP," pp. 113–14; "POR?" (*IPP*), pp. 295–98; *TOM*, pp. 11–12.

125. *NRH*, p. 124; *CM*, p. 119–21; *OT*, pp. 214–16; *OT* (rev.), pp. 200–202; "POR?" (*IPP*), p. 297; "JA" (*SPPP*), p. 149.

126. Strauss is, in my judgment, also speaking for himself; however, to be clear about what he is ostensibly doing in the quoted passage, he is merely proceeding to expound the spirit of Socrates' teaching as interpreted by Plato. See *NRH*, pp. 125–26.

127. The term is adapted from E. D. Hirsch, Jr., who applied it, in reverse, to Heidegger, whom he calls a "cognitive atheist." See *The Aims of Interpretation* (Chicago: University of Chicago Press, 1976), pp. 12–13. This designation remains valid, however one may put the emphasis in Strauss's final understanding of "the ideas," those "self-subsistent," transcendent entities that must first be apprehended in "a vision." Thus, Thomas L. Pangle rather overstates the case for Strauss's ultimate skepticism in regard to "the ideas" and the Socratic "teleotheology" concerning the whole. See Pangle's introduction to *SPPP*, pp. 2–5; and Strauss, *PG*, pp. 20, 23, *PL*, pp. 12, 15; *NRH*, pp. 7–8, 89 note 9, 94–95, 109–13, 124–26, 155, 171, 176–77; *TOM*, pp. 78, 298; *WIPP?*, pp. 38, 47, 286; "AE" (*IPP*), pp. 128–29, 152–53; *CM*, pp. 19–21, 118–21, 138; *XSD*, p. 160. Strauss's concern with "the whole" is itself already an expression of his "cognitive theism," since the philosophic intuition represented by "a vision of the articulated whole," whether "adequate" or not, is not the only or the necessary way in which the human or natural basis of philosophy has been postulated. Consider also that while "the ideas" may be a transitional pedagogical teaching to true and pure philosophizing, colored by the theological teaching which they are meant to supersede, and hence this teaching is not meant to be taken literally, nevertheless it is meant very seriously. For Strauss, as we also know, *only* the theological teachings give us our first access to "the articulated [or intelligible] whole" which philosophy is a striving to know. Inasmuch as we do not achieve that complete knowledge of "the whole," we are stranded in the transitional realm, which augments its value to us as the only unchanging reminder we possess of what we are striving for. Thus, the question may legitimately be asked: what remains of "theism" in Strauss's notion? Is there any element of divine will or of personality possible in "the ideas" which we cognize? How then is God ("theism") present? The soundest answer which we are bound to reach, if our original suggestion is correct, is: God is "the whole" or "nature"—which we cannot fully comprehend—hence his Being is beyond our comprehension, although this is not *necessarily* willed. He is the merely *intuited* unity of "the whole" (whose "character" is "elusive" or "mysterious"), which is expressed imaginatively but truly by "theistic" religion,

and especially by "monotheism." For a similar notion about Strauss, see Kojève's remarks about the *"theistic* conception of Truth (and of Being)," *OT,* pp. 160–62, or *OT* (rev.), pp. 150–53, a notion which Strauss does not directly address or refute, but which is more or less adequately covered by *OT,* pp. 209–10, and *DLT,* pp. 342–44 or *OT* (rev.), p. 212. For Kojève's critique of the "theistic" element in the Platonic tradition, see further *Introduction to the Reading of Hegel* (New York: Basic Books, 1969), pp. 100–130.

CHAPTER TWO

1.   *PG,* p. 10; *PL,* p. 4.
2.   Cf., e.g., "MITP," pp. 114–17; "POR?" (*IPP*), pp. 298–309.
3.   The Platonic derivation of the leading idea in Maimonides was rightly established for Strauss by Hermann Cohen—but for the wrong reasons. The clue which Cohen gave him did not take clear shape immediately. The correct connection was finally clarified for Strauss in a remark of Avicenna's, which he apparently discovered quite by accident. For Cohen, Plato, and Maimonides, see *PG,* pp. 9, 35–37, 67, 119–22; *PL,* pp. 3, 28–30, 58, 107–10; *PIHPE,* pp. xxvi, xxx–xxxii; *PSCR,* pp. 15–28; *JA,* pp. 22–24; "JA" (*SPPP*), pp. 167–68; "GA," pp. 2–3; "IERR" (*SPPP*), p. 244; IERR, pp. xxxv–xxxvi. Also see supra, chapter 1, notes 1 and 11, for Cohen and Maimonides; and note 6, for Strauss's remark on Avicenna quoted. For Strauss's connection to Cohen, see infra, chapter 4, the text between endnote markers 1 and 10, and notes 5 and 7. The differing views of A. Altmann and T. L. Pangle on Strauss and Cohen are quoted and contrasted infra in chapter 3, note 16. In spite of Strauss's youthful break with Cohen, it is by no means remote to suggest that Cohen continued to exercise a decided influence on Strauss's reading of Maimonides in his construction of a *primarily* political, nonmetaphysical Maimonides, whose theoretical bent was ultimately turned to establishing "the primacy of practical reason," albeit of a nonmoral type. This is, of course, the reading fully developed by Shlomo Pines in the revision of his views expressed in his essay, "The Limits of Knowledge According to al-Farabi, Ibn Bajja, and Maimonides," in *Studies in Medieval Jewish History and Literature,* edited by Isadore Twersky (Cambridge, Mass.: Harvard University Press, 1979), pp. 82–109. (This represents a dramatically changed point of view from the quite differently interpreted Maimonides in his Translator's Introduction to *The Guide of the Perplexed.*) It is, however, my judgment that this revised reading by Pines of Maimonides is not to be identified with Strauss's own deeper reading of Maimonides or with Strauss's own views. For a critique of Pines's revised "practical" reading of Maimonides, cf. R. Zev Friedman, "Maimonides and Kant on Metaphysics and Piety," *Review of Metaphysics* 45, no. 4 (June 1992): 773–801. But cf. *PG,* pp 120–22, and *PL,* pp. 109–10, for what I believe most concisely articulates Strauss's position on that issue.

4. "POR?," pp. 37–40; "POR?" (*IPP*), pp. 278–84.

5. *MMJA*, vol. 3, pt. 2, pp. xix, xxiii, xxv-xxviii, xxx, lvi-lvii, xc-xci, xcv.

6. *PG*, pp. 22–23; *PL*, pp. 14–15.

7. *PG*, p. 29; *PL*, p. 20.

8. In this context, one must recall that Strauss considered the multifarious attempted "harmonizations [*Vereinbarungen*] between the 'modern world picture' [*modernen Weltbild*] and the Bible, which ran wild especially in the 17th and 18th centuries, and which are still attempted often enough today," to be "vehicles of the Enlightenment and not dams against it." (*PG*, p. 22 and *PL*, p. 14)

9. *SCR*, pp. 134–36, 238–39, 262. Cf. also Spinoza's *Ethics*, the appendix to part 1, and the preface to part 4.

10. *SCR*, pp. 140–46, 205–6; *PSCR*, pp. 28–31.

11. *PG*, p. 20; *PL*, p. 12; idem, *PSCR*, p. 28.

12. Cf. *SCR*, pp. 37–39, 86, 107–9, 143–46, 204–14; *PG*, pp. 18–28, especially p. 23; *PL*, pp. 10–19, and especially p. 15; *PSCR*, pp. 28–31. Also consider "TS," pp. 322–24; *PIHPE*, pp. xxix-xxx.

13. The discovery at issue for Strauss would seem to have been made by Heidegger, whose radical historicism "made nature disappear completely, which however has the merit of consistency and compels one to reflect." ("CCM," p. 107) Or as he also puts this same point otherwise: "Certain it is that no one has ever questioned the premise of philosophy as radically as Heidegger." ("UP," p. 2) In other words, in attempting to complete the overcoming of nature—nature being for Strauss simply "the premise of philosophy" (*NRH*, p. 9)—one discerns that philosophy must have already undergone a gradual historicization. This commenced for Strauss with modern rationalism. (Cf., e.g., *SCR*, p. 181; *WIPP?*, pp. 58–60; "POR?," pp. 37–42; "POR?" [*IPP*], pp. 278–84.) Thus, one begins to wonder whether one has correctly comprehended what one has been trying to surpass historically. One next wonders whether a return to a previous teaching is possible once historicism itself is rendered problematic, for this possibility of return or "restoration" (e.g., of nature) is only excluded by historicism itself, which assumes "that every intended restoration necessarily leads to an essential modification of the restored teaching." (*WIPP?*, p. 60) Strauss credits his friend Jacob Klein with having first recognized, or first taught him, both Heidegger's greatness and his questionableness: "by uprooting and not simply rejecting the tradition of philosophy, he made it possible for the first time after many centuries—one hesitates to say how many—to see the roots of the tradition as they are and thus perhaps to know, what so many merely believe, that those roots are the only natural and healthy roots." ("UP," p. 2) Cf. also *WIPP?*, pp. 26–27, 56–77; *SPPP*, pp 29–30. Strauss also credits Klein with the following discovery: "Klein was the first to understand the possibility which Heidegger had opened without intending it: the possibility of a genuine return to classical philosophy, to the philosophy of Aristotle and of Plato, a return with open eyes and in full clarity about the infinite difficulties which it entails." Consider also the following

statement: "...a return to an earlier position is believed to be impossible. But one must realize that this belief is a dogmatic assumption whose hidden basis is the belief in progress or in the rationality of the historical process." (*CM*, pp. 10–11) Cf. also the review of Julius Ebbinghaus, p. 2453 (fully cited in chapter 1, note 6, supra); *PG*, pp. 13 note 1, 53 note 3, 116; *PL*, pp. 111–12 note 2, 119 note 71, 104; "FP," pp. 375–77, 393; "ONI," pp. 329–32; "OCPH," pp. 575–76, 578–79, 582–86; *NRH*, pp. 7, 61–62, 79–82; *PAW*, pp. 14–17, 155–56; *WIPP?*, pp. 73–77; *OT*, p. 27; *OT* (rev.), pp. 27–28; *CM*, pp. 10–12; "CCM," pp. 107, 109–10, 114; "GA," pp. 2–3; "UP," pp. 1–3.

14. This argument of Strauss's, directed both against the current dissolution of modern science and for the greater compatibility of the biblical teachings and classical-medieval philosophy and science, does not mean to suggest that Strauss was embracing or advocating unreason, i.e., what he aptly calls "fanatical obscurantism." (*NRH*, pp. 6–7) Rather, this argument is meant to suggest that classical notions of rationality might be worth reconsidering in the wake of "radical historicism," which has been successful in its destruction of the claim made by modern science to know or to be the final truth. According to Strauss, modern science is built on the ground of its denial of the possibility of miracles, as has previously been discussed: cf. supra, chapter 1, note 44, and near endnote marker 44 in the text. This is also not meant to suggest that miracles are simply knowable *as miracles* to classical philosophy and science. Classical philosophy and science certainly do not know miracles *as miracles*, but they may at least accept the events (which are referred to as "miracles" by the religious) as simple or brute facts. In other words, miracles are *possible* on the basis of classical philosophy and science insofar as highly inexplicable events are possible, as events whose causes do not seem to be knowable, e.g., because they occur only once. Modern science would deny both actuality and significance to such events. It would do so because it does not allow events to enter its purview which do not obey "natural law." Such events do not and cannot exist by the modern definition of "nature." Such events *seem* to occur for several reasons: either because the observer was naïve, lacking sanity, or unmethodical; or because the event did not occur as perceived by the observer since he was deluded by something like an optical illusion; or because the cause of the event is previously unknown but can be known. Once known it will be fully accounted for in the all-encompassing scheme of natural (mechanical) necessity, to whose "laws" it must conform. On the basis of classical philosophy and science, one may admit the facts (of an event) even when the causes remain inexplicable, since the highest or ultimate causes of things may not be fully knowable. In the "Maimonidean" view of Strauss, classical philosophy and science therefore provide a sounder basis for the reconciliation of science and religion. This issues in a certain circumscribed legitimacy for the religious thinker (or theologizing philosopher) calling such facts "miracles," in that his philosophic integrity and scientific honesty has not

been compromised by his denying something which he genuinely *knows* for the sake of his religious beliefs.

15. *WIPP?*, p. 38.

16. *PSCR*, p. 2; *NRH*, pp. 120–64; *WIPP?*, pp. 35–40.

17. *WIPP?*, pp. 60, 66–68, 76.

18. ". . .l'Être se crée lui-même au cours de l'Histoire." See *DLT*, p. 343; *OT* (rev.), p. 212. For the original statement of Kojève quoted by Strauss, see *OT*, p. 161; *OT* (rev.), p. 152.

19. See, e.g., *Guide*, Introduction to part I, 31, 34.

20. Strauss divides the *Guide* into two unequal halves, i.e., "views" and "actions," with regard to its essential argument. In this context, one should see properly Strauss's brilliant originality and interpretive virtuosity as they are revealed in his version of "the plan of the *Guide* as it [had] become clear to [him] in the course of about twenty-five years of frequently interrupted but never abandoned study." He brings to light hidden dimensions in the meaning of the *Guide* by highlighting the contrast between its apparent and its unapparent "formal" features, which deliberately conceal both significant regularities and significant irregularities. Further, his detections suggest hidden depths of its often obscure contents even in their very structure. Thus, what were supposed to have been "merely" formal matters (and hence were at most noted in passing by commentators) were for Strauss serious matters of the highest importance; he regarded them as keys to unlock gates, or as clues to resolve puzzles. In order to appreciate fully the genius of Strauss as an explicator of the text, it must be said that this dimension of the *Guide* was so unobvious as to have been mostly unnoticed by previous generations of often highly perspicacious readers through the last eight centuries. Certainly sharper readers were aware of a unit on prophecy (II, 32–48) and a unit on the reasons for the laws of the Torah (III, 25–50), as well as a unit on negative theology (I, 50–60), but no one ever divided the *Guide* into "sections" and "subsections" (or even alluded vaguely to the reasons for such divisions and arrangements), and no one ever made the number seven the concealed structural secret of the "plan"—although Strauss in his numerous works never actually divulged the secret of the number seven. This is probed by Marvin Fox, *Interpreting Maimonides*, pp. 54–55, who asks if it is appropriate to announce that there are secrets to be uncovered and then proceed to keep them as much covered as they were previously. A commentator as perspicacious as Alexander Altmann, who also deeply revered Strauss's work of the early and middle periods, was not as impressed with what he regarded as Strauss's interpretive excesses in the late works: "So much had he immersed himself in the attempt to disentangle Maimonides' presumed esotericism that he discovered strange keys and often abstruse answers. The comparison with Beethoven's last quartets may not be completely out of place. One finds a similar wilfulness of exegesis in his lecture *Jerusalem and Athens*. . ." ("Leo Strauss: 1899–1973," p. xxxvi) Certainly no other commentator preceding Strauss ever even suggested the *Guide* was

constructed on a secret architectonic "plan" of such precise, masterful, and subtle artistry. Cf. the still amazing first three pages of "HBSGP," pp. xi–xiii; idem, "On the Plan of *The Guide of the Perplexed*," pp. 775–77; and compare "MSPS," pp. 165–169. It is also worth considering whether Strauss's "plan" of the *Guide* may not be itself a sort of response to his friend Kojève's equally brilliant anatomy of the "structure" of Hegel's *Phenomenology of Spirit*. Cf. *Introduction to the Reading of Hegel*, pp. 261–87.

21.   *PAW*, pp. 90–92, 42–46; "HBSGP," pp. xviii–xx, xxiii–xxiv, li–lii, lv–lvi.

22.   We should not forget what Strauss refers to as "the virtue of not being trained in natural science" according to Maimonides. By avoiding the previously mentioned corruption, which is a possible result of an unguided training in natural science (which for him also encompassed metaphysics), it affords Maimonides two capital opportunities. On the one hand, for the sake of his "typical addressee," who remains loyally attached to the scriptural text, if also perplexed by it, he may boldly employ a fresh and radical approach to the difficult biblical terms, determined by his human science, in order to cure "the vicious habit" which is an "obstacle to speculation," namely, the habit of revering texts and hence remaining arrested in their literal meaning. On the other hand, he strives mightily to construct his approach so as to temper its radicalism until the properly guided "typical addressee" is prepared to receive its message moderately, precisely in order to preserve the hugely beneficial habits, moral and religious, which such pious habituation to authoritative texts also produces. As Strauss deciphers Maimonides' hidden purpose, "in the circumstances" of this habituation to texts, with its consequent tendency to literalism, "the natural substitute for natural science" seems to have been that "he simply tells the typical addressee what to believe regarding the meaning of the biblical terms" which, if taken literally, lead to "the gravest errors" as well as "the most tormenting perplexities." He moves deftly between obedience to authority and freedom from authority regarding natural science specifically and unaided human reason in general. As Strauss puts it in one passage, Maimonides "enters the ranks of the traditional Jewish [biblical] authorities," and this seems to suggest that Maimonides' purpose has nothing to do with natural science. Yet Strauss is also careful to emphasize that this fresh scriptural approach has a very specific and even radical aim: "Maimonides introduces Reason in the guise of Authority." Thus, it seems as if his fresh scriptural approach is determined in part by his human science, especially in order to give natural science a safe or traditional coloration as one among several true meanings which are hidden in many of the troublesome biblical terms, if not in Scripture as a whole. If eventually "the typical addressee" will be "compelled to be passionately concerned with demonstration," he is not brought to the point of deciding "whether or not he will turn altogether to the way of demonstration" until he has been thoroughly prepared by "the natural substitute for natural science"—a human science with its attendant method of scriptural interpretation which exegetically neutralizes

the threat represented especially by natural science. See "HBS*GP,*" pp. xx, xxiii–xxiv, xxxix, xiv, li; "OA," p. 100. Consider also the remark about "a certain very harsh lack of learning, which seems to be the greatest prudence" in book 10 of Plato's *Laws* (886b). In this context, Strauss would seem to be thinking of the contemporary world in subtly suggesting that to begin to philosophize with "divine science" or metaphysics or ontology or "talk about Being" is just as much of a threat to the well-being of the student, of society, and of philosophy, as what he says about beginning with natural science. For his Maimonidean model, see *Guide* I, 17, 33, for the light they shed on such statements as: "Know that to begin with this science is very harmful, I mean the divine science," and "Do not think that only the divine science should be withheld from the multitude. This holds good also for the greater part of natural science." Consider also *Guide* I, 31, for the rise of the habituation to texts, i.e., literalism, as the fourth and only new cause of philosophic discord. It also necessitates the development of new pedagogic strategies to surmount the new obstacle to philosophy.

23. If this seems to be overstating Strauss's case, one should recall what Strauss maintains can be "learned from Plato's natural philosophy," namely, "that the universe cannot be understood if it is not ruled by divine intelligence." (*NRH,* p. 170; cf. also *NRH,* pp. 120–24, 144–45, 149–52, and especially p. 150 note 24; "HBS*GP,*" pp. xix–xx, xxiii–xxiv; "ONI," p. 338; *Guide* I, 5, 17, 32–34, 62)

24. *CM,* pp. 41–43 as against *NRH,* pp. 174–75.

25. "HBS*GP,*" p. xlvi, with *Guide* I, 34.

26. Obviously the "greater evidence" is relative to modern criticism, for modern philosophy attacked both Maimonides' political and his theological teachings equally. And while "Maimonides does not know of theology as a discipline distinct from metaphysics" (*PAW,* p. 46), this theology or divine science does not make any sense if it does not presuppose natural science or physics. Thus, in this case of the contrast with his political or human science, what we conclude about his metaphysics embraces or is coordinated with his physics. (Cf. "HBS*GP,*" pp. xviii–xix, lv–lvi.) See also infra, chapter 6, note 85.

27. *NRH,* pp. 128–29; *OT,* pp. 213–16, 218–19; *OT* (rev.), pp. 199–202, 203–5.

28. These fundamental *natural* principles may be reduced to the single assumption that man is endowed with an unchangeable "nature," i.e., an essential form and a final end. This "nature" hence is definable only in terms of the virtue or perfection which manifests itself in the full actualization of his highest powers. Cf. *NRH,* pp. 145–46, 194–96.

29. See *NRH,* pp. 78–80, 90–91, 120–27, 150 note 24; *WIPP?,* pp. 38–40; *XSD,* pp. 147–50; *XS,* pp. 6–8, 22–26, 101–5, 123–24. For the most developed version of this teleotheology—that is also perhaps its least subtle presentation—together with a devastating critique in which traditional religion seems to be vindicated, cf. Cicero, *De natura deorum,* especially books 2 and 3. But cf. already Plato, *Timaeus* 40d–41a; *Laws* 886c–86d; *Phaedrus* 229c–30a.

30. *WIPP*, p. 38; *TOM*, pp. 207–23; *PG*, p. 29; *PL*, p. 20.

31. *Guide* I, 1, 18.

32. *NRH*, p. 170; *TOM*, p. 299: "It would seem that the notion of the beneficence of nature or of the primacy of the Good must be restored by being rethought through a return to the fundamental experiences from which it is derived." Cf. also *TOM*, pp. 222–23: "It is reasonable to assume that Machiavelli favored a cosmology which is in accordance with his analysis of morality. His analysis of morality will prove to be incompatible with a teleological cosmology."

33. *NRH*, pp. 7–8.

34. Ibid.

35. Maimonides in his day faced a medieval "crisis of the sciences." Strauss's muted call to reconstitute and to revive the fundamental principles of natural teleology in our day is faintly reminiscent of a similar call by Maimonides' contemporary Averroes in his Long (or Great) Commentary on Aristotle's *Metaphysics*, edited by M. Bouyges (Beirut: Imprimerie Catholique, 1948), III, 168. (Cited by S. Pines, Translator's Introduction, p. cx; cf. also pp. lxiii, cix–cxviii, for the medieval "crisis.") Strauss's "muted call" seems to have been heard, paradoxically enough, only by a Thomist—indeed by the leading Thomist of our century, Etienne Gilson. Although it is not clear that he heard this call from Strauss, he made with a full awareness of contemporary science the most powerful philosophic argument I know of in the last several decades in favor of restoring final causality and teleology in modern science. Among his last books is *From Aristotle to Darwin and Back Again: A Journey in Final Causality, Species, and Evolution* (Notre Dame, Ind.: Notre Dame University Press, 1984). (The original French version of *D'Aristote à Darwin et retour* was first published in 1971.) Though Strauss never commits himself unambiguously to a specific physics, he does occasionally identify himself with a specific metaphysics. For the best statement of this, consider the brief remarks he allows himself in the concluding paragraph of his debate with Alexandre Kojève. (This paragraph, until recently, only appeared in the French version, *De la tyrannie*, p. 343. See now *OT* [rev.], p. 212. Here I take the liberty, since it is such a crucial passage, of giving my own translation along with the French. The French "original" is itself a translation from the English, which has been lost.)

> La philosophie au sens strict et classique est la recherche de l'ordre éternel ou de la cause ou des causes éternelles de toutes choses. Je suppose alors qu'il y a un ordre éternel et inchangeable dans lequel l'Histoire prend place, et qui n'est, en aucune manière, affecté par l'Histoire. Cela laisse supposer, en d'autres termes, que tout "royaume de Liberté" n'est pas plus qu'une province qui dépend du "royaume de la Fatalité." Cela présuppose, dans les termes de Kojève, que "l'Être est essentiellement immuable en lui-même et éternellement identique à lui-même." Cette hypothèse n'est pas évidente par elle-même...

Philosophy, in the strict and classical sense, is the search for the eternal order, or for the eternal cause or causes of all things. I suppose, then, that there is an eternal and unchangeable order in which History takes place, and that it is not, in any way, affected by History. That allows one to suppose, in other words, that the entire "realm of Liberty" is no more than a province which depends upon the "realm of Fatality." This presupposes, in the words of Kojève, that "Being is essentially immutable in itself and eternally identical with itself." This hypothesis is not evident by itself . . .

For Kojève's remarks quoted by Strauss, cf. *OT*, pp. 160–61; *OT* (rev.), p. 151. See also: Kurt Riezler, *Physics and Reality: Lectures of Aristotle on Modern Physics* (New Haven: Yale University Press, 1940); and *WIPP?*, pp. 255–60, 284–86.

36. *NRH*, pp. 169–77; "CCM," pp. 107–8, 111–14. Consider also Hilail Gildin, Introduction to *IPP*, pp. xiii–xvii, and Victor Gourevitch, "Philosophy and Politics," pp. 289–93.

37. *WIPP?*, pp. 38–39.

38. *Guide* II, 24.

39. "HBSGP," pp. lv–lvi. As far as I know, Strauss was the first reader to notice that Maimonides uses this pregnant phrase in the *Guide* (II, 24). Strauss takes this as a vital clue given to us by Maimonides concerning his highest purposes. For an exploration of this crucial theme, a treatment that seems to have been inspired by Strauss's penultimate remark in "HBSGP," cf. Tzvi Langermann, "The 'True Perplexity': *The Guide of the Perplexed*, Part II, Chapter 24," in *Perspectives on Maimonides*, edited by Joel L. Kraemer (Oxford: Oxford University Press, 1991), pp. 159–74.

40. For all of the tentativeness with which I have been presenting Strauss's possible "cosmology," in my view it is only this approach that makes any sense of Strauss's position. I would argue further that, if pursued in greater detail, this Straussian cosmology could be definitively demonstrated from Strauss's writings. Though philosophy as Strauss so wisely rediscovered must be at bottom "skeptical," this does not mean that philosophers may not or should not hold opinions which they view as better grounded than alternate opinions; rather, it means they must always, "by profession," as it were, remember the fundamental ground on which their skepticism rests—the difference between genuine knowledge and uncertain opinion, however well-grounded. In spite of this, I am not claiming that for Strauss man or nature can necessarily be *fully* comprehended. I am only suggesting that for Strauss some of the *most* fundamental principles for understanding man and nature *can* be comprehended, so far as they make philosophy itself possible. This accounts for the need for such great tentativeness in my presentation, in order not to overstate the comprehensiveness of my claims about Strauss's position as an "absolute" one. As a result of this, I would also dispute from the opposite side Raymond Aron's counterargument to Strauss's critique of Max Weber. Weber does invite Strauss's

critique by his refusal to accept even a fundamental principle of the rule of rationality as natural, even in terms of possibly knowing it, while Strauss seems to accept the probability that the natural order is somehow rational, based on certain evidence. In this context, Aron drives Strauss's premises *too* far in order to exonerate Weber of the charge of nihilism. He puts his conclusion in the following pithy terms: "Strauss's philosophy could be reduced to a suprahistorical dogmatism, just as he reduces Weber's relativism to nihilism." Thus, according to Aron, Strauss's argument is merely a type of *reductio ad extremum*. See "Max Weber and Modern Social Science," chapter 12 in *History, Truth, and Liberty: Selected Writings of Raymond Aron*, edited by Franciszek Draus (Chicago: University of Chicago Press, 1985), pp. 355–73, and especially p. 354. For Strauss's original argument, cf. *NRH*, pp. 36–74, and especially pp. 42–50. For powerful textual evidence disproving the correctness of Aron's counterargument against Strauss's critique of Weber, cf. "Rel," pp. 141–45. Consider also the remark by Fred Dallmayr, *Polis and Praxis* (Cambridge, Mass.: MIT Press, 1984), p. 45: "Curiously, while insisting strongly on the separation of philosophy and theology, Strauss—in pleading the case of classical thought—also vindicates what Heidegger has described as the legacy of 'ontotheology.'"

41.   "UP," p. 2; "CCM," pp. 107–8.

42.   *NRH*, p. 123; *WIPP?*, p. 39. Cf. Victor Gourevitch, "Philosophy and Politics," pp. 281–88, 299–307.

43.   Even in Socrates' turn to "the human things," Strauss does not detect any diminution or neglect of "the divine or natural things"; he simply was the first who did not reduce the former to the latter, but studied the human things as a distinctive kind of being. In this light, Strauss does not overstate the case for Socrates' human orientation: there is in him a continuity of what philosophy always meant for his predecessors. "Socrates' study of the human things was then based on the comprehensive study of 'all things.' Like every other philosopher, he identified wisdom, or the goal of philosophy, with the science of all the beings: he never ceased considering 'what each of the beings is.'" Socrates only "deviated from his predecessors by identifying the science of the whole, or of everything that is, with the understanding of 'what each of the beings is.'" *NRH*, p. 122. Cf. also *XS*, pp. 6–8, 101–5, 116–24. Compare also with the pointed and significant last sentence of *DLT*, p. 344; *OT* (rev.), p. 212.

44.   What is Strauss's basic evidence for this, i.e., that man forms one part of the whole, which in itself seems to form a completed whole? Strauss seems to point to the civilized political life of men in ancient cities. (With a greater stress on the moral life, this is also known from the emergence of integral religious communities rooted in divine law.) As Strauss would seem to argue, the study of human beings teaches one thing beyond doubt: though the forms and conditions of "civilization" may vary greatly, it is in this direction, of cities and civilizations and laws, that human societies always seem by necessity to develop. Such a unity appears to represent the fully developed natural form of human life, in the sense that it manifests the most complete and highest possibilities of human actualization. (Both family and tribal life seem to be mere

way stations on the road either to the ancient city or to the divine law.) And any such developed human entity will form a unity which, on reflection, is comparable by a legitimate (though limited) analogy with a cosmos. There would then seem to be for Strauss a distinctive perfection which is clearly evident in the completed whole which is man. On the other side, a human "situation" or "condition" would seem by definition *not* to constitute a whole: can one speak about these things as one would about a "soul"? Strauss seems to use terms like these interchangeably in the historicist and "existentialist" context of contemporary thought, because ultimately they are talking about the same primary human "facts," which are endowed with different "values": thus is he able to use a phrase like "the human soul, or. . . the human condition." See "IHE" (*RCPR*), p. 35; and cf. also pp. 37, 39, 45. For man as a part of the whole, see also "SSH" (*RCPR*), pp. 7–8; "POR?" (*IPP*), pp. 297–98.

45. *WIPP?*, p. 39.

46. "CPP," pp. 92–93, 99–100, 103; "Rel," pp. 136–37; *TOM*, pp. 294–99. Cf. also *SA*, 6–7, 46–47, 52–53, 140, 158–59, 168, 189–93, 313. For a "Maimonidean" like Strauss, what the precise element of "divine ordination" in such a notion is must remain unsettled until the issue of "creation versus eternity," and hence of divine will, is resolved. For some discussion of a related matter, see supra, chapter 1, note 127.

47. *SCR*, pp. 155–56; *PG*, pp. 90, 99, 106; *PL*, pp. 83–84, 92, 96–97; *PAW*, pp. 9–10; *Guide* Introduction to part I, with II, 32.

48. *PG*, pp. 65–66, and *PL*, pp. 56–57, for a contrast between Maimonides' and Gersonides' views of divine providence in Platonic versus Stoic terms respectively. See also "OVL," pp. 97–101.

49. *PG*, pp. 117–22; *PL*, pp. 105–10.

50. *PG*, pp. 77–79; *PL*, pp. 69–71.

51. *SCR*, pp. 154–60; *PG*, pp. 44–67, 87–122, but especially 59–60, 64–65; *PL*, pp. 35–58, 79–110, but especially 50–52, 55–56; *NRH*, pp. 163–64.

52. "WILE?" (*LAM*), p. 8:

> As it seems to me, the cause of this situation [i.e., our need to judge, yet our lack of standards by which to judge, the great books in our Western tradition] is that we have lost all simply authoritative traditions in which we could trust, the *nomos* which gave us authoritative guidance, because our immediate teachers and our teachers' teachers believed in the possibility of a simply rational society. Each of us here is compelled to find his bearings by his own powers, however defective they may be.

A loss of wholehearted faith in the "simply rational society" as something possible to actualize by human effort alone cannot be partly remedied or rectified by a romanticism which similarly rejects all traditional religious authority as "irrational" or as historically surpassed:

Bowing to the principle of authority is sterile if it is not followed by surrender to authority itself, i.e., to this or that authority. If this step is not taken one will remain enmeshed in the religious longing or the religiosity so characteristic of our centuries, and will not be liberated by religion proper. (*TOM*, pp. 165–66)

As for whether this democratic and egalitarian Enlightenment is Spinoza's final position, Strauss himself obliquely raises doubts about this in his presentation of Cohen's critique of Spinoza. He shows how Cohen recognized that Spinoza

is concerned above everything else with what he calls philosophy, which he assumes to be wholly inaccessible directly or indirectly to the large majority of men. He has no compunction whatever about affirming the radical and unmodifiable inequality of men without ever wondering "how can nature, how can God answer for this difference among men?" Hence his sympathy for democracy is suspect. . . .There is no place in his thought for the enlightenment of the people. (*PSCR*, pp. 18–19)

53. *PG*, pp. 21–22; *PL*, pp. 13–14; *NRH*, pp. 175–76; *PSCR*, p. 30.
54. *PSCR*, p. 7.
55. "CA"; *SCR*, pp. 207–9; *PSCR*, pp. 18–28.
56. *PSCR*, p. 28.
57. *PG*, pp. 23, 26–27 with 26 note 1; *PL*, pp. 15, 17–19, 113–14 note 12; "AE" (*IPP*), pp. 148–49. Even if "intellectual probity" is not the same thing as "the love of truth," the former is surely one element of the latter, so that even if the genuine "love of truth" is recovered, this does not simply dissolve the difficulties raised by "intellectual probity" while operating in man by itself alone.
58. *SCR*, pp. 147–92, 198–200, 206–7.
59. "POR?," p. 33; "WWRJ," typescript, pp. 8, 11; "POR?" (*IPP*), pp. 272–73; *PSCR*, pp. 7, 15; *JA*, pp. 5–7; "JA" (*SPPP*), pp. 149–51, for various remarks and allusions made by Strauss to his own personal struggle with being a modern Jew. Strauss himself was raised in an Orthodox Jewish home, was "converted to Zionism" at seventeen, and remained passionately committed to Jews and Judaism during his entire life. He counted himself among those "who cannot be orthodox," but he also regarded it as an exigent task to reject "all attempts to interpret the Jewish past in terms of a culture."

In other words, for me the question is: truly either the Torah as understood by our tradition or, say, unbelief. And I think that is infinitely more important than every cultural interpretation which is based on a tacit unbelief and cannot be a substitute for the belief it has given up.

He immediately adds this as a clarification

When I say "the Jewish faith as our ancestors held it," I do not mean that every particular belief, even if entertained by the majority of Jews or by the large majority of Jews for centuries, must necessarily be binding.

Thus, what he means to express by the term "Jewish tradition" would seem to be in fact something very inclusive. Cf. "WWRJ," typescript, p. 9, and Question and Answer section, p. 11.

60. This does not mean at all to suggest that Spinoza disregarded the continuing *political* need of divine revelation for the multitude in order to control their passions and train them morally. The argument with Maimonides concerns whether such a "Machiavellian" use of divine revelation can even be efficacious if it does not ultimately take account of the elite's similar need for divine revelation in moral and in other terms, and if it does not recognize every society's need to be guided by theologically given truths.

61. *Theological-Political Treatise*, chapter 7.

62. Ibid., chapter 1.

63. *SCR*, p. 175.

64. Ibid., pp. 161–63, 185–91; *PG*, pp. 54–55; *PL*, pp. 45–47.

65. *SCR*, pp. 133, 138–56, 163, 210–14.

66. *PSCR*, pp. 15–16.

67. See the first chapter in *PG* (pp. 30–67) or *PL* (pp. 21–58), "The Quarrel Between the Ancients and the Moderns in the Philosophy of Judaism," which comprises Strauss's critique of Julius Guttmann. See Guttmann's reply to Strauss's critique in "Philosophie der Religion oder Philosophie des Gesetzes?" in the *Proceedings of the Israel Academy of Sciences and Humanities* 5 (1976): 146–73; with a Hebrew translation, pp. 188–207. The Strauss-Guttmann "controversy" focuses ostensibly on the proper interpretation of medieval Jewish philosophy, and especially on the correct explication of Maimonides' *Guide*. For two examinations of the scholarly differences and the philosophical issues involved in their "controversy," see: Moshe Schwarcz, "The Enlightenment and Its Implications for Jewish Philosophy in the Modern Period (in Light of the Controversy between Leo Strauss and Julius Guttmann)" (in Hebrew), *Daat* 1, no. 1 (Winter 1978): 7–16; and Eliezer Schweid, "Religion and Philosophy: The Scholarly-Theological Debate between Julius Guttmann and Leo Strauss," *Maimonidean Studies* 1 (1990): 163–95. Strauss, of course, also wrote an incisive critique of Isaac Husik (cf. *PIHPE*, pp. xxi–xxxii), who wrote the other leading history of Jewish philosophy in our century, and to whom Strauss was much closer in his approach to the reading of Maimonides. Strauss was not as much occupied with Husik's specific interpretation of Maimonides, although he is also critical of its tacit premise (pp. xxviii–xxix). He was concerned with extracting the chief difficulties which beset Husik's philosophic position in general, especially as it was directly applied to his Jewish scholarly researches. Strauss reduces these difficulties to the three "problems of objectivity, of historical evolution, and of the idea of a Jewish philosophy." In this context, it would be

more accurate to say that, surprisingly, what Strauss seems to carry through is a kind of "vindication" of Hermann Cohen, whom Husik sharply criticized, rather than Maimonides (pp. xxvi, xxx–xxxii). Indeed, Strauss discovers less ability to escape a *modern* Jewish philosophy than Husik would like to acknowledge, however much he denied both its actuality and its possibility. Strauss also considers Husik to have been ultimately forced to as "arbitrary" or "subjective" a principle in delimiting the field of who is a "Jewish philosopher" and what is "Jewish philosophy" as was his opponent Cohen (p. xxviii).

68. *PG*, p. 29; *PL*, p. 20.

69. *PG*, pp. 87–89; *PL*, pp. 81–82. Cf. also *PG*, pp. 82–83 and *PL*, pp. 74–75 for the difference between Maimonides and Gersonides concerning the exoteric and the esoteric.

70. Cf. the English translation, *Philosophies of Judaism*, translated by D. W. Silverman (Philadelphia: JPS, 1964), pp. 169–82, with p. 434 note 125. Unfortunately, it is difficult to rely on the English translation of Guttmann's book in the reading of Strauss's critique, a critique which pays careful attention to the language. One is well-advised to check the German original at all points.

71. *PG*, pp. 42–43, 61–67; *PL*, pp. 34–35, 52–58.

72. *PG*, pp. 33, 38–39; *PL*, pp. 26, 30–31.

73. *PG*, pp. 30–48, 57–67; *PL*, pp. 23–33, 48–58; *MMJA*, vol. 3, pt. 2, pp. lx–lxx.

74. *PG*, pp. 117–22, 62–67; *PL*, pp. 105–10, 53–58; "QR," pp. 1–6; "SR," pp. 4–7; "OA," pp. 95–100.

75. In this concluding paragraph, the term "Platonic" is used to designate a tradition of philosophic thought in the same sense that Strauss uses it in the title of *Studies in Platonic Political Philosophy*, a book which contains studies of thinkers from Thucydides to Hermann Cohen. An overview of Strauss's understanding of the term "Platonic" is discussed in chapter 1, supra; these issues are addressed in somewhat greater detail in chapter 6, infra. The question of whether the need for revelation is theoretical or practical, rational or political, cannot yet be answered in terms of such a simple disjunction; for Strauss, the two are (as in the nature of philosophy itself) inextricably conjoined. But *how* and *why* precisely that inextricable conjunction is so, and in what cases one might be subordinate to the other, are matters not dealt with in the present context. Cf. chapter 6, infra, toward the end. As for whether Strauss's reading of Maimonides is sustainable in these terms, cf. chapter 7, infra.

76. As will emerge with greater clarity in subsequent chapters, especially chapters 5 and 6, Strauss seems to present the *Guide* on one level as Maimonides' "Decisive Treatise," thus calling to mind Averroes' similar effort "to determine the nature of the connection between philosophy and religion." Strauss does indeed maintain that both Maimonides and Averroes agree about, among other significant matters, *the* decisive issue regarding philosophy and the divine law: the primacy of the divine law and its authority in rightfully commanding *all*

men, even philosophers. Moreover, the law is considered to be divine by both of them in great measure because it commands philosophizing for those naturally fitted to it, and hence because it provides for philosophy's freedom in the limit of the law (*PG*, pp. 77, 79; *PL*, pp. 69, 71). But, according to Strauss, they disagree about an equally fundamental issue, namely, about whether the prophet brings a suprarational *truth* which is unattainable by unaided human reason, yet which man is vitally in need of, as is Maimonides' opinion alone. In other words, they differ about whether the human intellect is "sufficient" in the attainment of the highest truths about "God and the angels," Averroes alone arguing in favor of man's "sufficiency." This difference revolves specifically around how centrally they locate the teaching about *creatio ex nihilo* for dogmatically maintaining the divine law's authority. Maimonides views it as absolutely crucial (*PG*, pp. 78–79; *PL*, pp. 70–71; cf. also *MMJA*, vol. 3, pt. 2, pp. lx–lxviii). But if there is such a deep difference between Maimonides and the "true" Averroes concerning man's need for the prophet, and if Strauss himself knowingly approaches a "Maimonidean" standpoint concerning "the connection between religion and philosophy" (cf. especially "POR?" and "MITP"), then it would seem to be doubly difficult to maintain that his approach amounts to "Averroism," whether this be the "true" or the "Latin" version. Strauss speaks about Machiavelli as one who proceeded "in the ways of Averroism," which I believe refers to its "Latin" version (cf. *TOM*, pp. 175, 202–3, 207–8, 333–34 note 68); he significantly defines such Averroism as comprising "those medieval Aristotelians who as philosophers refused to make any concessions to revealed religion." (*SPPP*, pp. 226; idem, *HPP*, p. 289) While both friend (implicitly) and foe (explicitly) have tried to characterize Strauss's (and "Straussian") religious and political thought as what might be called a kind of revived philosophic Averroism, I believe both attempts to be in error for reasons which should emerge in the course of our work. For the friend, see T. L. Pangle in his introduction to *SPPP*, especially pp. 20–24, with the subsequent debate between Pangle and Harry V. Jaffa, *Claremont Review of Books* 3, no. 3 (Fall 1984): 14–21, and 4, no. 1 (Spring 1985): 18–24; compare with the attempt at a mediation by David Lowenthal in *Interpretation* 13, no. 3 (1985): 297–320. For the "Thomist" foe, see F. D. Wilhelmsen, *Christianity and Political Philosophy*, chapter 8 (Athens: University of Georgia Press, 1978), pp. 209–25, 238–39. For two reviews of Christian Straussians in critical response to Wilhelmsen, see E. Fortin, *Review of Politics* 41 (1979): 578–82, and J. J. Carpino, *Interpretation* 9 (1979–80): 204–22. (Contrast with this entire debate a Catholic attitude to Strauss quite different from that of Wilhelmsen in James V. Schall, "Reason, Revelation, and Politics: Catholic Reflexions on Strauss," *Gregorianum* 62 [1981]: 349–65, 467–97. Cf. p. 351: "This is why not a few, including myself, have wondered whether Strauss's main service to our culture is not, in fact, to Christian thought itself, rather than to Judaism or classical political philosophy, whatever difficulties, and there are several, there might be with his overall position." But cf. also his critique of Strauss's Thomas in "A Latitude for

Statesmanship? Strauss on St. Thomas," *Review of Politics* 53, no. 1 [Winter 1991]: 126–45.) The "Thomist" attack has been continued by R. Sokolowski with a sophisticated critique in his *The God of Faith and Reason*, appendix to chapter 11 (Notre Dame, Ind.: University of Notre Dame Press, 1982), pp. 157–66. For Strauss's critique of both Thomas's and Averroes's theological-political teachings in terms which, I believe, tacitly vindicate the "Maimonidean" approach, see *NRH*, pp. 156–64; cf. also "*FP*," pp. 374–75 (idem, *PAW*, pp. 14–15). But cf. also, e.g., *WIPP?*, pp. 229–30, and *OT*, pp. 196–97, *OT* (rev.), pp. 183–84, for Strauss's appearing to identify his own teaching with Averroism. However, he himself refers to it in such obviously qualifying quotes, since the term is used most often erroneously to refer to "*Latin* Averroism." He speaks of scholars using such a designation "with pardonable ignorance" to refer to an ancient teaching first articulated by Plato with moderation and prudence, but radicalized, and hence transformed, by Latin Averroism, which for the sake of its philosophic freedom and rational pride vis-à-vis irrational dogmas paid too little attention to the human conditions from which the need for moderation and prudence arises, and in which the ancient-medieval "Platonic" teaching is firmly and self-consciously rooted. For a different view of Strauss, a blunter view of Plato presented fully as a "modern," and a critique of "Straussian politics," see Stanley Rosen, "Hermeneutics as Politics," in *Hermeneutics as Politics* (New York: Oxford University Press, 1987), especially p. 140. He argues that Strauss "did not fully appreciate the deep connection between theory and practice, or what one could call the application of Churchillian daring to the world-historical stage," or because "contrary to Xenophon, courage is in fact a Socratic virtue." In spite of these criticisms, see also Stanley Rosen, "Is Metaphysics Possible?" *Review of Metaphysics* 45 (1991): 235–57. I would suggest that this is the first serious attempt to think through consistently the metaphysical implications of what can only be called a Straussian position in philosophy. For one of the first attempts by a contemporary theologian to pay critical attention to the implications of Strauss's philosophic thought for theology, and especially for the school of thought rooted in Lonergan, see Robert M. Doran, *Theology and the Dialectics of History* (Toronto: University of Toronto Press, 1990), pp. 26–30, 459–67, 489–99.

    77. *SCR*, pp. 147–56, 161–63; *PG*, pp. 48, 58–60, 62–67, 108–22; *PL*, pp. 40–41, 50–51, 53–58, 98–110; "QR"; "SR"; "OVL," pp. 97–104; "OA," pp. 95–109; "FP"; "GA," pp. 3–4.

    78. *NRH*, p. 159; "POR?," pp. 38–40; "POR?" (*IPP*), pp. 281–84.

CHAPTER THREE

    1. See chapter 1, supra, between endnote markers 3 and 5.

    2. The original suggestion that Strauss's view of Maimonides passed through *three* distinguishable stages was made to me by the late Alexander Altmann in oral communication. However, as our discussion on this point did not proceed any further than fixing the number of stages at three, I cannot say

whether my scheme would conform with the one which he had in mind. Still, I am pleased to be able to acknowledge my debt to Professor Altmann for his fruitful suggestion, whether or not he would approve of how I have been moved to employ it in my own research.

3. Each of these three works represents one stage, but each work does not exhaust the contents of the stage it represents. Hence, as I would like to stress, other works will be used to elucidate and to interpret each stage in Strauss's developing views on Maimonides.

4. See "Correspondence Concerning *Wahrheit und Methode*," *Independent Journal of Philosophy* 2 (1978): 5–12, and especially 5–6, 9, 11.

5. See chapter 1, note 5, supra.

6. Review of "Das Heilige," *Der Jude* 7 (1923): 240–42.

7. *PSCR*, p. 3.

8. As Strauss observed, obviously Otto's concern with the radical transcendence of God in biblical religion, reflected by his using the Hebrew-derived term "the holy," cannot be entirely separated from epistemological issues related to post-Kantian philosophy, as these were raised and elaborated by Schleiermacher. Hence, the legitimation for our emphasizing Otto's connection to Kant by using the Kantian-derived term "the noumenal."

9. "Das Heilige," p. 242.

10. Ibid., p. 241.

11. Ibid., p. 242.

12. Ibid. The emphasis is added.

13. *PSCR*, p. 15. For retrospective testimony (1970) about the basic orientation of Strauss's thought in the 1920s, Jacob Klein, his closest lifelong friend (whom he met in 1920 at the University of Marburg), characterizes Strauss in the following terms: "His primary interests were two questions: one, the question of God; and two, the question of politics." ("GA," p. 1) Strauss, speaking of himself in 1922, comments: "My predominant interest was in theology." (Ibid., p. 2) Strauss in 1965 also speaks of his beginnings along similar lines: "My study of Hobbes began in the context of an investigation of the origins of biblical criticism in the 17th century, namely of Spinoza's *Theological-Political Treatise*. The reawakening of theology, which for me is marked by the names of Karl Barth and Franz Rosenzweig, appeared to make it necessary to investigate how far the critique of orthodox theology—Jewish and Christian—deserved to be victorious. Since then the theological-political problem has remained *the* theme of my investigations." ("PHPW," p. 1) By way of contrast with the approach to Strauss's Jewish thought articulated by the present writer, in 1974 Klein wrote the following words which in his view summarized the course of Strauss's Jewish spiritual life:

> There is something else that cannot remain unmentioned now as it did not remain unmentioned in the speeches delivered at Strauss's funeral. It is his profound awareness of being a Jew. Just as his thinking on man as a "political animal" had its roots in what the ancient Greeks

thought, had its focus in Athens, his preoccupation with the question of divinity and with the peculiar way of Jewish life and Jewish history tied his thinking and feeling to Jerusalem. He distinguished sharply— and did so always—the *political* programs and actions of the Jews from their *religious* background. There was a time when Leo Strauss was an orthodox Jew, while yet pursuing his political goals explicitly and determinedly in an unreligious way. He later changed his religious orientation radically, tying the question of god and of gods to his political reasoning, without letting his own life be dependent on any divinity or on any religious rites. But his being in a definite sense a Jew was all-important to him. Nothing could change that.

See Jacob Klein, "Leo Strauss, 1899–1973," *The College* 25, no. 4 (January 1974): 2. In "A Giving of Accounts," Strauss spoke, among other things, about the differences between himself and Klein. In this talk, Strauss said clearly that they "differ regarding the status of morality." (Pp. 4–5) However, from the story Strauss tells of their friendship (pp. 2–4), in spite of its being a lifelong and fruitful intellectual exchange, one distinct and overriding impression is conveyed: their most crucial difference (beside "the status of morality") almost from the moment they met was that Klein never understood Strauss on things Jewish, both political and religious. This matter is addressed from a different point of view again by Werner Dannhauser in "Leo Strauss as Citizen and Jew," *Interpretation* 17, no. 3 (Spring 1990): 433–47.

14. *PSCR*, p. 15. The other great fascination of Strauss's youth was with Nietzsche, who "dominated and bewitched" him in the 1920s. See "CLS," pp. 182–85. For very different attempts to read Strauss *primarily* as a disaffected or modified Nietzschean, consider essays by: A. Momigliano, "Ermeneutica e Pensiero Politico Classico in Leo Strauss" (1967); T. L. Pangle, Introduction to *SPPP* (1983); Rémi Brague, "Leo Strauss et Maïmonide" (1986); Shadia Drury, *The Political Ideas of Leo Strauss* (1988). In my opinion, all of these efforts have been unsuccessful. This is not to fail to note the tremendous influence that Nietzsche exercised on Strauss at a certain formative stage in his philosophical development. But the fundamental premises of Strauss and Nietzsche (on both the possibility of philosophy and on its possible rootedness in truth) are at odds with one another. This can only be gotten around by claiming that it is possible to "discover" a Nietzsche supposedly "concealed" in the teaching of Strauss. In the case of those hostile to Strauss, their motives for doing so cannot help but be reminiscent of Jacobi: he "discovers" the ill-famed Spinoza secretly concealed in Lessing, in order to discredit the Enlightenment and rationality by discrediting its greatest representative. See also supra, Introduction, note 1, chapter 1, note 6; infra, chapter 4, note 13.

15. "Cohens Analyse der Bibel-Wissenschaft Spinozas," *Der Jude* 8 (1924): 295–314. It is the conclusions reached by this study that received summarization, clarification, and further development in the central portion of *PSCR*, pp. 15–28. As might be expected, *PSCR* also legitimately qualifies "CA" on several points in the act of interpreting his earlier ideas in light of his later ideas.

16. Cf. one of Strauss's last works, IERR (1972), in which he still praises Cohen as

> a faithful warner and comforter to many Jews. At the very least he showed them most effectively how Jews can live with dignity as Jews in a non-Jewish, even hostile, world while participating in that world. ...It is a blessing for us that Hermann Cohen lived and wrote. (P. xxxviii; idem, "IERR" (SPPP), pp. 246–47)

According to Alexander Altmann, Strauss was closely bound to Cohen from beginning to end. Cohen started him thinking about Spinoza and the Enlightenment, about the Platonic character of Maimonides' thought, and about the dilemmas of modern Judaism. By Strauss's consenting to write the introductory essay to the translation of Cohen's *Religion of Reason*, as Altmann puts it, "the circle of his life's course was complete." See the full quotation from his "Leo Strauss: 1899–1973," *PAAJR* 41–42 (1973–74): xxxiii–xxxvi, and especially p. xxxvi, fully quoted in chapter 1, note 1, supra; and see also chapter 2, note 3, supra. The last book of his essays, which Strauss arranged to publish "in their present order" prior to his death (Joseph Cropsey), also finished with his introductory essay to Cohen's *Religion of Reason*. Alan Udoff quotes a letter Strauss wrote in 1931 in which, speaking of himself, he declares "as emphatically as possible": "I am in no way a Cohenian." Notwithstanding this unambiguous declaration, he proceeds to follow this with a revealing statement:

> Cohen is much too original and deep a thinker that the doubtfulness of his teaching can release us thereby from listening, in any event, to that which he says.

Cf. Udoff's entire essay for several suggestive remarks about Strauss's complex but positive relation to Cohen's thought: "On Leo Strauss: An Introductory Account," in *Leo Strauss's Thought*, pp. 1–29, and especially pp. 22–23, note 3. By way of contrast, Thomas L. Pangle in his introduction to *SPPP* reads the relation of Strauss to Cohen in quite a different, and mostly negative, light:

> ...there is a discernible kinship between the hopes of modern philosophy and the hopes for the Messiah. In the hands of the penetrating and truly noble Kantian Jew Hermann Cohen, that kinship became the leitmotif of a new, supposedly superior or "historically progressive" grand synthesis of Jerusalem and Athens. Strauss closes his last work by returning again to Cohen and demonstrating, with the greatest respect but with relentless clarity, what a delusion was thus constructed by the man who had been in a sense the hero of Strauss's youth. (P. 26)

17. "Cohen attracted me because he was a passionate philosopher and a Jew passionately devoted to Judaism." ("GA," p. 2) Cf. also "IERR" (SPPP), p. 233;

"JA" (*SPPP*), pp. 167–68; *WIPP?*, p. 242. But Strauss also calls himself even in 1922 "a doubting and dubious adherent of the Marburg school of neo-Kantianism." Cf. "PARSPP" (*SPPP*), p. 31, and "GA," pp. 2–3.

18. Cf. chapter 2, note 59, supra.

19. "In almost every sense," i.e., other than Spinoza's attitude to things Jewish. Strauss recognizes the unconditional superiority of Cohen as the nobler soul and the better Jew. Strauss certainly also praises Cohen not only for his freedom from the unqualified veneration of Spinoza common in modern Jewish theology and among modern Jews in general, but also for his willingness to judge Spinoza specifically guilty of betraying Judaism and the Jewish spirit by not even attempting to do full justice to the highest truths it teaches, though he could have been its great modern transformer. As Strauss later concisely comments on, and summarizes, his earlier work: "Far from rescinding the excommunication, Cohen confirmed it acting as a judge in the highest court of appeal." Cf. *PSCR*, p. 19, with pp. 24–25. Strauss, however, cannot assent to Cohen's despair of Spinoza in characterizing his betrayal as "surpassing human comprehension"— it is quite comprehensible in light of the Machiavellian political considerations which permitted him to tactically attack things Jewish if it helped him strategically win his battle to separate Christian religious faith and European political life. In Rosenzweig's spirit, Strauss also does not refrain from criticizing Cohen for his lack of a proper appreciation of Spinoza for originating the modern Jewish tradition which Cohen himself cherished and in which his Jewish philosophy was ultimately rooted. Strauss formulates the correct or "radical" question which Cohen should have been trying to answer: "Which Jewish motives are alive in Spinoza's Bible science?" ("CA," p. 314) Strauss subsequently summarized his own final appreciation of Spinoza's "Jewish motives" in the following words:

> However bad a Jew he may have been in all other respects, he thought
> of the liberation of the Jews in the only way in which he could think
> of it, given his philosophy.

Strauss refers directly to the two purely political "solutions to the Jewish problem" which Spinoza first suggested, namely, liberal "assimilationism" and Zionism. Both suggestions, according to Strauss's analysis, are in full conformity with "Spinoza's egoistic morality." Cf. *PSCR*, pp. 20–21, 26–27. The youthful Strauss himself, following Cohen, tried to make a final Jewish "break" with Spinoza, as is signalized by "Das Testament Spinozas" (1931), but it was a "break" which in a certain sense he reversed subsequently because of a greater appreciation for Spinoza's *conscious* contribution to changing modern Jewish life. However, in this brief essay he concludes that Jews must surrender all special claims to Spinoza as representing primarily or even essentially a unique event in the history of Judaism. To him, Spinoza belongs solely to Europe, and indeed he is one of the first greats in "the community of the 'good Europeans,'" borrowing Nietzsche's self-designation. (Cf. the Preface to *Beyond Good and Evil*, translated by Walter Kaufmann [New York: Randon House, 1966], p. 4.) Even Spinoza's suggestions for Jews and Judaism are not proffered in a Jewish spirit but as the work of a social scientist following conclusions dictated by his philosophy:

> . . . Spinoza did not at all wish or call for the restoration of the Jewish state. . . but only discussed it: he leaves it in a superior way from the heights of his philosophical neutrality, as it were, for the Jews to free themselves from their religion and to thus obtain for themselves the possibility of again establishing their state. . . . [H]e did not state this view as a Jew, but as a neutral, and he does not once state it, but only just drops it.

Strauss attempts to move beyond either "condemning" or "canonizing" Spinoza, and leaves the matter at valuing him for his fierce "independence," i.e., both of mind and of will. This he somewhat paradoxically equates with "the inscription on his signet-ring (*caute*)," by which he seems to mean that Spinoza did not always feel compelled to give full expression to the views which he took with the utmost seriousness, but such "caution" did not hinder his complete freedom of thought. In other words, it seems as if Strauss did not admire Spinoza for his moral character as a philosopher who was also a Jew and who could have been loyal to both, but he did continue to regard him as an exemplification of the intellectual freedom which is one fundamental characteristic of the philosopher. (Strauss renders a similar but perhaps even harsher judgment on F. H. Jacobi in his controversy with Moses Mendelssohn. As Strauss presents it, Jacobi was a somewhat deep thinker and had a probing, critical mind with regard to certain key issues which concerned him, and yet also was a man of substantial moral unscrupulousness and base deviousness, not to mention of subtle anti-Semitism. See *MMJA*, vol. 3, pt. 2, pp. lv–lviii. For a previous remark about Jacobi, cf. *SCR*, p. 204.) Subsequently, Strauss's view of Spinoza as entirely unconcerned with Jews and Judaism seems to have been moderated somewhat, for Strauss recognizes in Spinoza's suggestions for reforming Jewish society some vital remaining "sympathy with his people." See *PSCR*, pp. 20–21, and also 23–25, 27. For "caution," cf. also "HSS" (*PAW*), pp. 179–181, and *SCR*, p. 171.

   20.   To anticipate somewhat, Strauss's romance with Spinozism did not last long, i.e., beyond *Spinoza's Critique of Religion*, however decisive the interlude may have been in the course of his philosophic development. Strauss incisively discovered in Spinoza a fatal flaw (which has already been mentioned in our chapter 1): for all of Spinoza's success in ridiculing orthodoxy as rationally confused, he fails to disprove the *possibility* of divine revelation, but can only lay bare the difficulties to which it is exposed once it tries to prove rationally any single divine revelation as a historical actuality. As such, Spinoza's liberal philosophy and the Enlightenment which accompanies it stand on shaky ground, on a mere promise to prove man's radical autonomy and sufficiency which, it would seem, it can never deliver. This is, to be sure, the precise reason that would

compel Strauss to turn to Maimonides. If human rational and moral autonomy is undemonstrable, the question is whether a modern Jew can be both as philosophically rigorous as Spinoza, with reason as his final authority, and yet still remain as rationally and passionately committed as Cohen to Judaism, with its belief in the actuality of divine revelation.

21. "Dogmatism" for Spinoza refers to those like Maimonides who believe in the ultimate harmony of reason and revelation, but only because they also believe "Scripture should be made subservient to reason." Cf. *Theological-Political Treatise*, chapter 15, as well as chapters 7 and 13.

22. "CA," p. 312. Cf. also "HSS" (*PAW*), pp. 200–201.

23. "CA," pp. 312–14. Cf. also P*SCR*, pp. 18–21.

24. Strauss in fact discerns in Spinoza's statements about the "corporeal" notion of God in the Bible not only a concealed attack on the Bible for its purely imaginative form and content. He also detects an honest allusion by Spinoza to Rabbi Abraham ben David (Rabad), especially where Rabad through his strictures against Maimonides' rational theology defended the place of the belief in God's "corporeality." Rabad thought such a belief fully legitimate for, and consistent with, Jewish monotheism, if only for those simple-minded people whose intellectual defects prevent them from attaining to the true conception of the nature of God, and hence who do not deserve to be execrated as heretics. Indeed, an authentic and authoritative model for Spinoza's critique of Maimonides could have been identified by Cohen in Rabad, for it was Rabad who stood in decided opposition to Maimonides' towering theological authority on precisely this point, and yet who unlike Spinoza cannot be dismissed as a man who was moved by a hostility to Judaism and Jews that prevented him from viewing the Jewish tradition in an equitable light. Cf. "CA," pp. 308, 310. For a recent discussion of this famous criticism that occurs in Rabad's comments or glosses on Maimonides' *Mishneh Torah*, cf. I. Twersky, *Rabad of Posquieres* (Philadelphia: JPS, 1980), especially pp. 282–86.

25. "CA," pp. 299–301.

26. Ibid., p. 312. This argument is repeated with a somewhat astonishing consistency in the subsequent writings of Strauss on Spinoza. Spinoza chose to combat Maimonides not because he happened to study his works in his youth, but because he considered Maimonides' position the best articulation of a fundamental viewpoint which he utterly rejected and believed he could refute. Cf. *SCR*, p. 108, and "HSS" (*PAW*), pp. 200–201. Strauss makes a similar point against Leon Roth (*SCR*, p. 297, note 238), and against H. A. Wolfson ("HSS" [*PAW*], pp. 188–90): "Spinoza did not know of any authorities in philosophic investigation."

27. "CA," pp. 312–13.

28. Subsequently, Strauss seems to have been persuaded that this may well not at all have been Maimonides' true position: "How far Maimonides accepted the teaching of the *falasifa*, according to which a 'priestly city' is one of the

bad regimes, must here remain an open question." ("*LCGP*" [*PAW*], p. 91, note 156) Strauss seems to obliquely make a definite point about Maimonides' rejection of the "priestly city" in two other essays: "MSPS" (*WIPP?*), pp. 157–58; "NMLA" (*SPPP*), p. 207. As for the "priestly city," cf. *CM*, pp. 33–34; *TOM*, pp. 184–85; and "Marsilius of Padua," in *HPP*, pp. 252–57.

29. As Strauss perceived, if Spinoza's distortions of Judaism generally, and Maimonides specifically, are still in some sense caused by a polemical spirit animating an "alienated" Jew, Cohen too diverges occasionally from the Enlightenment norm of "honesty" in which he is as rooted as is Spinoza. However, Cohen is driven by an apologetic stance as a loyal and "committed" Jew; he needs to counteract modern Christian and secular attacks against Judaism. Strauss claims to be able to fairly judge them both in this regard, recognizing the two extreme intentions as vices, for he pointedly notes that surely "the objectivity of the investigation of Bible science can be endangered just as much by the skeptical coldness of the apostate as by the apologetic love of the faithful." ("CA," p. 313) For a related point, cf. *PSCR*, p. 22. This is not even to mention the fact that Cohen also neglects to recall the debt he owes to Spinoza, other than for his biblical criticism. Cf. *PSCR*, pp. 27–28. This reflects a fundamental principle of Strauss's own activity as scholar and thinker: that the human mind can only be free if it strives austerely for objectivity, something he regarded as both possible and necessary for the human mind to achieve. In a letter to Alexander Altmann of 7 Aug. 1970 concerning his work on the Mendelssohn-Jacobi controversy for the *MMJA*, vol. 3, pt. 2, Strauss wrote: "My introduction was written in 1936–37, at a time in which I regarded it as particularly important to preserve my intellectual freedom [geistige Freiheit] against lapses into apologetics." Strauss did not reach his conclusions determined by apologetic motives, but on objective grounds; he wanted to achieve objectivity as much as possible. Obviously the historical situation of 1936–37 tempted him to want to exonerate Mendelssohn, a representative Jew, on all grounds, but he would not let himself conceal the critical features of Mendelssohn just because of Hitler. On this point Altmann remarked to me that in his opinion perhaps Strauss's decided harshness vis-à-vis Jacobi in moral terms nevertheless may still show some remaining Jewish desire to "save" Mendelssohn.

30. That Strauss began his turn to Plato along with Maimonides as early as the 1920s is attested to by his own autobiographical statements in *PSCR*, pp. 30–31, and "GA," pp. 2–3. See also supra, chapter 1, note 6, chapter 2, note 3, and infra, chapter 5, note 23. If later personal testimony may serve as corroboration for the historical accuracy of these statements, it is available through the remarks of his friend Shlomo Pines, who knew Strauss well toward the end of the 1920s in Berlin. According to Pines, Strauss

> was in this period already familiar with Plato's *Laws*, and had begun to discover the medieval Jewish philosophers and their Islamic predecessors. As a result, he came to the conclusion that Maimonides

was a deeper thinker than Spinoza. Many of the opinions that he held until the end of his life crystalized already in those days, and I remember things that he said then which [I] find in writings that he wrote some thirty years later.

Cf. "On Leo Strauss" (in Hebrew), *Molad* 30, no. 247–48, n.s. 7, no. 37–38 (1976): 455–57, and especially p. 455; and *Independent Journal of Philosophy* 5/6 (1988): 169–71, especially p. 169.

31. "Biblische Geschichte und Wissenschaft," *Jüdische Rundschau* 30, no. 88 (1925): 744–45.

32. Strauss elaborates his critical argument as follows: Simon's "dogmatic and scholastic" assumption about Orthodoxy's basis, even as he reasonably presents it, would exact the price of a certain literalism, which has never been able to provide or to sustain a sound and fully convincing argument for Orthodoxy. By contrast, the *need* for the Law is acknowledged by Strauss to be the most essential point in Orthodoxy's favor: as Strauss seems to suggest, Simon may be right to believe that "only divine guidance preserves mankind from the 'madness of genocide.'" This indeed seems to have been to the youthful Strauss the most morally compelling argument for Orthodoxy. Perhaps it is in this that Strauss reveals himself already as not actually a full convert to Spinozism; he lacks absolute faith in "natural morality" as a power to be reckoned with. But as he further concedes, even that powerful moral need, evoked by Simon in favor of Orthodoxy, cannot by itself command either rational assent or true belief. Perhaps we should also recall Strauss's mature statement about "vital need" and the possible return to Orthodoxy as a matter of faith in *the* truth. It evinces much greater sympathy for the claims of such "vital need":

> Some of our contemporaries believe such a return to be altogether impossible because they believe that the Jewish faith has been overthrown once and for all, not by blind rebellion, but by evident refutation. While admitting that their deepest problem would be solved by that return, they assert that intellectual probity forbids them to sacrifice intellect in order to satisfy even the most vital need. Yet they can hardly deny that a vital need legitimately induces a man to probe whether what seems to be an impossibility is not in fact only a very great difficulty. (*PSCR*, p. 7)

Strauss also adds another reason why the argument for the Law is to be preferred in support of Orthodoxy. Jewish Orthodoxy is simply not refutable by history, as the modern Enlightenment once believed, and hence Orthodoxy need not fear history in the form of modern biblical science, if the Law is its chief support. Using a Maimonidean argument, Strauss maintains it is the form and substance of the Law which is holy, not its historical origin. He quotes Lessing as his decisive authority in rejecting any such claims to historical refutation of biblical faith, citing Lessing's critical notes to H. S. Reimarus's classical attempt at such a refutation.

33. This is, of course, mainly true only of *The Guide of the Perplexed*. It should be noted that neither in his "Thirteen Fundamental Principles" of the Jewish faith (in the Introduction to the tenth chapter of Sanhedrin, "Perek Helek," in his *Commentary on the Mishnah*) does Maimonides make *creatio ex nihilo* one of the thirteen basic beliefs, nor in his "Laws of the Fundamental Principles of the Torah" in the *Mishneh Torah's* "Book of Knowledge" does he use the terms "God created the world out of nothing." What this means for Maimonides, and how Strauss would have interpreted these strange facts, is something that cannot be explained in the present context. On this point, it should be noted that in Joseph Kafih's edition of the Arabic original and Hebrew translation of the *Commentary on the Mishnah* (Jerusalem: Mossad ha-Rav Kook, 1964), which is based on a revision of the text in Maimonides' own hand, "creation out of nothing" is made a specifically implied article of faith as an additional comment to the fourth article of faith, the eternity of God. Consider the illuminating discussion of these issues in Marvin Fox, "Creation or Eternity: God in Relation to the World," in *Interpreting Maimonides* (Chicago: University of Chicago Press, 1990), pp. 251–96, and especially pp. 252–54. See also the still-debated article of Herbert Davidson, "Maimonides' Secret Position on Creation," in *Studies in Medieval Jewish History and Literature*, edited by I. Twersky (Cambridge: Harvard University Press, 1979), pp. 16–40. In this article, Davidson takes issue with the approach of Strauss, but he also gives arguments in favor of a secret Platonic dimension to Maimonides' position on creation. For a contrasting view of Maimonides as holding a thoroughly agnostic or skeptical position on creation versus eternity—a position which, however, does not necessarily contradict the esotericist view of what Maimonides is doing in the *Guide*—see Sarah Klein-Braslavy, "The Creation of the World and Maimonides' Interpretation of Genesis i–v," in *Maimonides and Philosophy*, edited by S. Pines and Y. Yovel (Dordrecht: Martinus Nijhoff, 1986), pp. 65–78. For a critique of both Davidson and the esoteric reading of the *Guide*, see William Dunphy, "Maimonides' Not-So-Secret Position on Creation," in *Moses Maimonides and His Time*, edited by E. L. Ormsby (Washington, D. C.: Catholic University of America Press, 1989), pp. 151–72.

34. "Zur Bibelwissenschaft Spinozas und seiner Vorläufer," *Korrespondenzblatt* (des Vereins zur Gründung und Erhaltung einer Akademie für die Wissenschaft des Judentums) 7 (1926): 1–22.

35. For similar statements, see *SCR*, pp. 151–52, 166; "TS," pp. 322–23; *PSCR*, pp. 15–18.

36. Cf. *Guide* II, 25 with I, 31; *Theological-Political Treatise*, chapter 7; "CA," p. 313; "ZBWS," p. 4. Spinoza (as Strauss's suggestive approach leads us to perceive) turns upside down Maimonides' "open-mindedness" in his refusal to be bound by the apparent or literal meaning of (biblical) texts. He makes it

into a reproach that Maimonides does not show sufficient respect for the (biblical)
text. In this context, Spinoza is using Maimonides as a foil to prove two things:
the literal or apparent meaning is obvious and readily accessible, and has just
been ignored or concealed by unscrupulous readers; and the literal or apparent
meaning is the text's *only* meaning, and anyone who claims otherwise is just
a dishonest reader.

37.   "ZBWS," p. 5.

38.   In other words, Strauss maintained that this rationalist debate between
Maimonides' "allegorical" (i.e., cognitive and lexicographical) method and
Spinoza's "critical" (i.e., historical and philological) method with regard to
Scripture is never the most fundamental issue. It is always derivative from, or
subordinate to, a higher concern which is purely philosophical and theological.
Thus, the debate revolves around the ultimate conceptions, such as of the nature
of God and prophecy, in which hermeneutical assertions about the primary
approach to Scripture are actually grounded.

39.   It is plainly evident that, at this point in Strauss's development, he
is prepared to explain the basic positions of Maimonides and Spinoza as in a
significant measure determined by their different historical situations (i.e.,
twelfth-century Spain and Northern Africa versus seventeenth-century Holland
and Western Europe), and by their different speculative and scientific cosmologies
(i.e., medieval versus modern). He is not yet ready to interpret their fundamental
moral principles and perhaps even their theological convictions as guided by the
"mere" fact of their both being philosophers, and having hence a prior interest
and experience in common, as he would seem to maintain in *PAW*. Philosophy
does not yet bring in its wake basic and prior "moral" imperatives to which all
philosophers do or should adhere, irrespective of their distinctive philosophic
positions. Strauss does not yet maintain this because he does not yet believe,
or perhaps has not been so liberated from "historicism" as to know, that what
unites the philosophers as a class or type in their common condition as
philosophers is always greater than what divides them by their philosophic
positions.

> In the common view the fact is overlooked that there is a class interest
> of the philosophers qua philosophers, and this oversight is ultimately
> due to the denial of the possibility of philosophy. Philosophers as
> philosophers do not go with their families. (*NRH*, p. 143)

Cf. also p. 34, and *WIPP?*, pp. 92–94. In this context, the most complete and
also rhetorically powerful statement that Strauss made on "the philosopher"
should be considered: *OT*, pp. 205–26; *OT* (rev.), pp. 191–212. For his changed
view of the role to be played by history in the understanding of the great
philosophic writers, consider the following:

> Historical understanding, as it is frequently practiced, seduces one into
> seeing the author whom one studies, primarily as a contemporary

among his contemporaries, or to read his books as if they were primarily addressed to his contemporaries. But the books of men like the mature Spinoza, which are meant as possessions for all times, are primarily addressed to posterity.... The flight to immortality requires an extreme discretion in the selection of one's luggage. ("HSS" [*PAW*], pp. 159–60)

It is precisely "the denial of the possibility of philosophy," and the consequent ignorance of the conditions of human life in which philosophy is grounded, which will serve in *PAW* and most of his subsequent works as the basis for Strauss's critique of modern historicism in all of its guises. Cf., e.g., *PAW*, pp. 26–35, 136–41, 151–62; *NRH*, pp. 11–34; *WIPP?*, pp. 17–27, 56–77. Cf. also already "ET," pp. 51–52, 55, 59.

40. *Ethics*, part 2, proposition 47.

41. *Guide* I, 54.

42. Ibid., I, 59; cf. also I, 31.

43. Strauss does not yet wonder whether there might be a Platonic philosopher's primary *political* motivation driving Maimonides' entire theological position. It was precisely the discovery of this primary *political* motivation, i.e., the need to justify and account for their life as philosophers among nonphilosophers who did not regard the philosophic life as fully in accord with the requirements of the divine law, that would serve as the basis for Strauss's critique of Guttmann. (See, e.g., *PG*, pp. 33–40, 50–58, as well as 98–110 or *PL*, pp. 25–32, 42–49, as well as 91–100.) Strauss holds at this early stage in his development a position asserting the primacy of the theological, and even purely religious, motives for the comprehension of the medieval Jewish philosophers. This is identical with the position that is maintained constantly by Guttmann, and for which Strauss himself would eventually criticize Guttmann. Strauss later began to recognize that such a position is maintained precisely in order to prove the superiority of the moderns to the medievals, a superiority which he ceased to regard as self-evident. But Strauss subsequently continued to stay alert to the difficulties with arguing for the superiority of the classical-medieval philosophic position, to "the difficulties to which classical philosophy was and is still exposed." These difficulties called for the rise of modern philosophy, and, in a sense, still justify it. Strauss summarizes these "difficulties," especially as related to medieval philosophy, as follows:

Classical science, one may say in order to simplify the discussion, ultimately depends on the possibility of natural theology as a science.... One would have to have the courage to call Luther and Calvin sophists before one could dare to assert that only sophists can question the satisfactory character of the reconciliation attempted by Maimonides and Thomas Aquinas between the biblical and the Aristotelian teaching. ("ONI," pp. 337–39)

Cf. also *NRH*, pp. 6–8; "CPP," pp. 92–93; "COT," pp. 41–42, 54; "TWM" (*IPP*), pp. 87–88. For Strauss's last word on Spinoza's philosophy, in which is grounded his "novel account of man's end (the life of contemplation)," though as something "not natural, but rational," cf. *PSCR*, pp. 15–17, 28–29.

44. "ZBWS," p. 6.

45. Ibid., p. 7.

46. Ibid., p. 8.

47. Ibid., pp. 7–8. Strauss briefly discusses the key function of the imaginative faculty in Maimonides' prophetology, and even isolates the essential issue (or contradiction): Maimonides' claim that "the cooperation of the imaginative faculty with the intellect in the prophetic comprehension is not detrimental to the theoretical dignity of prophecy because the imaginative faculty does not thereby influence the intellect, and therefore does not hinder and interfere with it." But to this, at least according to Strauss, Maimonides also attaches this further spectacular claim: "theory operating by means of the intellect alone is surpassable." This suggests that it is the imaginative faculty which contributes to, and even makes possible, the higher theoretical comprehension attained in prophecy. (Whether Strauss was right in his youthful view of Maimonides on this point is not at all clear. It remains controversial whether Maimonides ever actually said anything like this, or anything that could be so construed to mean or imply that. For a recent treatment of this issue, which tries to prove definitively that Maimonides' view of prophecy is entirely naturalistic, cf. A. Altmann, "Maimonides and Aquinas: Natural or Divine Prophecy?" *AJS Review* 3 [1978]: 1–19.) Strauss also acknowledges Spinoza's "decisive objection"—"with the contrariness of intellect and imaginative faculty, . . . an extraordinary increase of the imaginative faculty must entail an extraordinary decrease of the capacity for pure intellection"—but he relegates it to Spinoza's "entirely different conception and valuation of the 'imaginative faculty,'" which leads him to "mistake the point of Maimonides' prophetology." The debate between Maimonides and Spinoza on prophecy, at the present point in Strauss's development, is apprehended as solely reflecting "the opposition between the Aristotelian and the Cartesian conceptions of truth and knowledge." Spinoza's critique is merely grounded in his Cartesian epistemology, while Maimonides' doctrine simply adds theologically to the basic Aristotelian notions. To be sure, Strauss is already aware of the political necessity for the imaginative form in which revelation conveys theoretical and practical truths to the multitude, but the defensive need of philosophy in itself does not yet make sense for him of the apparent contradiction glaringly present in Maimonides' epistemology.

> The aim of revelation, insofar as it is not simply identical with theory, is therefore the social organization of the multitude. However, for Maimonides the solicitude about the multitude with regard to theory

is not only as a means to an end— in the sense that social organization, the outer security of life, is the *conditio sine qua non* for the theoretical life—but it is of concern to him as something essential that the fundamental truths as such be acknowledged by the multitude; that is, without his having his eye on the social organizational function of these truths. The acknowledgement of a truth is supposed to unite all men—the wise and the unwise. ("ZBWS," pp. 5–6)

For a slightly different notion, cf. *SCR*, p. 171, in which Strauss also discusses how "recognition of *one* truth is to unite all men, the wise and the foolish." Also compare with the discussion infra in chapter 4, notes 56, 60, and 64. Guttmann's approach to medieval Jewish philosophy was obviously still exercising a decisive influence on Strauss at this stage, since it is Guttmann who argues that, for Maimonides, it is theology which precedes in dignity and significance his political views.

48. "ZBWS," pp. 7–8.

49. Ibid., p. 9.

50. Ibid., p. 10.

51. Ibid., p. 11.

52. These doubts are repeated often in Strauss's subsequent work, and seem to lay the basis for the approach to philosophy which he pursued in all of his philosophic thinking. Consider especially the two decisive statements on Spinoza, P*SCR*, pp. 27–29, "MITP," p. 117, "POR?" (*IPP*), pp. 307–8, and the one virtually identical statement on Hegel, "OIG," p. 7, regarding "the absolute and final philosophic system":

I regard the existence of such a system as at least as improbable as the truth of the Bible. But, obviously, the improbability of the truth of the Bible is a contention of the Bible whereas the improbability of the truth of the perfect philosophic system creates a serious difficulty for that system.

The gist of Strauss's view would seem to lie in what he might call the "Socratic" conviction that philosophy can never possess the whole of wisdom but can only attain to parts of wisdom. Philosophy must, however, love or desire such complete wisdom, since this love or desire is a legitimate and even necessary aspect of true philosophic ambition. The doubt about the "sufficiency" of the human intellect to truly know "God and the angels" is the medieval formulation of the same basic issue, and the dubiousness of the search for "the absolute and final philosophic system" is the modern equivalent. No philosopher can dogmatically dismiss such attempts, and perhaps much can be learned from such attempts even if they result in failure. But he also must be very careful about accepting their claims, i.e., "to possess the binding power peculiar to the known" rather than the merely believed. Indeed, the Maimonidean formulation, focusing on and emphasizing the limited powers of the human mind while not denying "the natural harmony between the human mind and the universe," manifests a peculiar precision in pinpointing perhaps *the* most decisive dilemma, for Strauss, facing the philosopher.

CHAPTER FOUR

1. "OF" (*WIPP?*), p. 230.

2. The three-stage scheme in the development of Strauss's views about Maimonides, because it unfolds in an opposition to Spinoza, seems to necessitate a certain kind of simplification in the treatment of Strauss's views about Spinoza, which were in fact by no means simple. Strauss certainly never dispensed with the true insights which he learned, or critically extracted, from Spinoza; indeed, these probably helped guide him to those very "deeper" truths which he discovered in the thinking of Maimonides. Not only did he follow Spinoza with regard to the need for biblical criticism as well as concerning the critique of orthodoxy in its claim to *know* the Bible to be divinely revealed (see *PSCR*, pp. 27–29), but even with reference to the peculiarly modern "solutions" to "the Jewish problem," which he regarded as necessary though not sufficient responses to modern liberalism, in so far as these too were first suggested by Spinoza. Strauss's own defense of liberal democracy as the most decent available modern regime, and not only for Jews (see, e.g., *PSCR*, pp. 1–7), cannot help but owe a sizable debt to Spinoza. He designated Spinoza as "the first philosopher who was both a democrat and a liberal," and as the philosopher who first established liberal democracy as something which is *philosophically* defensible. As "a specifically modern regime," Spinoza's liberal democracy combines "classical republicanism," to which he was according to Strauss the first to make a partial return, with "modern speculation." Strauss considered Spinoza by no means "a revolutionary thinker," for he was indeed "only the heir of the modern revolt and the medieval tradition as well"; but Spinoza "thus was the first great thinker who attempted a synthesis of premodern (classical-medieval) and of modern philosophy." (Ibid., pp. 15–16, 20–21. But cf. already "TS" [1932], p. 322) To be sure, for Strauss, in whom no great reverence for syntheses abides, it seems as if Spinoza's "systematic" synthesis, of all the great modern syntheses, preserves whole and original some of the most fundamental classical principles better than any subsequent syntheses. Thus, even if Strauss never judged Spinoza's system to be theoretically perfect, he did perhaps recognize it as the least philosophically fallible modern approach (if only through his conditional and qualified return to certain key classical notions). And for all practical purposes, Spinoza and his liberalism remained for Strauss a decisive though qualified guide to the philosophic life, to morality, and also to wisdom—and even to Jewish thought, in his devising of liberal democracy and originating biblical criticism. (See especially *PSCR*, pp. 2–3, 17, 21.) It will be of some substantial interest, and worth careful and detailed examination in a subsequent study which I hope

to write, to consider how much of Spinoza remains in Strauss's Maimonides. Cf. also "MITP," p. 117; "POR?" (*IPP*), pp. 307–8. For Strauss's first doubts about the efficacy of philosophical "systems" in his encounter of Spinoza with orthodoxy and Calvin, cf. *SCR*, pp. 139–40, 204–14. Strauss also recalls his effort to surpass Cohen's critique of Spinoza (pp. 207–9), but with a sharper formulation of his essential conclusion. While Cohen correctly points to "the very foundation of Spinoza's mind" as the only way to explain "Spinoza's [hostile] attitude to Judaism," Cohen resorted to a faulty psychological assessment of that "very foundation" in ultimately blaming this attitude on Spinoza's resistance to divine transcendence. Strauss interprets the "mind" of Spinoza differently, tracing the causes to a theological-moral source, to "a battle against fear of God," "a revulsion against the jealous God of wrath in Scripture." Such is the source of "this truly world-historical opposition to Judaism," which opposition to the biblical God primarily occurs in the history of Christianity insofar as it is the chief bearer in the West of that theological-moral legacy of Judaism.

3. *PSCR*, p. 31. And if, as Strauss's mature self-reflection puts it, "the present study was based on the premise . . . that a return to premodern philosophy was impossible," this premise was also severely impaired by the same work. By seemingly demonstrating the superiority of Maimonides' position to Spinoza's in almost every significant respect (except for modern natural science), it also seemed to make a return to the "premodern" Maimonides desirable, even if not yet truly possible. For Strauss's reasoning in favor of the *possibility* of such a "return," refer to the discussion in chapter 2. Strauss believed that he first reached the idea of the possibility of a return to classical political philosophy in his Carl Schmitt review (1932) (cf. *PSCR*, p. 31). Christopher Bruell in his "A Return to Classical Political Philosophy," *Review of Politics* 53, no. 1 (Winter 1991): 173–86, especially p. 186, note 47, isolates a passage (with a decidedly moral-theological emphasis) in the Carl Schmitt review (p. 345) which, he seems to suggest, is the one to announce the possibility and the intention of this return: "In order to launch the radical critique of liberalism . . . Schmitt must first eliminate the conception of human evil as animal evil, and therefore as 'innocent evil,' and find his way back to the conception of human evil as moral depravity." He even locates a passage written prior to that review (*SCR*, p. 204) which he believes also anticipates the possibility of such a return: "There is in [Spinoza's critique of religion] no continuous transition from Scripture, from the spirit of Scripture, to denial of sin." But cf. already the remark which Strauss makes in his review of Julius Ebbinghaus (1931). Thus, *SCR* may legitimately and with certainty be called "the first stage" in Strauss's return to Maimonides at the very least because it elucidates why such a return would be desirable. He makes a similar point about another return—return to Jewish faith—which for him had also been proven to be vitally needed or desirable: one "can hardly deny that a vital need legitimately induces a man to probe whether what seems to be an impossibility is not in fact only a very great difficulty." (*PSCR*, p. 7) This is exactly what Strauss

seems to have been led to do by the present work with respect to that very "premodern philosophy" which serves as the basis for Maimonides' Jewish thought. Cf. ibid., p. 31.

4. If the position still stands, a return to it is rendered possible; or in any case, if the possibility of "a return to the premodern" has been rendered conceivable it may not necessarily be deemed desirable at first and may seem to entail enormous difficulties and even impassable obstacles, but perhaps it has to be considered with the utmost seriousness as possibly the only credible option remaining to escape the modern crisis of rationality in philosophy and in religion—especially if it is a theological rationalism which has never actually been refuted. Indeed, as Strauss then viewed the two great contenders, it is the Maimonidean position (in opposition to the Spinozistic) which claimed to achieve a unity, a harmony, and a synthesis between the two sides of the dilemma, the Jewish and the philosophic. If the Maimonidean position is sufficiently hardy to survive the withering Spinozist attack, it would seem to offer an integral theological resolution of the modern crisis in Judaism and in philosophy, while providing the philosophical yet loyal Jew with a stand which would not require him to surrender or even to compromise either reason or revelation.

5. This is not to say that Strauss recognized "presuppositions" which needed to remain "unarguable." By his own rigorous standards of what a philosopher is, he could not accept things unthinkingly. This is rather meant to observe that Strauss remained to the end of his life with the faith and people with which he began in life, whatever his reasons were for doing so. Certainly prior to his showing a lucid comprehension of what it fully entails to be a philosopher, he manifested an unyielding loyalty at the highest level to the spiritual legacy with which he was endowed, to his Judaism. That he held tenaciously to his Judaism even following what might be called his "conversion" to philosophy is, if nothing else, evidence of his nobility of character. Further, his Jewish loyalty, even if subsequently a reasoned loyalty, supported a commitment which it also might have been possible to reason his way around—a possibility which, I would venture, he never seriously contemplated in personal terms, although he tried to comprehend the motives for modern Jewish people doing so. (Cf. "WWRJ" for his most detailed and "personal" treatment of these issues.) His Jewish commitment may well have been subsequently turned into something which was mostly thought through, though still held tenaciously and passionately. To be sure, his thinking through his commitments is, in a certain measure, the chief topic of the present work. This should, I hope, bring a somewhat sharper focus to what I meant to say in referring to Strauss's "unarguable presupposition." As for whether his commitment as a Jew necessarily vouches for his commitment to "Judaism as a revealed religion," this is certainly a crucial difficulty which can only be approached in an exploratory and initial way in the present context. What was the precise shape and substance of his final commitment to Judaism? But it should be remembered that he himself

was emphatic about the need for modern Jews to deal with Judaism primarily and ultimately as a religion, even as a "revealed" religion, however comprehended, rather than solely as a culture. See supra, chapter 1, notes 27 and 49; chapter 2, note 59.

6. In his youth, "Cohen was the center of attraction for philosophically minded Jews who were devoted to Judaism; he was the master whom they revered." ("IERR" [SPPP], p. 233) In the most personal terms, Cohen exercised a spiritual influence upon Strauss, as upon his non-Jewish friend Kurt Riezler, "by the fire and power of his soul." (WIPP?, p. 242) Or as Strauss eloquently put it, "Cohen attracted me because he was a passionate philosopher and a Jew passionately devoted to Judaism." See "GA," p. 2.

7. As previously mentioned (chapter 3, notes 16 and 17), in 1922 Strauss was what he calls "a doubting and dubious adherent of the Marburg school of neo-Kantianism." Husserl seems to have been responsible for turning him away from Cohen and toward "phenomenology," while Heidegger turned him away from Husserl. Heidegger "radicalized Husserl's critique of the school of Marburg and turned it against Husserl: what is primary is not the object of sense perception but the things which we handle and with which we are concerned, *pragmata*. What [Strauss] could not stomach was his moral teaching." Cf. "PARSPP" (SPPP), p. 31, as well as "GA," p. 3. See, for a fuller treatment, infra, chapter 5, note 3.

8. PIHPE, pp. xxx–xxxii.

9. "GA," p. 3; "TS," p. 322; PSCR, pp. 18–19.

10. Besides writing "Cohens Analyse der Bibel-Wissenschaft Spinozas" (1924), Strauss had already "led an analytical reading of Hermann Cohen's *Religion of Reason*" in the 1923–24 term of Franz Rosenzweig's Frankfurt "Freies Jüdisches Lehrhaus." He had also taught a course in which he "analysed Spinoza's *Theological-Political Treatise*" in the sixth academic year, 1924–25, of the Lehrhaus. These facts are reported by Nahum N. Glatzer, "The Frankfurt Lehrhaus," in his *Essays in Jewish Thought* (University: University of Alabama Press, 1978), pp. 265–66. Cf. also "GA," pp. 2–3.

11. Consider PSCR, pp. 18–29, and SCR, pp. 162–65, 178–81, 205–8. One must confine this reasoning in favor of Strauss's turn to Spinoza's *Treatise* to his earlier self-comprehension. His later view discovers in the *Treatise* a priority to the *Ethics* because of its greater correctness and self-assertiveness in the attack against its opponent. It needed to argue for its own presuppositions as philosophy rather than just proceeding as if revelation may be simply presupposed to have been refuted. In the *Treatise*, "Spinoza starts from premises that are granted to him by the believer in revelation." He tries to prove these premises to be self-contradictory and hence to liberate his reader from them: "the *Treatise* is Spinoza's introduction to philosophy." See PSCR, pp. 27–29.

12. "GA," p. 3. Cf. also PSCR, p. 31, "UP," p. 2, and Alexander Altmann, "Leo Strauss: 1899–1973," pp. xxxii-xxxvi, and especially p. xxxiii. Cf. also "THE" (RCPR), pp. 27–35, 43–44.

13.   Strauss could, of course, have been persuaded to move the other way—to follow Heidegger and his turn to what Strauss calls "ultramodern thought," as the only authentic response to Nietzsche. Why did he choose not to follow Heidegger's way? Why did he try to pioneer his own way? One factor, which may perhaps have been decisive in this, was precisely that Strauss "could not stomach his moral teaching." Cf. *PG*, p. 28 or *PL*, p. 19 together with "IHE" (*RCPR*), pp. 28, 30–31, 41–42. (This would seem to put the lie to any claim, even tacitly asserted by Strauss himself, that as a philosopher he held to no specific moral teaching.) To begin with, however, one thing must be stated unambiguously. Whatever greatness Strauss acknowledged in Heidegger, he also recognized an enormous difference between Heidegger and Nietzsche, both in terms of philosophic depth and moral integrity. But this by itself obviously does not answer the question of how Strauss is related to Nietzsche. As improbable as it might first appear to some, is it the case that Strauss was actually a follower of Nietzsche in a definite sense? Rémi Brague makes the assertion that this may have been precisely what Strauss was: his "return" to Maimonides, and with him to Plato and Aristotle, makes for one "ultramodern" response to Nietzsche (p. 104), and Heidegger provides the other response. I do not believe that the evidence which he provides to substantiate this assertion is convincing, if a radical dependency is implied in the notion of such an "ultramodern" response. From a different angle, this is the hidden core of Shadia Drury's reading of Strauss (beyond her simple animus against Strauss, which energizes her work)—that he tries to do for Nietzsche what in Strauss's reading of the history of modern political philosophy Hobbes did for Machiavelli: he "mitigated Machiavelli's scheme," because of its "revolting character," to make it acceptable and to "guarantee its success." (Cf. her *The Political Ideas of Leo Strauss*, pp. 170–81; compare with *WIPP?*, pp. 47–49.) In my judgment, Strauss is only an "ultramodern" thinker, i.e., a true disciple of Nietzsche, if everything which he wrote in criticism of Nietzsche is not as important as his appreciation of Nietzsche. It is true that Strauss represents Nietzsche's philosophy as "the third wave" of modernity, our present "wave." But this assertion of Strauss's rootedness in Nietzsche, whether it is meant to praise Strauss or to bury him, cannot be established from the mere fact that Strauss learned a great deal from Nietzsche, and even used him as the necessary point of departure on several key points, since this has been the case with several important thinkers from whom Strauss learned a good deal (e.g., Spinoza, Cohen, Lessing, Plato). As things stand, I do not believe that a convincing or even plausible case has yet been made to prove Strauss's radical dependency on Nietzsche. The only way in which this assertion that Strauss's teaching is integrally related to Nietzsche's teaching makes even some fragmentary sense, and is not entirely farfetched, is to look at Strauss as trying to provide the antidote to Nietzsche's poison. If this were the case, I would further suppose that Strauss's relation to Nietzsche is not at all the same as the relation of Sherlock Holmes to Professor Moriarty, as Strauss himself puts it about Hobbes and Machiavelli,

since it would still put him in the dependent and derivative relation of Hobbes to Machiavelli. As his debate with Kojève makes plain, Strauss believes in the actuality of truth, in the eternality of Being, and hence in the possibility of philosophy, all of which he strives to truly know or comprehend. In other words, at least as I read him, Strauss's philosophic position, whether well-grounded or not, differs on the most *fundamental* points from the position of Nietzsche. See David R. Lachterman, "Strauss Read from France," *Review of Politics* 53, no. 1 (Winter 1991): 224–45 (especially pp. 236–37), for judicious remarks on this topic in his comments on Pierre Manent ("Strauss et Nietzsche," *Revue de Metaphysique et de Morale* 94, no. 3 [July-September 1989]: 337–45). Lachterman rightly issues a caution that "a full-dress study of Strauss and Nietzsche will have to reckon with . . . true and false resemblances." See also supra, Introduction, note 1, chapter 1, note 6, chapter 3, note 14.

14. Two reviews, which shortly followed *SCR*'s publication (1930), distinctly manifest Strauss's tentative answer in favor of the need for a return to the premodern. First, in his review of Julius Ebbinghaus's *Über der Fortschritte der Metaphysik* (1931), he praises the author for his attempt at a truly "Socratic" point of departure in philosophizing, but corrects him by maintaining we must first recover "the natural ignorance with which philosophy must begin; for it may first be in need of a long detour, a great effort, in order to return, generally speaking, to the state of natural ignorance." This programmatic statement is followed by that striking image already quoted of the "second much deeper [unnatural] cave" in which we are trapped, causing the crisis in philosophy, even though our predicament is of our own making. He then speaks of our great need to ascend to the first natural cave of "blissful ignorance" with which Socrates contended, and "from which Socrates can lead us to the light." Second, in Strauss's "Anmerkungen zu Carl Schmitts *Der Begriff des Politischen*" (1932), translated and reprinted in *SCR*, pp. 331–51, he speaks of Schmitt's flawed critique of Hobbes and liberalism. It is flawed because it is infected by a polemical spirit colored by his failure to extricate himself from "the horizon of liberalism" even in fighting against it. The true critique of liberalism, "this urgent task," cannot be expected to occur *in* "the horizon of liberalism," irrespective of whether one is for it or against it. Rather, a truly radical critique must somehow transcend its horizon. Indeed, it must achieve a completely superior horizon, i.e., classical philosophy, in the higher light of which Hobbes himself originally established the basis for liberalism. Now Strauss puts the same point somewhat obliquely: "the critique of liberalism that Schmitt has initiated can therefore be completed only when we succeed in gaining a horizon beyond liberalism." Strauss's growing dedication to Plato and classical, or premodern, philosophy emerges here. In a sense, his life's great mission became the attempt to recover precisely such "a horizon beyond liberalism." For Strauss's critique of Schmitt in its larger context, cf. Heinrich Meier, *Carl Schmitt, Leo Strauss, und "Der Begriff des Politischen"* (Stuttgart: Metzler, 1988). For an analysis of Meier's approach to Strauss and

Schmitt, see Susan Shell, "Meier on Strauss and Schmitt," *Review of Politics* 53, no. 1 (Winter 1991): 219–23.

15. *SCR*, pp. 148–49, 151, 161, 176–78, 191. See also p. 251: "Spinoza, disciple of Maimonides as he was, never doubted the legitimacy of science."

16. Ibid., pp. 208–9. Cf. also p. 50: "a great gulf yawns between the fear of the gods known to the ancients and the fear of God known in the Bible."

17. Ibid., p. 35.

18. It is no accident to Strauss that "revealed religion is *positive* religion, grounded in experience." (*SCR*, p. 126) This in some measure accounts for the rise and development of *positive* science, according to Strauss, because it is so useful in the attack on revealed religion. The express intent of positive science is to construct and explain the empirical world so as to prevent any inference to a divine agency—even if it be only as a final cause, because that can too readily be accommodated to divine activity. Cf. also *SCR*, pp. 123–36, 136–44.

19. Cf. ibid., pp. 37–47.

20. Ibid., p. 38.

21. Cf. ibid., p. 130: "The denial of revelation is the result of the system developed in the *Ethics*," as contrasted with *PSCR*, p. 28.

22. Ibid., pp. 37–38.

23. Cf. ibid., pp. 37–52, and 274–75, note 10, for a qualifier with regard to how the moderns used (or misused) his philosophy for their own purposes.

24. Ibid., pp. 204–6, 143–46.

25. Ibid., p. 148. Cf. also pp. 241–45, 251–52.

26. Ibid., p. 49.

27. Strauss is aware that "desire for peace" need not reflect Epicurean motives, even if it results in a critique of key revealed religious doctrines which lead to "senseless conflict," for this is consistent with religious motives. (Cf. *SCR*, pp. 51–52.) At the opposite end, the defense of revealed religious doctrines may also be essayed on Epicurean grounds, as with Moses Mendelssohn's defense of the immortality of the soul as entirely an expression of a consolatory teaching. "Mendelssohn does not contest the legitimacy of the Epicurean interest. He aims only at determining which system of metaphysics—the materialist or the spiritualist—best serves that interest. This interest is common to all the efforts made in the Age of Enlightenment." Cf. *SCR*, pp. 59–60. The "moderate" Enlightenment, as he will call it, seems to represent an extenuation of Epicurean motives by combining them with Christian (or biblical) motives, and hence enabling them to "form an alliance," allegedly to "counter the trend against religion present in Epicureanism." Cf. pp. 49–50. According to Strauss's present understanding, "the effect of the Epicurean doctrines [on modern philosophy and science] is not easily overestimated." *PSCR* seems to qualify this historical conclusion, for he relates that in order to comprehend "the [moral] antagonism between Spinoza and Judaism, between unbelief and belief...the Jewish

designation of the unbeliever as Epicurean *seemed to be helpful."* (The emphasis is added.) Cf. *PSCR*, pp. 29–30.

28. *SCR*, p. 38.

29. Ibid., pp. 101, 204–6.

30. Ibid., pp. 86, 48–49, 224–29.

31. Ibid., pp. 101, 204–14, 215–50.

32. Ibid., pp. 101, 47–49. Spinoza's closeness to Averroes's attitude to theory, as the "classical" attitude, is recognized with greater clarity in *PSCR*, pp. 15–16. This same attitude was shared by Epicurus, and in that Spinoza was "closer to original Epicureanism" than was Hobbes, whose critique of religion primarily diverges from Spinoza in this regard. (That also leads them to a political divergence, according to Strauss.) Cf. *SCR*, pp. 229–45. Spinoza is closer to Epicurus because "he holds fast to the classical view of *beatitudo,* a stable condition complete in itself." (P. 210) Both Hobbes and Spinoza "see self-preservation as the essence of man, but they mean very different things by the same term. Self-preservation, truly understood according to Spinoza, compels to theory." (P. 229) According to Strauss in *SCR*, Hobbes was the first to carry through a modern critique of religion based on all three motives, since he "established the lacking connection" between the three, "and brought it into full light." Cf. *SCR*, pp. 86–87, as well as the entire section pp. 86–104. Hobbes "grasps afresh—and in a manner entirely different"—the opposition between religion and science, because he, unlike Epicurus, views them "as two opposed *attitudes of mind."* (The emphasis is in the original.)

33. *SCR*, pp. 220–22, 252–55.

34. Ibid., pp. 47, 245–50, 240–41, 228–29, 222–23, 100–101.

35. Ibid., pp. 225–29, 48–50.

36. Ibid., pp. 207, 212. Cf. also chapter 3, note 52, supra.

37. *SCR*, p. 204.

38. Ibid., p. 176.

39. Precisely because the encounter between Maimonides and Spinoza issues in a certain type of stalemate, it represents a decisive turning point, for it prepares Strauss's willingness to consider Maimonides as a still powerful guide to Jewish philosophical theology. As Strauss began to discern, Maimonides' continuing power as a guide derives from the fact that his basic analysis of the relations between theology and science, and his essential approach to the resolution of the tension between these two claims to *the* truth, transcend his operating in a "medieval" framework. Maimonides may be relevant to our modern conditions, if we do not presuppose the truth of modern conditions as if they were rooted in supposedly "evident and necessary" premises. Indeed, this preceding suggestion about Maimonides' relevance may further help prove that his "medieval" approach rests on sounder premises than does the basic approach embraced by his "modern" successors. At least he does not carry a brief for one side or the other, science or theology, until each side's evidence is considered

fairly. Thus, Maimonides may be a "deeper thinker" than Spinoza because he honestly assumes in this conflict that each side, on first view and prior to further enquiry, possesses a reasonable claim which must be considered on its merits. Such a commitment to consider the possible truth of both claims represents a prior commitment to the honest search for truth over and above everything else, rather than the desire to vindicate science at all costs. The desire to vindicate science, as Strauss learned about Spinoza, actually conceals a prior commitment to "peace of mind," i.e., to certain and secure pleasure in the pursuit of science, which may not be a necessary concomitant of the genuine search for knowledge of the truth in the purest and most original sense. This seems to be one of the key lessons that Nietzsche taught Strauss: the search for truth may require the most warlike man on the spiritual plane, and it may also be accompanied by suffering and misery. In no sense, however, does Strauss (unlike Nietzsche) forget the vital difference between theoretical and practical virtues. He shows such awareness most succinctly in his critique of Cohen: "Is the conservatism which is generally speaking the wise maxim of practice also the sacred law of theory?" (*PSCR*, p. 25)

40.   Strauss seems to have been "liberated" already from the view of modern science so prevalent in modern philosophy until Nietzsche and Heidegger that this science represents the "evident and necessary" truth about nature. Cf. supra, chapter 2. As Strauss puts it in one passage, the "promise" which has not been kept by modern science is to "reveal to us the true character of the universe and the truth about man." ("IHE" [*RCPR*], p. 32, and the entire essay, pp. 27–46) Hilail Gildin observes that for Strauss this active dissolution of modern science, abandoning its great and final claims for itself, is not just the work of critics like Nietzsche and Heidegger, but is heralded and celebrated by scientists themselves, insofar as they transform science into positivism, which will "necessarily transform [itself] into historicism." Cf. Gildin's introduction to *IPP*, pp. xiii–xviii.

41.   *SCR*, p. 172.

42.   Ibid., p. 185.

43.   Ibid., pp. 160–62.

44.   Cf. ibid., pp. 173–76, together with *Guide* II, 25 and *Theological-Political Treatise*, chapter 7. See also supra, chapter 3, note 36.

45.   *SCR*, pp. 123, 148–52, 160–63.

46.   Ibid., pp. 181–86, 165–76.

47.   Ibid., pp. 184, 172.

48.   Ibid., p. 185.

49.   Ibid., p. 182.

50.   Ibid., p. 181.

51.   Ibid., p. 184.

52.   Ibid.

53.   Ibid., p. 172.

54. Ibid., pp. 183–85, 172–73.

55. "Prophetology" as a technical term seems to have been Strauss's coinage, as far as I can determine. It has not been widely accepted. However, in a sense this is a peculiarly felicitous and well-chosen coinage, in that it fits well the relation of the study of prophecy to science rather than to theology, i.e., it is supposed to be grounded in the sciences of psychology, political science, and metaphysics.

56. *SCR*, pp. 155, 161–62. Strauss is fully aware that Maimonides chooses to "make one reservation" to the doctrine of "the Islamic philosophers, in whose footsteps Maimonides followed": God's miraculous prevention of a man who is properly endowed and trained from achieving prophecy. But this must be put beside Strauss's equal awareness of Maimonides' exertions to bring about a "decline of interest" in miracles. (Cf. *SCR*, pp. 155, 186–91.) In no sense, however, should such exertions at bringing about a "decline of interest" in miracles be construed as necessarily entailing any attempt to "refute the possibility of miracles," which are fully made possible by "the assertion of the creation of the world." Strauss seems to believe this to be the case about Maimonides in the present work. (Cf. p. 191.) Perhaps Maimonides' "negative" condition for prophecy (i.e., only if God does not prevent it) should be seen in the light of his "negative theology," his "negative" argument for creation (i.e., no demonstration refutes it), and his "negative" approach to providence (i.e., providence is consequent on intellect if and only if man loses his passion for extraneous worldly conditions of happiness). Could it be that this all conforms with some deeper pattern in Maimonides' thought, which might be dubbed "the power of negative thinking"?

57. Ibid., pp. 165–74.

58. Ibid., pp. 177 161–63, 157, 150–51, 181–82.

59. Ibid., pp. 172–73.

60. If we were to make so bold as to relate this epistemological contrast between Maimonides and Spinoza to subsequent developments in Strauss's unique notion of the history of philosophy, we might suggest that for him modern philosophy begins with Descartes's overestimation of reason and underestimation of imagination in the cognitive process, with all its theological and political ramifications, and it ends with Heidegger reversing this order in the estimation of the faculties, and thus ceasing to be philosophy. It should be remarked that already for Strauss, the medievals and especially Maimonides penetrated to a deeper comprehension of the relations between intellect, imagination, and sensation, which perhaps reflects an Aristotelian leaning. Cf. *SCR*, pp. 172–73, 183–85, for Cartesian epistemology which "reflects the *absolute* preference for waking as against dreaming," i.e., the rejection of what in Aristotle is judged to be the natural, divinatory dream, or of what in Maimonides is similarly called "the veridical dream." Consider also how Strauss traces "the considerable differences" between Spinoza's and nineteenth/twentieth-century biblical criticism "to their difference in regard to the evaluation of the imagination." For the

former, it is "simply subrational," while for the latter it is "assigned a much higher rank," since it is interpreted as "the vehicle of religious or spiritual experience" through "symbols and the like." Cf. *JA*, pp. 5–6; idem, "JA" (*SPPP*), p. 150. These remarks are anticipated by *SCR*, pp. 263–64. See also especially supra, chapter 3, note 47.

    61.   *SCR*, pp. 174–76.

    62.   Ibid., p. 173.

    63.   Ibid., pp. 175, 181, 163.

    64.   Ibid., p. 163. It is also worth noting that with regard to Maimonides' idea of science in its possible relations with Scripture, Strauss makes this following succinct remark:

> the type of theory with which Maimonides is confronted refuses itself far less to the identification with revelation than does the opposite type which Spinoza has in mind. This holds quite apart from the difference in the substantive assertions. (*SCR*, p. 175)

Strauss seems to believe this not only because of the Aristotelian scientific basis for Maimonides' prophetology, but also because he recognizes in the classical philosophic search for the one eternal truth a basis for accord between philosophy and revealed religion. Such philosophy can acknowledge in revealed religion a rival with another possible source of the same, or similar, eternal truth. To be sure, Strauss also admits the basic merit concealed in Spinoza's *positivist* critique of Maimonides' idea of science as employed in his hermeneutics: that Maimonides still assumes a completed science.

> Only on the assumption of such a completion of science is the principle of interpretation adopted by Maimonides capable of application.... Not until science is completed and perfect can it unlock the mysteries of Scripture. (*SCR*, p. 175)

But Spinoza's own modern Cartesian, i.e., metaphysical, idea of science also transcends positivism. Such modern philosophy is no exception to the idea expounded by ancient philosophy, for it too "is intended as completed science," even if it pursues a different approach to such "completion." Cf. also *SCR*, p. 181.

    65.   *SCR*, pp. 163, 191, 140–44.

    66.   Ibid., pp. 236–50, 252–58. As Strauss grasped, Spinoza did not come to this conclusion about the need for history to criticize "facts," beliefs, and texts transmitted by tradition, and about Maimonides' deficiency in recognizing this need, merely because of a keener alertness to the unreliability of tradition. Such alertness is evident in the Reformation attitude to history as a necessary aid in the correction of a corrupt tradition, but its motives in turning to history are fully consistent with fidelity to revealed religion. (Cf. pp. 251–54, 140–44.) Spinoza's alienation from revealed religion alone leads to his need for history,

for he turns to it just in order to "clarify" how the tradition's originally *political* grounding for religion has been obscured by falsifying priests.

67. Ibid., pp. 186, 188.

68. Ibid., p. 163. Strauss detects "the positive critique of miracle's" limit in two fundamentally different modes of viewing the world: as open to divine encroachment and as closed to the same. Hence, the difference does *not* lie in a critical, doubting, unbelieving attitude versus a credulous, naïve, believing attitude to nature, as positivism and the Enlightenment claim. Strauss cites the case in the Bible of Elijah and the Baal prophets (*SCR*, pp. 213–14). The same theme has been invoked, and expanded upon, by E. L. Fackenheim, "Elijah and the Empiricists," in *Encounters Between Judaism and Modern Philosophy* (New York: Basic Books, 1973), pp. 9–29.

69. *SCR*, pp. 123–36.

70. Ibid., pp. 188–91.

71. Ibid., p. 143.

72. Ibid., pp. 143, 157. Strauss applies the same insight to the attack on Maimonides' exegesis: "In principle, no critique of Scripture can touch Maimonides' position, since such critique is capable of no more than establishing what is *humanly* possible or impossible, whereas his opponent assumes the divine origin of Scripture." (P. 157)

73. For Spinoza and miracles, cf. ibid., pp. 123–36, 140–44, 160–65, 185–91, 196–99, 212–14.

74. Ibid., p. 199.

75. Ibid., p. 214.

76. Ibid., p. 157.

77. Ibid., p. 199.

78. Ibid., p. 161.

79. Ibid. It would seem that in this way of framing Maimonides' enterprise with respect to science and reasoning, he recognizes the need to correctly define their precise limits prior to proceeding further. As such, Strauss continues to use the conceptual terminology of Cohen's approach, which indeed characterizes what we are calling the entire "first stage" in Strauss's developing views of Maimonides. However, Strauss clearly understands the contents of Maimonides' teaching in a fashion which is not truly Kantian or neo-Kantian, i.e., he consciously overturns Cohen's approach.

80. Ibid., pp. 159–60.

81. Ibid., p. 155.

82. If there are still true "Spinozists" in philosophy, who are persuaded of the complete adequacy of the *Ethics* as the final philosophic system, in which all its truths about God, man, and the world are fully and properly demonstrated by its geometrical method, then to them Strauss's entire argument and ultimate conclusions will appear to be specious logic. Strauss briefly summarizes his own doubts about Spinoza's *Ethics* as follows:

But is Spinoza's account of the whole clear and distinct? Those of you who have ever tried their hands, for example, at his analysis of the emotions, would not be so certain of that. But more than that, even if it is clear and distinct, is it necessarily true? Is its clarity and distinctness not due to the fact that Spinoza abstracts from those elements of the whole which are not clear and distinct and which can never be rendered clear and distinct?

See "MITP," p. 117; "POR?" (IPP), pp. 307–8.

83. PSCR, pp. 28–29; SCR, pp. 144–46, 204–14, 42.

84. In retrospect, Strauss will deny that in this work he attained to a precise, complete, or accurate comprehension of either Maimonides' or Spinoza's positions.

85. Thus, the first stage in Strauss's view of Maimonides represents such a decisive breakthrough not only because of what it would yield in the future, but also because he already recognized this essential point: "the basis of Maimonides' position . . . remains unimpaired by all the changes that have occurred" in the history of philosophy from Maimonides' era to Spinoza's era. And since, as Strauss discovered further, Spinoza never actually refuted Maimonides, "the basis of Maimonides' position" seemingly remains intact and sound until the present, because it is based on the belief in revelation which is not destroyed with the demolition of Aristotelianism. (P. 163) To Strauss, Spinoza's "fundamental alienation from Judaism" seems to refer to his deaf and blind refusal, based on dogmatic belief in modern positive science (which is itself driven by "Epicurean" motives), to accept or even to consider anything which "fosters, or even merely tolerates, the concern with supernatural guidance of human life." (P. 160) Since Strauss argues on moral grounds that "concern with revelation precedes belief in revelation" (p. 158), from this it would seem to follow that unconcern with revelation precedes disbelief in revelation. A moral position precedes any positions with respect to either theology or science, as well as with respect to their possible reconciliation. In other words, the denial of revelation seems to be necessarily connected with the desire to deny the hidden God, whose omnipotence allows him to act freely and hence to reveal himself as he will, since "only a God who is free and unfathomable wisdom can truly reveal himself." (P. 155) Man does not need to consider such a God and his revelations—he has no interest in him and hence is not exposed to his caprice, which is the breeding-ground of fear (p. 150)—if he can so construct the world through reason as to render nothing possible which is not actual: "the actual is of necessity such as it is; the rules of actual events are necessary laws, eternal truths; the modifications of nature, the annulling of a law of nature, the miracle is an absurdity." Cf. SCR, pp. 151–52, as well as 38, 140, 178.

86. I refer to "the historical" and its proper use, as first enunciated by Strauss in the review of Ebbinghaus, op. cit., and to be differentiated from its modern

misuse: "we are in need of history first of all. . .in order to get up into the cave from which Socrates can lead us to the light; we are in need of a propaedeutic, of which the Greeks were not in need, precisely of learning through reading." See supra, note 14, and also chapter 1, note 49. Cf. also James F. Ward, "Political Philosophy and History: The Links Between Strauss and Heidegger," *Polity* 20, no. 2 (Winter 1987): 273–95.

87. *SCR*, pp. 178–82. For the specifically Jewish context, in which the matter of "prejudice" is discussed, cf. pp. 162–65. For the Bible and "the prejudices of an ancient people," cf. pp. 251–55. For "theological prejudices" versus philosophical freedom, cf. pp. 111–16. Consider also *PSCR*, p. 28. For Maimonides' tacit and "preemptive" rejection of "prejudice" as a determinative notion, and for his unambiguous rootedness in Jewish life and faith, cf. *SCR*, pp. 163–64. Thus:

> Maimonides is not setting up a pedagogic program by virtue of sovereign philosophy. . . . As a Jew, born, living, and dying with Jews, he pursued philosophy as a Jewish teacher of Jews. . . . He defends the context of Jewish life which is threatened by the philosophers in so far as it is threatened by them. He enlightens Judaism by means of philosophy, to the extent that Judaism can be enlightened.

However much Spinoza learned from Maimonides, it was overruled for Strauss by the basis for Spinoza's critique of Maimonides, which derives from "considering as typical the philosopher living 'cautiously' remote from the crowd." By contrast, Maimonides recommends the "intermediary stage" of correct opinions imitative of "the fundamental truths." He assumes that those who are encompassed by this stage will "remain dependent on trust in the wise men who possess true knowledge." In other words, Maimonides, "by a standard by no means utopian," conceives of "the philosophically enlightened rabbi" who regards it as his duty to be "responsible for the guidance of the multitude and who enjoys the people's confidence." (*SCR*, p. 171) Spinoza rejects "idealist" philosophers because he considers them to be too much like the religious, whose principle of not acting with sufficient vigor and cunning is rooted in "wishfulness," while his political doctrine claimed to be the first truly "realistic" one. However, Strauss regards his view as "in the final analysis. . .not at all political" but rather connected with, and furthering of, his whole philosophy, "which consists in the unqualified affirmation of reality." Thus, Strauss is able to explain Spinoza's hostility to utopias. He recognizes there is a deep and exact connection between all previous philosophy and the religious attitude, in the mind of Spinoza: "The opposition to utopia is thus nothing other than the opposition to religion," and "his opposition to utopia is then not so much in the interest of politics as in the interest of philosophy." Cf. also Strauss's remarks in regard to Spinoza's "denial of sin," *SCR*, pp. 202–4, and see note 3, supra.

88. *SCR*, pp. 181, 172, 205–6. As Strauss puts it: "with a view to the radical meaning of revealed religion it must be said" that this belief in "the unfathomable

God" who is also a lawgiver is itself "*the* prejudice pure and simple." In other words, by dogmatically denying the possibility of discovering *anything* of cognitive value in religion, Spinoza is "unreasonably" prevented from attributing to opinion the status of the necessary starting point for all philosophizing, and hence from appreciating revealed religion as, if nothing else, an opinion which may be salutary for nurturing the search for truth in man.

89.   According to Strauss, the Epicurean *eudaemonia* of man is to be located for Spinoza also in contemplation, as the highest human pleasure, although only for the wise few, since it will never appeal to the ignorant many. But Spinoza allows greater tolerance for the multitude's inferior bodily pleasures than had been previously allowed by philosophers, since hostility to them is also a "prejudice" fostered by, and thus supporting, revealed religion, which is "*the* prejudice pure and simple." Revealed religion, in its recalling the possibility of truth which transcends ordinary human life, denies man's sufficiency to attain *the* whole truth by his own effort and ability, and thus suggests the needs of the human soul are rooted in a "need" higher than pleasure, indicating higher exigencies than self-preservation.

90.   *SCR*, p. 181.

91.   Ibid., pp. 177, 182.

92.   Ibid., p. 182. Contrast this with Strauss's growing awareness of the natural primacy of "opinion" as rooted in political life, an awareness that will be further expanded on once he recognizes the possibility of a "return" to premodern philosophy, and especially as no longer held in check by modern natural science, since it too has itself been fatally enmeshed in historicism. Cf. chapter 2, supra.

93.   *SCR*, p. 178.

94.   Ibid., p. 180. Cf. T. L. Pangle's introduction to *SPPP*, p. 26, for an attribution of this "messianic" component of modern philosophy to its apotheosis in Cohen. (See also supra, chapter 3, note 16.) It is my view that Strauss attributed a "messianic" religious component or residual faith to modern philosophy in its very beginnings, irrespective of whether these were Machiavellian or Hobbesian.

95.   *SCR*, p. 165.

96.   Ibid., 175–76.

97.   Ibid., pp. 159–60.

98.   Ibid., pp. 175, 157–58.

99.   Ibid., pp. 157–58.

100.   Ibid., p. 171.

101.   Ibid., pp. 191–92.

102.   Ibid.

103.   Ibid., pp. 163–65.

104.   Ibid., pp. 163–64.

105.   Ibid., p 164.

106. Ibid., pp. 149, 191. As Strauss was already well-aware, Maimonides goes to the length of asserting that revealed texts must teach what is genuinely known, where something is known by scientific demonstration, even if this contradicts traditional beliefs based on a literal reading of those revealed texts. Cf. *SCR*, pp. 160–63; *Guide* II, 25; *Theological-Political Treatise*, chapter 7.

107. *SCR*, p. 161. Cf. also pp. 162–64 for miracles versus physics versus the "true" Jewish position.

108. Ibid., pp. 177, 149, 151.

109. Ibid., p. 191.

110. Ibid., pp. 191–92.

111. Ibid., p. 106.

112. Ibid., p. 158.

CHAPTER FIVE

1. See supra, chapter 4, between endnote markers 79 and 83, and between endnote markers 11 and 14.

2. See supra, chapters 1 and 3. For the Introduction to *Philosophy and Law* in the development of Strauss's Jewish thought, see especially supra, chapters 1 and 2.

3. *DLT*, p. 334; *OT* (rev.), p. 212. In his "GA," p. 3, Strauss tells how he read Heidegger very seriously until 1933. Once Heidegger sided with the Nazis, Strauss apparently did not bother with his writings again until the 1950s. Further to what was said in chapter 4, note 7, about Heidegger and Husserl, and how Heidegger "radicalized" Husserl's critique of Cohen, the following should also be considered in order to comprehend how Strauss's critique "radicalized" and reversed Heidegger's apotheosis of historicism, and indeed perhaps tried to provide an antidote to it: "Among the many things that make Heidegger's thought so appealing to so many contemporaries is his accepting the premise that while human life and thought is radically historical, History is not a rational process. As a consequence, he denies that one can understand a thinker better than he understood himself and even as he understood himself: a great thinker will understand an earlier thinker of rank creatively, i.e., by transforming his thought, and hence by understanding him differently than he understood himself. *One could hardly observe this transformation if one could not see the original form.*" (The emphasis is added.) See "PARSPP" (*SPPP*), p. 30. Similarly, Heidegger "intended to uproot Greek philosophy, especially Aristotle, but this presupposed the laying bare of its roots, *the laying bare of it as it was in itself* and not as it had come to appear in the light of the tradition and of modern philosophy." (The emphasis is added.) See "GA," p. 3. As it happened, Strauss with his friend "Klein was more attracted by the Aristotle brought to light and life by Heidegger than by Heidegger's own philosophy." However, Heidegger's deconstruction project was, from the epistemological point of view, a fruitful error for Strauss.

In studying it he learned to turn afresh to "the original form," however great and difficult an effort it might require. For if the route from Kant to Heidegger in the history of philosophy does help to definitively prove the untenability of the Kantian position, especially in its crucial epistemological phase, and if Heidegger is correct in raising the prospect of a return to sounder ancient positions, the decisive though paradoxical contribution which Heidegger's thought makes to Strauss's thought is the recognition that a previous thinker's position may still be correctly and accurately understood just as he understood it himself, and just as he meant it to be understood. This must be because History, which Strauss also concedes is not rational, also does not refute anything—it merely overlays the original position with traditional accretions. (It is true that Strauss had already been taught this lesson by Lessing.) But notwithstanding this decisive contribution, Heidegger's history of philosophy must still remain in doubt, according to Strauss, for only through it do we presuppose that the classical "Socratic" philosophic position is untrue and closed to us because it is not properly or adequately "open to Being." Thus, the true character of what is unique in the classical approach to Being, its approach through "nature," would actually seem to have been obscured by Heidegger's historicism, i.e., his continuing belief in a Hegelian "absolute moment of history." This belief is rooted in his own claim to the first full apprehension of "the true ground of all grounds, the fundamental abyss." Cf. "PARSPP" (*SPPP*), pp. 30–34. As Strauss concludes: "This assertion [i.e., Heidegger's apprehension of "the true ground" as "the fundamental abyss"] implies the claim that in the decisive respect Heidegger understands his great predecessors better than they understood themselves."

The ultimate conflict between Heidegger's radical modern historicism, on the one hand, and Strauss's restored classical naturalism or rationalism, on the other hand, may be said to have been prepared by Husserl in his critique of Cohen. What Strauss seems to mean by tracing the conflict to Husserl is something like the following. Husserl recognized with profundity the fact that "the scientific understanding of the world," which for Cohen is simply primary, is actually "derivative" from "our natural understanding of the world," and this is "prescientific." Hence, in order to understand this "prescientific" or "natural" ground, which is the true basis for all "scientific understanding," we must first understand how we arrive at the idea of "nature" as something that can and should be scientifically understood, and especially also what the human conditions are which lead to such a breakthrough to "science." For Strauss, Husserl raised the right question in asking whether the dubious, specifically modern "separation of the ideas of wisdom [i.e., the approach to man] and of rigorous science [i.e., the approach to nature]" is tenable. Hence, Husserl also correctly asked about the proper relation between "the two kinds of philosophy," the human and the natural, and about whether one is necessarily prior to the other. Husserl's answer, however, Strauss rejects. Husserl asserts that this separation cannot be surpassed and properly ordered, and thus maintains there is no comprehensive or universal "natural" approach to man (i.e., the "idea of philosophy") which is presupposed by what is merely considered at present to be the prior eternal "idea of science" with regard to nature. It is then, according to Husserl, only in the arbitrary sphere of *Weltanschauungen*, i.e., in particular and historically relative acts of faith by one man or some men or by a human society about how best to construe the world, that this relation must be ordered. For Husserl, modern Western man just happened to choose "science." Strauss, in contrast to Husserl, maintains that it is the possibility of philosophy as "wisdom" or as "search for wisdom" which should be the key to a "natural" or "prescientific" approach to man and the world. Indeed, in Strauss's view, it is only this necessary priority of the question of what man is and about what a philosopher is which will enable one to adequately explain, and to offer an answer to, why "rigorous science" about the world, or even the "scientific approach to nature," as a pursuit is an intelligible and even a necessary choice for man as such. Cf. "PARSPP" (*SPPP*), pp. 31, 34–37; "GA," pp. 2–3; "IHE" (*RCPR*), pp. 28–35. For a further allusion to the importance of Husserl in Strauss's thought, see also now "CLS," pp. 189–90.

    4. Cf., e.g., *PG*, pp. 26–29, *PL*, pp. 17–20, with "GA," pp. 2–3, "UP," p. 2, and "PARSPP" (*SPPP*), pp. 29–37, and especially p. 30.

    5. These well-known Maimonidean qualifications, which differentiate the teaching of the Torah from the teaching of "the philosophers," may be summarized briefly as follows: the creation of the world out of nothing as opposed to the eternity of the world; the supraphilosophical knowledge obtained in true prophecy; the special providence of God with respect only to human beings; and most importantly, their difference not about the existence but about the essence or character or "name" of God. Curiously, as Strauss subsequently noted in "NMLA" (*SPPP*), pp. 205–7, in Maimonides' *Letter on Astrology* he mitigates or "reduces the difference, as stated in the *Guide*, between philosophy and the Torah" on both creation and universal providence, in order "to present as it were a unitary front of philosophy and the Torah against astrology." However, as Maimonides stresses "according to the *Letter on Astrology*, they are divided by what they teach regarding providence": it seems as if *the* difference between philosophy and the Torah rests on their views of particular providence as grounded in freedom, and as issuing in the just fate of the human individual.

    6. See infra, chapter 6, and also supra, chapter 4, between endnote markers 101 and 106.

    7. Cf. supra, chapter 4, between endnote markers 79 and 83, and between endnote markers 38 and 61.

    8. For the relevance of prophecy to *both* the philosophic and religious positions, i.e., even to those who believe in the world's eternity rather than its createdness, consider the following statement by Maimonides: "For as we shall make clear, prophecy is not set at nought even in the opinion of those who believe in the eternity of the world." (*Guide* II, 16) Cf. also II, 32, 36–38, 40, 48. Further, Strauss recognized in this concern to present prophecy as acceptable to philosophy

a similarity to the attitude of the moderate Enlightenment, but with a crucial difference: for Maimonides, the prophet is intellectually as well as morally perfect, while in the modern view, the prophet is just an imaginative teacher of rational or natural religion and morality, which may indeed on the surface be closer to the literary form in which the message of prophecy is conveyed. Nevertheless, Maimonides reconciles his medieval "enlightenment" attitude to prophecy, i.e., as acceptable to philosophy, with the imaginative and hence popular form essential to prophecy, through a different notion of what his own, as well as what prophetic, "enlightening" is aimed at: their "enlightenment" is esoteric, or aimed at the few, while the moderns are exoteric, or aimed at the many. That difference will, of course, become more and more decisive in Strauss's view of Maimonides, especially as it unfolds in the third stage. For why should those who aim at the few seem to speak so directly and predominantly to the many?

9.   The budding awareness of the connection between literary form and philosophical purpose in the first stage (*SCR*, pp. 163–64) only bears fruit in the second stage with the preliminary notion that Maimonidean medieval "enlightenment" is ultimately esoteric, while the Spinozistic modern version is primarily exoteric. See *PG*, pp. 88–90; *PL*, pp. 82–83. However, this insight is not carried through to any final conclusion in the present stage: the literary expression is not as yet for Strauss the key to any specific philosophic views, only to a general philosophic tendency.

10.   See supra, chapter 4, between endnote markers 106 and the end of the chapter, as well as between endnote markers 65 and 67.

11.   Cf., e.g., G. E. Lessing, "On the Proof of the Spirit and of Power," for a possible antecedent for Strauss.

12.   *SCR*, pp. 191–92.

13.   For an elaborate assertion of the "historical proof," and a pedagogical argument for the crucial role it plays in bolstering Jewish belief and Jewish loyalty, see Maimonides' *Letter to Yemen*.

14.   *Guide* III, 27–28. Cf. also "ET," pp. 57–59; *PG*, pp. 50–52, 59–60; *PL*, pp. 42–44, 50–51. Cf. already *SCR*, pp. 170–71.

15.   See supra, chapter 4, between endnote markers 94 and 101.

16.   *PG*, pp. 108–22; *PL*, pp. 98–110.

17.   Cf. *Guide* II, 11–12, 36–38, together with *PG*, pp. 87–99; *PL*, pp. 81–92. Maimonides hopes to vindicate the belief in the rationality of God as lawgiver, which is *the* true difficulty from the Platonic-Aristotelian perspective (just as much as from the Spinozist perspective), in a fashion which will not contradict anything actually *known* from the Platonic-Aristotelian perspective. That this is enough to convince a Platonic-Aristotelian philosopher of its *truth* is not self-evident. Hence it still remains an unresolved difficulty, a question not fully answered, in the second stage of Strauss's developing views on Maimonides.

18.   If all the signs seemed to point Strauss to Maimonides' prophetology as the royal gateway to the *Guide* (as a book which he was to call "an enchanted

and enchanting forest"), his focusing upon it transformed his comprehension of Maimonides' Jewish thought in its essential aim and purpose. To summarize briefly and in anticipation "the change of orientation" (*PSCR*, p. 31) accompanying his turn to premodern reason as it is presented by *Philosophy and Law*: not Aristotle but Plato is the key to Maimonides' *Guide*; not Christian scholastic theology in the manner of Thomas but Islamic political philosophy in the manner of Averroes (or Alfarabi) is the model for comprehending Maimonides as thinker and writer; not primarily supernatural grace or religious experience but just as much natural achievement or philosophical intellect is the exemplar for Maimonides' intention in his treatment of prophecy and revelation; not "simple" synthesis between reason and revelation, whose fierce quarrels have been construed as mostly caused by errors in construction of the one eternal truth, but rather "complex" harmonization at best of two things which are locked in a fundamental tension about the conception of the eternal truth in its very nature; and not prophecy and revelation as pertaining to purely "religious" matters, but the highest lawgiving prophet as philosopher-king whose concern is "political," i.e., to establish the perfect or virtuous city which is also hospitable to philosophy.

19. For whether a premodern "natural theology" (original or reconstituted) would support Maimonides' "prophetology" or any like it, see supra, note 8; chapter 1, notes 37, 44, 49, 70; chapter 2; chapter 3, note 43.

20. See supra, chapter 2, note 3, with *PG*, pp. 9, 66–67, 119–22; *PL*, pp. 3, 57–58, 107–10.

21. See supra, chapter 1, notes 7, 49, 78, 98, 99, 105.

22. See supra, chapter 2, note 13.

23. See supra, chapter 1, note 6. For the continuing fruitfulness of Avicenna's remark as it is reflected in the last work Strauss prepared for publication himself, cf. *AAPL*, p. 1, the epigraph. According to Shlomo Pines, Strauss already in the 1920s recognized the centrality of Plato's *Laws* for the understanding of Maimonides and his Islamic philosophic predecessors. See "On Leo Strauss," pp. 455–57. Compare also supra, chapter 1, note 6 with note 1, and with chapter 2, note 3, and chapter 3, note 30.

24. See supra, chapter 1, note 80, as well as *PG*, pp. 99–108; *PL*, pp. 92–98.

25. *PG*, p. 62; *PL*, p. 53. For a careful and probing analytical discussion of the contents of *Philosophy and Law*, chapter by chapter, and for a cogent critique of the English translation, see Eve Adler, "Leo Strauss's *Philosophie und Gesetz*," in *Leo Strauss's Thought*, edited by Alan Udoff (Boulder, Colo.: Lynne Rienner, 1991), pp. 183–226.

26. *PG*, pp. 61–64, 112–18; *PL*, pp. 52–55. 102–7.

27. *PG*, p. 89; *PL*, pp. 82–83.

28. *PG*, pp. 63–64, 117–18; *PL*, pp. 54–55, 106–7. It might be asked whether Strauss (or Maimonides or the Muslim philosophers) ever treats Jesus as one of the lawgiving prophets. I will not presume to speak for all of the great Islamic philosophers whom Strauss studied (Alfarabi, Avicenna, Averroes), but so far as

I know they do not treat Jesus in precisely the same way as they treat Moses
and Mohammed, because they are constrained by specific Muslim beliefs about
Jesus. But Maimonides is a different case entirely. To be sure, in his works he
treats the two non-Jewish monotheistic religions quite distinctly from one
another in certain key respects, e.g., on the purity of their monotheisms, on the
ethical teachings and ethical conduct of their prophets, and on their holy books
(what their attitude to the Hebrew Bible is, and what it reflects), among other
things. But on one matter, Maimonides makes it crystal clear that none of this
makes any difference whatsoever in defining what Jesus and Mohammed were—
they were the "founders" of their religious communities, i.e., prophetic lawgivers.
Consider what I would regard as Maimonides' definitive statement: the censored
paragraphs toward the end of the *Mishneh Torah*, in book 14 ("Book of Judges"),
treatise 5 ("Laws of Kings and Their Wars"), chapter 11, section 4. (It is translated
by Abraham M. Hershman in the Introduction to his edition of *The Code of
Maimonides, Book 14: The Book of Judges* [New Haven: Yale University Press,
1949], pp. xxii–xxiv.) I make the assumption that Strauss follows Maimonides
on this point. I so assume because the writings of Maimonides represent to
Strauss the highest and most perfect articulation of the medieval philosophic
doctrine on prophets with which he is concerned in *Philosophy and Law*, and
hence such a view of Jesus does not require that Maimonides contradict himself
in any way. (As has been noted, Strauss is especially careful to declare that this
is his attitude toward Maimonides' prophetology in *Philosophy and Law*. Cf.
PG, p. 65; *PL*, pp. 56–57.) Also I have not been able to locate any direct evidence
in Strauss's scholarly writings, nor have I been able to generate any contrary
reasoning from his philosophic thought, to suggest that Strauss would have been
prevented from pursuing this comparative approach to Jesus as a lawgiving
prophet. Further, I can perceive no serious theological reason why Jesus would
not have been so viewed by Strauss himself. While I would not presume to speak
on this with religious authority, it seems to me that it does no harm to the
sensibilities of a Christian to acknowledge that this is a key aspect of his faith—
Jesus established his religious community. As Strauss keenly observed,
Christianity on the one hand, Judaism and Islam on the other hand, may be
differentiated by the contrasting *priority* they put on law versus doctrine. But
this is no proof that a different status necessarily appertains to Jesus, for this
observation of Strauss's relates to a *subordinate* and even *extraneous* difference,
insofar as the philosophical analysis of revealed religions is concerned with
prophetology. (Refer to the context in which it is discussed in the Introduction
to *PAW*, pp. 17–21.) The medieval Christian empire is still essentially a law-based
and law-ruled religious polity (and not just in terms of canonical law), even if
divine law does not take the pride of place given to it by Judaism and Islam.
At the same time, Jesus lays the foundations of the faith, and as such must also
be regarded as the "founder," i.e., legislator, of the way of life, the community,
and the state established in his name and based on his faith. Cf. also *Guide* I,
71, p. 177.

29. *PG*, pp. 88–90; *PL*, pp. 82–84.

30. See supra, chapter 2, note 52. Maimonides will thus appeal to modern man who has also been disillusioned about the possibility of actualizing "a simply rational society." The difficulties involved were plainly evident to Strauss from the history of modern political philosophy from Rousseau to Nietzsche, and especially from the political history of our century. This is to separate as an entirely different question his appeal to modern Jews, in that they will look at him also from the specific perspective and problematics of modern Judaism.

31. Whether according to Strauss the "Socratic" position on truths about the superlunar sphere is that, rather than man being in need of prophets, such truths are simply unavailable to man, or whether this position would imply an undue dogmatism in Socrates about the availability of even superlunar truth to man, is something which cannot be addressed in the present context. Strauss's researches on "the problem of Socrates" will only emerge in the decade following *Philosophy and Law*. At the moment, we can only concern ourselves with what the Platonic position is as it is elaborated by Maimonides, according to the present view of Strauss.

32. *PG*, pp. 65, 76–79; *PL*, pp. 56–57, 68–71.

33. *PG*, pp. 118–22; *PL*, pp. 107–10. Strauss in his second stage did not lay as much stress on a possibly significant gap between the true Platonic teaching and what Maimonides says. Does Plato mean by philosopher-king precisely the same thing as Maimonides means by prophet? Is Plato's "prophetology" concerned only with the possible appearance of prophetic revelation, and not at all with its actuality, i.e., is it not merely the *question*, and what it implies for the human mind, which is his focus, rather than as a guide to action? And finally, is the "truly virtuous city," even for Maimonides, not an oxymoron? Is it not only the philosopher-king (or prophet) who is "truly virtuous"? And even if it is the philosopher-king (or prophet) who alone can discern the needs of political life and theological doctrine in terms of a specific community, does this very insight into the truth not teach him that it can never be fully expressed in actuality?

34. *PG*, pp. 78, 55–56; *PL*, pp. 70, 46–48.

35. *PG*, p. 54; *PL*, pp. 45–46.

36. Cf. *SCR*, pp. 177, 161–63, 157, 150–51, 181–82, together with *PG*, pp. 51–58, 76–79, 88–97, 120; *PL*, pp. 43–49, 68–71, 82–90, 108–9.

37. Gersonides, who according to Strauss in *PG/PL* was the most radical medieval Jewish rationalist, "neither acknowledges suprarational truths in principle which can be guaranteed by revelation alone, nor ascribes to prophecy an essentially political meaning." Hence, for Strauss, he represents "the disintegration of Platonism" through his notion that divine providence is fully evident and proven in the governance of the natural world alone, since this detaches divine providence from necessarily being fulfilled in "a prophetic lawgiving and state-grounding" as was true for "the Islamic Aristotelians and Maimonides." Cf. *PG*, pp. 65–66; *PL*, pp. 56–57. Strauss delineates several other divergences of Gersonides from Maimonides in the direction of Averroes,

especially concerning the sufficiency of human reason to answer *all* fundamental questions for which it has a "natural desire," however difficult it may be to attain the final answer to these questions. Even so, Gersonides also acknowledges the Torah as a divinely granted imaginative map of the world, which is established in the world "prior to philosophy," i.e., prior cognitively and morally as a divine authority whose scope is all things, however one may finally decide on what its proper meaning is. Thus Strauss concludes: "The primacy of the law is just as established for Levi as it was for Maimonides and Ibn Rushd." The prophet, even if not fulfilling an "essentially political" function for Gersonides, certainly *also* serves as such; this means that we must obey his law. The diminution of the prophet's political function in Gersonides' view may well be adequate to account for his similar divergence from Maimonides about concealing the Torah's esoteric meaning. He claims the full right to freely communicate these meanings is justified by the Torah's aim of perfecting men's souls, i.e., in cognizing physical and metaphysical truth, and thus it would be a sin to refuse to communicate to others the cognitions one has been able to apprehend. Cf. *PG*, pp. 79–86; *PL*, pp. 71–78.

38.   *PG*, p. 65; *PL*, pp. 56–57.

39.   It seems that Strauss did already in some measure recognize the implications of this term, but only in the case of Averroes—he makes no attempt to apply it to Maimonides. Cf. *PG*, pp. 47–48, 57–58, 69–75, 77–79; *PL*, pp. 39–41, 48–49, 62–68, 69–71.

40.   *PG*, pp. 48, 69–78; *PL*, pp. 40–41, 62–71.

41.   *PSCR*, p. 31.

42.   The return to the premodern wisdom may yield the possibility of saving the modern tradition itself because it promises to recover a sounder basis for reason. With due modifications to the notion of what reason itself means, it was in the name of, and for the sake of, the same reason which caused the modern tradition to arise in the first place. In their essence and their origins, modern philosophy and science were an attempt to vindicate reason, and to restore it to its ancient glory, if not also to revise it at the same time. Cf. *PG*, p. 13, note 1; *PL*, pp. 111–12, note 2.

43.   Cf. *PSCR*, p. 30, for the phrase "complex- simple philosophy." The same "philosophy" is already diagnosed in the Introduction to *Philosophy and Law*: see *PG*, pp. 26–28, and *PL*, pp. 17–19.

44.   Certainly we may want to question not just the details of Maimonides' scheme, but the very idea of it. And it is entirely fitting for some of us to want to do so, as Strauss would certainly acknowledge. Is it not radically problematic for us in our modern situation? Perhaps it is appropriate to now repeat things which I said at the beginning of chapter 1. Although I have been speaking about Strauss's notion of a "return to Maimonides" (in its developing stages), I do not believe that Strauss means this in any simplistic way. In other words, I do not want to overstate Strauss's argument here in *Philosophy and Law*, or even in

his Jewish thought *per se*. Strauss is not asking modern Jews to forget or abandon their modern tradition, or to adopt Maimonides' scheme as the one and only guide to future Jewish thought. He only asks us to take it seriously as a potential (though neglected and often dismissed) source of wisdom, to try to understand the hidden depths of its reasoning, and hence to learn critically from it. In his view, it still retains the power to teach us important lessons not only about Jews and Judaism, but also about God, man, and the world.

45. See supra, chapter 1, note 49, toward the end.

46. Cf. *Guide* III, 28, with *PG*, pp. 76–79, 54–56, 96–97, 116, 120; *PL*, pp. 68–71, 45–47, 89–90, 104–5, 108–9. See also, *CM*, p. 139.

CHAPTER SIX

1. The grounds for Strauss's rejection of "historicism" had already been formulated in "Political Philosophy and History" (1949), and culminated in his analysis and critique of the historian and philosopher Collingwood (1952). See "PPH" (*WIPP?*) and "OCPH." He also rejects the assumption which prevents those who believe in historicism from considering the possibility of a "return" to an ancient, "prehistorical" philosophic truth by historically later men: "Equally characteristic of historicism is the assumption that restorations of earlier teachings are impossible, or that every intended restoration necessarily leads to an essential modification of the restored teaching. This assumption can most easily be understood as a necessary consequence of the view that every teaching is essentially related to an unrepeatable 'historical' situation." Cf. "PPH" (*WIPP?*), p. 60. See also supra, chapter 2, note 13; chapter 3, note 39; chapter 4, notes 3 and 4; chapter 5, note 3.

2. "PHPW," p. 1. The transition to the third stage in the development of Strauss's views on Maimonides is distinguished by his growing attentiveness to what might be called Maimonides' *theologia politica*, which Strauss discovered by focusing on the "deliberate contradictions" in the writing of the *Guide*. For the phrase *theologia politica*, cf. "OVL," p. 104, note 34. As Strauss notes, the term is used by Solomon Maimon to characterize the *Guide* with regard to its "plan, purpose, and method." As has been made clear, however, the conjoining phrase "theological-political" commonly used by Strauss is undoubtedly adopted from Spinoza.

3. *PPH*, p. xv.

4. *PG*, p. 28; *PL*, p. 19.

5. Strauss often speaks about the radical transformation which may be expected to occur to the historian who is "seriously interested" in his study of classical philosophy. "When he engages in the study of classical philosophy he must know that he embarks on a journey whose end is completely hidden from him. He is not likely to return to the shores of our time as exactly the same man who departed from them." But Strauss defines this interest as truly serious

only if the historian is "prepared to consider the possibility that its teachings are simply true, or that it is decisively superior to modern philosophy." In other words, he must explore it on its own terms, not on modern terms, because modern terms distort the possible truth of the classical teachings. To simplify considerably, the classical teachings are primarily oriented to what is true theoretically, while the modern teachings are primarily oriented to what is true practically. Thus, the lessons Strauss supposes Plato teaches may be radical theoretically, but he is equally convinced they will be moderate practically: ". . . in an imperfect society the [Platonic] philosopher is not likely to engage in political activity of any kind, but will rather lead a life of privacy." Cf. "ONI," pp. 331, 361; "OCPH," p. 583; "ET," pp. 52–53; *OT*, pp. 219–22; *OT* (rev.), pp. 204–7; *PAW*, pp. 15–18.

   6.   Cf. *PPH*, pp. 155–70, and especially 159–60.

   7.   Cf. "GA," pp. 2–3, and his letter to Cyrus Adler, of 30 Nov. 1933. Archives, University of Chicago Library (box 3, folder 8).

   8.   Cf. *Guide* III, 51.

   9.   *PG*, p. 24; *PL*, p. 16, for an allusion to the volcano lying beneath the house built by modern rationalism.

   10.   See his letter to Cyrus Adler, cited in note 7 supra.

   11.   See "ET" (1939), with the introductory note. Cf. also *PAW*, pp. 28, 33, 47, 70, 182. For such "flashes," consider the following passages from essays written between *PG* and *PAW*, as the *PAW* approach was first fully developed by "ET," i.e., between 1935 and 1939:

> "QR" (1936), p. 14: "the subtle allusions are perhaps more important than the doctrines developed in an explicit manner." Cf. also pp. 22, 30–31, 34–35, and especially 31–32 for the "usefulness" of esoteric speech.

> "OVL" (1937), pp. 98, 99–101 (with note 20), 101–102 (with notes), 104–105 (with note 35): how the exoteric arrangement of topics in the *Guide* is determined by the Kalam, but for esoteric reasons; how Maimonides' exoteric and esoteric views on providence are hinted at by different language, using "my view" versus "our view"; how the political significance of providence is demonstrated by its location in the *Guide*, i.e., why it follows prophetology and precedes the discussions on the laws.

> "OA" (1937), pp. 100–102, 97–100: on Maimonides' view of revelation as rooted in philosophic considerations; how one must always differentiate between "a literal meaning" which is often moderate, and "a secret meaning" which is often radical; Strauss puts in doubt whether Maimonides' view of creation is truly his "own opinion."

> "RMH" (1939), pp. 453–454: "an exoteric work such as the *Sepher ha-Madda* (or the *Mishneh Torah* as a whole) is much more esoteric than are most esoteric works."

12. For the Platonic basis of esotericism, see Strauss's remarks on Plato's *Seventh Letter* in "ONI," pp. 348–55. (Strauss's own estimation is that the only truly serious portion of "ONI" is this section: "The only thing I did not write only for students is the interpretation of the, in a certain sense decisive, passage of the *Seventh Letter.*" ["CCM," p. 108]) Maimonides' own pointed remarks reiterating the appropriateness of *deliberate* concealment (in the "two preambles" to his one chapter solely devoted to a commentary on the crucial *maaseh bereshit, Guide* II, 30) should also be carefully considered. See *Guide* II, 29, pp. 346–48.

13. To be sure, Strauss scarcely originated the notion of esotericism as *the* key to understanding the *Guide*. Not to mention Maimonides' plain statements in his Introduction about the proper method for penetrating to his book's innermost secrets, the same notion partially or wholly guided some of the best medieval commentators in their diverse readings, from Samuel Ibn Tibbon through Joseph Ibn Kaspi and Moses Narboni to Shem Tov ben Joseph Ibn Shem Tov. Strauss's "originality" consisted in bypassing the orthodox conventional wisdom of modern Maimonidean studies, whose basis was laid by Salomon Munk, and returning to the original texts as well as to the sounder readings by the medieval commentators, who paid greater attention to Maimonides' own directions for reading his book. While Salomon Munk clearly inaugurated the modern critical-historical study of Maimonides' *Guide*, he also cannot be exculpated from the charge of simply burying awareness of the key esoteric-exoteric distinction. See "HBSMP" (*RCPR*), p. 214. For a "second stage" comment by Strauss on the limits of Munk's approach to Maimonides, see "QR," pp. 2–4, "SR," pp. 5–7, which faults him for not appreciating both the determining political and Platonic dimensions in Maimonides' thought. ("For Munk and those who followed him, the teaching of Maimonides and the *falasifa* is an Aristotelianism contaminated or corrected by neo-Platonic conceptions.") As far as I can determine, the last modern Jewish scholar or thinker prior to Strauss who seems to have been somewhat aware of the decisive significance of esotericism and deliberate contradictions in penetrating to the secret teachings concealed in the *Guide* was Solomon Maimon. See his *Autobiography*, appendix 3, chapter 1, toward the end, with Strauss's remark on Maimon in "OVL," p. 104, note 34. Strauss's view of the conventional modern scholarly wisdom, as this may be reduced to historicist overreaching which is blind to Maimonides' esoteric purposes, is summarized in the following remark: "... to recognize that a scholarly criticism of Maimonides is unreasonable is equivalent to progressing in the understanding of his thought." ("MSPS" [*WIPP?*], p. 168) See also supra, note 1. Of course, what is exceptionally original about Strauss in his reading of Maimonides is how much further than his medieval predecessors he carried the implications of esotericism, both in terms of literary interpretation and philosophic teaching.

14. But consider already "ET" with respect to Lessing. In this regard, a story that was told to me by Alexander Altmann perhaps bears recording. Altmann

visited the University of Chicago in about 1957 to lecture on Jewish philosophy, and in conversation with Strauss asked him, "Do you happen to know Lessing's work *On Eternal Punishments?*" to which Strauss replied, "Do I know it?! It lies constantly open on my desk." For a similar remark about Strauss's youth, cf. "GA," p. 3. For Lessing, and Strauss's remark in "GA" quoted, see supra, chapter 1, note 14.

15. See Maimonides' Introduction to the *Guide*, as the best evidence for Strauss's thesis and approach. In my view, the differences between *PAW* and "HBS*GP*" are not great enough to justify speaking about separate stages, as does Allan Bloom, "Leo Strauss: 1899-1973," pp. 383–87; idem, *Giants and Dwarfs*, pp. 246–50. The differences, at least viewed from the perspective of his studies in Maimonides, are mostly in mode of expression rather than in fundamental intellectual development. *PAW*, it is true, conforms to more generally accepted scholarly conventions, but it is not for that reason less esoteric. As a proof for this contention about *PAW*'s esoteric character, see my article, "Religion, Philosophy, and Morality: How Leo Strauss Read Judah Halevi's *Kuzari*," *Journal of the American Academy of Religion* 61, no. 2 (Summer 1993): 225–73. With regard to the beginning and continuity of the third stage, and Strauss's own dating of the great change in his view of Maimonides, Strauss refers in "HBS*GP*" (1963) to "about twenty-five years" of continuous study of Maimonides' *Guide*, i.e., since about 1938. But it is clear that his close study of this book began in earnest in about 1923, along with the work on his analysis of Cohen's treatment of Spinoza's Bible science. About fifteen years have been lost. Obviously Strauss meant by this remark that an entirely different type of study of Maimonides' *Guide* began in 1938.

16. "LC*GP*" (*PAW*), pp. 68–70, 74. Consider the following statements: "Contradictions are the axis of the *Guide*" (p. 74); "And if the objection is made. . .we answer by referring to Maimonides' emphatic declaration concerning the extreme care with which he had written every single word of his book and by asking the objectors to produce similar declarations from those books of other philosophers which they may have in mind" (p. 69); "It is for this reason that the whole work has to be read with a particular care, with a care, that is, which would not be required for the understanding of a scientific book" (p. 54). Cf. also Strauss's very useful elaborations of his thesis in "OF" (*WIPP?*) and especially pp. 223–25, 230–31.

17. For Strauss as a "typological" thinker, refer to Nathan Rotenstreich, "Between Athens and Jerusalem," in *Studies in Contemporary Jewish Thought* (in Hebrew), pp. 139–43. For the theory of human "types" as something he learned from Nietzsche, see Pierre Manent, "Strauss et Nietzsche," *Revue de Metaphysique et de Morale* 94, no. 3 (July-September 1989): pp. 337–45.

18. *PAW*, p. 11. Cf. also pp. 17, 19, 42–43.

19. *TOM*, p. 14.

20. *PAW*, p. 56.

21. *TOM*, pp. 120, 173.
22. Ibid., p. 173.
23. *WIPP?*, p. 47.
24. Cf. *WIPP?*, pp. 43, 47; *SPPP*, pp. 227–28; *TOM*, p. 295; *OT*, pp. 195–97; *OT* (rev.), pp. 183–85. This gradual modern "disappearance" of rigorous theology is a variation on a theme that recurs often in Strauss's mature writings—a contraction of the philosophic horizon poses as an enlargement. His most succinct statement is as follows: "In Machiavelli's teaching we have the first example of a spectacle which has renewed itself in almost every generation since. A fearless thinker seems to have opened up a depth from which the classics, in their noble simplicity, recoiled. As a matter of fact, there is in the whole work of Machiavelli not a single true observation regarding the nature of man and of human affairs with which the classics were not thoroughly familiar. An amazing contraction of the horizon presents itself as an amazing enlargement of the horizon." (*WIPP?*, p. 43) For a comparison between Maimonides and Machiavelli specifically along these lines, see especially *OT*, pp. 195–97; *OT* (rev.), pp. 183–85. According to Strauss, Machiavelli's basic premises amount to a rejection of "Aristotle's doctrine of the whole" as rooted in "nature," and hence he leaves no room "in his cosmology for a ruling Mind." (*TOM*, pp. 221–22) Cf. also pp. 175, 201–11. But Strauss himself, in his critique of the moderns, does not attempt a restoration of Aristotle's cosmology in any simple sense. To say nothing of his keen alertness to the genuine difficulties raised by modern science in its break with Aristotelian science (*NRH*, pp. 7–8), Strauss surely also learned from Maimonides to doubt some of the fundamental principles basic to Aristotle's cosmology. Thus, see the opening remark in his letter to Helmut Kuhn, p. 23, and the closing remark of "HBSGP," p. lvi about "the true perplexity," as well as "IHE" (*RCPR*), pp. 32–39. See also supra, chapter 2. Strauss suggests that one of the most enduring aspects of Aristotle's philosophic thought may reside in his theological teaching. He puts this as follows:

> Philosophy, we have learned, must be on its guard against the wish to be edifying—philosophy can only be intrinsically edifying. We cannot exert our understanding without from time to time understanding something of importance; and this act of understanding may be accompanied by the awareness of our understanding, by the understanding of our understanding, by *noesis noeseos*, and this is so high, so pure, so noble an experience that Aristotle could ascribe it to his God. This experience is entirely independent of whether what we understand primarily is pleasing or displeasing, fair or ugly. It leads us to realize that all evils are in a sense necessary if there is to be understanding. It enables us to accept all evils which befall us and which may well break our hearts in the spirit of good citizens of the city of God. By becoming aware of the dignity of the mind, we realize

the true ground of the dignity of man and therewith the goodness of the world, whether we understand it as created or as uncreated, which is the home of man because it is the home of the human mind. ("WILE?" [LAM], p. 8)

The phrase, "philosophy must beware of the wish to be edifying," is from the Preface to Hegel's *Phenomenology of Spirit*, translated by A.V. Miller (New York: Oxford University Press, 1977), p. 6. For the philosopher, the "well-ordered soul," and the eternal order, see *OT*, pp. 211–16; *OT* (rev.), pp. 197–202.

25. *TOM*, p. 297.

26. See, e.g., *NRH*, p. 317.

27. Cf. *WIPP?*, pp. 46–47; *SPPP*, pp. 212–14; *TOM*, pp. 296–97.

28. *OT*, p. 197; *OT* (rev.), p. 184.

29. *TOM*, pp. 292–96.

30. For Strauss it was Nietzsche who recalled with unparalleled modern clarity the fate which science cannot completely neutralize, i.e., its *morally* destructive power. See e.g., *On the Genealogy of Morals* III, 23–25. However, Rousseau's *First Discourse, on the Sciences and Arts*, as well as his *Letter to D'Alembert* already issue in a somewhat similar analysis. Cf. Strauss's "On the Intention of Rousseau," *Social Research* 14 (1947): 455–87.

31. *TOM*, pp. 173, 298. The "moderateness" of the original Enlightenment is obviously only relative to recent developments in the history of philosophy. In absolute terms, it cannot compare with the genuine moderateness of the ancient-medieval position with respect to changing man and society. It is in contrast with this that the Enlightenment appears fiercely radical, especially with regard to its estimation of man's vital need for religion. This leads to the modern Enlightenment's break with ancient Epicureanism, which recognized the need for religion on political grounds even if it did not believe any religion was true. "No premodern atheist doubted that social life required belief in, and worship of, God or gods." (*NRH*, p. 169)

32. The charges preferred against Socrates perhaps best represent the threat which the philosopher poses: the philosopher corrupts the youth, i.e., he leads them away from wholehearted devotion to the city by introducing them to philosophy; he does not appear to believe in the gods of the city. Cf. "OPAS" (*SPPP*), pp. 38–66.

33. *PPH*, p. xvi.

34. *TOM*, pp. 232–34.

35. Ibid., pp. 120–22, 294–97.

36. As a result of this permanent division in human nature, Strauss maintains that the Platonic philosophers can never envision a day in which the necessity of esotericism might actually be dispensed with or rendered obsolete. Even if the philosophers should, by some miraculous chance, be asked to rule in a perfectly virtuous city of the future, esotericism (or "noble lies") would still be in accord with the basic needs of unchangeable human nature. In other words, it is not possible for such philosophers to imagine a day in which "no one would

suffer any harm from hearing any truth," which means "they must conceal their [true] opinions from all but philosophers." Cf. *PAW*, pp. 33–37; "ET," pp. 55–57. The theological-political conseqence of this truth is that "even the absolutely best civil constitution is necessarily imperfect" ("ET," p. 58), i.e., Platonic philosophers should only hope for relative relief from the fate to which they have been consigned, either through changes in the political order or through reforms of theological opinion or through "enlightening" education. Thus, like Lessing, a modern philosopher who returned to the Platonic tradition, Strauss too seems to argue for this position, in that esotericism in one form or another must still be accepted "not merely as a strange fact of the past, but rather as an intelligible necessity for all times." See "ET," p. 52; *PAW*, p. 34.

37. *PAW*, pp. 9–10.

38. "HFRPL" (*WIPP?*), pp. 147–50; *AAPL*, pp. 4, 7, 11, and 149.

39. *PAW*, pp. 8–11.

40. Ibid., p. 17.

41. See *OT*, p. 220; *OT* (rev.), pp. 205–6.

42. *OT*, pp. 80–94, and especially 85–90; *OT* (rev.), pp. 78–91, and especially 83–87.

43. See, e.g., *OT*, pp. 206–7; *OT* (rev.), pp. 193–94.

44. *NRH*, p. 75.

45. Ibid., p. 74.

46. Ibid.

47. Ibid.

48. *OT*, p. 196; *OT* (rev.), p. 184; *WIPP?*, pp. 229–30, 102, 41; *TOM*, pp. 175, 202–3; *SPPP*, pp. 209, 226; *PAW*, p. 14.

49. *PAW*, p. 35; "ET," pp. 56–57.

50. *NRH*, p. 84.

51. *WIPP?*, pp. 221–22.

52. *PAW*, p. 36, and pp. 32–37 as a whole.

53. *OT*, pp. 206–26; *OT* (rev.), pp. 193–212; *WIPP?*, pp. 92–96, 27–40.

54. *PAW*, pp. 139, 36.

55. Ibid., p. 139.

56. *WIPP?*, pp. 221–22. For Strauss's own "esoteric" views on philosophy as in its essence radically ambivalent with regard to the character and finality of moral virtue, cf. "QR," pp. 9–12; "SR," pp. 8–10; *PG*, pp. 120–22; *PL*, pp. 108–10; "FP," pp. 385–89; *PAW*, pp. 13–17, 20–21, 32–37, 95–141, 173–75, 193; "ET," pp. 55–57; *WIPP?*, pp. 138–39, 145, 147, 149, 152, 167; *OT*, pp. 217, 213–14; *OT* (rev.), pp. 202–3, 199–200; and especially "GA," pp. 4–5.

57. *PAW*, pp. 137–41; *OT*, pp. 211–13, 220–21; *OT* (rev.), pp. 197–99, 205–6.

58. *PAW*, p. 95.

59. Strauss also encountered the conflict in his personal life as a conflict between Jewish loyalties in purely *political* terms and the exigencies of the intellectual life. He tells the story of a meeting in his youth between himself,

a "political Zionist," and Vladimir Jabotinsky, who was then his mentor. Strauss proudly reported on the studies of Hebrew, classical Jewish texts, and Jewish history in which his circle of friends was engaged; instead of praising them, Jabotinsky asked him whether they were learning how to shoot a rifle. Strauss seems to have been alerted thereby to the radical difference between the theoretical life and the practical life; the one makes absolute claims on man which conflict with the most pressing needs arising from the other. Cf. "WWRJ," typescript, p. 10.

   60.   *TOM*, p. 232:

> In his teaching concerning morality and politics Machiavelli challenges not only the religious teaching but the whole philosophic tradition as well. This novelty is compatible with the fact that the teaching in question contains many elements which were known before him to all men or some men; for Machiavelli integrates those elements into a new whole or understands them in the light of a new principle. Even if it were true that that whole or that principle were known to certain earlier thinkers but not set forth by them coherently or explicitly, or in other words, if it were true that Machiavelli differed from those predecessors only by his boldness, his claim would be wholly justified: that boldness as considered boldness would presuppose a wholly new estimate of what can be publicly proposed, hence a wholly new estimate of the public and hence a wholly new estimate of man.

   61.   For the "restoration" of philosophy in Alfarabi, see *PAW*, p. 12; "FP," pp. 375–77, 393.

   62.   "ET," p. 53; and cf. also pp. 55, 59; *PAW*, pp. 32–35.

   63.   By looking closely at Strauss's approach to Maimonides, with its other applications, one would undoubtedly be able to isolate certain difficulties on specific points and to localize their philosophic or literary causes, but I believe one would not touch the general thrust. Strauss's rediscovery of Maimonides' esotericism *of some kind* is almost an irrefutable truth, even if one only takes Maimonides' words at their face value. Given that irrefutable truth, nevertheless to some degree one may want to legitimately limit its conseqences in allowing Strauss either to draw far-reaching textual conclusions about the measure of intentionality in Maimonides' literary expression, or to make radical assertions about Maimonides' hidden teachings as "necessarily" following from his literary method. Thus, Alexander Altmann, who maintained an immense regard for Strauss's achievements in illuminating the hidden depths of Maimonides' *Guide* (as previously quoted), draws the line at Strauss's "strange excursions" into numerology:

> [Strauss] even ventures to read symbolical significance into the numbers designating the sequence of chapters (pp. xxx and xviii). Here he

obviously enters into a realm of pure speculation, and few will follow
in a credulous mood this kind of "kabbalistic" exegesis. It seems far
remote from Maimonides' way of thinking. (Review of *The Guide of
the Perplexed*, *Journal of Religion* 44 [1964]: 260–61)

A recent article by Raphael Jospe, researching the origin of the division and
numbering of the chapters in the *Guide*, raises some very serious difficulties
for Strauss's type of numerological interpretation. Cf. "The Number and Division
of Chapters in *The Guide of the Perplexed*" (in Hebrew), *Jerusalem Studies in
Jewish Thought* 7 (1988): 387–97.

    64. *PG*, p. 30; *PL*, p. 23.

    65. *PAW*, p. 19.

    66. It is because Maimonides the philosopher knew all of this so well,
according to Strauss's assumptions, that his attempt to resolve the contradiction
between the two needed things is never called by Strauss a "synthesis" (in the
mode of Hegel), and is even hesitantly and sparingly called a "harmonization."
As Strauss finally views Maimonides, his was an attempt only to discover a
humanly necessary *modus vivendi* for the two antagonists, rather than a final
settlement between them. (To be sure, each one can *use* the other in a subordinate
function, "but what is so used in each case rebels against such use, and therefore
the conflict is really a radical one." Cf. "POR?," p. 33; "POR?" [*IPP*], p. 273.) Thus,
Strauss rejects any tacit efforts by modern exegetes of the medievals to
anachronistically interpret their attempts at some fragmentary "resolution" in
moral, political, and theological terms (which may itself have been an exoteric
teaching) in light of a modern Hegelian logic, in which a higher plane, a "third
thing" (such as "history") is discovered to serve as the basis for a final "synthesis"
between the two antagonists. Cf., e.g., "OIG," p. 19; "POR?," pp. 31–32; "POR?"
(*IPP*), pp. 269–72.

    67. These are the words of Winston Churchill, which he used to
characterize what is both necessary and proper for the defense of truth during
war. (They were delivered in a speech made at Teheran, November 1943.) I will
quote the full sentence because I believe it neatly lays bare what Strauss thought
was the ancient view of the perennially defensive condition of philosophy in
every human society: "In wartime, truth is so precious that she should always
be attended by a bodyguard of lies." It might be argued by a critic of Strauss's
attitude to the history of philosophy that this takes a partial truth and gives it
as the whole truth. Were philosophers always so enormously threatened by their
societies? And even if in some cases they were, how can it help us, i.e., how can
we move from a principle of the legitimacy of concealment in certain
circumstances to any type of *sound* and *reliable* interpretive rule for the
explication of texts written by authors who accepted such a principle? Or is
Strauss generalizing from the unusual conditions of medieval society, from the
particular status of Jewish philosophers (who may well have been in a precarious

position), and perhaps especially from the specific case of Maimonides? Is it true that this is the *universal* condition of philosophers, i.e., to necessarily be at war, as it were, with their societies? And should this "state of war" be the model or archetype, even though it may also be true that most philosophers do not at all expose themselves through deliberately provocative speech so as to invite such attack? I believe Strauss would respond to such criticism with the same arguments which he made in *PAW* (pp. 7–37) and "OF" (*WIPP?*). Are the critics not generalizing from their beliefs, experience, and interest in their own society, i.e., from the modern West, to other very different societies of the past (or even of the present, as his imagined case of the philosopher in a totalitarian society illustrates)? And if so, is not Strauss's mode of interpretation of philosophic writers from the past the one most in harmony with "the [modern] tradition of historical exactness"? Hans-Georg Gadamer is unlike the recent hostile critics of Strauss because of his distinct note of friendliness and because of his open-mindedness, but his critique of Strauss's reading of the history of philosophy actually turns on the same point:

> Is not conscious distortion, camouflage and concealment of the proper meaning in fact the rare extreme case of a frequent, even normal situation? —just as persecution (whether by civil authority or the church, the inquisition, etc.) is only an extreme case when compared with the intentional or unintentional pressure that society and public opinion exercise on human thought. Only if we are conscious of the uninterrupted transition from one to the other are we able to estimate the hermeneutic difficulty of Strauss's problem. How are we able to establish clearly that a distortion has taken place? Thus, in my opinion, it is by no means clear that, when we find contradictory statements in a writer, it is correct to take the hidden meaning—as Strauss thinks—for the true one. There is an unconscious conformism of the human mind to considering what is universally obvious as really true. And there is, against this, an unconscious tendency to try extreme possibilities, even if they cannot always be combined into a coherent whole....Contradictions are an excellent criterion of truth but, unfortunately, they are not an unambiguous criterion when we are dealing with hermeneutics.

Cf. "Hermeneutics and Historicism," in *Truth and Method* (New York: Crossroad, 1982), pp. 482–91. In their letters on *Truth and Method*, written prior to Gadamer's "Hermeneutics and Historicism," Strauss isolates what he regards as "the fundamental difference between us: *la querelle des anciens et des modernes*, in which *querelle* we have taken different sides; our difference regarding hermeneutics is only a consequence of this fundamental difference." See "Correspondence Concerning *Wahrheit und Methode*," *Independent Journal of Philosophy* 2 (1978): 5–12. In further understanding the "fundamental difference" between Strauss and Gadamer, insofar as it touches on the possibility of the complete freedom of the philosopher from his own time and place, it helps to recall what Strauss considers the defining characteristic of philosophy: "philosophy requires the greatest possible awareness of what one is doing." Cf. "NM*BK*" (*SPPP*), p. 198.

68. It seems, based on what has been argued previously, that Strauss regarded this Maimonidean prophetology as quite an adequate *practical* resolution of the dilemma. However, it is my further assumption that Strauss did not regard the adequate *theoretical* resolution of this dilemma as simply impossible. I so assume because Strauss says:

> [T]he core, the nerve of Western intellectual history, Western spiritual history, one could almost say, is the conflict between the biblical and the philosophic notions of the good life.
>
> [I]t seems to me that this unresolved conflict is the secret of the vitality of Western civilization. ("POR?," p. 44; "POR?" [IPP], p. 289)

This is also why I assume that Strauss regarded it as desirable to *try* to resolve the dilemma.

69. *PAW*, p. 21.

70. *OT*, p. 220–21; *OT* (rev.), pp. 205–6.

71. See Thomas L. Pangle's introduction to *SPPP* for just such an approach to both Maimonides and Strauss himself, and especially pp. 19–21, 24.

72. "ET," p. 59.

73. To make this point clearer: I am suggesting that even if it were true that this Maimonidean (and Straussian) position does represent a primary adherence to pure philosophy or unaided reason in the sphere of truth, not only is it the adherence of a deeply loyal, nobly pious, and high-minded Jewish citizen, and not only does he see no truer or nobler light evident in any other religious and political tradition, but also he may well regard the Jewish tradition as a repository of the highest, most essential truths, which to be sure no one tradition can entirely contain or convey. For Strauss's "noble piety" and his "profound reverence for the Jewish tradition," see the two remarks of Alexander Altmann quoted above, in the Introduction, p. 1, and in note 4 to the Introduction. For the phrase about Maimonides' "high-minded citizenship," I borrow from Ralph Lerner, who used it in oral communication with me to characterize the position of Strauss as a Jewish thinker. As for Strauss seeing no truer or nobler light evident in any other religious or political tradition, permit me to quote from "Why We Remain Jews." Following his piously refraining from reading the *Aleynu* prayer ("It would be absolutely improper for me to read it now"), Strauss adds poetically and rather obscurely, but still piously, about the prayer's Jewish high theological vision:

> No nobler dream was ever dreamt. It is surely nobler to be a victim of the most noble dream than to profit from a sordid reality and to

wallow in it. Dream is akin to aspiration. And aspiration is a kind of divination, of an enigmatic vision. And an enigmatic vision in the emphatic sense is the perception of the ultimate mystery, of the truth of the ultimate mystery. The truth of the ultimate mystery, the truth that there is an ultimate mystery, that being is radically mysterious cannot be denied even by the unbelieving Jew of our age. ("WWRJ," typescript, pp. 16–17)

74. It could be argued rationalistically that something of universal significance must also of necessity be of particular Jewish significance. Such an approach obscures the true Jewish theological interest in this matter: Judaism makes a claim to the truth just as comprehensive as the claim of philosophy. If all Maimonides' position implies is a subordination of revelation to reason, and perhaps also its use by reason, revelation will not long allow itself to be so used and subordinated, as it was Strauss's wont to emphasize. Strauss well knew of the medieval Jewish historical conflict called the "Maimonidean controversy," which turned on just such issues as these, and he could not have been asking Jewish thought to repeat the experience. He is determined to engage in a radical encounter of reason with revelation, in terms of thinking through their shared as well as their different meanings.

75. Clearly Strauss does not regard Thomas as sharing the same basic approach as Averroes to the relation between philosophy and theology. It is much more reasonable to link the Muslim Averroes with the Christian Marsilius: cf., e.g., *PAW*, p. 97, note 5; and *LAM*, pp. 185–202, and especially pp. 185, 189. But see especially *NRH*, pp. 156–66, for Averroes and Thomas treated together, with respect to their common roots in the natural right teaching of Aristotle. For Strauss, however differently they resolve their difficulties with Aristotle's teaching, the solutions are to a commonly held set of problems. Both recognize them as primary and ultimate, and both resolve them in a common framework of Aristotelianism.

76. *PAW*, p. 198.

77. *TOM*, p. 14; "OIG," p. 19.

78. *PSCR*, p. 30.

79. On the one hand, for the "rational" character of the Hebrew Bible in this presentation of Strauss's view, see "OIG," p. 14, top:

These considerations show, it seems to me, how unreasonable it is to speak of the mythical or prelogical character of biblical thought as such. The account of the world given in the first chapter of the Bible is not fundamentally different from philosophic accounts; that account is based on evident distinctions which are as accessible to us as they were to the biblical author. Hence we can understand that account; these distinctions are accessible to man as man. We can readily understand why we should find something of this kind in the Bible. An account of the creation of the world, or more generally stated, a cosmogony, necessarily presupposes an articulation of the world, of the completed world, of the cosmos, that is to say, a cosmology. The biblical account of creation is based on a cosmology. All the created things mentioned in the Bible are accessible to man as man regardless of differences of climate, origin, religion, or anything else.

On the other hand, for the qualifying quotation marks I put around "argument" in this sentence, see also "OIG," p. 15, bottom:

> The Bible is distinguished from all philosophy because it simply asserts that the world is created by God. There is not a trace of an argument in support of this assertion. How do we know that the world was created? The Bible declared it so. We know it by virtue of declaration, pure and simple, by divine utterance ultimately. Therefore, all knowledge of the createdness of the world has an entirely different character than our knowledge of the structure or articulation of the world.

Strauss does add the most important argument: "There is no argument in favor of creation except God speaking to Israel." (p. 16) Thus the biblical claims are based on the chosenness of Israel, which is itself supported by the continuing history of the Jews, their "miraculous" survival. Knowing that, Spinoza tried to entirely naturalize this survival. (See *Theologico-Political Treatise*, chapter 3.)

80. "OIG," pp. 14–15, and especially p. 19; *PAW*, pp. 19–21. T. L. Pangle rejects any such notion as attributable to Strauss. In his view of Strauss, monotheism does not change anything. Philosophers never believed they could "refute" even the most primitive argument for revelation, since it is based on an experience always accessible to man as man. As Pangle reads Strauss's views on revelation, the different religious interpretations of it do not change what is conveyed in it, according to the ancient philosophers. See his introduction to *SPPP*, pp. 19–24. Werner Dannhauser tries to explode this type of reading of Strauss on "Jerusalem and Athens" by insisting that for Strauss

> [w]hen one equates Homer with the Bible one does violence to both, and when one equates the gods with God one demonstrates incomprehension of both. Jerusalem is not to be understood as the pale imitation of, or unreasonable substitute for, Athens. In the thought of Leo Strauss it shines forth as the great alternative, and one does less than full justice to the pristine open-mindedness of Leo Strauss when one implies that for him the alternative was less than a genuine alternative. ("Leo Strauss as Citizen and Jew," *Interpretation* 17, no. 3 [Spring 1991]: 433–47, and especially p. 445)

As for whether Strauss believed the Greek poets could be equated generally with the Hebrew prophets, he makes unambiguous statements which deny such a notion for a very specific reason:

> The perfect book is an image or an imitation of that all-comprehensiveness and perfect evidence of knowledge which is aspired to but not reached [by Greek philosophy]. The perfect book acts, therefore, as a countercharm to the charm of despair which the never satisfied quest for perfect knowledge necessarily engenders. It is for this reason that *Greek philosophy is inseparable from Greek poetry.* ("OIG," p. 20; emphasis added)

Cf. also *NRH*, p. 90; *TOM*, pp. 205–8; "POR?," pp. 39–40, 43; "POR?" (*IPP*), pp. 281–83, 287. Certainly he stresses the same point from the opposite angle by saying about the name of God (Exod. 3:14):

> It is indeed the fundamental biblical statement about the biblical God, but we hesitate to call it metaphysical, since the notion of *physis* is alien to the Bible. (*JA*, p. 17; "JA" [*SPPP*], p. 162)

Harry V. Jaffa has expressed a view of Strauss's notion of the relation between reason and revelation which is similar to the view which informs the present work. This has led Jaffa to argue that Strauss "was uncompromising in defending, on Socratic grounds, the integrity of the way of life represented by the Bible and biblical faith." (See, e.g., "Crisis of the Strauss Divided: The Legacy Reconsidered," *Social Research* 54, no. 3 [Autumn 1987]: 579–603, and especially p. 583.)

81. For Maimonides' supreme mastery of the art of writing as rooted in his acute alertness to what Strauss calls "the precarious status of philosophy in Judaism," see *PAW*, pp. 19–21, 34–37, 92–94, 101–12, 139–41. Consider also Strauss's remark about how Maimonides fits himself in the line of tradition by stressing "the fundamental similarity between the prophet, the bringer of the secret teaching, and the interpreter of the secret teaching." (*PAW*, p. 91)

82. It might be thought that Strauss would follow Socrates on this issue. Socrates would seemingly not recognize such a fundamental distinction because it breaks with his famous saying, "virtue is knowledge." Further, while the striving for moral perfection might tend to lead on to only one thing, religion, does not the striving for intellectual excellence alone already *presuppose* moral virtue for Socrates and Plato, which would seem to transcend or bypass religion entirely? It is my opinion that Strauss reads this Socratic-Platonic saying, "virtue is knowledge," as the sign and possession only of the perfect knower—the philosopher—and not of every knower, from the sophist to the potential philosopher to the "half-philosopher." In other words, most human beings are only on the way to "virtue is knowledge." As a result, an additional virtue, religion or piety, is essential in the ordinary life and in the education of every human being—even the knowers—precisely in order to help them reach their human

perfection. Although the very rare knower, the perfect philosopher (or in terms of Maimonidean wisdom, the highest prophet) may achieve the perfection of "virtue is knowledge," for everyone else virtue is *not* knowledge alone. As such, the fundamental distinction discussed in the text takes on an even graver significance: how does one give an account of the need for moral virtue as categorical imperatives to those who are rightly striving for knowledge, but who are not yet perfect philosophers, and who may be tempted to think that in this knowing they are beyond the constraints or the concerns of "mere" morality. They will be tempted to think that in their very knowing they already attain to "virtue is knowledge." To Strauss, Maimonidean enlightenment about both wisdom and piety is the necessary correction to such ever-present possible corruption of the knowers. Still, one may want to reflect on the following passage from Plato's *Epinomis* 989a–b:

> THE ATHENIAN STRANGER: "The source of the trouble, as I am strongly persuaded by our recent discussion, is that our practice in the very chief point of virtue is amiss. There is no human virtue—and we must never let ourselves be argued out of this belief—greater than piety, and piety, I must tell you, thanks to our incredible folly, has failed to show itself in the most nobly endowed natures. By the most nobly endowed I mean those which are most difficult of production, but once produced, of the highest service to mankind."

Consider also the following remark by Strauss:

> I am having a correspondence with Kendall, who. . .also is writing a review article on my *Machiavelli*. He is of the opinion that just as Machiavelli compels his readers to think blasphemies, by themselves, I am compelling my readers to perform acts of piety by themselves.

Cf. Leo Strauss, in a letter to Harry V. Jaffa, written 11 February 1960. For Willmoore Kendall's review of *Thoughts on Machiavelli* by Leo Strauss, see *Philosophical Review* 15 (1965–66): 247–54. This phase of the argument must be completed with the aid of what is to follow: it seems that for Strauss, as for Maimonides, only biblical religion and morality can be combined with the search for knowledge in such a way as enable the greatest human perfection to be achieved in both realms, morality and knowledge.

    83. *CM*, p. 125.

    84. "POR?," pp. 37–40, 26–28; "POR?" (*IPP*), pp. 278–84, 262–65; "OIG," pp. 14–19. An analysis of several key passages in these two essays could lay the basis for the essential arguments against what I believe is Pangle's faulty thesis about Strauss.

    85. Certainly Maimonides never actually speaks about "natural laws," but he implies that they exist in the *specific* sense in which we are using this term. He implies, then, that there are guides to morality, articulated as general

principles by practical reason, which are only "natural" in the sense of devolved from human nature, and aimed to help it achieve its two perfections, of the body and of the soul. As Maimonides puts it, "the law, although it is not natural, enters into what is natural." (*Guide* II, 40; cf. also III, 27–28; and *PAW*, pp. 131–35) They are not "natural laws," however, in any ordinary sense of the term—either as necessary ethical and legal rules dictated by right reason, or as artificially constructed social conventions whose essence is to serve as binding commands to ensure order—but guidelines or advisements or recommendations, which a wise man might proffer based on a prudent regard for what is as a rule best for most human beings in most circumstances. Certain utilitarian and advantageous rules are bound to appear in any list composed by wise men. Their rational standard is, as Strauss puts it, "evident usefulness." (*PAW*, p. 122; cf. also *Guide* III, 28) But this is in no way, shape, or form the same absolute quality of morality as what is encountered in, e.g., the Ten Commandments. Nor do these "natural laws" in any sense receive a theoretical rational standing—they are only "evidently useful" for facilitating life among human beings and for helping in the perfection of human beings. They are "natural" in the ends they serve, but otherwise most or all of their actual contents as means are purely conventional. For a detailed analysis of these distinctions, as Strauss treats them in "LRK" (*PAW*), see my "Religion, Philosophy, and Morality: How Leo Strauss Read Judah Halevi's *Kuzari*," *Journal of the American Academy of Religion* 61, no. 2 (Summer 1993): 225–73. This uncertainty about the absolute contents of morality, by the way, does not necessarily extend to the political principles. It would seem reason can be much surer and can reach a greater definiteness on the specific political truths. The opposite is true about theology—as compared with morality, to the humanist at least, it would seem that morality can speak with a clearer rational voice than theology:

> There is, finally, another implication of the term "humanism"—viz., the contradistinction of human studies to divinity. Provisionally I limit myself to the remark that humanism may be said to imply that the moral principles are more knowable to man, or less controversial among earnest men, than theological principles. ("SSH" [*RCPR*], p. 7)

Cf. *NRH*, p. 164; see also chapter 2, notes 26 and 28, supra. Whether Strauss sees himself as simply a "humanist," however, must be reflected on in light of the complete argument in "SSH." Also, while my discussion is meant to suggest that morality is central and primary for Strauss, basing himself on Maimonides, this is not to say it is necessarily also ultimate. *The* original and fundamental problem for Strauss may be put as follows. *Either* morality is "merely" central and primary to human life, meaning, it is only central and primary if it is on the way to and subserves something else, something higher, which sustains it; *or*, it is simply ultimate, meaning it can stand on its own, whether with a correlated rational or a correlated natural basis. The Maimonidean view radically questions both the rationality and the naturalness of what is contained in so-called rational and natural moralities, as a claim about their being ultimate, and hence he also doubts whether these moralities are truly sanctioned as a result. This is a view, then, that would put the latter, greatly elevated notion of morality as ultimate into doubt. The former, still dignified notion of morality as central and primary is in the Maimonidean view regarded as the sounder notion of morality, but it only raises the equally crucial and perplexing matter: on the way to what and subserving what? As I understand Strauss's reading of the Maimonidean view, insofar as it overrides the rational and natural basis of morality, it also demolishes the philosophic claim to provide morality with the higher basis which it needs. Morality even as "merely" central and primary still would seem to need religion rather than philosophy to sustain it, because in the notion of it as central and primary, it can only be made something absolute, as it should be, by the biblical religious faith, by the divine commander, by God as lawgiver. The possible exception of the very rarest individuals, whose knowledge alone is enough to make them perfectly morally virtuous, is only apparent, because their knowledge, if it is genuine and complete in the true sense, will encompass knowledge of God. Thus, Moses did not need the Ten Commandments written on the tablets in order to reach his perfection, but he did need his connection with God. (Socrates is a different case entirely—Strauss does not regard him as the highest *moral* type. Cf., e.g., "JA" [*SPPP*], pp. 169–73.) This is because the natural or rational basis of the innermost core of morality, while perhaps there is something actual to it, is so slender and tenuous that it is not enough to sustain it as a "genuine" morality for almost every human being who is not directly linked to God mind to mind, by knowledge alone.

> The only universally valid standard is the hierarchy of ends. This standard is sufficient for passing judgment on the level of nobility of individuals and groups and of actions and institutions. But it is insufficient for guiding our actions. (*NRH*, p. 163)

In other words, my argument about what Strauss learned from Maimonides is this. It is no matter that morality may be central and primary to human life for decent people, and perhaps also possesses a very thin rationally knowable natural grounding. Morality as we know it would still seem to require biblical religion, and perhaps only biblical religion, in order to make itself "genuine" morality, because only from such a divine source can those tenuous and slender threads of what is natural and rational in morality be made into the iron rope of one set of absolutely binding divine commands, promises, and sanctions. Otherwise it would not command our obedience to it as *the* single, absolute moral code. The perfect justice of the philosopher even at his highest is not the *perfection* of "what we would call moral virtue," because moral virtue is "only the condition or by-product" of his life, the life of "the quest for knowledge of the good, of the idea of the good." It is not the all-consuming passion it was for the Hebrew prophets, who alone teach us what "genuine" morality, as we know it, is and requires. Though little has been written on Strauss's views on morality and religion, for further discussion of these matters in Maimonides, see: Ralph

Lerner, "Maimonides," in *HPP*, pp. 203–22; Steven Schwarzschild, "Do Noachites Have to Believe in Revelation?" in *The Pursuit of the Ideal*, edited by M. Kellner (Albany: SUNY Press, 1990), pp. 29–59, 266–72; Marvin Fox, *Interpreting Maimonides* (Chicago: University of Chicago Press, 1990), pp. 93–226. Schwarzschild concludes his article with a statement which focuses the contemporary Jewish philosophical (and scholarly) debate on the following issues, of which I believe Strauss would have been able to approve:

> To us [Maimonides] says: the law of nature must be preserved if only so that we will not always be restricted to the fallibilities of the positive law, but this natural law cannot be relied on to reside in the nature around us or in the nature within us; it must come from a higher source. To Maimonides this source was, of course, divine revelation; to Cohen it was reason, or the nature which humanity will in the future make for itself. It is another question—perhaps the most important one—whether on this last score Maimonides or Cohen has more to teach us. (P. 59)

86. Cf. e.g. *PAW*, pp. 96–97, note 4, with 139–41. Although I cannot possibly prove this in the context of the present discussion, I try to demonstrate it in my "Religion, Philosophy, and Morality: How Leo Strauss Read Judah Halevi's *Kuzari*." For some further evidence, see "GA," pp. 4–5; and supra, chapter 6, note 56.

87. *TOM*, pp. 133, 32; "POR?," pp. 42, 37; "POR?" (*IPP*), pp 286–87, 278–79; *NRH*, p. 125; *SCR*, pp. 256, 176; "HBSGP," pp. xxvi, xxxiv, xlix, li, lii–liii. I believe it would not be entirely misguided with respect to Strauss to recall the remark of Nietzsche in *Human, All Too Human* (aphorism 475), who acknowledged the uniqueness of the biblical teachings as "the most powerful book [and] the most effective moral code in the world."

88. Cf. "OIG," pp. 7–9, 14–20; "POR?," pp. 34–45; "MITP," pp. 111–12, 116–17; "POR?" (*IPP*), pp. 274–94, 305–9; *NRH*, p. 144; "HBSGP," p. xxii; and "JA" (*SPPP*), especially pp. 168–73. Consider also "NM*BK*" (*SPPP*), pp. 199–200, 201–4, for Strauss's subtle comments on "repentance" in the view of Maimonides.

89. Strauss fully appreciated that this is not so very simple for most unbelievers, philosophical or nonphilosophical: to just "assume the biblical faith" in order to be achieve a "genuine" morality. I am certain Strauss knew that this yields some very grave moral implications, to say nothing of the difficulties which arise from the important religious differences between the biblical faiths. Strauss dealt with these moral implications by writing *Natural Right and History*, which offers as sound a grounding for morality as unaided reason can provide. But is such an alternative finally preferable for those who are truly serious about morality, which he believed all decent human beings will be? Compared with biblical religion and morality, it may not provide categorical imperatives; but for these biblical imperatives one must pay a price which some philosophers may consider

too high. It remains for debate which price is too high to pay, reason's or revelation's, and I do not believe that Strauss's final personal position in this debate is beyond all ambiguities—although the ambiguities are ones which he taught those who study his works to recognize.

CHAPTER SEVEN

1. With as subtle a philosophic thinker as Leo Strauss, it is tempting either to overstate a seemingly deliberate ambiguity, or to simplify his thought in order to resolve the tension of a tantalizing ambiguity and bring it closer to his equally impressive lucidity. Notwithstanding such temptations, we have been attempting in this work to articulate Strauss's clear understanding and distinctive teaching on numerous issues, with all of the qualifications, hesitations, and nuances which it requires. As previously argued, I believe Strauss's position as philosopher and Jew may be characterized as "cognitive theism." This means that on the crucial issue of God, which preoccupied Strauss's thought from his youth, Strauss may also be called a "theologizing philosopher," to employ a Maimonidean term. (*Guide* I, 68) I make this point so emphatically only in order to differentiate him decisively from his friend Kojève. It is uncontroversial that Kojève announced his atheism, not just as deaf and blind rebellion, but as philosophically necessary. It is in this specific sense that I call Strauss a "theologizing philosopher," precisely because he would in no way accept Kojève's position on these matters as philosophically necessary. For Kojève's unambiguous enunciation of his philosophic atheism, see: *OT*, pp. 161–62, 171; *OT* (rev.), pp. 152, 161; "A Note on Eternity, Time, and the Concept," in *Introduction to the Reading of Hegel*, edited by Allan Bloom, translated by James H. Nichols, Jr. (New York: Basic Books, 1969), pp. 100–130; "Kojève-Fessard Documents," *Interpretation* 19, no. 2 (Winter 1991–92): 185–200. See also supra, Introduction, note 2. Strauss is radically different in this respect, in that he not only regards it as philosophically justifiable to appear in the guise of a defender of orthodox religious faith, and he not only argues a position which seemingly can be made consonant with such faith, but he genuinely seems to have been persuaded by a "theistic" belief of sorts, albeit of a Maimonidean and philosophical persuasion. In the only statement he made about his "personal" religious belief of which I am aware, which unfortunately he did not publish, he saw it as meet to sketch a defense of himself against an accuser, who in a review made the passing remark that "Strauss rejects God." This is the sketch, written probably in 1959:

> A friend showed me a passage in an article by Professor David Spitz which reads "Strauss rejects God." I could not help laughing when I read it but did not know why I laughed. Another friend explained to me that the three words read like a manifestly absurd headline, say, "Nixon (or Stephenson) Declines Presidency." On reflection I sketched

the following letter to the Editor which I did not for a moment intend
to send to the periodical in which Spitz's utterance appeared:

"Spitz has said that Strauss is a great fool. If he had limited himself
to saying that I would not have reason to protest. Apart from the fact
that I have some awareness of my limitations, no one is under a moral
obligation to be intelligent; the fact that there are and always have been
so many fools in the world, would seem to show that there is a natural
necessity for that, and with such necessity even gods fight in vain. But
Spitz has said 'Strauss rejects God.' If one says of a man that he rejects
the sun, the moon and the stars, one says in effect that he is a fool.
Hence, considering the proportion of everything finite to the Infinite,
if one says of a man that he rejects God, one says in effect that he is
not only foolish but infinitely foolish. In addition, however, if the
accuser is not himself foolish, he accuses the accused by such a
statement of something like turpitude. Such accusations at any rate
require proof. My accuser has not even tried to prove his accusation.
If he should be induced by this remark to try to prove his accusation,
I warn him in advance to keep in mind the difference between revealed
theology and natural theology or to make himself familiar with it."

The original reply by Strauss is available in the Leo Strauss Archive, University
of Chicago Library (box 13, folder 16). Strauss construes the remark, first, as an
accusation of foolishness, and second, as an accusation of turpitude, both of
which charges he rejects. On the first count, Strauss seems to allude to Ps.
14:1—"The fool says in his heart 'There is no God.' " He only once mentioned
this biblical verse ("JA" [SPPP], pp. 150–51, JA, p. 6, but cf. also "MITP," p. 116,
"POR?" [IPP], pp. 304–5) to suggest that he knows the biblical faith legitimately
views the philosophical atheist as a fool: "Not theology, but philosophy, begs
the questions." Strauss also cites Bacon's essay "Of Atheism," in which he says:
"God never wrought miracle to convince [i.e., refute] atheism, because his
ordinary works convince [i.e., refute] it." These admittedly brief and allusive
remarks seem to suggest a theological position in which Strauss acknowledges
"the Infinite" as authoritative (cf. also "WWRJ," toward the end), and perhaps
should be related to what Strauss also maintains about the unity of "the whole."
(See supra, chapter 1, note 127.) This truth is somehow supported by what can
be learned from "the difference" between natural and revealed theologies, which
suggests that in spite of doubts about its cogency Strauss still recognizes the
essential truth of natural theology, and respects the unrefuted power of the
argument of revealed theology. Together, though they contradict one another,
they combine to make a compelling case for God not readily dismissed. Strauss
seems to regard the second implied charge of turpitude as gratuitous and merely
accusatory, because Spitz makes not even the slightest attempt to prove or
substantiate it. The original remark to which Strauss was responding occurred

in a review by David Spitz, *Commentary* 28, no. 10 (October 1959): 313–21. It has been reprinted as "Freedom, Virtue, and the 'New Scholasticism': The Supreme Court as Philosopher-Kings," in *The Liberal Idea of Freedom*, by David Spitz (Tucson, Ariz.: University of Arizona Press, 1964), chap. 16, pp. 163–74.

2. In this light, it would appear that Strauss's distinctive attitude toward Western civilization is rooted in his reading of Maimonides' attitude toward reason and revelation:

> . . . it seems to me that this unresolved conflict [between the biblical and the philosophic notions of the good life] is the secret of the vitality of Western civilization. . . .There is therefore no reason inherent in the Western civilization itself, in its fundamental constitution, why it should give up life. But this comforting thought is justified only if we live that life, if we live that conflict, that is. No one can be both a philosopher and a theologian or, for that matter, a third which is beyond the conflict between philosophy and theology, or a synthesis of both. But every one of us can be and ought to be either the one or the other, the philosopher open to the challenge of theology or the theologian open to the challenge of philosophy. ("POR?" [*IPP*], pp. 289–90)

For us in the West, the two options of our thought which remain vital (in spite of their contemporary sickness) are philosophy and theology. By clear implication, "ultramodern thought" (like the Hegelian synthesis) cannot succeed in its effort to get beyond these options to some third thing. Strauss believes we must choose between these two distinct options. The point, however, is that this choice for one thing should not close us to its opposite. It is *only* by authentic encounter and critical dialogue with the other that we remain true to ourselves as citizens of Western civilization. This is the "blessing" which we bear, he seems to say, and we do well not to forsake it.

3. Strauss's position on the conflict is most fully expounded, and the "higher perspectives" indicated, in "JA" (*SPPP*) and especially in "POR?" with "MITP." (For the first complete edition of "POR?" and "MITP" together, see "POR?" [*IPP*].) By employing the term "higher perspectives," I do not suggest that this means the submission of one claim to truth to the claim of the other, even on specific points, which would seemingly make one side "superior" to the other. This would mean that three things follow, which are crucially important in the notion of "higher perspectives": one side receives from the other a sharper and clearer picture of what the fundamental differences between them on the truth imply, which should compel both sides to distinctly focus on the areas of keenest dispute; one side learns from the other how deeply and how far it is necessary to penetrate the innermost parts of truth in order to present the whole adequately, and hence to meet the challenge of its opponent; each side is taught to proceed most cautiously in claiming total victory against its opponent. I make this point also in light of Strauss's related remarks, which he states in qualified terms rather than absolutely, about the ability of a later thinker or interpreter to provide

an expansion of the *fundamental* thought of an earlier thinker of profundity: the deepest thinkers set the standard and provide the most synoptic vision, irrespective of historical time and place, i.e., "hermeneutic situation." There are, then, as Strauss would like to persuade us, "fundamental alternatives" in the realm of truth. These are few in number, but many in manifestation. Modifications may be made to the periphery of the teaching, but as such they do not touch the fundamental core. A subsequent thinker either simply surpasses his predecessor in terms of truth; or he accepts the previous original truth, and just fills in the details, however important, on specific points, and applies or adapts the teaching to different circumstances. As Strauss puts it in his debate with Gadamer:

> I agree with your demand that the interpreter must reflect on his hermeneutic situation and he must apply the text to that situation; but I contend that prior to modern historicism all intelligent people whom I have studied and who spoke about the understanding of old and foreign books have done this; my last experience in this matter was Maimonides. I agree with your view according to which a doctrine cannot be an object of contemplation, to be interpreted as the "expression" of a certain kind of life, but must be understood in its claim to be true and this claim must be met. Meeting it means that I can, nay, must accept it as true or reject it as untrue or make a distinction *or recognize my inability to decide and therefore the necessity to think or learn more than I know at present.* . . . I do not believe however that this state of affairs is brought out when one speaks of "a fusion of horizons." Surely my horizon is enlarged if I learn something important. But *it is hard to say that Plato's horizon is enlarged if a modification of his doctrine proves to be superior to his own version.* ("CCWM," p. 6; emphasis added)

4. "PGS" (*LAM*), p. 266. Strauss articulates a view of Jewish-Christian relations which is suggestively Maimonidean. (See especially *The Code of Maimonides*, Book 14: *The Book of Judges*, edited by Abraham M. Hershman (New Haven: Yale University Press, 1949). Most relevant are the censored paragraphs from "Laws of Kings and Their Wars," pp. xxiii–xxiv. With respect to the ways of God in the economy of truth, i.e., teaching it through several religions, Maimonides concedes: "But it is beyond the human mind to fathom the designs of the Creator; for our ways are not His ways, neither are our thoughts His thoughts. All these matters relating to Jesus of Nazareth and the Ishmaelite [Mohammed] who came after him, only served to clear the way for King Messiah, to prepare the whole world to worship God with one accord. . . . Thus the messianic hope, the Torah, and the commandments have become familiar topics—topics of conversation [among the inhabitants] of the far isles and many peoples, uncircumcized of heart and flesh." In my judgment, Strauss's position

on Judaism and philosophy is similar, and it is similarly Maimonidean. He continues with a passage about the virtues and the limits of "mutual recognition" between Jew and Christian, which can be applied directly to his chief concern, the relation between Judaism and philosophy. Beyond the need to "recognize each the noble features of its antagonist," such mutual recognition also

> cannot but be accompanied by the certainty on the part of each of the two antagonists that in the end the other will lower its head. Recognition of the other must remain subordinate to recognition of the truth. Even the pagan philosophers Plato and Aristotle remained friends, although each held the truth to be his greatest friend, or rather because each held the truth to be his greatest friend.

Strauss adds something significant about Judaism and Christianity which can also be applied in essence directly to his view of Judaism and philosophy:

> The Jew may recognize that the Christian error is a blessing, a divine blessing, and the Christian may recognize that the Jewish error is a blessing, a divine blessing. Beyond this they cannot go without ceasing to be Jew or Christian.

Finally, and related to this, Strauss is careful to record a view, which he suggests was laid down by Alfarabi, that "conformity with the opinions of the religious community in which one is brought up is a necessary qualification of the future philosopher." (*PAW*, p. 17)

BIBLIOGRAPHY

JEWISH PHILOSOPHICAL SOURCES

Cohen, Hermann. *Religion of Reason out of the Sources of Judaism.* Translated by Simon Kaplan. New York: Frederick Ungar, 1972.

———. *Religion der Vernunft aus den Quellen des Judentums.* Edited by Bruno Strauss. Darmstadt: Joseph Melzer, 1966.

Halevi, Judah. *The Kuzari.* Translated by Hartwig Hirschfeld. New York: Schocken, 1964.

———. *Sefer ha-Kuzari.* Translated by Yehuda Ibn Tibbon. Edited by A. Tzifroni. Jerusalem: Schocken, 1970.

Maimonides, Moses. *The Code of Maimonides,* Book 14: *The Book of Judges.* Translated by Abraham M. Hershman. New Haven: Yale University Press, 1949.

———. *The Guide of the Perplexed.* Translated by Shlomo Pines. Chicago: University of Chicago Press, 1963.

———. *The Mishneh Torah,* Book 1: *The Book of Knowledge.* Translated by Moses Hyamson. Jerusalem: Philipp Feldheim, 1981.

———. *Mishneh Torah,* Book 1: *Sefer ha-Madda.* Edited by Mordechai D. Rabinowitz. Jerusalem: Mossad Harav Kook, 1958.

———. *Mishneh Torah,* Book 14: *Sefer Shoftim.* Edited by Mordechai D. Rabinowitz. Jerusalem: Mossad Harav Kook, 1966.

———. *Moreh ha-Nevuchim.* Translated by Shmuel Ibn Tibbon. Edited by Yehuda Ibn Shmuel. Jerusalem: Mossad Harav Kook, 1981.

Mendelssohn, Moses. *Gesammalte Schriften, Jubiläumsausgabe.* Volume 8. Edited by Alexander Altmann. Stuttgart-Bad Cannstatt: Friedrich Frommann Verlag (Günther Holzboog), 1983.

———. *Jerusalem.* Translated by Allan Arkush. Hanover, N. H.: University Press of New England, 1983.

Rosenzweig, Franz. *The Star of Redemption.* Translated by William W. Hallo. Boston: Beacon Press, 1972.

———. *Der Stern der Erlösung*. The Hague: Martinus Nijhoff, 1976.
Spinoza, Benedict. *Ethics*. Translated by R. H. M. Elwes. New York: Dover, 1951.
———. *A Theologico-Political Treatise*. Translated by R. H. M. Elwes. New York: Dover, 1951.
———. *Opera*. Volumes 2 and 3. Edited by Carl Gebhardt. Heidelberg: Carl Winter, 1925.

PRIMARY SOURCES: WORKS BY LEO STRAUSS

Strauss, Leo. "Anmerkung zur Diskussion über 'Zionismus und Antisemitismus.'" *Jüdische Rundschau* 28, nos. 83/84 (1923): 501.
———. "Antwort auf das 'Prinzipielle Wort' der Frankfurter." *Jüdische Rundschau* 28, no. 9 (1923): 45.
———. *The Argument and the Action of Plato's "Laws"*. Chicago: University of Chicago Press, 1975.
———. "Biblische Geschichte und Wissenschaft." *Jüdische Rundschau* 30, no. 88 (1925): 744–45.
———. *The City and Man*. Chicago: University of Chicago Press, 1964.
———. "Cohens Analyse der Bibel-Wissenschaft Spinozas." *Der Jude* 8 (1924): 295–314.
———. "Correspondence between Karl Löwith and Leo Strauss." *The Independent Journal of Philosophy* 5/6 (1988): 177–92.
———, with Karl Löwith. "Correspondence Concerning Modernity." *The Independent Journal of Philosophy* 4 (1983): 105–19.
———, with Hans-Georg Gadamer. "Correspondence Concerning *Wahrheit und Methode*." *The Independent Journal of Philosophy* 2 (1978): 5–12.
———. "The Crisis of Our Time" and "The Crisis of Political Philosophy." In *The Predicament of Modern Politics*, edited by Harold J. Spaeth, 41–54, 91–103. Detroit: University of Detroit Press, 1964.
———. *De la tyrannie*. Paris: Librairie Gallimard, 1954.
———. "Eine vermisste Schrift Farâbîs." *Monatsschrift für Geschichte und Wissenschaft des Judentums* 80 (1936): 96–106.
———. *Essays on Judaism* (in Hebrew). Edited by Ehud Luz. Jerusalem: Bialik Institute. Forthcoming.
———. "Exoteric Teaching." Edited by Kenneth Hart Green. *Interpretation* 14, no. 1 (January 1986): 51–59.
———. *Faith and Political Philosophy. The Correspondence Between Leo Strauss and Eric Voegelin*. Edited and translated by Barry Cooper and Peter Emberley. Introduction by Thomas L. Pangle. University Park, Pa.: Pennsylvania State University Press, 1993.
———. "Farabi's *Plato*." In *Louis Ginzberg Jubilee Volume*, edited by Alexander Marx, Saul Lieberman, et al, 357–93. New York: American Academy for Jewish Research, 1945.

————. "Franz Rosenzweig und die Akademie für die Wissenschaft des Judentums." *Jüdische Wochenzeitung für Kassel, Hessen, und Waldeck*, 13 December 1929.

————. "Freud on Moses and Monotheism." Lecture delivered at the Hillel House, University of Chicago. Publication by State University of New York Press forthcoming in *The Jewish Writings of Leo Strauss*, edited by Kenneth Hart Green.

————, with Jacob Klein. "A Giving of Accounts." *The College* 22, no. 1 (April 1970): 1–5.

————. "Das Heilige." *Der Jude* 7 (1923): 240–42.

————. "How to Begin to Study *The Guide of the Perplexed*." In *The Guide of the Perplexed*, by Moses Maimonides, translated by Shlomo Pines, xi–lvi. Chicago: University of Chicago Press, 1963.

————. "The Idea of the Holy." In *The Jew: Essays from Martin Buber's Journal "Der Jude," 1916–1928*, edited by Arthur A. Cohen, and translated by Joachim Neugroschel, 232–36. University, Ala.: University of Alabama Press, 1980.

————. "Introduction," "Plato," "Marsilius of Padua," and "Machiavelli." In *History of Political Philosophy*, 2d ed., edited by Leo Strauss and Joseph Cropsey, 1–6, 7–63, 251–70, 271–92. Chicago: University of Chicago Press, 1963.

————. Introductions to "Pope ein Metaphysiker!," "Sendschreiben an den Herrn Magister Lessing in Leipzig," "Kommentar zu den 'Termini der Logik' des Mose ben Maimon," "Abhandlung über die Evidenz," XV–XXIII, XLI, XLV–LIII. In *Moses Mendelssohn Gesammelte Schriften: Jubiläumsausgabe*. Volume 2. Berlin: Akademie-Verlag, 1931.

————. Introductions to "Phädon," "Abhandlung von der Unkörperlichkeit der menschlichen Seele," "Über einen schriftlichen Aufsatz des Herrn de Luc," "Die Seele," XIII–XLI. In *Moses Mendelssohn Gesammelte Schriften: Jubiläumsausgabe*. Volume 3, part 1. Berlin: Akademie-Verlag, 1932.

————. Introductions to "Sache Gottes oder die gerettete Vorsehung," "Morgenstunden," "An die Freunde Lessings," XI–CX. In *Moses Mendelssohn Gesammelte Schriften: Jubiläumsausgabe*. Volume 3, part 2. Stuttgart-Bad Cannstatt: Friedrich Frommann (Günther Holzboog), 1974.

————. *An Introduction to Political Philosophy: Ten Essays by Leo Strauss*. Edited with an introduction by Hilail Gildin. Detroit: Wayne State University Press, 1989.

————. Introductory Essay to *Religion of Reason out of the Sources of Judaism*, by Hermann Cohen, translated by Simon Kaplan, xxiii–xxxviii. New York: Frederick Ungar, 1972.

————. *Jerusalem and Athens*. The First Frank Cohen Public Lecture in Judaic Affairs. New York: The City College, 1967.

————. *The Jewish Writings of Leo Strauss*. Series Edited by Kenneth Hart Green. Publication by State University of New York Press forthcoming.

———. "Letter to Helmut Kuhn." *The Independent Journal of Philosophy* 2 (1978): 23–26.

———. *Liberalism Ancient and Modern.* New York: Basic Books, 1968.

———. "Machiavelli and Classical Literature." *Review of National Literatures* 1, no. 1 (Spring 1970): 7–25.

———. *Maïmonide.* Edited and translated by Rémi Brague. Paris: Presses Universitaires de France, 1988.

———. "The Mutual Influence of Theology and Philosophy" (in Hebrew). *Iyyun* 5 (1954): 110–23.

———. "The Mutual Influence of Theology and Philosophy." *The Independent Journal of Philosophy* 3 (1979): 111–18.

———. *Natural Right and History.* Chicago: University of Chicago Press, 1953.

———. "On Abravanel's Philosophical Tendency and Political Teaching." In *Isaac Abravanel,* edited by J. B. Trend and H. Loewe, 93–129. Cambridge: Cambridge University Press, 1937.

———. "On Collingwood's Philosophy of History." *Review of Metaphysics* 5, no. 4 (June 1952): 559–86.

———. "On Isaac Husik's Work in Medieval Jewish Philosophy" (in Hebrew). *Iyyun* 2 (1951): 215–23.

———. "On a New Interpretation of Plato's Political Philosophy." *Social Research* 13 (1946): 326–67.

———. "On the Intention of Rousseau." *Social Research* 14 (1947): 455–87.

———. "On the Interpretation of Genesis." *L'Homme* 21 (1981): 5–36.

———. "On the Plan of *The Guide of the Perplexed.*" In *Harry Austryn Wolfson Jubilee Volume,* edited by Saul Lieberman, Shalom Spiegel, et al, 775–91. Jerusalem: American Academy for Jewish Research, 1965.

———. *On Tyranny.* Ithaca, N. Y.: Cornell University Press, 1963.

———. *On Tyranny.* Rev. Ed. Edited by Victor Gourevitch and Michael S. Roth. New York: The Free Press, 1991.

———. "Der Ort der Vorsehungslehre nach der Ansicht Maimunis." *Monatsschrift für Geschichte und Wissenschaft des Judentums* 81 (1937): 93–105.

———. "Paul de Lagarde." *Der Jude* 8 (1924): 8–15.

———. *Persecution and the Art of Writing.* Glencoe, Ill.: The Free Press, 1952.

———. *Philosophie und Gesetz: Beiträge zum Verständnis Maimunis und seiner Vorläufer.* Berlin: Schocken, 1935.

———. *Philosophy and Law: Essays Toward the Understanding of Maimonides and His Predecessors.* Translated by Fred Baumann. Philadelphia: Jewish Publication Society, 1987.

———. "Philosophy as Rigorous Science and Political Philosophy" (in Hebrew). *Iyyun* 20 (1969): 14–22.

———. "Political Philosophy and History" (in Hebrew). *Iyyun* 1 (1946): 129–46.

———. *The Political Philosophy of Hobbes: Its Basis and Its Genesis.* Translated by Elsa M. Sinclair. Chicago: University of Chicago Press, 1952.

———. "Preface to *Hobbes Politische Wissenschaft.*" Translated by Donald J. Maletz. *Interpretation* 8 (1979–80): 1–3.

———. Preface to *Isaac Husik's Philosophical Essays: Ancient, Medieval, and Modern*, edited by Milton Nahm and Leo Strauss, vii–xli. Oxford: Basil Blackwell, 1952.

———. "Progress or Return?" *Modern Judaism* 1 (1981): 17–45.

———. "Quelques remarques sur la science politique de Hobbes." *Recherches Philosophiques* 2 (1933): 609–22.

———. "Quelques remarques sur la science politique de Maïmonide et de Fârâbî." *Revue des Études Juives* 100 (1936): 1–37.

———. *The Rebirth of Classical Political Rationalism: Essays and Lectures by Leo Strauss.* Selected and edited with an introduction by Thomas L. Pangle. Chicago: University of Chicago Press, 1989.

———. "Relativism." In *Relativism and the Study of Man*, edited by Helmut Schoeck and J. W. Wiggins, 135–57. Princeton: Van Nostrand, 1961.

———. *Die Religionskritik Spinozas als Grundlage seiner Bibelwissenschaft.* Berlin: Akademie-Verlag, 1930.

———. "Remarques sur *Le Livre de la connaissance* de Maïmonide." Translated by Olivier Berrichon-Sedeyn. *Revue de Metaphysique et de Morale* 94, no. 3 (July-September 1989): 293–308.

———. "Replies to Schaar and Wolin." *American Political Science Review* 57 (1963): 152–55.

———. Review of Julius Ebbinghaus, *Über die Fortschritte der Metaphysik. Deutsche Literaturzeitung* no. 52 (27 December 1931): 2451–53.

———. Review of A. Levkowitz, *Religiöse Denker der Gegenwart. Der Jude* 8 (1924): 432.

———. Review of Moses Hyamson's edition of Maimonides, *The Mishneh Torah, Book 1. Review of Religion* 3, no. 4 (May 1939): 448–56.

———. "Social Science and Humanism" (in Hebrew). *Iyyun* 7 (1956): 65–73.

———. "Sociologische Geschichtschreibung?" *Der Jude* 8 (1924): 190–2.

———. *Socrates and Aristophanes.* Chicago: University of Chicago Press, 1966.

———. "Some Remarks on the Political Science of Maimonides and Farabi." Translated by Robert Bartlett. *Interpretation* 18, no. 1 (Fall 1990): 3–30.

———. *Spinoza's Critique of Religion.* Translated by Elsa M. Sinclair. New York: Schocken, 1965.

———. "The Spirit of Sparta or the Taste of Xenophon." *Social Research* 6 (1939): 502–36.

———. "The State of Israel." *National Review* 3, no. 1 (5 January 1957): 23.

———. *Studies in Platonic Political Philosophy.* With an Introduction by Thomas L. Pangle. Chicago: University of Chicago Press, 1983.

———. "Das Testament Spinozas." *Bayerische Israelitische Gemeindezeitung* 8, no. 21 (1 November 1932): 322–26.

———. *Le Testament de Spinoza.* Edited and translated by Gérard Almaleh, Albert Baraquin, and Mireille Depadt-Ejchenbaum. Paris: Les Editions du Cerf, 1991.

————. *Thoughts on Machiavelli.* Glencoe, Ill.: The Free Press, 1958.

————. "An Unspoken Prologue to a Public Lecture at St. John's College (In Honor of Jacob Klein, 1899–1978)." *Interpretation* 7, no. 3 (1978): 1–3.

————. "What Is Political Philosophy?" (in Hebrew). *Iyyun* 6 (1955): 65–99.

————. *What Is Political Philosophy?* New York: The Free Press, 1959.

————. "Why We Remain Jews." Lecture delivered at the Hillel House, University of Chicago. Publication by State University of New York Press forthcoming in *The Jewish Writings of Leo Strauss,* edited by Kenneth Hart Green.

————. *Xenophon's Socrates.* Ithaca, N. Y.: Cornell University Press, 1972.

————. *Xenophon's Socratic Discourse: An Interpretation of the 'Oeconomicus'.* Ithaca, N. Y.: Cornell University Press, 1970.

————. "Zionism in Max Nordau." In *The Jew: Essays from Martin Buber's Journal "Der Jude," 1916–1928,* edited by Arthur A. Cohen, and translated by Joachim Neugroschel, 120–126. University, Ala.: University of Alabama Press, 1980.

————. "Der Zionismus bei Nordau." *Der Jude* 7 (1923): 657–60.

————. "Zur Auseinandersetzung mit der europäischen Wissenschaft." *Der Jude* 8 (1924): 613–17.

————. "Zur Bibelwissenschaft Spinozas und seiner Vorläufer." *Korrespondenzblatt* (des Vereins zur Gründung und Erhaltung einer Akademie für die Wissenschaft des Judentums) 7 (1926): 1–22.

Note: Letters to and from Leo Strauss, and unpublished writings by Leo Strauss, are stored in the Archives of the University of Chicago Library. They are cited according to the system of storage used in the Archives, i.e., by box number and folder number.

SECONDARY SOURCES: SELECTED WORKS ON LEO STRAUSS

Adams, James Ring. "The Power of Strauss." *Forward,* 24 April 1992, pp. 1, 11.

Adler, Eve. Review of *Philosophy and Law,* by Leo Strauss. *AJS Review* 14 (1989): 263–88.

————. "Leo Strauss's *Philosophie und Gesetz.*" In *Leo Strauss's Thought,* ed. Alan Udoff, 183–226. Boulder, Colo.: Lynne Rienner, 1991.

Almaleh, Gérard, Albert Baraquin, and Mireille Depadt-Ejchenbaum. "Présentation." In *Le Testament de Spinoza,* by Leo Strauss, 9–39. Paris: Les Editions du Cerf, 1991.

Altizer, Thomas J.J. "The Theological Conflict Between Strauss and Voegelin." In *Faith and Political Philosophy,* eds. Barry Cooper and Peter Emberley, 267–77. University Park, Pa.: Pennsylvania State University Press, 1993.

Altmann, Alexander. Review of *The Guide of the Perplexed,* by Moses Maimonides, translated by Shlomo Pines, with an introductory essay by Leo Strauss. *Journal of Religion* 44 (1964): 260–61.

————. "Leo Strauss: 1899–1973." *Proceedings of the American Academy for Jewish Research* 41–42 (1975): xxxiii–xxxvi.

————. "Maimonides and Thomas Aquinas: Natural or Divine Prophecy?" *AJS Review* 3 (1978): 1–19.

————. "Maimonides on the Intellect and the Scope of Metaphysics." In *Von der mittelalterlichen zur modernen Aufklärung,* 60–129. Tübingen: J. C. B. Mohr, 1987.

Altwicker, Norbert. Foreword to *Die Religionskritik Spinozas als Grundlage seiner Bibelwissenschaft,* by Leo Strauss, ix–xii. Hildesheim: Georg Olms, 1981.

Anastaplo, George. "On Leo Strauss: A Yahrzeit Remembrance." *University of Chicago Magazine* 67 (Winter 1974): 30–38.

————. "Shadia Drury on Leo Strauss." *The Vital Nexus* 1, no. 1 (May 1990): 9–28.

Andrew, Edward. "Descent to the Cave." *Review of Politics* 45 (1983): 510–35.

Aron, Raymond. "Max Weber and Modern Social Science." Chapter 12 in *History, Truth, and Liberty: Selected Writings of Raymond Aron,* edited by Franciszek Draus, 335–373. Chicago: University of Chicago Press, 1985.

Baraquin, Albert. *See* Almaleh, Gérard.

Becker, Jacob. *The Secret of "The Guide of the Perplexed": A Reevaluation of the World View of the Rambam* (in Hebrew). Tel Aviv: J. Shimoni, 1955.

Belaval, Yvon. "Pour une sociologie de la philosophie." *Critique* 9, no. 77 (October 1953): 852–66.

Benardete, Seth. "Leo Strauss's *The City and Man.*" *Political Science Reviewer* 8 (1978): 1–20.

Ben-Asher, Mordechai. "Religion and Reason in Maimonides. Contribution to an Explanation of the Views of Julius Guttmann and Leo Strauss" (in Hebrew). *Bash-Sha'ar* 4 (1961): 78–87.

Berman, Lawrence. "A Re-examination of Maimonides' 'Statement on Political Science.'" *Journal of the American Oriental Society* 89 (1969): 106–11.

————. "The Structure of *The Guide*: Reflections Occasioned by L. Strauss and S. Rawidowicz." In vol. 3 of *Proceedings of the Sixth World Congress of Jewish Studies,* edited by Avigdor Shinan, 7–13. Jerusalem: World Union of Jewish Studies, 1977.

————. "Maimonides, the Disciple of al-Farabi." *Israel Oriental Studies* 4 (1974): 154–78.

Berns, Laurence. "Leo Strauss: 1899–1973." *Independent Journal of Philosophy* 2 (1978): 1–3. idem, *The College* 25, no. 4. *See* Klein, Jacob.

————. "Aristotle and the Moderns on Freedom and Equality." In *The Crisis of Liberal Democracy,* eds. Kenneth L. Deutsch and Walter Soffer, 148–66. Albany: State University of New York Press, 1988.

————. "The Prescientific World and Historicism: Some Reflections on Strauss, Heidegger, and Husserl." In *Leo Strauss's Thought,* ed. Alan Udoff, 169–81. Boulder, Colo.: Lynne Rienner, 1991.

————. "The Relation Between Religion and Philosophy: Reflections on Leo Strauss's Suggestion Concerning the Source and Sources of Modern Philosophy." *Interpretation* 19, no. 1 (Fall 1991): 43–60.

Berns, Walter, Herbert J. Storing, Harry V. Jaffa, and Werner Dannhauser. "The Achievement of Leo Strauss." *National Review* 25 (1973): 1347–57.

———. *See* Storing, Herbert J.

Bertman, Martin A. "Hobbes' Science of Politics and Plato's *Laws*." *Independent Journal of Philosophy* 2 (1978): 47–53.

Best, Judith A. "The Innocent, the Ignorant, and the Rational: The Content of Lockian Consent." In *The Crisis of Liberal Democracy*, eds. Kenneth L. Deutsch and Walter Soffer, 167–79. Albany: State University of New York Press, 1988.

Biale, David. "Leo Strauss: The Philosopher as Weimar Jew." In *Leo Strauss's Thought*, ed. Alan Udoff, 31–40. Boulder, Colo.: Lynne Rienner, 1991.

Blanchard, Kenneth C. "Philosophy in the Age of Auschwitz: Emil Fackenheim and Leo Strauss." In vol. 2 of *Remembering for the Future*, edited by Yehuda Bauer, et al, 1815–29. Oxford, England: Pergamon, 1989.

Blanton, Ted A. *See* Klein, Jacob.

Bloom, Allan. "Leo Strauss: September 20, 1899—October 18, 1973." *Political Theory* 2 (1974): 373–92. idem, *Giants and Dwarfs*, 235–55. New York: Simon and Schuster, 1990.

———. "Aristophanes and Socrates: A Response to Hall." *Political Theory* 5 (1977): 315–30. idem, *Giants and Dwarfs*, 162–76. New York: Simon and Schuster, 1990.

———. Foreword to *Liberalism Ancient and Modern*, by Leo Strauss, v–vi. Ithaca, N.Y.: Cornell University Press, 1989.

Bluhm, William T. "Platonism versus the Natural Science of Politics: Leo Strauss and His 'Academy'." In *Theories of the Political System*, 3d ed., 63–70. Englewood Cliffs, N. J.: Prentice-Hall, 1978.

Bodéüs, Richard. "Deux propositions aristotéliciennes sur le droit naturel chez les continentaux d'Amérique." *Revue de Metaphysique et de Morale* 94, no. 3 (July-September 1989): 369–89.

Bouganim, Ami. "Une desillusion héroïque: Une étude de la pensée de Léo Strauss." *Pardès* 4 (1986): 54–72.

Brague, Rémi. "Leo Strauss et Maïmonide." In *Maimonides and Philosophy*, edited by Shlomo Pines and Yirmiyahu Yovel, 246–68. Dordrecht, The Netherlands: Martinus Nijhoff, 1986.

———. "Athènes, Jérusalem, La Mecque. L'interprétation 'musulmane' de la philosophie grecque chez Leo Strauss." *Revue de Metaphysique et de Morale* 94, no. 3 (July-September 1989): 309–36.

———. "Leo Strauss and Maimonides." In *Leo Strauss's Thought*, ed. Alan Udoff, 93–114. Boulder, Colo.: Lynne Rienner, 1991.

Bruell, Christopher. "Strauss on Xenophon's Socrates." *Political Science Reviewer* 13 (1983): 99–153; 14 (1984): 263–318.

———. "A Return to Classical Political Philosophy and the Understanding of the American Founding." *Review of Politics* 53, no. 1 (Winter 1991): 173–86.

Buijs, Joseph A. "The Philosophical Character of Maimonides' *Guide*—A Critique of Strauss's Interpretation." *Judaism* 27 (1978): 448–57. idem, *Maimonides: A Collection of Critical Essays*, edited by Joseph A. Buijs, 59–70. Notre Dame, Ind.: University of Notre Dame Press, 1988.

Burnyeat, Myles F. "Sphinx Without a Secret." Review of *Studies in Platonic Political Philosophy*, by Leo Strauss. *New York Review of Books* 32, no. 9 (30 May 1985): 30–36. For responses to the review in letters to the editor, and replies of the reviewer, see *New York Review of Books* 10 October and 24 October 1985; 24 April 1986; 31 March 1988.

Cantor, Paul A. "Leo Strauss and Contemporary Hermeneutics." In *Leo Strauss's Thought*, ed. Alan Udoff, 267–314. Boulder, Colo.: Lynne Rienner, 1991.

Caranfa, Angelo. *Machiavelli Rethought: A Critique of Strauss's Machiavelli.* Washington, D. C.: University Press of America, 1978.

Carpino, Joseph J. Review of *Christianity and Political Philosophy*, by Frederick Wilhelmsen. *Interpretation* 8 (1979–80): 204–22.

Caton, Hiram. "Der hermeneutische Weg von Leo Strauss." *Philosophisches Jahrbuch* 80 (1973): 171–82.

Clay, Diskin. "On a Forgotten Kind of Reading." In *Leo Strauss's Thought*, ed. Alan Udoff, 253–66. Boulder, Colo.: Lynne Rienner, 1991.

Colmo, Christopher A. "Reason and Revelation in the Thought of Leo Strauss." *Interpretation* 18, no. 1 (Fall 1990): 145–60.

Cooper, Barry, and Peter Emberley, eds. *Faith and Political Philosophy: The Correspondence Between Leo Strauss and Eric Voegelin*. With an Introduction by Thomas L. Pangle. University Park, Pa.: Pennsylvania State University Press, 1993.

Cox, Richard H. "Aristotle and Machiavelli on Liberality." In *The Crisis of Liberal Democracy*, eds. Kenneth L. Deutsch and Walter Soffer, 125–47. Albany: State University of New York Press, 1988.

Cropsey, Joseph. "Reply to Rothman." *American Political Science Review* 56 (1962): 353–59.

———. "Leo Strauss on His Sixty-fifth Birthday" and Preface to *Ancients and Moderns: Essays on the Tradition of Political Philosophy in Honor of Leo Strauss*, edited by Joseph Cropsey. New York: Basic Books, 1964.

———. "Leo Strauss: A Bibliography and Memorial." *Interpretation* 5, no. 2 (Winter 1975): 133–47.

———. "Leo Strauss." In vol. 18 of *The International Encyclopedia of the Social Sciences*, edited by David Sills, 746–50. New York: The Free Press/ Macmillan, 1979.

Cubeddu, Raimondo. *Leo Strauss e la filosofia politica moderna*. Naples: Edizioni scientifiche italiane, 1983.

Dallmayr, Fred R. "Political Philosophy Today." Chapter 1 in *Polis and Praxis*, 15–46. Cambridge, Mass.: MIT Press, 1984.

———. "Politics Against Philosophy: Strauss and Drury." *Political Theory* 15, no. 3 (August 1987): 326–37.

Dannhauser, Werner J. "Leo Strauss: Becoming Naïve Again." *American Scholar* 44 (1974–75): 636–42. idem, *Masters: Portraits of Great Teachers*, edited by Joseph Epstein, 253–65. New York: Basic Books, 1981.

———. "Leo Strauss as Citizen and Jew." *Interpretation* 17, no. 3 (Spring 1991): 433–47.

———. *See* Berns, Walter.

Davidson, Herbert. "Maimonides' Secret Position on Creation." In *Studies in Medieval Jewish History and Literature*, edited by Isadore Twersky, 16–40. Cambridge, Mass.: Harvard University Press, 1979.

Deane, Herbert A. Review of *What Is Political Philosophy?*, by Leo Strauss. *American Political Science Review* 55 (1961): 149–50. See also letter to the editor, by Harry V. Jaffa, 55 (1961): 599.

Depadt-Ejchenbaum, Mireille. *See* Almaleh, Gérard.

Deutsch, Kenneth L., and Walter Nicgorski, eds. *Review of Politics* 53, no. 1 (Winter 1991). Special Issue on Leo Strauss.

———, and Walter Soffer, eds. *The Crisis of Liberal Democrary: A Straussian Perspective*. Albany: State University of New York Press, 1988.

Doran, Robert M. *Theology and the Dialectics of History*. Toronto: University of Toronto Press, 1990.

Drury, Shadia B. "The Esoteric Philosophy of Leo Strauss." *Political Theory* 13 (1985): 315–37.

———. "Leo Strauss's Classic Natural Right Teaching." *Political Theory* 15, no. 3 (August 1987): 299–315.

———. *The Political Ideas of Leo Strauss*. New York: St. Martin's Press, 1988.

———. "Leo Strauss on the Nature of the Political" and "Reply to My Critics." *The Vital Nexus* 1, no. 1 (May 1990): 29–47, 119–34.

East, John P. "Leo Strauss and American Conservatism." *Modern Age* 21 (1977): 2–19.

Eden, Robert. "Why Wasn't Weber A Nihilist?" In *The Crisis of Liberal Democracy*, eds. Kenneth L. Deutsch and Walter Soffer, 212–42. Albany: State University of New York Press, 1988.

Edmond, Michel-Pierre. "Machiavel et la question de la Nature." *Revue de Metaphysique et de Morale* 94, no. 3 (July-September 1989): 347–52.

Eidelberg, Paul. *Jerusalem vs. Athens*. Lanham, Md.: University Press of America, 1983.

Emberley, Peter. "Leo Strauss: Machiavellian or Moralist?" *The Vital Nexus* 1, no. 1 (May 1990): 49–59.

———. *See* Cooper, Barry.

Enegrén, André, ed. *Revue de Metaphysique et de Morale* 94, no. 3 (July-September 1989). Special Issue on Leo Strauss.

Fackenheim, Emil L. "Leo Strauss and Modern Judaism." *Claremont Review of Books* 4, no. 4 (Winter 1985): 21–23.

———. *To Mend the World*. New York: Schocken, 1982.

————. "Reply to My Critics: A Testament of Thought." In *Fackenheim: German Philosophy and Jewish Thought*, edited by Louis I. Greenspan and Graeme Nicholson, 251–300. Toronto: University of Toronto Press, 1992.

Ferry, Luc. "The Rejection of Historicist Modernity: Leo Strauss." In *Political Philosophy*. Volume 1, *Rights—The New Quarrel between the Ancients and the Moderns*, 29–70. Chicago: University of Chicago Press, 1990.

Feuchtwanger, Ludwig. Review of *Philosophie und Gesetz*, by Leo Strauss. *Jüdische Rundschau* 29, no. 9 (9 April 1935): 7.

Fortin, Ernest L. "Christian Political Theory." *Review of Politics* 41 (1979): 578–82.

————. "Rational Theologians and Irrational Philosophers: A Straussian Perspective." *Interpretation* 12 (1984): 349–56.

————, ed. "Interview with Hans-Georg Gadamer on Leo Strauss." *Interpretation* 12 (1984): 1–13.

————. "Faith and Reason in Contemporary Perspective." *Interpretation* 14 (1986): 371–87.

————. "Was Leo Strauss a Secret Enemy of Morality?" *Crisis* 7, no. 12 (December 1989): 19–26.

————. "Dead Masters and Their Living Thought." *The Vital Nexus* 1, no. 1 (May 1990): 61–71.

Fox, Marvin. Review of *The Guide of the Perplexed*, by Moses Maimonides, translated with an introduction and notes by Shlomo Pines, with an introductory essay by Leo Strauss. *Journal of the History of Philosophy* 3 (1965): 265–74.

————. Prolegomenon to *The Philosophy of Maimonides*, by Abraham Cohen, xv–xliv. New York: KTAV, 1968.

————. *Interpreting Maimonides: Studies in Methodology, Metaphysics, and Moral Philosophy*. Chicago: University of Chicago Press, 1990.

Fradkin, Hillel. "Philosophy and Law: Leo Strauss as a Student of Medieval Jewish Thought." *Review of Politics* 53, no. 1 (Winter 1991): 40–52.

————. "Leo Strauss and Contemporary Jewish Thought." In *Contemporary Jewish Thinkers*, edited by Steven T. Katz. New York: B'nai Brith. Forthcoming.

Fuller, Timothy. "Philosophy, Faith, and the Question of Progress." In *Faith and Political Philosophy*, eds. Barry Cooper and Peter Emberley, 279–95. University Park, Pa.: Pennsylvania State University Press, 1993.

Gadamer, Hans-Georg. "Hermeneutics and Historicism." In *Truth and Method*, 482–91. New York: Crossroad, 1982.

————. "Interview on Leo Strauss." *Interpretation* 12 (1984): 1–13.

————. "Philosophizing in Opposition: Strauss and Voegelin on Communication and Science." In *Faith and Political Philosophy*, eds. Barry Cooper and Peter Emberley, 249–59. University Park, Pa.: Pennsylvania State University Press, 1993.

Galston, Miriam. "Philosopher-King vs. Prophet." *Israel Oriental Studies* 8 (1978): 204–18.

Germino, Dante. "Second Thoughts on Leo Strauss's Machiavelli." *Journal of Politics* 28 (1966): 794–817.

————. "Blasphemy and Leo Strauss's Machiavelli. "*Review of Politics* 53, no. 1 (Winter 1991): 146–56.

Gildin, Hilail. "Leo Strauss and the Crisis of Liberal Democracy" and "A Response to Gourevitch." In *The Crisis of Liberal Democracy*, eds. Kenneth L. Deutsch and Walter Soffer, 91–103, 114–23. Albany: State University of New York Press, 1988.

————. Introduction to *An Introduction to Political Philosophy: Ten Essays by Leo Strauss*, edited by Hilail Gildin, vii–xxiv. Detroit: Wayne State University Press, 1989.

————. "The First Crisis of Modernity: Leo Strauss on the Thought of Rousseau." *Interpretation* 20, no. 2 (Winter 1992–93): 157–64.

Gilson, Etienne. *From Aristotle to Darwin and Back Again*. Translated by John Lyon. Notre Dame, Ind.: University of Notre Dame Press, 1984.

Gourevitch, Victor. "Philosophy and Politics." *Review of Metaphysics* 22 (1968): 58–84, 281–328.

————. "The Problem of Natural Right and the Fundamental Alternatives in *Natural Right and History*" and "A Reply to Gildin." In *The Crisis of Liberal Democracy*, eds. Kenneth L. Deutsch and Walter Soffer, 30–47, 104–13. Albany: State University of New York Press, 1988.

————, and Michael S. Roth. Introduction to *On Tyranny*, by Leo Strauss, ix–xxii. Revised Edition. Edited by Victor Gourevitch and Michael S. Roth. New York: The Free Press, 1991.

Grant, George P. "Tyranny and Wisdom: The Controversy Between L. Strauss and A. Kojève." *Social Research* 31 (1964): 45–72. idem, *Technology and Empire*, 81–109. Toronto: Anansi, 1969.

Grayzel, Solomon. Review of *Persecution and the Art of Writing*, by Leo Strauss. *Annals of the American Academy of Political and Social Sciences* 285 (1953): 204–05.

Green, Kenneth H. " 'In the Grip of the Theological-Political Predicament': The Turn to Maimonides in the Jewish Thought of Leo Strauss." In *Leo Strauss's Thought*, ed. Alan Udoff, 41–74. Boulder, Colo.: Lynne Rienner, 1991.

————. "Religion, Philosophy, and Morality: How Leo Strauss Read Judah Halevi's *Kuzari*." *Journal of the American Academy of Religion* 61, no. 2 (Summer 1993): 225–73.

Gunnell, John G. "The Myth of the Tradition." *American Political Science Review* 72 (1978): 122–34.

————. "Political Theory and Politics: The Case of Leo Strauss." *Political Theory* 13 (1985): 339–61.

————. "Political Theory and Politics: The Case of Leo Strauss and Liberal Democracy." In *The Crisis of Liberal Democracy*, eds. Kenneth L. Deutsch and Walter Soffer, 68–88. Albany: State University of New York Press, 1988.

————. "Strauss Before Straussianism: The Weimar Conversation." *The Vital Nexus* 1, no. 1 (May 1990): 73–104.

————. "Strauss Before Straussianism: Reason, Revelation, and Nature." *Review of Politics* 53, no. 1 (Winter 1991): 53–74.

Guttmann, Julius. *Die Philosophie des Judentums*. Munich: E. Reinhardt, 1933.

————. *The Philosophy of Judaism* (in Hebrew). Translated by Y. L. Baruch. Jerusalem: Bialik Institute, 1951.

————. Introduction to *Philosophia Judaica: The Guide of the Perplexed*, by Moses Maimonides, 1–36. Translated by Chaim Rabin. London: East and West Library, 1952.

————. *Philosophies of Judaism*. Translated by David W. Silverman. Philadelphia: Jewish Publication Society, 1964.

————. "Philosophie der Religion oder Philosophie des Gesetzes?" *Proceedings of the Israel Academy of Sciences and Humanities* 5 (1976): 146–73 (in Hebrew translation, pp. 188–207).

Hall, Dale. "The Republic and the 'Limits of Politics.' " *Political Theory* 5 (1977): 293–313.

Hall, Robert W. "Plato's Just Man: Thoughts on Strauss's Plato." *New Scholasticism* 42 (1968): 202–25.

Hallowell, John. Review of *Natural Right and History*, by Leo Strauss. *American Political Science Review* 48 (1954): 538–41.

————. Review of *Thoughts on Machiavelli*, by Leo Strauss. *Journal of Politics* 3 (1959): 300–303.

Harbison, Warren. "Irony and Deception." *Independent Journal of Philosophy* 2 (1978): 89–94.

Hartman, David. *Maimonides: Torah and the Philosophic Quest*. Philadelphia: Jewish Publication Society, 1976.

Harvey, Steven. "Maimonides in the Sultan's Palace." In *Perspectives on Maimonides*, edited by Joel L. Kraemer, 47–75. Oxford: Oxford University Press, 1991.

Harvey, Warren Zev. "The Return of Maimonideanism." *Jewish Social Studies* 42 (1980): 249–68.

————. "Why Maimonides was not a *Mutakallim*." In *Perspectives on Maimonides*, edited by Joel L. Kraemer, 105–14. Oxford: Oxford University Press, 1991.

Havard, William C. "The Method and Results of Political Anthropology in America." *Archiv für Rechts- und Sozialphilosophie* 47 (1961): 395–415.

Herberg, Will. "Athens and Jerusalem: Confrontation and Dialogue." *The Drew Gateway* 28, no. 3 (Spring 1958): 178–200.

Himmelfarb, Milton. "On Leo Strauss." *Commentary* 58, no. 8 (August 1974): 60–66. For responses to the article in letters to the editor, and a reply by the author, see *Commentary* 59, no. 1 (January 1975): 14, 16.

Holmes, Stephen. "Truths for Philosophers Alone?" Review of *The Rebirth of Classical Political Rationalism*, by Leo Strauss. *Times Literary Supplement*, 1–7 December 1989, 1319–24. For responses to the review in letters to the editor, see *Times Literary Supplement*, 5–11 January and 12–18 January 1990.

Horwitz, Robert H. *See* Storing, Herbert J.

Hyman, Arthur. "Interpreting Maimonides." *Gesher* 5 (1976): 46–59.

Ivry, Alfred L. "Leo Strauss on Maimonides." In *Leo Strauss's Thought*, ed. Alan Udoff, 75–91. Boulder, Colo.: Lynne Rienner, 1991.

Jaffa, Harry V. "The Primacy of the Good: Leo Strauss Remembered." *Modern Age* 26 (1982): 266–69.

———. "The Legacy of Leo Strauss." *Claremont Review of Books* 3, no. 3 (Fall 1984): 14–21.

———. " 'The Legacy of Leo Strauss' Defended." *Claremont Review of Books* 4, no. 1 (Spring 1985): 20–24.

———. "Crisis of the Strauss Divided: The Legacy Reconsidered." *Social Research* 54 (1987): 579–603.

———. "Dear Professor Drury." *Political Theory* 15, no. 3 (August 1987): 316–25.

———. "Humanizing Certitudes and Impoverishing Doubts: A Critique of *The Closing of the American Mind* by Allan Bloom." *Interpretation* 16, no. 1 (Fall 1988): 111–38.

———. *See* Berns, Walter.

Jospe, Raphael. "The Number and Division of Chapters in *The Guide of the Perplexed*" (in Hebrew). *Jerusalem Studies in Jewish Thought* 7 (1988): 387–97.

Jung, Hwa Yol. "Leo Strauss's Conception of Political Philosophy: A Critique." *Review of Politics* 29 (1967): 492–517.

———. "The Life-World, Historicity, and Truth: Reflections on Leo Strauss's Encounter with Heidegger and Husserl." *Journal of the British Society for Phenomenology* 9 (1978): 11–23.

———. "Two Critics of Scientism: Leo Strauss and Edmund Husserl." *Independent Journal of Philosophy* 2 (1978): 81–88.

Kendall, Willmoore. Review of *Thoughts on Machiavelli*, by Leo Strauss. *Philosophical Review* 15 (1965–66): 247–54.

Kennington, Richard. "Strauss's *Natural Right and History.*" *Review of Metaphysics* 35 (1981–82): 57–86.

———. "Strauss's *Natural Right and History.*" In *Leo Strauss's Thought*, ed. Alan Udoff, 227–52. Boulder, Colo.: Lynne Rienner, 1991.

Klein, Jacob, J. Winfree Smith, Ted A. Blanton, Laurence Berns. "Memorials to Leo Strauss." *The College* 25, no. (January 1974): 1–5.

Kleven, Terence. "A Study of Part I, Chapters 1–7 of Maimonides' *The Guide of the Perplexed.*" *Interpretation* 20, no. 1 (Fall 1992): 3–16.

Klosko, George. "The 'Straussian' Interpretation of Plato's *Republic.*" *History of Political Thought* 7 (1986): 275–93.

Kojève, Alexandre. "Tyranny and Wisdom." In *On Tyranny*, by Leo Strauss, 143–88. Ithaca, N. Y.: Cornell University Press, 1963. Revised edition (with the addition of the Strauss-Kojève correspondence), edited by Victor Gourevitch and Michael S. Roth, 135–176. New York: The Free Press, 1991.

———. "The Emperor Julian and His Art of Writing." In *Ancients and Moderns: Essays in the Tradition of Political Philosophy in Honor of Leo Strauss*, edited by Joseph Cropsey, 95–113. New York: Basic Books, 1964.

———. *Introduction to the Reading of Hegel*. Edited by Allan Bloom. Translated by James H. Nichols, Jr. New York: Basic Books, 1969.

———. "Hegel, Marx, and Christianity." Translated by Hilail Gildin. *Interpretation* 1, no. 1 (Summer 1970): 21–42.

———. "The Idea of Death in the Philosophy of Hegel." Translated by Joseph J. Carpino. *Interpretation* 3, nos. 2 and 3 (Winter 1973): 114–56.

———. "Kojève-Fessard Documents." Translated by Hugh Gillis. *Interpretation* 19, no. 2 (Winter 1991–92): 185–200.

Kraemer, Joel L. "Maimonides on the Philosophic Sciences in his *Treatise on the Art of Logic*." In *Perspectives on Maimonides*, edited by Joel L. Kraemer, 77–104. Oxford: Oxford University Press, 1991.

Kravitz, Leonard. *The Hidden Doctrine of Maimonides' "Guide for the Perplexed": Philosophical and Religious God-Language in Tension*. Lewiston, N. Y.: Edwin Mellen, 1988.

Krüger, Gerhard. Review of *Die Religionskritik Spinozas als Grundlage seiner Bibelwissenschaft*, by Leo Strauss. *Deutsche Literaturzeitung* 51 (1931): 2407–12.

———. Review of *Die Religionskritik Spinozas als Grundlage seiner Bibelwissenschaft*, by Leo Strauss. Translated by Donald L. Maletz. *Independent Journal of Philosophy* 5/6 (1988): 173–75.

Kuhn, Helmut. "Naturrecht und Historismus." *Zeitschrift für Politik* 3 (1956): 289–304. idem, *Independent Journal of Philosophy* 2 (1978): 13–21.

Lachterman, David R. "Strauss Read from France." *Review of Politics* 53, no. 1 (Winter 1991): 224–45.

———. "Laying Down the Law: The Theological-Political Matrix of Spinoza's Physics." In *Leo Strauss's Thought*, ed. Alan Udoff, 123–53. Boulder, Colo.: Lynne Rienner, 1991.

Lampert, Laurence. "The Argument of Leo Strauss in 'What Is Political Philosophy?' " *Modern Age* 22 (1978): 38–46.

Lefort, Claude. "Le restauration et la perversion de l'enseignement classique ou la naissance de la pensée politique moderne: Une interprétation de Leo Strauss." In *Le travail de l'oeuvre: Machiavel*, 259–309. Paris: Gallimard, 1972.

Lerner, Ralph. "Leo Strauss." In vol. 15 of the *Encyclopedia Judaica*, edited by Cecil Roth, 434. Jerusalem: Keter, 1971.

———. "Leo Strauss (1899–1973)." *American Jewish Year Book* 76 (1976): 91–97.

———. Foreword to *Philosophy and Law*, by Leo Strauss, ix–xiii. Philadelphia: Jewish Publication Society, 1987.

Levine, David L. "Without Malice but With Forethought: A Response to Burnyeat." *Review of Politics* 53, no. 1 (Winter 1991): 200–218.

Lichtheim, George. "Xenophon versus Hegel." Review of *On Tyranny*, by Leo Strauss. *Commentary* 36, no. 11 (November 1963): 412–16.

Liebich, André. "Straussianism and Ideology." In *Ideology, Philosophy, and Politics*, edited by Anthony Parel, 225–45. Waterloo, Ont.: Wilfrid Laurier University Press, 1983.

Lowenthal, David. Review of *Studies in Platonic Political Philosophy*, by Leo Strauss. *Interpretation* 13 (1985): 297–320.

———. "The Case for Teleology." *Independent Journal of Philosophy* 2 (1978): 95–105.

———. "Comment on Colmo." *Interpretation* 18, no. 1 (Fall 1990): 161–62.

Luz, Ehud. "The Judaism of Leo Strauss" (in Hebrew). *Daat* 27 (Summer 1991).

MacCormack, John R., ed. *The Vital Nexus* 1, no. 1 (May 1990). Special Issue on Leo Strauss.

Malherbe, Michel. "Leo Strauss, Hobbes et la nature humaine." *Revue de Metaphysique et de Morale* 94, no. 3 (July-September 1989): 353–67.

Manent, Pierre. "Strauss et Nietzsche." *Revue de Metaphysique et de Morale* 94, no. 3 (July-September 1989): 337–45.

———. "Notre Destin Libéral." Preface to *Carl Schmitt, Léo Strauss, et la notion de politique*, by Heinrich Meier, 7–12. See Meier, Heinrich.

Mansfield, Jr., Harvey C. "Strauss's Machiavelli" and "Reply to Pocock." *Political Theory* 3 (1975): 372–84, 402–5.

Marshall, Terence. "Leo Strauss, la philosophie et la science politique." *Revue francaise de science politique* 35 (1985): 605–38.

———. Review of *Political Philosophy*. Vol. 1, *Rights—The New Quarrel between the Ancients and the Moderns*, by Luc Ferry. *Interpretation* 20, no. 2 (Winter 1992–93): 217–24.

Masters, Roger D. "Evolutionary Biology and Natural Right." In *The Crisis of Liberal Democracy*, eds. Kenneth L. Deutsch and Walter Soffer, 48–66. Albany: State University of New York Press, 1988.

McCoy, Charles N. R. "On the Revival of Classical Political Philosophy." *Review of Politics* 35 (1973): 161–79.

McShea, Robert J. "Leo Strauss on Machiavelli." *Western Political Quarterly* 16 (1963): 782–97.

Meier, Heinrich. *Carl Schmitt, Leo Strauss, und "Die Begriff des Politischen": Zu einem Dialog unter Abwesenden*. Stuttgart: J. B. Metzler, 1988.

———. *Carl Schmitt, Léo Strauss, et la notion de politique: Un dialogue entre absents*. Translated by Françoise Manent. Preface by Pierre Manent. Paris: Commentaire/Julliard, 1990.

Mendes-Flohr, Paul. "The Theological-Political Predicament of Modern Judaism. Leo Strauss's Neo-Maimonidean Political Ethic." Unpublished manuscript, 40 pp.

Midgley, E. B. F. "Concerning the Modernist Subversion of Political Philosophy." *New Scholasticism* 53 (1979): 168–90.

Miller, Eugene F. "Leo Strauss: The Recovery of Political Philosophy." In *Contemporary Political Philosophers*, edited by Anthony de Crespigny and Kenneth Minogue, 67–99. London: Methuen and Co., 1976.

———. "On Rules of Philosophic Interpretation: A Critique of Ryn's 'Knowledge and History.' " *Journal of Politics* 44 (1982): 409–19.

Momigliano, Arnaldo. "Ermeneutica e Pensiero Politico Classico in Leo Strauss." *Rivista Storica Italiana* 79 (1967): 1164–72.

———. Review of *Socrates and Aristophanes*, by Leo Strauss. *Commentary* 44, no. 10 (October 1967): 102–4.

Morgan, Michael L. "The Curse of Historicity: The Role of History in Leo Strauss's Jewish Thought." *Journal of Religion* 61 (1981): 345–63. idem, *Dilemmas in Modern Jewish Thought*, 40–54. Bloomington, Ind.: Indiana University Press, 1992.

———. "Leo Strauss and the Possibility of Jewish Philosophy." In *Dilemmas in Modern Jewish Thought*, 55–67. Bloomington, Ind.: Indiana University Press, 1992.

Morrisey, Will. Review of *Jerusalem vs. Athens*, by Paul Eidelberg. *Interpretation* 14 (1986): 441–47.

———. Review of *The Crisis of Liberal Democracy: A Straussian Perspective*, edited by Kenneth L. Deutsch and Walter Soffer. *Interpretation* 16, no. 3 (Spring 1989): 481–87.

———. Review of *An Introduction to Political Philosophy*, by Leo Strauss, edited by Hilail Gildin; and of *The Rebirth of Classical Political Rationalism*, by Leo Strauss, edited by Thomas L. Pangle. *Interpretation* 17, no. 3 (Spring 1990): 465–67.

Motzkin, Aryeh Leo. "On the Interpretation of Maimonides." *Independent Journal of Philosophy* 2 (1978): 39–46.

Neumann, Harry. "Civic Piety and Socratic Atheism: An Interpretation of Strauss's *Socrates and Aristophanes*." *Independent Journal of Philosophy* 2 (1978): 33–37.

———. Review of *Xenophon's Socratic Discourse*, by Leo Strauss. *Journal of the History of Philosophy* 9 (1971): 239–43.

———. Review of *Xenophon's Socrates*, by Leo Strauss. *Journal of the History of Philosophy* 12 (1974): 252–56.

Nicgorski, Walter. "Leo Strauss." *Modern Age* 26 (1982): 270–73.

———. "Leo Strauss and Liberal Education." *Interpretation* 13, no. 2 (May 1985): 233–50.

———. "Reason, Politics, and Christian Belief." Review of *The God of Faith and Reason*, by Robert Sokolowski. *Claremont Review of Books* 4, no. 2 (Summer 1985): 18–21.

———. *See* Deutsch, Kenneth L.

Niemeyer, Gerhart. "Humanism, Positivism, and Immorality." Review of *Thoughts on Machiavelli*, by Leo Strauss. *Political Science Reviewer* 1 (1971): 277–94.

———. "What Is Political Knowledge?" Review of *What Is Political Philosophy?*, by Leo Strauss. *Review of Politics* 23 (1961): 101–7.

Norton, Paul. "Leo Strauss: His Critique of Historicism." *Modern Age* 25 (1981): 143–54.

Orwin, Clifford. "Leo Strauss: Moralist or Machiavellian?" *The Vital Nexus* 1, no. 1 (1990): 105–13.

———. Review of *The Political Ideas of Leo Strauss*, by Shadia Drury. *Polis* 9, no. 1 (1990): 104–18.

Pangle, Thomas L. Introduction to *Studies in Platonic Political Philosophy*, by Leo Strauss, 1–26. Chicago: University of Chicago Press, 1983.

———. "The Platonism of Leo Strauss: A Reply to Harry Jaffa." *Claremont Review of Books* 4, no. 1 (Spring 1985): 18–20.

———. "Nihilism and Modern Democracy in the Thought of Nietzsche." In *The Crisis of Liberal Democracy*, eds. Kenneth L. Deutsch and Walter Soffer, 180–211. Albany: State University of New York Press, 1988.

———, and Nathan Tarcov. "Epilogue—Leo Strauss and the History of Political Philosophy." In *History of Political Philosophy*, 3d ed., edited by Leo Strauss and Joseph Cropsey, 907–38. Chicago: University of Chicago Press, 1988.

———, ed. Introduction to *The Rebirth of Classical Political Rationalism*, by Leo Strauss, vii–xxxviii. Chicago: University of Chicago Press, 1989.

———. "On the Epistolary Dialogue Between Leo Strauss and Eric Voegelin." *Review of Politics* 53, no. 1 (Winter 1991): 100–125.

———. Introduction and "Platonic Political Science in Strauss and Voegelin." In *Faith and Political Philosophy*, eds. Barry Cooper and Peter Emberley, ix–xxvi, 321–47. University Park, Pa.: Pennsylvania State University Press, 1993.

Pines, Shlomo. Introduction to *The Guide of the Perplexed*, by Moses Maimonides, lvii–cxxxiv. Translated by Shlomo Pines. Chicago: University of Chicago, 1963.

———. "Spinoza's *Tractatus Theologico-Politicus*, Maimonides and Kant." *Scripta Hierosolymitana* 20 (1968): 3–54.

———. "On Leo Strauss" (in Hebrew). *Molad* 30, nos. 247–48 / n. s. 7, nos. 37–38 (1976): 455–57.

———. "The Limitations of Human Knowledge according to al-Farabi, ibn Bajja, and Maimonides." In *Studies in Medieval Jewish History and Literature*, edited by Isadore Twersky, 82–109. Cambridge, Mass.: Harvard University Press, 1979.

———. "On Leo Strauss." Translated by Aryeh Leo Motzkin. *Independent Journal of Philosophy* 5/6 (1988): 169–71.

Pippin, Robert B. "The Modern World of Leo Strauss." *Political Theory* 20, no. 3 (August 1992): 448–72.

Platt, Michael. "Leo Strauss: Three Quarrels, Three Questions, One Life." In *The Crisis of Liberal Democracy*, eds. Kenneth L. Deutsch and Walter Soffer, 17–28. Albany: State University of New York Press, 1988.

Pocock, J. G. A. "Prophet and Inquisitor, or, A Church Built Upon Bayonets Cannot Stand: A Comment on Mansfield's 'Strauss's Machiavelli.'" *Political Theory* 3 (1975): 385–401.

Prufer, Thomas. "Juxtapositions: Aristotle, Aquinas, Strauss." In *Leo Strauss's Thought*, ed. Alan Udoff, 115–21. Boulder, Colo.: Lynne Rienner, 1991.

Ravitzky, Aviezer. "Samuel Ibn Tibbon and the Esoteric Character of the *Guide of the Perplexed.*" *AJS Review* 6 (1981): 87–123.

———. "The Secrets of *The Guide of the Perplexed*: Between the Thirteenth and Twentieth Centuries." In *Studies in Maimonides*, edited by Isadore Twersky, 159–207. Cambridge, Mass.: Harvard University Press, 1991.

Riedel, Manfred. "Political Language and Philosophy." *Independent Journal of Philosophy* 2 (1978): 107–112.

Riezler, Kurt. *Physics and Reality: Lectures of Aristotle on Modern Physics.* New Haven: Yale University Press, 1940.

Rosen, Stanley. "Hermeneutics as Politics." In *Hermeneutics as Politics*, 87–140. New York: Oxford University Press, 1987.

———. "Is Metaphysics Possible?" *Review of Metaphysics* 45 (1991): 235–57.

———. "Leo Strauss and the Quarrel Between the Ancients and the Moderns." In *Leo Strauss's Thought*, ed. Alan Udoff, 155–68. Boulder, Colo.: Lynne Rienner, 1991.

———. Review of *Xenophon's Socrates*, by Leo Strauss. *Classical World* 66 (1973): 470–71.

———. "Politics or Transcendence? Responding to Historicism." In *Faith and Political Philosophy*, eds. Barry Cooper and Peter Emberley, 260–66. University Park, Pa.: Pennsylvania State University Press, 1993.

Rotenstreich, Nathan. "Between Athens and Jerusalem" (in Hebrew). In *Studies in Contemporary Jewish Thought*, 139–43. Tel Aviv: Am Oved, 1978.

Roth, Michael S. *See* Gourevitch, Victor.

Rothman, Stanley. "The Revival of Classical Political Philosophy: A Critique" and "A Rejoinder to Cropsey." *American Political Science Review* 56 (1962): 341–52, 682–86.

Ryn, Claes G. "Knowledge and History" and "Strauss and Knowledge: A Rejoinder." *Journal of Politics* 44 (1982): 394–408, 420–25.

Sabine, George H. Review of *Persecution and the Art of Writing*, by Leo Strauss. *Ethics* 63 (1953): 220–22.

Salkever, Stephen G. "The Crisis of Liberal Democracy: Liberality and Democratic Citizenship." In *The Crisis of Liberal Democracy*, eds. Kenneth L. Deutsch and Walter Soffer, 245–68. Albany: State University of New York Press, 1988.

Sandoz, Ellis. "Medieval Rationalism or Mystic Philosophy? Reflections on the Strauss-Voegelin Correspondence." In *Faith and Political Philosophy*, eds. Barry Cooper and Peter Emberley, 297–319. University Park, Pa.: Pennsylvania State University Press, 1993.

Schaar, John R., and Sheldon Wolin. Review of *Essays on the Scientific Study of Politics*, edited by H. J. Storing. *American Political Science Review* 57 (1963): 125–50.

Schaefer, Jr., David L. "The Legacy of Leo Strauss: A Bibliographic Introduction." *Intercollegiate Review* 9 (1974): 139–48.

———. "Leo Strauss and American Democracy: A Response to Wood and Holmes." *Review of Politics* 53, no. 1 (Winter 1991): 187–99.

Schall, James V. "Revelation, Reason and Politics: Catholic Reflexions on Strauss." *Gregorianum* 62 (1981): 349–65, 467–97.

———. "A Latitude for Statesmanship? Strauss on St. Thomas." *Review of Politics* 53, no. 1 (Winter 1991): 126–45.

Schram, Glen N. "Strauss and Voegelin on Machiavelli and Modernity." *Modern Age* 31, nos. 3–4 (Summer-Fall 1987): 261–66.

———. "The Place of Leo Strauss in a Liberal Education." *Interpretation* 19, no. 2 (Winter 1991–92): 201–16.

Schwab, George, ed. Introduction to *The Concept of the Political*, by Carl Schmitt, 3–16. New Brunswick, N. J.: Rutgers University Press, 1976.

Schwarcz, Moshe. "The Enlightenment and Its Implications for Jewish Philosophy in the Modern Period, in Light of the Controversy between L. Strauss and J. Guttmann" (in Hebrew). *Daat* 1, no. 1 (Winter 1978): 7–16.

Schwarzschild, Steven. "Moral Radicalism and 'Middlingness' in the Ethics of Maimonides." In *The Pursuit of the Ideal: Jewish Writings of Steven Schwarzschild*, edited by Menachem Kellner, 137–60. Albany: State University of New York Press, 1990.

Schweid, Eliezer. "Religion and Philosophy: The Scholarly-Theological Debate Between Julius Guttmann and Leo Strauss." *Maimonidean Studies* 1 (1990): 163–95.

Shell, Susan. "Meier on Strauss and Schmitt." *Review of Politics* 53, no. 1 (Winter 1991): 219–23.

Smith, J. Winfree. *See* Klein, Jacob.

Smith, Steven B. "Leo Strauss: Between Athens and Jerusalem." *Review of Politics* 53, no. 1 (Winter 1991): 75–99.

Soffer, Walter. *See* Deutsch, Kenneth L.

Sokolowski, Robert. "Revelation and Political Philosophy." Appendix to Chapter 11 in *The God of Faith and Reason*, 157–64. Notre Dame, Ind.: University of Notre Dame Press, 1982.

Steintrager, James. "Political Philosophy, Political Theology, and Morality." *Thomist* 32 (1968): 307–32.

Stone, Robert. "Drury Against Aristotle." *The Vital Nexus* 1, no. 1 (May 1990): 115–17.

Storing, Herbert J., Leo Strauss, Walter Berns, Leo Weinstein, and Robert Horwitz. "Replies to Schaar and Wolin." *American Political Science Review* 57 (1963): 151–60.

———. *See* Berns, Walter.

Sturm, Douglas. "Politics and Divinity." *Thought* 52 (1977): 333–65.

Tarcov, Nathan. "Philosophy and History: Tradition and Interpretation in the Work of Leo Strauss." *Polity* 16 (1983–84): 5–29.

————. "Philosophy and History: John Gunnell and Leo Strauss on Tradition and Interpretation." In *Truth, Interpretation, and Science: Essays in Honor of John G. Gunnell*, edited by John S. Nelson, 69–112. Albany: State University of New York Press, 1986.

————. "On a Certain Critique of 'Straussianism.'" *Review of Politics* 53, no. 1 (Winter 1991): 3–18.

————. *See* Pangle, Thomas L.

Tolle, Gordon J. Review of *The Political Ideas of Leo Strauss*, by Shadia Drury. *Review of Politics* 50 (1988): 467–70.

Tucker, George Elliott, ed. *The Independent Journal of Philosophy* 2 (1978). Special Issue on Leo Strauss.

Udoff, Alan, ed. *Leo Strauss's Thought: Toward a Critical Engagement*. Boulder, Colo.: Lynne Rienner, 1991.

————. "On Leo Strauss: An Introductory Account." In *Leo Strauss's Thought*, ed. Alan Udoff, 1–29. Boulder, Colo.: Lynne Rienner, 1991.

————. Review of *The Rebirth of Classical Political Rationalism*, by Leo Strauss. *Review of Metaphysics* 63, no. 3 (March 1990): 648–50.

Umphrey, Stewart. "Natural Right and Philosophy." *Review of Politics* 53, no. 1 (Winter 1991): 19–39.

Vajda, Georges. Review of *The Guide of the Perplexed*, by Moses Maimonides, translated with an introduction and notes by Shlomo Pines, with an introductory essay by Leo Strauss. *Revue des Études Juives* 123 (1964): 209–16.

————. "La pensée religieuse de Moïse Maïmonide: unité ou dualité?" *Cahiers de civilization médiévale* 9 (1966): 29–49.

Veatch, Henry B. "Law and Ethics in Search of a Physics or Metaphysics." Chapter 4 in *Human Rights—Fact or Fancy?*, 213–49. Baton Rouge, La.: Louisiana State University Press, 1985.

————. "Telos and Teleology in Aristotelian Ethics" and "Natural Law: Dead or Alive?" In *Swimming Against the Current*, 99–116, 254–68. Washington, D. C.: Catholic University of America Press, 1990.

Voegelin, Eric. Review of *On Tyranny*, by Leo Strauss. *Review of Politics* 2 (1949): 241–44.

Walsh, David. "The Reason-Revelation Tension in Strauss and Voegelin." In *Faith and Political Philosophy*, eds. Barry Cooper and Peter Emberley, 349–68. University Park, Pa.: Pennsylvania State University Press, 1993.

Ward, James F. "Experience and Political Philosophy: Notes on Reading Leo Strauss." *Polity* 13 (1980): 668–87.

————. "Political Philosophy and History: The Links Between Strauss and Heidegger." *Polity* 20, no. 2 (Winter 1987): 273–95.

Weber, Stanley G. *Leo Strauss on Jerusalem and Athens*. Ph.D. diss., McMaster University. Hamilton, Ont., 1975.

Weinstein, Leo. *See* Storing, Herbert J.

Weiss, Raymond L. *Maimonides' Ethics: The Encounter of Philosophic and Religious Morality.* Chicago: University of Chicago Press, 1991.

West, Thomas G. "Leo Strauss and the American Founding." *Review of Politics* 53, no. 1 (Winter 1991): 157–72.

Wilhelmsen, Frederick D. "Jaffa, The School of Strauss, and the Christian Tradition." Chapter 8 in *Christianity and Political Philosophy*, 209–25. Athens, Ga.: University of Georgia Press, 1978.

Wiser, James L. "Reason and Revelation as Search and Response: A Comparison of Eric Voegelin and Leo Strauss." In *Faith and Political Philosophy*, eds. Barry Cooper and Peter Emberley, 237–48. University Park, Pa.: Pennsylvania State University Press, 1993.

Wood, Gordon S. "The Fundamentalists and the Constitution." *New York Review of Books* 35, no. 2 (18 February 1988): 33–40.

Yaffe, Martin D. "On Leo Strauss's *Philosophy and Law*: A Review Essay." *Modern Judaism* 9 (1989): 213–25.

———. "Leo Strauss as Judaic Thinker: Some First Notions." *Religious Studies Review* 17, no. 1 (January 1991): 33–41.

———. "Autonomy, Community, Authority: Hermann Cohen, Carl Schmitt, and Leo Strauss." In *Autonomy and Judaism*, edited by Daniel H. Frank, 143–61. Albany: State University of New York Press, 1992.

———. "On the Merit of Hermann Cohen's Critique of Spinoza: Franz Rosenzweig and Leo Strauss." Unpublished manuscript, 15 pp.

Youlton, John. "Criticism and Histrionic Understanding." *Ethics* 65 (1955): 206–12.

———. "Locke on the Law of Nature." *Philosophical Review* 67 (1958): 477–98.

Zuckert, Michael. "Of Wary Physicians and Weary Readers: The Debates on Lockes' Way of Writing." *Independent Journal of Philosophy* 2 (1978): 55–66.

INDEX

Accusation and defense, 238 n. 1

Activities vs. pleasures, philosophic, 166 n. 119

Addressees, of *Guide*, 32–33, 89–92, 172 n. 22

Adler, Eve, 155 n. 32, 160 n. 70, 215 n. 25

Africa, North, 192 n. 39

Aleynu prayer, 229 n. 73

Alfarabi (Abu Nasr), 96, 101, 128, 161 n. 80, 215 nn. 18, 28, 226 n. 61, 241 n. 4

Alienation from Judaism, 79–82, 186 n. 19, 189 n. 29, 190 n. 32, 206 n. 66, 208 n. 85

Allegorical method, 43–46, 55–56, 77, 79–82, 171 n. 20, 172 n. 22, 191 n. 36, 192 n. 38, 220 n. 11, 221 n. 13, 222 n. 16, 228 n. 67, 240 n. 3

Allison, Henry E., 161 n. 78, 164 n. 99, 165 n. 114

Altmann, Alexander, ix–x, 146 nn. 1, 4, 149 n. 7, 168 n. 3, 171 n. 20, 182 n. 2, 185 n. 16, 189 n. 29, 194 n. 47, 199 n. 12, 221 n. 14, 226 n. 63, 229 n. 73

Ancients and moderns, 22, 45–48, 54, 115–126 passim, 144 n. 2, 163 nn. 98, 99, 182 n. 76, 193 n. 43, 196 n. 2, 224 n. 31, 228 n. 67

Antibiblical spirit, 95–96, 159 n. 49

Anti-Goeze (Lessing), 159 n. 49

Anti-Semitism, 53, 187 n. 19

Antitheism, 165 n. 116

Antitheological ire, 15, 19, 67, 73, 118, 160 n. 55

Apologetics, 69, 189 n. 29

Argument and Action of Plato's "Laws" (Strauss), 215 n. 23

Aristotle: and the Bible, 18, 30, 40, 193 n. 43, 214 n. 17; Maimonides and, 47, 76–79, 96–97, 100–101, 104, 112–113, 148 n. 6, 151 n. 11, 205 n. 60, 206 n. 64, 208 n. 85, 215 n. 18, 217 n. 37, 221 n. 13, 223 n. 24, 241 n. 4; and the medievals, 181 n. 76, 217 n. 37, 221 n. 13, 230 n. 75; modern critique of, 43–44, 117, 211 n. 3, 223 n. 24; science of, 44, 65, 84, 96–97, 194 n. 47, 205 n. 60, 206 n. 64, 208 n. 85; Strauss's return to Plato and, 70, 87, 130, 132, 147 n. 4, 158 n. 49, 169 n. 13, 200 n. 13, 205 n. 60; theology of, 30, 36, 118, 223 n. 24

Aron, Raymond, 175 n. 40

Art of writing, 232 n. 81

Astrology, 213 n. 5

Ataraxia, 73

Atheism, 10–11, 24, 25–26, 58, 107–108, 145 n. 2, 165 n. 116, 166 n. 119, 237 n. 1

Authority, 26, 33, 65, 105, 123–124, 125, 172 n. 22, 178 n. 52, 188 nn. 24, 26, 218 n. 37

Autobiography, Strauss's, 148 n. 6, 189 n. 30

Autobiography (Solomon Maimon), 221 n. 13

Autonomy, 187 n. 20

Averroes (Ibn Rushd), 48, 73–74, 104–105, 123, 129, 174 n. 35, 180 n. 76, 203 n. 32, 215 nn. 18, 28, 217 nn. 37, 39, 230 n. 75

Avicenna (Ibn Sina), 69, 96, 100–101, 148 n. 6, 161 n. 80, 168 n. 3, 215 nn. 23, 28

Bacon, Francis, 120, 154 n. 24, 238 n. 1

Barth, Karl, 163 n. 96, 183 n. 13